BUSINESS ETHICS
TODAY

FOUNDATIONS

Additional Services in the publishing of the *Business Ethics Today: Conference Papers:*
Publishing services by KLO Publishing Service, LLC (www.KLOPublishing.com).
Cover design by Roark Creative Group (www.RoarkCreative.com).
Interior design by Katherine Lloyd (www.TheDESKonline.com).

THE CENTER FOR CHRISTIAN BUSINESS ETHICS

TODAY

The Center for Christian Busienss Ethics Today was established in

2009 to address the need for the application of Christian principles

to strengthen business operations. The Center's research shows that

Christianity, as found in the Westminster Confession of Faith, laid

the foundations for the commercial world, as we know it today. The

current movement of society across the world risks the abandonment of

these business practices. To reinvigorate the study of founding business

principles, the Center challenges those sharing God's calling to business,

to use God's Word and His principles to shape their engagement in

business.

Visit us at www.cfcbe.com.

FORWARD AND ACKNOWLEDGEMENTS

This anthology is the result of the vision of John (Jack) Templeton, Jr., in seeing the need to look into the contribution of Christianity to our communities. In 2003, Templeton challenged Philip J. Clements, a fellow board member of the National Bible Association, to consider the contribution of Christianity to commerce. That challenge led to six years of research and analysis based upon both Clements' experience in business and his connection with Christianity personally and through his obtaining a Masters in Theological Studies at the Reformed Theological Seminary. The conclusion was that Templeton was right – Christianity that came out of the Reformation did create much of the commercial environment we experience today.

As part of their work on the National Bible Association, both Templeton and Clements connected with Peter A. Lillback, president of Westminster Theological Seminary (WTS). Clements and Lillback explored the possibility of a business ethics conference to begin the process of creating a business, seminary and church discourse on this important topic. That possibility bore fruit June 11-12, 2010 in Philadelphia. The Business Ethics Today: Adding a Christian Worldview as Found in the Westminster Confession of Faith conference, co-hosted by WTS and the Center for Christian Business Ethics Today (Center), took place before some 250 participants. Many of the papers in this text were developed and presented for this conference.

*The conversion of conference papers into a text requires exten-
sive efforts by many people. Acknowledgement goes to Jon Coo-
per, the Center's director, who tirelessly worked to organize the
conference and to oversee the conversion to this text. Next special
thanks goes to the many encouragers for both this text and the
work of the Center, particularly Andrew J. Peterson, president of
RTS Virtual campus; Chuck Stetson, partner of Private Equity Investors, Inc, who regularly reached out with inspiration and encouragement on the importance of this work in our business community;
Jody Wood, who added thinking to the potential use of material for
small groups; all of the speakers and moderators who traveled from
around the country to be at the conference and gave encouragement after the conference; and last but not least, Julie Clements, my
wife, who patiently endured the normal distractions of these kinds
of projects and aided through many a reread.*

Philip J. Clements, January 8, 2011

AUTHORS

Arranged by Chapter

Philip J Clements, JD, LLM, Managing Director, Center for Christian Business Ethics

Peter Lillback, PhD, President, Westminster Theological Seminary

Charles Colson, JD, Founder, Prison Fellowship Ministries

K. Scott Oliphint, PhD, Professor of Apologetics and Systematic Theology, Westminster Theological Seminary

Richard B. Gaffin Jr., ThD, Professor of Biblical and Systematic Theology, Emeritus Westminster Theological Seminary

Michael Wykes, DPhil, REF and Impact Manager, University of Exeter

Wayne A. Grudem, PhD, Research Professor, Theology and Biblical Studies, Phoenix Seminary

John Weiser, currently Board Member to Westminster Theological Seminary

Barry Asmus, PhD, Senior Economist, National Center for Policy Analysis

William Edgar, DrThéol, Westminster Theological Seminary

Mac McQuiston CEO, CEO Forum

Lou Giuliano, Former CEO, ITT, currenlty Senior Advisor to the Carlyle Group

Julius Kim, PhD, Associate Professor of Practical Theology, Westminster Seminary California

Phillip Kim, PhD, Assistant Professor of Management and Human Resources, University of Wisconsin School of Business

Galen Radebaugh, PhD, Retired Executive, Formerly Vice President, Pfizer Research, Pharmaceutical Sciences

Vern Poythress, PhD, Professor of New Testament Interpretation, Westminster Theological Seminary

Jeff Conway, Former CFO, Ruth's Chris Steak House

Andrew Peterson, PhD, President, Reformed Theological Seminary, Virtual Campus

Chuck Stetson, Co-founder and Managing Director, PEI Funds

Ron Ferner, Dean of the School of Business and Leaership, Philadelphia Biblical University

Philip Ryken, DPhil, President, Wheaton College

Fran McGowen, Founder and President, CarSense

Mark Futato, PhD, Maclellan Professor of Old Testament, Reformed Theological Seminary, Orlando

CONTENTS

INTRODUCTION TO BUSINESS ETHICS TODAY: FOUNDATIONS

PHILIP J. CLEMENTS AND PETER LILLBACK

After that whole generation had been gathered to their fathers, another generation grew up, who knew neither the LORD nor what He had done for Israel. Then the Israelites did evil in the eyes of the LORD and served the Baals. (Judges 2:10-11 NIV)

Business Ethics Today: Foundations endeavors to respond to the warning of Judges 2:10-11, that we can fail to remember what God has done for us. In this Introduction, we review the contribution Christianity made to commerce so that business is a blessing in God's world and the principles underlying this blessing. The worry is that we will forget these principles and lose the blessing. Much of this discussion is framed in the arena of business ethics.

This text has three sections: 1. Foundations, with six papers, 2. Workplace Ethics, with six papers, and 3. Church Support for Those Doing Business in God's World, with two papers. This Introduction will incorporate the themes of these different papers into the overall role of Christianity in developing commerce ethics. Preceding each section is an editorial comment on the group of papers and a specific comment on each paper. This Introduction and these comments are designed to aid the reader in using this text for individual and small group study.

Today, is there a business ethics problem?

The world has moved from modernism to post-modernism. Business sees the same changes in the global market place. Post-modernism comes with differing values and mores. These differences follow our young people into the companies they join. Companies need to hold on to the values and practices that make commerce work well. But these practices are grounded in a prior time. So we worry about the current generation's not knowing from whence great business practices come. Added to the loss of ethical grounding are the pressures of the current economic environment. Economic stress always tests the foundations of any enterprise, especially the ethical foundation. Is it a surprise that the leaders of companies and their staffs turn to practices that are described as unethical in order to meet these challenges?

Have business ethics gotten worse over the decades? To get a better understanding of what has transpired over the past forty years, we undertook a review of *BusinessWeek* articles for the month of March for 1980, 1990, 2000, and 2010 [1]. March was chosen because March 2010 allowed for a consistent four decades. Otherwise, March was not viewed as a notable month in the year. Each decade had its business issues: 1980 had continued fallout from the Vietnam War and some federal bailouts; 1990 had the savings and loan crisis, the collapse of Drexel Burnham Lambert and junk bonds, and a recession; 2000 had the .com era in full swing; and 2010 had the continuing discussion of the sources of the 2007-2008 financial crisis, Bernard Madoff, and Toyota quality problems. The tone of the magazines over the 40 years did shift to a more hostile style of writing relative to business. The business ethics articles results were:

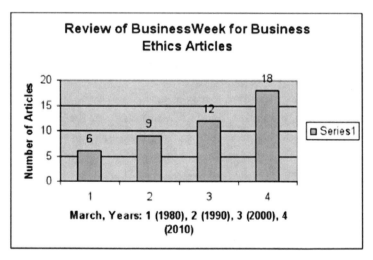

The new millennium has seen a continuous stream of ethical breakdowns in previously respected companies. Starting with Enron, Worldcom, Tyco, and

Arthur Anderson scandals in 2001 - 2002, the new millennium's first decade ended with Madoff, a Food and Drug Administration warning letter to Johnson and Johnson [2] , and the melt-down of the financial system[3]. In chapter 10, "Some Biblical contributions to Business Ethics," the authors delve into the recent Johnson and Johnson matters as well as other drug company operating issues. The United States Congress enacted the Sarbanes-Oxley Act of 2002 (Sarbox) to address the then perceived sources of the problems, primarily governance, accounting firm independence, and financial reporting responsibility. Post-modernism looks to the government for the answer and solution to all behavior problems. Sarbox is such a governmental response to the ethics crisis. Yet, the financial crisis of 2007 to 2009 reveals that Sarbox did not get the job done. Other ethicists recommend proper leadership, or proper corporate governance, or proper corporate mission statements, or proper sense of corporate social responsibility. As seen above none of this has had success. Is there a clear path out of the business ethics problem?

Where to find the answer?
In chapter 1, Charles Colson explores whether a society that has moved away from the foundations of Christianity can teach business ethics. In his paper, "The Problem of Ethics: 'Why Good People Do Bad Things'", [4] Colson finds that the post-modern society has a religion, and it is humanism. Therefore, the U.S. continues to be affected by religion, just not the Anglo-Protestant faith it was founded on. Humanism's key distinctive is that every view has merit, resulting in a community without ethical direction. Colson would challenge us to see that this is precisely why business today has ethical problems.

In chapter 2, "Prolegomena to the Practice of Ethics in Business" articulates the next step in Colson's answer – the Bible. The *Confession* starts with the Bible as the source of God's revelation for mankind of the truth of God and His world. Oliphint's paper develops this into an understanding of why we must stay with the Bible as the source of truth. The Bible contains many directives for behavior. Psalm 1:1-3 says that the righteous man loves God's law and meditates on it. Joshua was encouraged to study God's law, meditate on it and not depart from it [5]. So the Christian is challenged in his or her business activities to know what the Bible provides by way of instruction on various activities

Starting with the Bible as the source of truth, the text papers point in a different direction for the answer to the continuing business ethics problems.

We suggest that the Christian faith holds better guidance on both the source and the solution to business ethics problems. Specifically, we recommend Christianity as found in the *Westminster Confession of Faith* (the *Confession*).

Why Christianity as found in the *Confession*? We acknowledge that the discussion in this text centers on business and commerce and not on the salvation dimension of Christianity. We encourage the reader to explore the relationship of Christianity as found in the *Confession* to the question of salvation of the soul and community. However, the authors hold that, in business, the Christian faith found in the *Confession* creates a distinctive and blessed orientation in the conduct of business.

Did the Reformation really change business ethics?

In support of this premise, we point to several authors: Max Weber, Samuel P. Huntington, Lawrence E. Harrison, and David S. Landes. In 1904, Max Weber wrote *The Protestant Ethic and the Spirit of Capitalism* [6], in which he cited the *Confession* as the articulation of the Christian faith that he felt changed commerce. Weber specifically distinguishes between various Christian traditions in arriving at his conclusion. Huntington wrote a series of books on the effect of faith on society, including economics. *Clash of Civilizations and the Remaking of World Order* [7] contrasted the world before the fall of communism with the world post-fall. Huntington's prediction was that faith will form the central cultural framework that will distinguish one culture from another. In *Culture Matters: How Values Shape Human Progress* [8] co-editors Lawrence E. Harrison and Huntington assembled an anthology on the question of how faith affects a country's economy. The first paper opens with "Max Weber was right." [9] As will be explored below, culture in *Culture Matters* is essentially a worldview concept. Huntington goes on to write *Who Are We?: The Challenges to America's National Identity* [10] in 2004, where he further explored the effect of Protestant heritage in the United States on the values and culture of the United States, including commerce. Of particular interest are his views on the impact of this Protestant heritage on other denominations of the Christian faith, including Catholicism, and the way members of such faiths undertake commerce. [11]

We note here a divergence of views exists in the socio-economic arena on the principles expressed by both Max Weber and Samuel Huntington. Weber creates a continuing flurry of contra-publications. [12] It is not the intent of this Introduction or this text to engage in this debate. [13] Rather the authors are comfortable that Weber, Landes, and Huntington properly shed light on a change in commerce that arose from the Christian faith of the Reformation.[14]

Why does Christianity change business ethics?

Why are we so confident that Christianity as found in the *Confession* (herein-after referred to as Christianity) has a dramatic effect on commerce? We would touch on two aspects of how Christianity affects commerce: 1. A change in the operating rules, and 2. A change in faith that leads to a change in the way people live. Many economists find that it was the Reformation change in the view of usury that enabled the flow of capital required for the industrial revo-lution. In chapter 4, "Devaluing the Scholastics: Calvin's Ethics of Usury,"
the reader will find an excellent discussion both of the historical setting and of how Calvin wrestled with the principles of usury and the proper biblical in-terpretation of passages on usury. The editorial comments preceding Section 1 expand the biblical principles on why Calvin's theology on usury is more consistent with God's requirements in His world. Landes in his book *Wealth and Poverty of Nations* adds to the change in usury, the change in the under-standing of time.[15] Landes would ascribe the change in the view of time as grounded in the faith of the individuals. The Reformation Christian believed that his or her time was part of the resources that God had entrusted to him or her. Therefore, he or she was to use this time wisely. The Reformation also added the theology of assurance, which meant that, since the believer was sure to be in heaven, he or she should practice living in the presence of God here on earth. J.I. Packer describes this in his course, *English Puritans,*[16] as being dual minded, living the Christian life here on earth in the presence of God, while anticipating living in heaven in the presence of God.

Both Weber and Huntington hold that as a person believes, so he or she lives.[17] Belief is foundational to a person's values, and values are founda-tional to behavior, and behavior is foundational to ethics. Therefore, differ-ent religions will lead to different conduct in commerce, to different business ethics. Over and above addressing the subject of salvation, faiths determine the core values of a person, and the person in turn contributes those values to his or her community, including his or her business activity. In his "For-ward" for *Culture Matters,* Huntington defines culture as "the values, attitudes, beliefs, orientations, and underlying assumptions prevalent among people in a society."[18] This works quite well for defining the term "worldview." Harrison in his "Introduction" notes that Alan Greenspan's perspective changed after the fall of Russia, from the assumption that the free-market entrepreneurial system was inherent in all peoples, to it is culture that creates such a system of commerce.[19]   Culture here is "worldview." This is why Landes opens his paper, "Culture Makes Almost All the Difference," in *Culture Matters*, with "Max Weber was right."[20]   Landes notes the importance of Weber's work in studying cultures, particularly the faith interplay with culture, and Weber's observations on the importance of Protestant ethics in commercial development. Landes closes his paper with

> "… it is fair to say that most historians today would look upon the Weber thesis [the role of Christianity in commerce] as implausible and unacceptable: it had its moment and it is gone.

> I do not agree. Not on the empirical level, where records show that Protestant merchants and manufacturers played a leading role in trade, banking and industry. Nor on the theoretical. The heart of the matter lay indeed in the making of a new man – rational, ordered, diligent, productive. These virtues, while not new, were hardly commonplace. Protestantism generalized them among its adherents, who judged one another by conformity to these standards."[21]

Landes then notes two important characteristics of Protestantism in community that contributes to his view that the Protestant Ethic did change commerce. First was literacy, because Protestants believed that everyone needed to read their Bible to know their God. The second was the value of time, noted above.[22]

Chapter 3, "Total Depravity and Business Ethics," explores the problem of what a person believes from the Reformation concept of total depravity, the fallen nature of man. One of the hardest struggles for business ethicists is why we cannot just wish away or teach away the problems of bad business ethics. The Reformation articulated what is obvious to us all, but we deny, that man is fallen and has a constant propensity to do bad. Yet, we also see that man does good some of the time. So the frustration elevates. The Reformation explanation of total depravity answers this dilemma. It also affirms Weber, Huntington, and Landes' observations that people's ethics are founded on their faith. We point the reader to the clear fact that Christianity is a distinctively different faith, which is why the Christian has distinctly different ethics.

Why does the distinctiveness of Reformation Christianity affect business ethics?

The *Confession* sets forth a series of fundamental theological principles that form a faith that is distinctive.[23] While the footnoted summary of Christianity would seem to have no application to business, Landes notes that this Christianity does indeed cause changed lives, a new man, and affects business activities. It was this change in behavior that Weber identifies in his work. Hereinafter, Christian will be understood to refer to those who hold to the principles found in the *Confession* and live by the Christian worldview these principles create.

Why and what changes in behavior are created by this Christian worldview, especially as this behavior relates to business? Landes noted two behavioral differences, literacy and time management, but there are a number of other principles that are more fully explored in this text's papers. Here we look at two other sets of Christian principles that have an effect on behavior. First, the Christian worldview holds that God created the world and continues to sustain the world, making God present throughout the world.[24] Because God created the world and everything in it, the world and everything in it, including humans, belong to God. The Christian's business activity must be seen as belonging to God. Therefore, the Christian is a steward of all that God has given to him or her, including time (cited by Landes), talents and the business, itself. Such a perspective changes behavior relative to governance, self-interest, the need for incentive pay, etc.

Second, because of God's presence throughout the world, the Christian conducts his or her business activity under God's eyes, under God's direct attention. This means that God is watching and will hold the Christian accountable for his or her actions. Therefore, the Christian has a boss who is always present. Because God is the boss and always watching, the effect should be the same as when the human boss walks on the factory floor – everyone is a bit sharper in his or her conduct. Another analogy is the presence along the side of the highway of a state patrol car that causes traffic both to go the speed limit and to become less aggressive. Believing that God is present in every aspect of one's life, including business, has a similar effect. In chapter 6, Barry Asmus and Wayne Grudem in their paper, "What is at Risk for Business If We Lose a Christian Worldview?," present a rich description of the principle of God's presence in the world. Both of these principles directly affect a Christian's behavior or ethics in business. There are many other principles; some have been covered in the papers included in this text.

Does Christianity create good business ethics?

Too often ethics become a description of bad behavior. Christianity celebrates good behavior and models the behavior that is a blessing to the community, even as God has blessed us, His creatures. The two principles, above, look to be negative and constraining, but to the Christian, the presence of God is a blessing; it is what we were made to share. Therefore, the Christian, in feeling the blessed presence of God, is joyous in being more diligent in his or her business dealings. It is this blessing that Weber, Landes and Huntington do not seem to understand. In chapter 8, "Doing Business in God's World: Business is a Calling," the authors highlight the importance of understanding the purpose we have been created to fulfill in God's world. Mac McQuiston relays his experiences in working with executives as they are called to higher positions in understanding both God's will and the blessing that they can be in stepping up in answer to the call.

The Reformation also created a change in perspective that work is indeed part of God's purpose for our lives and thus part of our calling. Coming into the period of the Reformation, being a priest or monk carried the aura of greater holiness.[25] In addition, several groups of monks, such as the Franciscans, adopted vows of poverty and used begging as their means of obtaining sustenance. The Reformers challenged begging based upon their reading of the Bible. As a result, the Reformation affirmed the merit of work in God's calling to the Christian's life. In chapter 7, William Edgar's paper, "Work and Rest: God's Perspective," addresses this dynamic of work and the merit of work in a Christian life. The Section 2 papers further explore the workplace and the Christian's ethics while engaged in the workplace. This calling to work challenges us to the highest performance every day, because all performance is unto God.

In chapter 11, Jeffrey A. Conway and Andrew J. Peterson in their paper, "Courage and Conviction in the Public Company: Adding a Christian Worldview as Found in the *Westminster Confession of Faith*," explore the implications of running a public company as a Christian. Today many are challenged by the oversight environment and the litigious nature of business. The risks are real, but so also is the call of God to service in leading the public company. In chapter 12, Chuck Stetson in his paper, "The Importance of a Business Leader's Contribution to community Leadership," explores the effect of the changing nature of our communities and the contribution that Christian business leaders need to have in their community.

Does Christianity affect commerce as a whole?

But can we really assert that Christianity affects commerce as a whole rather than just an individual's activity? We are quite comfortable with this assertion. From its beginning two thousand years ago, Christianity has impacted daily lives, which in turn impacted the community. In the first three hundred years of Christianity, the Roman Empire did not embrace it. Yet, Christianity flourished and without aggression became the accepted faith for the Empire.[26] For business ethics, the same impact can be seen. A look at the world of commerce shows that Christians changed the way commerce was conducted during the period between 1550 and 1800. Today, the whole world is wrestling with the blessings that have flowed from the changes wrought during this period. Some call the changes capitalism,[27] some the industrial revolution, some creative destruction, but all note that today commerce is different from that engaged in throughout the period of human history before the Reformation. This text views Christianity as the source of this change, the source of commerce as we know it today.

We worry that Huntington is correct in his book *Clash of Civilizations*. Huntington asserts that the culture impact of the different religions in the world will strengthen, thereby creating differing value systems, resulting in differing civilizations. Evidence confirms Huntington's premise. As the world moves away from a Christian worldview, what does this mean to business ethics? In chapter 5, "Are Profits Moral?" demonstrates the shift in social thinking that is impacting our business community. "Are Profits Moral?" presents a series of texts for comparison, starting with the *Westminster Larger Catechism* from 1647,[28] to the *Communist Manifesto* of 1848, with some editorial comments. These texts show how our rhetoric has shifted from godly principles to humanistic principles. The world at large voices negative concerns about business being exploitive,[29] environmentally damaging, and immoral in its creation of private wealth.[30] The contrast between Christian and the current post-modern worldviews could not be sharper than on this point. Having a strong Biblical foundation for why engaging in business is a moral activity is fundamental to Christian business ethics and creates a good template for addressing other business ethic situations using the Bible. The reader is referred to Wayne Grudem's book, *Business for the Glory of God*,[31] which articulates well the principles and theology underlying the concept that business done right is part of God's blessing.

In chapter 6, Barry Asmus and Wayne A. Grudem in, "What Is at Risk for Business If We Lose a Christian Worldview?," explore the implications of the future where the Christian foundations have been abandoned, as was shown in chapter 5, "Are Profits Moral?." Asmus' and Grudem's discussion is gripping in its implications to the business community.

In chapter 10, Galen Radebaugh and Vern S. Poythress in their paper, "Some Biblical Contributions to Business Ethics," explore the implications of company ethics statements and policies in the daily operations of a business. While the company ethics statement provides a measure of ethical guidance, both application consistency and voids in coverage force the Christian back to the Bible for firmer guidance. Using three actual public cases, Radebaugh and Poythress explore biblical guidance that all readers will find insightful.

How can the Church aid the business leader?

An underappreciated aspect of Christianity is its community dynamic. While the *Confession* is clear that it is the individual that must address his or her relationship to God, the individual, as a Christian, becomes part of God's people, His Church.[32] How should the church support the Christian as he or she goes forth to do business?

The modern church has projected an environment that business is not part of church oversight or even church practice. Part of the reason for this state of affairs is the passage, "You cannot serve God and mammon."[33] To this add the general notion of separation of church and state. In modern business, the law now requires further separation of church, or religion, and business. When all of these are combined, the modern church becomes a place for only spiritual matters. This orientation of separation of church and business can be seen as a step backwards from that progress made in the Reformation. Therefore this text has two papers specifically designed to aid the pastor in the challenge of how the church should minister to those engaged in commerce or business. Chapter 14, "Church Support for Doing Business in God's World: Adding a Christian Worldview as Found in the *Westminster Confession of Faith*," gives specific actions for a church to undertake to minister and support those in the congregation engaged in business.

Chapter 15, "How To Get Fat In 90 Days! : The Relationship Of Generosity and Prosperity In Business," uses a measure of the lighter side to explore the important topic of generosity in a competitive world and God's blessings.

To these two papers should be added the final portion of chapter 9,

"Three Offices and the Entrepreneur: How the Church Community Helps the Business Leader Do Well by Doing Good." This paper presents an innovative discussion of the Christian business leader's role in God's world as prophet, priest and king. The authors also address how the Church can establish programs to aid the business leader entrepreneur. Redeemer Presbyterian Church in New York City has a series of programs that the paper cites as examples of what a church can develop in this part of its ministry.

Conclusion

Business Ethics Today: Foundations' papers lay a foundation that each of us can build upon. Paul in 1 Corinthians 3:10-13 challenges us with this counsel:

> By the grace God has given me, I laid a foundation as an expert builder, and someone else is building on it. But each one should be careful how he builds. For no one can lay any foundation other than the one already laid, which is Jesus Christ. If any man builds on this foundation using gold, silver, costly stones, wood, hay or straw, his work will be shown for what it is, because the Day will bring it to light. It will be revealed with fire, and the fire will test the quality of each man's work. (NIV)

Notes

1. Business ethics articles were those listed in the table of contents that contained the following descriptions: a. Negative ethical behavior (the scan revealed few positive articles), b. Product problems which had a management/quality orientation (Toyota's recall reaction as an example), c. Lawsuits, d. Scandals or investigations, and e. Corruption. Each month of March had four magazines.

2. Johnson and Johnson is cited here because its response to a 1982 crisis with its Tylenol product is still cited as the standard for ethical behavior. For a brief summary see http://iml.jou.ufl.edu/projects/Fall02/Susi/tylenol.html.

3. See the white paper, "The Credit Crisis of 2007 and 2008," by Phil Clements for more background on principles outlined in the Bible that were ignored by the financial industry, http://www.cfcbe.com/wp-content/uploads/2009/12/Credit-Crisis-of-2007-and-2008-Phil-Clements.pdf.

4. Charles Colson, "The Problem of Ethics: 'Why Good People Do Bad Things,'" edited from Charles Colson's address to Harvard Business School, April 4, 1991.

5. Joshua 1:1-9

6. *Max Weber, The Protestant Ethic and the Spirit of Capitalism, New York: Scribner, 1958. The Protestant Ethic* was first published in German in 1904.

7. Samuel P. Huntington, *Clash of Civilizations and the Remaking of World Order,* New York: Touchstone, 1996.

8. Lawrence E. Harrison and Samuel P. Huntington, eds, *Culture Matters*, New York: Basic, 2000.

9. David Landes, "Culture Makes Almost All the Difference," *Culture Matters*, Lawrence E. Harrison and Samuel P. Huntington, eds, New York: Basic, 2000, p 2.

10. Samuel P. Huntington, *Who Are We?: The Challenges to America's National Identity*, New York: Simon & Schuster, 2004.

11. Huntington, *Who Are We?*, p. 30 summarizing the centrality of Anglo-Protestant culture in America; p. 65 summarizing the Protestant attributes of the American Creed, which are consistent with the Confession; p. 92-98 describes the Americanization of Catholicism, wherein American Catholics have adopted similar values to Protestants while maintaining their religious practices.

12. Amintore Fanfani, *Catholicism, Protestantism, and Capitalism*, 1934; repr., Norfolk, VA: IHS Press, 2003. George O'Brien, *An Essay on the Economic Effects of the Reformation*, 1923; repr., Norfolk, VA: IHS Press, 2003. R. H. Tawney, *Religion and the Rise of Capitalism*, New York: Harcourt, Brace & Co., 1924. Kenneth Hooper and William Hooper, *Puritan Gift*, London: I.B. Tauris, 2007. Articles in the *Journal of Business Ethics* routinely challenge Weber's findings. One notable article exception by Donald E. Frey, "Individualist Economic Values and Self-Interest: The Problem in the Puritan Ethic," *Journal of Business Ethics*, 17: 1573-1580, 1998, supports Weber's basic premises.

13. The underlying reasons for the protest over Weber center on points such as his research methods, or lack thereof, and the lack of including other economic principles, because Weber is more of a social scientist. This is why the findings in *Culture Matters* and other Landes and Huntington works are so relevant to this question. These are the rare texts of current times that affirm Weber. The reader should not be surprised that the world cries out against findings showing that Christianity plays a key role in a great society, including its business activity. The Bible says man has been doing this since the Garden of Eden – rejecting God and His ways, even if God's ways are a blessing. In business, we would say that the amount of disagreement, and the continuation of this disagreement, suggests that indeed Weber touched a truth nerve. In Acts 5:33-42 Gamaliel spoke to his fellow Jewish leaders that if Christianity was not of God, then it would come to naught; but if it was of God, they could not stand against it. Perhaps Weber, Huntington and Landes, who were not known to be Christian, identified a continuing truth. The authors of this Introduction believe this to be the case.

14. The Reformation is used to refer to the Protestant Reformation with the Westminster Confession of Faith being the capstone statement of its theology.

15. David S. Landes, *The Wealth and Poverty of Nations: Why some are so Rich and Some so Poor*, New York: Norton, 1999, p.178. This book fully develops much of Landes thinking found in his paper in *Culture Matters*, cited herein.

16. J.I. Packer, *English Puritan*, Reformed Theological Seminary Virtual Campus, virtual course lectures.

17. Huntington, *Who We Are?*, p. 30.

18. Harrison and Huntington, *Culture Matters*, p.xv.

19. *Ibid*, p. xxiv, xxv.

20. *Ibid*, p. 2.

21. *Ibid*, p. 11, 12.

22. *Ibid*, p. 12

23. A list of essential Christian principles from the Confession could be a) The Bible is the source for revelation, b) God is creator and sovereign of the world, c) God's providence provides sustaining sustenance for all His creatures here on earth, d) Man is created in God's image, yet fallen with a corrupted nature and is in need of redemption, e) God's provision of that redemption is through

the finished work of God's only Son, Jesus Christ, f) God's unmerited favor, grace, provides for the application of this redemption to the individual believer solely through the individual's faith, g) Faith is also a gift from God and not based on merit or works, and g) The individual believer is assured of salvation, therefore practices living in God's presence and lives in anticipation of being with God in heaven after this life.

24. Psalm 139 gives an extensive description of God's presence in all the earth and knowledge even of our very thoughts.

25. Other religions have similar holiness positional orientations. Buddhists, Hindus, and most animist religions attribute to the priest special holiness status.

26. A full exploration of the impact of Christianity on culture is beyond the scope of this Introduction. In addition to the referenced Huntington books, we would point the reader to some of the many books on Christian history.

27. Since the flourishing of capitalism, many have endeavored to define the term. Weber defined it, "Capitalism is distinguished by the striving for profit, indeed, profit is pursued in a rational, continuous manner in companies and firms, and then pursued *again* and *again*, as is *profitability*." Max Weber, "Prefatory Remark's to *Collected Essays in the Sociology of Religion (1920)*," *Protestant Ethic & Spirit of Capitalism* (trans. Stephen Kalberg; Los Angeles: Roxbury, 2002) 152-3. Other definitions do not contain the foundational "spirit" concept of Weber. The spirit notion provides an important cultural explanation that is playing out today as societies become more divided by their religious foundations. On one hand, we see capitalistic enterprises spanning cultures and the globe. This could leave one with the impression that we have indeed moved beyond a "spirit" issue. On the other hand, the world wherein capitalism and global enterprises were founded no longer exists. *The Puritan Gift*, noted elsewhere, adopts the framework that religion has nothing to do with the status of commerce as we see it today. Rather the Puritan gift is just good management techniques. But what if *The Puritan Gift* is wrong? Can it be that indeed faith makes all the difference and that without it commerce will go in the direction of pre-Reformation ethics? There are a number of places in the world today that function in the same way as commerce in Roman times. For example, many developing countries such as found in Africa or Latin America have commercial activities that are quite consistent with pre-Reformation practices.

The following are definitions which illustrate the spectrum of thinking on capitalism. Stark, *The Victory of Reason*, 55 defines capitalism as "an economic system wherein privately owned, relatively well organized, and stable firms pursue complex commercial activities within a relatively free (unregulated) market, taking a systematic, long-term approach to investing and reinvesting wealth (directly or indirectly) in productive activities involving a hired workforce, and guided by anticipated and actual returns." 56. Novak, *Business as a Calling*, 80-84 summarizes Karl Marx's definition as, "a system of market exchange, private property, and private accumulation or profit." Novak then defines capitalism as, "an economic system, dependent on an appropriate political system and supportive moral-cultural system that unites a large variety of social institutions (some new, some old) in the support of human economic creativity. It is a system oriented to the human mind: *caput* (L. "head"), wit, invention, discovery, enterprise. It brings institutional support to the inalienable right to personal economic initiative." Novak then notes that free markets and private property are not sufficient to equate to capitalism, citing Biblical Jerusalem, which had free markets and private property. Finally, Novak summarizes the heart of capitalism as, "creative wit, and the sheer joy of creating something solid, substantial, lasting and worth losing one's shirt for… The money that may (or may not) follow is more akin to public recognition than it is end in itself." Milton Friedman, *Capitalism and Freedom* (Chicago: University of Chicago Press, 1962 renewed 2002) 13, uses the term "competitive capitalism" and defines it as a society organized through voluntary exchange, provided the transaction is bi-laterally voluntary and informed. This leads to division of labor and specialization of function. O'Brien, *Effects of the Reformation*, 61-64, has these observations on capitalism: "... what really distinguishes the present age, which we call capitalistic,... - is that nowadays the capital employed in industry is not owned by the worker, and that the profits which that capital earns ... accrue for the benefit of persons not actually working in the industry." But O'Brien notes that this distinctive and 3 others, usury, avarice and large-scale activities, are not traits of a capitalistic society. O'Brien says the capitalistic spirit "is that the accumulation of wealth is looked on as a good in itself. ... In other words, business for business' sake has become the watchword of the modern capitalist." Fanfani, *Catholicism, Protestantism*, 49 cites "...Vito, the Italian economist, held that capitalism could be identified with 'economic system characterized by (a) free choice of activity on the part of economic agents; (b) private ownership of the means of productions; (c) competition'(F. Vito, *Il problema della stabilita*.)" Fanfani notes the difference in definitions between economists and sociologists, such as Weber. Fanfani concludes "that the capitalist spirit is the essence of capitalism." 51. "Since the capitalist spirit is nothing but the prevailing economic spirit of a given period, ... By economic spirit we mean that complex inner attitude, conscious or subconscious, in virtue of which a man acts in a certain determined manner in business matters. ... the economic spirit of a given age is necessarily inseparable from the current idea of wealth and its ends. " 56. Fanfani then notes a comparison with the historic views of economic spirit with a negative view of the capitalist spirit, since it amounts to the "unlimited use of all means of acquiring wealth." 58-59.

This summary has been provided to highlight the godless orientation to the discussion of business. If we add the Christian worldview to this discussion, capitalism looks very different. Perhaps the following three principles might help: 1) Privately owned enterprises in response to seeing a need in God's world decide what and how much to produce and at what price to sell in order to be profitable. 2) Labor is free to develop and sell its skills and services to enterprises. 3) As God's stewards, owners, including laborers, reinvest profits in their enterprises rather than using them for personal consumption.

28. The *Confession* was completed in 1647, and ratified by Parliament in 1649 and 1690.
29. See Leonardo Boff and Clodovis Boff, *Introducing Liberation Theology*, New York: Orbis Books, first printing 1987, 2005; Gustavo Gutierrez, *A Theology of Liberation*, New York: Orbis Books, first printed 1973, 2003, for a foundation and Michael Novak, *Will It Liberate: Questions About Liberation Theology*, New York, Madison Books, 1986, 1991, for a more balanced explanation of the implications of Liberation Theology. For an Introduction to the current administration's perspective on the application of Liberation Theology to U.S. policy see Jerome R. Corsi, *The Obama Nation: Leftist Politics and the Cult of Personality*, New York: Threshold Editions, 2008.
30. See the discussion of capitalism in footnote 22, especially Novak's views which tend to be socialistic. Modern politics have adopted the humanistic notions of equal distribution of earth resources. Therefore, private wealth creation is not appropriate. Much of Christendom has adopted these views as well.
31. Wayne Grudem, Business for the Glory of God: The Bible's Teaching on the Moral Goodness of Business," Wheaton: Good News, 2003
32. The theology that discusses the differences between the Church universal, the Church of faith, and the visible Church are beyond the scope of this Introduction.
33. Matthew 6:24.

SECTION 1
FOUNDATIONS

SECTION 1:
FOUNDATIONS

PHILIP J. CLEMENTS

A ssembled in this section are six papers. Each touches on a topic that forms part of the foundational principles for a Christian Ethics framework for business. The first three papers give grounding on the importance of the Bible and its revelation of God to all ethical discussions, including business ethics. The next three papers consider the shifts in thinking starting with the Reformation as first regarding usury, then moving from Reformation to modernity as shown with profits and property rights, and then considering the future, if Christianity is abandoned by commercial society. The changes in the community' thinking about commerce recorded in these three papers is shocking. The following are brief high lights of each paper, with some additional editorial comments.

THE PROBLEM OF ETHICS - WHY GOOD PEOPLE DO BAD THINGS

Chuck Colson sets the stage in "The Problem of Ethics." Speaking before a Harvard Business School assembly in 1991, Colson responds to the challenge of "Why do good people do bad things." Harvard's former President Bok decried the loss of ethics in the American business community. Surveys of American business school students have found that, by a two to one margin, businesses are viewed as unethical. Colson says America is experiencing "a crisis of character: a loss of those inner restraints and virtues that prevent Western civilization from pandering to its own darker instincts." A society's values must have a consensus and that consensus must have transcendence. Colson cites Margaret Thatcher's speech where she professed her own faith and noted that the Judeo-Christian tradition provides the moral impulse that causes people to rise above themselves and do something greater than themselves. How this moral impulse works is then analyzed. Colson closes with our biggest challenge

– finding the will to do what is right. Colson cites Solzhenitsyn that the line between good and evil passes not between principalities and powers, but it oscillates within the human heart. Even the most rational approach to ethics is defenseless, if there isn't a will to do what is right. Colson declares that he only has this will through Christ.

For the business person trying to create a culture that allows the business to perform above the individual selves, these passages are instructive. While Colson touched on a number of the core principles of ethics, including the concept that ethics are about what ought to be rather than what is, the next paper sets the anchor for where we as Christians believe that these ethical principles are to be found.

PROLEGAMENA TO THE PRACTICE OF ETHICS IN BUSINESS

K. Scott Oliphint drills down on the problem of relativism in our society, then sets up Christianity as the "impossibility of the contrary" (IC). Oliphint goes on to apply the implication of IC to society and business using marriage and demographics. As he drills into the problem of relativism, four examples are used to show how there can be no consensus on truth, affirming Colson's observations that America has lost that essential consensus. But Oliphint goes further to note that philosophy, which is widely studied in America, has not come to "one iota of consensus" in four millennia of rational thinking. Oliphint goes further to declare that relativism is by definition weak and insular, lacking the power to proclaim. As business people, we see this problem as a lack of leadership and vision. Business knows that the truth of a business does not allow for every differing view on strategy or practice.

IC, impossibility of the contrary, is a useful tool for discussing absolute truth. "Christians believe that Christianity *alone* is true." This is Oliphint's IC and it forms the distinctive of Christianity. The bedrock foundations of this worldview are the Scripture and God. The Westminster Confession of Faith's first two chapters articulate what the Christian believes about Scripture and God. "Unless we begin with God and his revelation to us in Scripture, there is no proper way to ground and found anything else that we do."

Oliphint ends his paper with a discussion of the significance of the Bible itself in this IC perspective. Of particular importance is Oliphint's coverage of the role of the Holy Spirit. No other paper in this text touches on the Holy Spirit and Oliphint captures this critical point perfectly:

As and when Scripture speaks, God Himself, in the person of the

Holy Spirit, speaks. The Spirit does not speak "though" the Word; He does not speak as one who "appropriates" the Word; the Word is not, for Him, an "instrumentality." Rather, the Word is just the Spirit speaking.

Too often the role of the Holy Spirit is underexplored in understanding how the Bible is effective in aiding the Christian in developing ethical practices. Jesus said that when He went away the Father would send the Holy Spirit, who would guide us in all truth.[1] The Christian businessperson needs to see that regular Bible study is the foundation for allowing God to affect Christian business ethics. Prayer and meditation based on God's Word, bringing it to bear on the business issues of each day, allow the Holy Spirit to administer answers and guidance. Psalm 1:1-3 summarizes the importance of this process.

In the middle of his paper, Oliphint considers the implications of IC to our society and business community. Using the example of marriage, he shows how God's perspectives on man and woman and marriage have been abandoned, with enormous economic implications to the business community. Similar observations are given about the implications of abortion and the decline in populations on the business community.

In this section, Oliphint gives an important warning about what is called the prosperity gospel. The Christian businessperson is "not to succumb to a secular, pragmatic mind-set – a mind-set that thinks that doing things God's way is bound to lead to earthly rewards." The Christian is to recognize that "*everything* ... is to be conducted for and to the glory of God,... *even if it happens that we reap no ... earthly rewards.*" Success is to practice our activities so as to honor and glorify God. Having said this, IC means that it is impossible to truly prosper without starting with God and His revelation, the Bible.

TOTAL DEPRAVITY AND BUSINESS ETHICS

Richard B. Gaffin, Jr. takes us to a critical next step in his paper, "Total Depravity and Business Ethics." This paper was published in *Christians in the Marketplace* [2]. Gaffin addresses a core set of issues for the Christian: total depravity and common grace. Total depravity is the theological concept that man is fallen and cannot aid himself relative to understanding and exercising the things of God. But then why do non-believers have success? Colson, in his paper, puts the question, why do bad people do good things? The answer is common grace. Gaffin explains in easy to follow language the importance of understanding God's patience and benevolence towards mankind. In His creation, God gave to man a measure of understanding of what is right. Man rejects this, but that does not mean that man cannot do right things on occasion. Colson closed his paper with this warning: the will to do right does not lie in the heart of man; rather it must be placed there by faith in Christ.

Gaffin goes on to further explain common grace's negative and positive types. The negative are the restraints that God places on both His righteous wrath and the restraints on evil in the world. Total depravity points to the fact that without God's grace in restraining mankind, the level of evil in the world would be unimaginable. Genesis 6 describes this condition and the necessary flood to clean it up. Gaffin briefly summarizes the theology around why the world's condition is part of this negative of common grace. The positive side to common grace is seen in God's goodness towards all creatures. The outcome of this positive side is unbelievers undertaking what is right, the blessings that come from arts and science, and the general well-being of the human race.

God's common grace has direct bearing on business and economics. Gaffin addresses a number of the paradoxes raised by common grace. The problem of the unbeliever doing good and not being able to do good is nicely covered in understanding the fallen nature of man and his relationship to God. Gaffin's second observation points out that Common grace sounds like it is common to all, but God deals with different individuals in their uniqueness. Gaffin also touches on the paradox of the unbeliever that meets expectations and the believer that fails.

Unfortunately, Gaffin does not fully cover two hard paradoxes for Christian business people. Solomon touches on the first in Ecclesiastes, that unbelievers can be successful, while believers struggle. Common grace is a key answer to this dilemma. The second is the ability to train people in a measure of proper behavior. While Gaffin touches on mission statements in his business ethics application, not covered is the affect that common grace has on being able to train members of a company in these ethical principles with some success. Gaffin's negative perspective is consistent with Calvinistic total depravity theology, but leaves the business person too pessimistic for the real world of business. God's common grace abides in both the fact, noted by Gaffin, that man has a measure of knowledge of what is right and that this knowledge can be stimulated into a measure of action. Businesses count on this training fact of common grace. Gaffin does properly warn the business person that "*de facto* conformity to God's law is not true obedience. To think of this conduct as somehow ethically superior is risky at best."

Gaffin concludes the paper with a specific discussion on application to business ethics. He observes that natural revelation adds nothing to the capacity to develop good business ethics. This confirms Oliphint's and Colson's observations. Gaffin points out that seeming compliance with good behavior by the unbeliever is not necessarily true ethics, as noted above. Finally, Gaffin summarizes that any economic system, including capitalism, is subject to exploitation by the deceit and perversity of the human heart.

DEVALUING THE SCHOLASTICS: CALVIN'S ETHICS OF USURY

Michael Wykes in "Devaluing the Scholastics: Calvin's Ethics of Usury" takes the reader through a thorough look at usury. This paper is a challenging read because of the depth of the analysis and the terminology used. This paper can properly be called a scholarly work. The paper is included in this Foundations text for two reasons. First, the change in the view of lending and interest from usury did contribute to the industrial revolution. Second, Wykes captures the level of thinking and analysis that Aquinas and Calvin brought to everyday issues. When business people approach Christian business ethics, we need to see the intensity of these principles, because God deserves this level of discipline. Therefore, the reader will find it well worth the effort to go through this paper.

In addressing the shift of thinking and theology on usury between Aquinas and Calvin, Wykes discusses a series of business practices. The refinements in practice are not dissimilar to those experienced today. As we consider business ethics, this level of refinement of business practice as shown in the usury analysis is worthy of consideration. The Center for Christian Business Ethics Today believes that crisp and refined business practice analysis is very much part of what made the Reformation Christians different. They were not sloppy in their thinking and struggled hard with what was a right practice and what was not.

Unfortunately, Wykes does not add to the usury analysis a discussion of Jesus' parables of the mina or talents. In both parables, Jesus indicated that the master had the right to at least the interest to be earned by putting the master's funds in the bank. Neither Aquinas nor Calvin addressed this point as recorded by Wykes. Yet, it is a fundamental principle of business. Further, the principles articulated by Wykes based on Aristotle and Roman law that affected the development of Aquinas' theology of usury are not supported by these parables. Calvin does not seem to address this distinction in his analysis, but effectively incorporates Jesus' views in his conclusions. Wykes would come to some interestingly different perspectives by incorporating these parables in his analysis. The short answer might be that Aristotle and Aquinas did not understand the basics of business and lending, but both got caught in some interesting cultural concepts as outlined by Wykes. On the other hand, perhaps Jesus and the Jews of his day did understand the basics of business finance, so that the lessons to them were therefore fundamentally different, all be it much closer to Calvin's conclusions. The reader is left to ponder this question as he or she works through the paper.

ARE PROFITS MORAL?

"Are Profits Moral? Answers from a Comparison of Adam Smith, Max Weber, Karl Marx, and the Westminster Larger Catechism" captures the movement of thinking in the Western world by reprinting with limited commentary pertinent texts from the various sources. If the Reformation thinking, as found in the Westminster Larger Catechism, is critical to the Industrial Revolution and commerce as we know it today, which is what the Center holds, then the trend as highlighted in this paper is most troubling. In commerce we talk much about Adam Smith and the invisible hand, but it is clear that Western society uses the language found in the Communist Manifesto. Today, neither commerce nor community use the language of the Catechism. What does this mean?

WHAT IS AT RISK FOR BUSINESS IF WE LOSE A CHRISTIAN WORLDVIEW?

Barry Asmus and Wayne Grudem nicely step in to answer this question with their chapter, "What is at Risk for Business, If We Lose a Christian Worldview?" With clarity and precision, these authors zero in on a series of fundamental values that are at risk. Every business person should know these and be prepared to address them in their planning. More importantly, the business person should not lose heart, but go back to the first three papers to be sure he or she has the comfort that this is indeed God's world and He is in control.

Briefly, Asmus and Grudem cover the potential loss of accountability. The business person depends on accountability as a fundamental trait for his people. This loss begs for alternative solutions. One of these should be seeing Christians as standing out because of their continued sense of accountability. The loss of in the belief in the moral goodness of business is the next point. Clearly in America there is much banter about the evils of various businesses and industries. But the paper goes on to note the resulting loss of blessings. The Christian business person needs to see that business for him is his calling as is discussed in the next section. For the Christian, business is a mission, captured nicely by the paper in its section titled "Business Transactions as a Way of Loving

Your Neighbor as Yourself." Loss of respect for private property is the next "at risk." A good series of Bible passages are set forth validating the views of private property rights in God's world. For this part the reader may wish to revisit the prior paper's presentation of the communist view – abolish private property. The loss in the belief in the goodness of productive work helps us understand what happens when some in community labor and achieve success, while others lounge. Additionally the authors note the potential decline in the quality of work. The next section of this text further explores the theology of work and these issues are more fully developed. However, the fact that work ethic is at risk should not be missed by any business person, for business counts on the work ethic of its people. The final section is the loss of a hopeful view of time and history. Businesses need hope that there is a point and a future. We will see this in the next section on work ethics. Christianity uniquely brings a hopeful perspective to the world. The authors note that the "Christian worldview encourages attempts to improve our lives, to bring change and improvement to the human situation," because we have faith that we will receive God's blessings. Weber, included in the prior paper, noted that as long ago as the 1600s Christian workers brought a different perspective to their job; they made suggestions for improvements, because they worked for God first, then the company. Business is blessed by this sense of hope and improvement. The community then is blessed by the business that is bringing positive opportunities for improvement.

Asmus and Grudem set up the next section well. The foundations have been framed. Now they will be applied to work.

Notes

1. John 14:26.
2. R. C. Chewning, ed. *Christians in the Marketplace: Biblical Principles and Business: The Foundations*, Colorado Springs: NavPress, 1989, p139-54, herein slightly revised and edited, 2010, used with permission.

THE PROBLEM OF ETHICS

Why Good People Do Bad Things

CHARLES COLSON

Chuck Colson is a popular and widely known author, speaker, and radio commentator. A former presidential aide to Richard Nixon and founder of the international ministry Prison Fellowship, he has written several books—including Born Again, Loving God, How Now Shall We Live?, The Good Life *and* The Faith Given Once, for All—*that have shaped Christian thinking on a variety of subjects. His radio broadcast* BreakPoint *airs daily to two million listeners.*

In 1993, Colson was awarded the prestigious Templeton Prize for Progress in Religion; the $1 million prize—along with all speaking fees and book royalties—are donated to Prison Fellowship. In 2008, President Bush conferred on him the second highest civilian award of the U.S. government, the Presidential Citizen Medal for his humanitarian work with Prison Fellowship.

The following copy is an adaptation of an address that I gave at Harvard Business School on April 4, 1991. It is the first speech I gave on the subject of ethics, and I've been giving it ever since. It is what triggered my interest in ethics, and it remains as pertinent today as it did twenty years ago when you consider events such as the 2008 financial crash, which was caused by ethical failures of government, Wall Street, lenders, and the public. It is vital that people understand there is a moral law to be known, and that it is possible to cultivate character and virtue within ourselves and the fabric of society. Ethics applies to the great life issues of our day, regardless of who you are where you work—be it in medicine, business/commerce, government, or elsewhere.[1]

THE PROBLEM OF ETHICS

Harvard well deserves its reputation as a very liberal university—liberal in the best sense of the word—because you have as a lecturer in the university today someone who is an ex-convict.

Harvard also deserves the reputation for being a liberal university, in the best sense of the word, because over the last three years, I have written articles that here at Harvard could be considered quite impertinent, in which I have described my views on why it is impossible to teach ethics at Harvard. And you've invited me to speak anyway.

I'm no longer in politics. I've done my time, literally and figuratively. But it's awfully hard not to watch what is happening on the political scene without a certain sense of dismay. Look at the Keating Five—five United States senators, tried, in effect, by their own tribunal. Just before that, Senator Dave Durenberger, who happens to be a good friend of mine, was censured by the Senate. I also spent some time with Marion Barry, the former mayor of the District of Columbia, who was arrested for drug use. And in South Carolina and Arizona, scams in the legislatures have been exposed by federal prosecutors.

I saw a press release in which the Department of Justice boasted that last year they had prosecuted and convicted 1,150 public officials, the highest number in the history of the republic. They were boasting about it, yet I read it with a certain sadness because it seems that kind of corruption has become epidemic in American politics.

We have seen congressmen, one after another: Coehlo, Wright, Frank, Lukens—both sides of the aisle—either being censured or forced out of office. We see probably the most cynical scandal of all—the HUD scandal—where people were ripping off money from the public treasury that was designed to help the poor. Then, we've seen more spy scandals during the past five years than in all previous 195 years of American history combined—people selling their national honor for sexual favors or money.

Business is not immune. The savings and loan scandals are bad enough on the face of them, but the fact that they're so widespread has fostered almost a looter's mentality. Ivan Boesky, speaking at UCLA Business School five years ago, said, "Greed is a good thing," and ended up spending three years in a federal prison. Just last week one of the major pharmaceutical firms was fined $10 million for covering up violations of criminal statutes.

It affects athletics. If you picked up a newspaper this week, you saw that Sugar Ray Leonard has just admitted to drug use. He's been a role model for lots of kids on the street. Pete Rose spent time in prison for gambling.

Academia has been affected. Stanford University's President Kennedy was charged with spending $7,000 to buy a pair of sheets—they must be awfully nice bed linens—and charging them improperly to a government contract. One day a Nobel Prize winner was exposed for presenting a fraudulent paper, and the very next day a professor at Georgetown University was charged with filing a fraudulent application for a grant from the National Institutes of Health. Probably saddest of all, at least from my perspective, are the cases of certain religious leaders like Jimmy Swaggart and Jim Bakker. Bakker—whom I've also visited in prison—was prosecuted for violating what should be the most sacred trust of all: to speak for God and to minister to people in their spiritual needs.

The first question that comes to mind is whether these are simply examples of rotten apples or of better prosecutors. Maybe you can dismiss these by saying, "This is simply the nature of humanity." I think it was Bishop Fulton Sheen, in paraphrasing G. K. Chesterton, who once said that the doctrine of original sin is the only philosophy empirically validated by 3,500 years of human history. Maybe you dismiss this, too, and say, "this is just the way people are."

But is there a pattern here?

A CRISIS OF CHARACTER

Time magazine, in its cover story on ethics, said what's wrong: "Hypocrisy, betrayal and greed unsettle a nation's soul." The *Washington Post* said that the problem has reached the point where "common decency can no longer be described as common." The *New Republic* magazine said, "There is a destructive sense that nothing is true and everything is permitted."

I submit to you that when the *Washington Post*, the *New Republic* magazine, and *Time* magazine—which have never been known as bastions of conservative, biblical morality—begin to talk about some sort of ethical malaise, a line has been crossed. These aren't simply isolated instances, but rather a pattern emerging in American life.

No institution has been more sensitive to this than Harvard. Former President Bok has given some extraordinary speeches decrying the loss of ethics in the American business community. I think some of you have seen the recent polls finding that business school students across America, by a two-to-one margin, believe that businesses are generally unethical. It's a very fragile consensus that holds together trust in our institutions. When most business school students believe there aren't any ethical operations, you begin to wonder if something isn't affecting us a lot more broadly than isolated instances of misbehavior that have been exposed.

I believe we are experiencing today in our country what I choose to call a crisis of character: a loss of those inner restraints and virtues that prevent Western civilization from pandering to its own darker instincts.

If you look back through the history of Harvard, you'll see that President Elliott was as concerned about the development of character as he was about education. Plato once said, if you asked why we should educate someone, "We educate them so that they become a good person, because good persons behave nobly." I believe we should be deeply concerned about the loss of what Edmund Burke called the traditional values of republican citizenship—words like valor, honor, duty, responsibility, compassion, civility. Words that sound quaint when uttered in these surroundings.

Why has this happened? I'm sure many of you studied philosophy in your undergraduate courses, and, if so, you are well aware that, through twenty-three centuries of Western civilization, we were guided by a shared set of assumptions that there was a transcendent value system. This was not always the Judeo-Christian value system, though I think the Judeo-Christian values were, as the eminent historian Christopher Dawson wrote, "the heart and soul of Western civilization."

It goes back to the Greeks and Plato's saying that if there were no transcendent ideals, there could be no concord, justice, and harmony in a society. There is through twenty-three centuries of civilization—the history of the West—a strain of belief in a transcendent value system. Whether it was the unknown god of the Greeks, the Christ of the Scriptures revealed to the Christian, Yahweh of the Old Testament revealed to the Jew, or, as Enlightenment thinkers chose to call it, natural law—which I believe to be not inconsistent with Judeo-Christian revelation—this belief guided our conduct for twenty-three centuries until a great cultural revolution began in America.

This revolution took place in our country in the 1960s. Some think it goes back further. Paul Johnson—who happens to be one of my favorite historians—wrote a history of Christianity, a history of the Jew, and a classic book called *Modern Times*. Johnson says that gradually, through the 1920s and 1930s, people began to challenge what had been the fixed assumptions by which people lived—the set of fixed and shared common values.

In the 1960s it exploded. Those of you who were on college campuses in the sixties will well remember that the writings of Camus and Sartre invaded American campuses. Basically, they were what Camus said when he came to America and spoke at Columbia University in 1947. To the student body assembled he said, "There is nothing." The idea was introduced that there is no God. In this view there is no transcendent value; life is utterly meaningless, and the only way that we can derive meaning out of life is if we overcome the nothingness of life with heroic individualism. The goal of life is to overcome that nothingness and to find personal peace and meaning through your own autonomous efforts.

Most of the people of my generation dismissed what was happening on the campuses as a passing fad—as protest. It was *not*. The only people who behaved logically in the sixties were the flower children. They did exactly what they were taught; if there were no other object in life than to overcome the nothingness, then go out and smoke pot, make love, and enjoy personal peace.

Then, America came through the great convulsion of Watergate and Vietnam—a dark era—and into the seventies. We thought we shook off those protest movements of the sixties. We did not; we simply embraced them into the mainstream of American culture. That's what gave rise to the "me" decade.

If you look at the bestsellers of the 1970s they are very revealing: *Winning Through Intimidation; Looking Out for Number One;* and *I'm Okay, You're Okay.* Each of these were saying, "Don't worry about *us*." We emerged into a decade that Tom Wolfe, the social critic, called "the decade of Me." Very logically that graduated into the 1980s and what some have cynically called "the golden age of greed."

Sociologist Robert Bellah wrote a book titled *Habits of the Heart*—a phrase he borrowed from Tocqueville's classic work on American life. Bellah examined the values of several hundred average, middle-class Americans. He came to the conclusion that the reigning ethos in American life in the eighties was what he called "ontological individualism," a radical individualism where the individual is supreme and autonomous and lives for himself or herself. He found that Americans had two overriding goals: vivid personal feelings and personal success.

Bellah tried to find out what people expected from the institutions of society. From business they expected personal advancement. Okay, that's fair enough. From marriage, personal development. No wonder marriages are in trouble. And from church, personal fulfillment! But the "person" became the dominant consideration.

Now, I would simply say—and I'll try to be as brief with this as I possibly can—that this self-obsession destroys character. It has to! All of those quaint-sounding virtues I talked about, which historically have been considered the elements of character, are no match for a society in which the exaltation and gratification of self becomes the overriding goal of life.

Rolling Stone magazine surveyed members of the baby-boom generation, to which many of you emerging leaders in this room belong. Forty percent said there was no cause for which they would fight for their country. If there's nothing worth dying for, there's nothing worth living for. Literally the social contract unravels when that happens, and there can be no ethics.

How can you have ethical behavior? The crisis of character is totally understandable when there are no absolute values. The word *ethics* derives from the Greek word *ethos,* which literally meant "stall"—a hiding place. It was the one place you could go and find security. There could be rest and something that you could depend upon; it was immovable.

Morals derives from the word *mores,* which means "always changing/" *Ethics* or *ethos* is the normative; what *ought* to be. "Morals" is what *is.* Unfortunately, in American lives today we are totally guided by moral determinations.

So, we're not even looking at ethical standards. Ethical standards don't change. It's the *stall,* it's the ethos, it's the environment in which we live. Morals change all the time. So with shifting morals, if 90 percent of the people say that it's perfectly all right to do this, then that must be perfectly all right to do because 90 percent of the people say it is. It's a very democratic notion.

Ethics is not—*cannot* be—democratic. Ethics by its very definition is authoritarian. That's a very nasty word to utter on any campus in America, and particularly at Harvard, where Arthur Schlesinger has written a magnificently argued assault on the perils of absolutism.

In a relativistic environment ethics deteriorates to nothing more than utilitarian or pragmatic considerations. If you're really honest with yourselves and look at the ethical questions you're asked to wrestle with in your courses here at Harvard, you will see that you are being taught how to arrive at certain conclusions yourself, and to make certain judgments yourself, which ultimately are going to be good for business. That's fine, and you should do that. That's a prudential decision that has to be made. That's being a responsible business leader. It just isn't ethics and shouldn't be confused with ethics.

Ethics is what *ought* to be, not what is, or even what is prudential.

There was a brilliant professor at Duke University, Stanley Hauerwas, who wrote that "moral life cannot be found by each person pursuing his or her options." In relativism, all you have is a set of options. The only way moral life can be produced is by the formation of virtuous people of traditional communities. That was the accepted wisdom of Western civilization until the cultural revolution of the sixties, with which we are still plagued.

What is the answer? I'd like to address two points: first, how each of us, individually, might view our own ethical framework, and second, why some set of transcendent values is vital.

OUR ETHICAL FRAMEWORK

We live in a pluralistic society. I happen to be a Baptist—and believe *strongly* that, in a pluralistic environment, I should be able to contend for my values as you should be able to contend for your values, and out of that contention can come some consensus we can all agree to live by. That' s the beauty of pluralism. It doesn't mean extinguishing all ideas; it means contending for them and finding truth out of that consensus.

Out of the battle comes some consensus by which people live. But I would argue that there must be some values; and I would take the liberty of arguing for my belief in a certain set of historic values being absolutely essential to the survival of society.

First, let me address the question of how we find it ourselves. If you studied philosophy courses as an undergraduate, you read about Immanual Kant and the categorical imperative. You read about rationalism and the ways in which people can find their own ethical framework. I guess the only thing I can tell you is that in my life—and I can't speak for anyone else—it didn't work.

I grew up in America during the Great Depression and thought that the great goal of life was success, material gain, power, and influence. That's why I went into politics. I believed I could gain power and influence how people live. If I earned a law degree—as I did at night—and accumulated academic honors and awards, it would enable me to find success, power, fulfillment, and meaning in life.

I had a great respect for the law. When I went through law school, I had a love for the law. I learned the history of jurisprudence and the philosophy underlying it.

I studied Locke, the Enlightenment, and social contract theories as an undergraduate at Brown, and had a great respect for the political process. I also had a well-above average I.Q. and some academic honors. I became very self-righteous.

When I went to the White House, I gave up a law practice that was making almost $200,000 a year (and that was back in 1969, which wasn't bad in those days). It's kind of ordinary now for graduates of Harvard Business School, but then it was a lot of money.

I had accumulated a little bit of money, so I took a job in the White House at $40,000 a year. I took everything I had and I stuck it in a blind trust at the Bank of Boston. Now let me tell you, if you want to lose money, that's the surest way to do it!

After three and a half years, when I saw what the Bank of Boston had done to my blind trust, I realized I was a lot poorer when I came out of the government than I was when I went *into* the government.

But there was one thing about which I was absolutely certain—that no one could corrupt me. *Positive!* And if anybody ever gave me a present at Christmas time, it went right to the driver of my limousine. They used to send in bottles of whiskey, boxes of candy, and all sorts of things. Right to the driver of my automobile. I wouldn't accept a thing.

Patty and I were taken out on someone's boat one day. I discovered it was a chartered boat, and ended up paying for half of it because I didn't want to give the appearance of impropriety. Imagine me, worried about things!

I ended up going to prison. So much for the categorical imperative. The categorical imperative says that with our own rational process we will arrive at that judgment, which, if everyone did it, would be prudential and the best decision for everyone. In other words, that which we would do, we would do only if we could will it to be a universal choice for everybody.

I really thought that way, and I never once in my life thought I was breaking the law. I would have been *terrified* to do it because I would jeopardize the law degree I had worked four years at night to earn. I had worked my way onto the Law Review, Order of Coif, and Moot Court—all the things that lawyers do—and I graduated in the top of my class. I wouldn't put that in jeopardy for anything in the world.

I was so sure. But, you see, there are two problems. Every human being has an infinite capacity for self-rationalization and self-delusion. You get caught up in a situation where you are absolutely convinced that the fate of the republic *rests* on the reelection of, in my case, Richard Nixon. I'm sure that next year people will think the same thing about George Bush. There's an *enormous* amount of peer pressure, and you don't take time to stop and think, *Wait a minute. Is this right by some absolute standard or does this seem right in the circumstances? Is it okay?*

I was taught to think clearly and carefully. As a lawyer that's what you do—you briefcase it, you spend four years in law school, and you go like a monkey. You're briefing cases, briefing cases. We used the case method, as you use the case method here in business. The case method in law school, however, is a little bit different, because you always have a fixed conclusion, so at least I knew there was a fixed law that you would arrive at. I had all the mental capacity to do that. I was capable of infinite self-delusion.

Second, and even more important—and this goes to the heart of the ethical dilemma in America today—even if I had known I was doing wrong, would I have had the *will* to do what is right? It Isn't hindsight. I have to tell you the answer to that is no.

The greatest myth of the twentieth century is that people are good. We aren't. We're not morally neutral. My great friend, Professor Stan Samenow, happens to be an orthodox Jew. I asked him one day, "Stan, if people were put in a room and no one could see what they were doing or no one knew what they were doing, would they do the right thing half the time and the wrong thing half the time? Would they do the wrong thing all the time, or would they do the right thing all the time?" He said they would *always* do the wrong thing.

We aren't morally neutral. I know that's a terribly unpopular thing to say in America today, but it happens to be true. The fundamental problem with learning how to reason through ethical solutions is that it doesn't give you a mechanism to override your natural tendency to do what is wrong. This is what C. S. Lewis—whose writings have had such a profound influence on my life—says.

My blessed friend Tom Phillips gave me the book *Mere Christianity* when I came to him in the summer of 1973 at a moment of great anguish in my life. I wasn't so worried about what was going on in Watergate, but I knew I didn't like what was going on in my heart. But something was different about him. So I went to see him one evening.

I went, and that was the evening that this ex-Marine captain, White House tough guy, Nixon hatchet man (and all kinds of things you can't write about in print or wouldn't say in polite company that I was called in those days—much of it justifiably) found myself unable to drive the automobile out of the driveway when I left his home, after he had told me of his experience with Jesus Christ. I was crying too hard.

I took that little book he had given me, *Mere Christianity*, and began to read it and study it as I would study for a case. I'd take my yellow legal pad and get down all the arguments—both sides. I was confronted with the most powerful mind that I had ever been exposed to, I saw the arguments for the truth of

Jesus Christ, and I surrendered my life eighteen years ago. My life has not been the same since and can never be the same again.

I discovered that Christ coming into your life changes that will. It gives you that will to do what you know is right, where even if you know what is right— and most of the time you won't—you don't have the *will* to do it. It's what C. S. Lewis wrote in that tremendous little book *Abolition of Man.* I'd love for you to read *Mere Christianity,* but if you had to read just *Mere Christianity* or *Abolition of Man* for today's cultural environment, read *Abolition of Man.* Wonderful book!

I don't know how to say this in language that is inclusive, but he wrote a marvelous essay called "Men Without Chests." It's a wonderful article about the will. He said the intellect can't control the passions of the stomach except by means of the will—which is the chest. But we mock honor—and then we are alarmed when there are traitors in our midst. It is like making geldings, he said, and then bidding them to multiply. He was talking about the loss of character in 1947 and 1948, long before the results we are witnessing today of the loss of character in American life.

So much for the individual. What about society as a whole? Margaret Thatcher delivered what I consider to be one of the most remarkable speeches in modern times two and a half years ago before the Church of Scotland. You'll find it reprinted only in the *Wall Street Journal.* Margaret Thatcher said—and I'll paraphrase that marvelous, eloquent speech—that the truth of the Judeo-Christian tradition is infinitely precious, not only because she believes it is true—and she professed her own faith—but also, she said, because it provides the moral impulse that causes people to rise above themselves and do something greater than themselves, without which a democracy cannot survive. She went on to make the case—I think quite convincingly—that without Judeo-Christian values at the root of society, society simply can't exist.

Our founders believed this. We were not formed as a totally tolerant, neutral, egalitarian democracy. We were formed as a republic with a certain sense of republican virtue built into the citizenry, without which limited government simply couldn't survive. No one said it better than John Adams: "Our constitution was made only for a moral and religious people. It is wholly inadequate for the government of any other."

SOME VALUES ARE INVALUABLE

There are four ways in which that moral impulse works. Someone sent me a letter suggesting the topic for this speech, "Why Good People Do Bad Things." I didn't have time to write back and say I really think that it would be more appropriate to address "Why Bad People Do Good Things," because that's a more difficult question.

Why do we do good things? If we live in an age of ontological individualism, if radical individualism is the pervasive ethos of the day, if we simply live for the gratification of our senses, of our personal success, and vivid personal feelings, why do anything good? Who cares? It won't make a particle of difference unless it's important to your balance sheet. But that's pragmatism, that isn't doing good things. That's pure utilitarianism.

First, we do good things because there is something in us that calls us to something greater than ourselves.

Prison Fellowship is, of course, a ministry in the prisons—not a very glamorous place to be. I visited three prisons this weekend. I was so moved in one prison because there were six hundred inmates that came out and saw their lives change. Now those were people who were lost and forgotten. One man stood up and said, "Ten years ago I was in the prison, and two of your volunteers came in, Mr. Colson, and they befriended me, this couple from Akron, Ohio." He said, "You know, they've been visiting me every month and writing to me ever since, for ten years." He continued, "I get out of prison in September, and they've invited me to live in their home." He said, "I'm going to make it."

Why do people do things like this? Why do they go to the AIDS wards? One of my friends goes into the AIDS ward of a prison all of the time, and people die in his arms. Do we do it because we have some good instinct? No! It is a moral impulse.

Why did William Wilberforce stand up on the floor of the Parliament in the House of Commons and denounce the slave trade? He said it was barbaric, and it cost him the prime ministership of England when he said it! But, he said, I have no choice as a Christian. He spent the next twenty years battling the slave trade and brought it to an end in England because of his Christian conscience.

What is it that makes us, as otherwise self-centered people disposed to evil—if the history of the twentieth century and civilization is correct—what is it that makes us do good?

Second, Margaret Thatcher is absolutely right. A society cannot survive without a moral consensus.

I tell you this as one who sat next to the president of the United States and observed our nation's fragile moral consensus during the Vietnam era. We did some excessive things, and we were wrong. But we did it feeling that if we didn't, the whole country was going to fall apart. It was like a banana republic having the 82nd Airborne down in the basement of the White House. One night my car was firebombed on the way home. They had 250,000 protesters in the streets: You almost wondered if the White House was going to be overrun.

The moral consensus that holds our country together was in great peril during that era and during the entire Watergate aftermath of Vietnam. A free society can't exist without it.

Now, what gives it to us? Thomas Aquinas wrote that without moral consensus, there can be no law. Chairman Mao gave the other side of that in saying that morality begins at the muzzle of a gun. Every society has two choices: whether it wants to be ruled by an authoritarian ruler, or whether there can be a set of shared values and certain things we hold in common that give us the philosophical underpinnings of our value system in our life.

I submit to you that without that—call it natural law if you wish, call it Judeo-Christian revelation, call it the accumulated wisdom of twenty-three centuries of Western civilization—I don't believe a society can exist.

The reason we have the most terrible crime problem in the world in America today is simple: We've lost our moral consensus. We're people living for ourselves.

We doubled the prison population in America during the 1980s. We are today number one in the rate of incarceration per capita in the world. When I started Prison Fellowship fifteen years ago, the United States was number three. We trailed the Soviet Union and South Africa. Today we're number one. While we build more prisons and put more people in, the recidivism rate remains constant at 74 percent. Those people go right back in.

The answer to it is very simple. There are kids being raised today from broken families who are not being given values. Remember that Stanley Hauerwas said the way you foster ethics is in tradition-formed communities. They're not being given values in the home, they're not being given values in the school, they're watching the television set for seven hours and thirty-six minutes a day, and what they're seeing is, "You only go around once, so grab for all the gusto you can." Now if that's the creed by which you live, then at twelve years old you're out on the streets sniffing coke. We arrest them and put them in jail. They think we're crazy. So do I.

Until you have some desire in society to live by a different set of values, we'll be building prisons in America until, as is the case today, 25 percent of the black, male inner-city population in America is either in prison or on probation or parole. We can't make it without that moral consensus. It will cost us dearly if we can't find a way to restore it.

Professor James Wilson, formerly at Harvard Law School, wrote one of the most telling pieces I've ever read, and I refer to it in one of my books, *Kingdoms in Conflict*. He wrote a primer, while he was here at Harvard, about the relationship between spiritual values and crime. It is really interesting.

The prevailing myth is that crime goes up during periods of poverty. Actually, it went down during the 1930s. He found that, during periods of industrialization, it went up as what he called Victorian values began to fade. When there was a resurgence of spiritual values, crime went down. He saw a direct correlation. Crime went up whenever spiritual values went down; when spiritual values went up, crime went down.

Third, I think we often miss the basis of sound policy because we have become secularized in our views in America and afraid to look at biblical revelation. We're terrified of it.

When Ted Koppel gave the commencement speech at Duke University a few years ago, in which he said the Ten Commandments weren't the Ten Suggestions, and that God handed the Commandments to Moses at Mt. Sinai, you know what the press did to him. It was horrible. A fellow like Ted Koppel couldn't possibly say something like that! So we blind ourselves to what can often be truth.

I have spoken to over half of the state legislators in America and have spoken with many of the political leaders around this country. I always make the same argument to them about our prisons. We have way too many people in prison. Half of them are in for non-violent offenses, which to me is ludicrous. They should be put to work. People should not be sitting in a cell at a cost of $20,000 a year to tax payers while doing absolutely nothing, and while their victims get no recompense. Offenders ought to be put in a work program paying back their victims. Whenever I speak about that, the response I get from political officials is amazing. It really is.

In the Texas legislature, I gave that talk and they all applauded. Afterward the Speaker of the House said, "Mr. Colson, wait here. I'm sure some of the members would like to talk to you." They came flooding in afterward. They all said that restitution is a wonderful idea—where did that come from? I asked,

"Have you got a Bible at home?" They said, "Have I got a Bible at home?" "Well," I responded, "you go home and dust it off and you'll see that's exactly what God told Moses on Mt. Sinai."

That's biblical truth. That's the lesson of Jesus and Zacchaeus. We blind ourselves to it because we think there's something wrong with that in today's tolerant society. But in a pluralistic society that ought not to be wrong. We ought to be seeking that out. If we can find wisdom, find it. So often we find wisdom in the teachings of the Holy Scriptures.

Fourth, no society exists in a vacuum. Vacuums don't remain vacuums— they get filled. In a vacuum, a tyrant will often emerge. You've just seen seventy years of that crumble in the former Soviet Union. Isn't it interesting that when it crumbles, it so often crumbles because people have an allegiance to a power above the power of that earthly potentate?

I remember when Pope John Paul II said that he would return to Poland if the Soviets invaded during Poland's period of martial law in the early eighties. Years earlier Stalin had said, "Hah! The Pope! How many divisions does he have?" Well, as a result of the Solidarity movement, we saw how many divisions he had—a whole lot more than the Soviets.

I remember getting on a plane and coming up to Boston to see our first grandson when he was born, back in 1981. A man got up in the aisle of the plane and was all excited to see me. He said, "Chuck Colson!" He was blocking the people coming behind me, so I finally got him into his seat.

He was talking so fast that I couldn't understand him. To make a long story short, he introduced himself as Benigno Aquino.

Aquino told me that when he was in jail for seven years and seven months, as a political prisoner of Marcos, he had read my book *Born Again*. He was in a prison cell and had gotten down on his knees and surrendered his life to Jesus Christ. He said after that his entire experience in prison changed. Well, Nino and I became pretty good friends. We did some television programs together, and we visited frequently.

He called me up one day and said, "I'm going back to the Philippines." I said, "Nino, do you think that's wise?" He said, "I have to, I am going back because my conscience will not let me do otherwise." He was safe here in America, he had a fellowship at Harvard, and he could lecture anywhere he wanted. He and his wife had everything they could possibly want.

But he knew he had to go back to the Philippines. "My conscience will not let me do otherwise." He said, "If I go to jail, it'll be okay, I'll be president of Prison Fellowship in the Philippines." He said, "If there are free elections, I'll be elected president. I know I can beat Marcos. And if I'm killed, I know I'll be with Jesus Christ." He went back in total freedom. And he was shot and killed as he got off the airplane.

But an extraordinary thing happened—what's known as people power. People went out into the streets. The tanks stopped. People went up and put flowers down the muzzles of guns: A tyrant was overthrown. A free government was reasserted because people believed in a power above themselves.

I was in the former Soviet Union last year and visited five prisons, four of which had never been visited by anyone from the West. I met with Soviet officials. It was really interesting. I met with Vadim Bakatin, then minister of interior affairs. When talking about the enormous crime problem in the Soviet Union, he said to me, "What are we going to do about it?" I said, "Mr. Bakatin, your problem is exactly the one that Fyodor Dostoyevsky, your great novelist, diagnosed. In *Brothers Karamazov,* he had that debate between the older brother, who is unregenerate, and the younger brother, Alexis, who is the priest, over the soul of the middle brother, Ivan. At one point, Ivan yells out and says, *'Ah, if there is no God, everything is permissible.'* Crime becomes inevitable." I said, "Your problem in the Soviet Union is seventy years of atheism." He said, "You're right. We need what you're talking about. How do we get it back in the Soviet Union?"

All I could think was how foolish we are in America to be squandering our heritage. In a country where they've ignored the king of greater power for seventy years, they're losing it all.

FINDING THE WILL TO DO WHAT IS RIGHT

I can only leave you with a very simple message, as someone who had thought he had it all together and attained a position of great power. I never thought I'd be one of the half-dozen men sitting around the desk of the president of the United States, with all of that power and influence. I discovered that there was no restraint on the evil in me. In my self-righteousness, I was never more dangerous.

I discovered what Solzhenitsyn wrote so brilliantly from a prison—that the line between good and evil passes not between principalities and powers, but it oscillates within the human heart. Even the most rational approach to ethics is defenseless if there isn't the will to do what is right. On my own—and

I can only speak for myself—I do not have that will. That which I want to do, I do not do; that which I do, I do not want to do.

It's only when I can turn to the One whom we celebrate at Easter—the One who was raised from the dead—that I can find the will to do what is right. It's only when that value and that sense of righteousness pervade a society that there can be a moral consensus. I would hope I might leave with you, as future business leaders, the thought that a society of which we are a part—and for which you should have a great sense of responsibility and stewardship—desperately needs those kind of values. And, if I might say so, each one of us does as well.

Notes

1. This entire chapter was copied from Charles Colson's *The Line Between Right and Wrong: Developing a Personal Code of Ethics* (Uhrichsville, Ohio: Barbour Publishing, Inc., 1997). Used by permission.

PROLEGAMENA TO THE PRACTICE OF ETHICS IN BUSINESS

K. SCOTT OLIPHINT

Doctor Oliphint is professor of apologetics and systematic theology at Westminster Theological Seminary in Philadelphia. He earned the MAR (1983), ThM (1984), and PhD (1994) from Westminster Theological Seminary. Before moving to Westminster in 1991, he was in pastoral ministry in Texas from 1984. He is the author of The Battle Belongs to the Lord: The Power of Scripture for Defending Our Faith (P&R, 2003), Reasons for Faith: Philosophy in the Service of Theology (P&R, 2006), *and coauthor, with Rod Mays, of* Things That Cannot Be Shaken: Holding Fast to Your Faith in a Realistic Way (Crossway, 2008).

The topic of business ethics and how people in the workplace can add a Christian worldview using the Westminster Confession of Faith is not only appropriate, but, I believe, is central to any discussion of what a "successful" business is. In order to discuss the notion of "business ethics," it is necessary, first, to try to outline just exactly *how* a Christian worldview is molded and shaped by the Westminster Confession of Faith. Once we have ventured into that discussion, it should become clearer just exactly how that worldview can, and must, shape any and every discussion of business, generally, and of business ethics, more specifically. My task, then, will be to provide a framework within which business ethics can flourish. Let's begin by noticing what the basic problem is.

A TROUBLING TREND

One of the most persistent problems, in the history of thought and of society, is *relativism*. Relativism holds that truth is what it is only *relative* to a particular person. It is to be distinguished from any view that holds that differing views should be *tolerated*, but it is a very short step from the *toleration* of different truths to the *affirmation* that truths that differ are *all true*. Four examples may help illustrate this.

1. In his groundbreaking book, *The Closing of the American Mind*, Alan Bloom began by affirming what has been obvious to most of us—that every student entering college assumes, as a bedrock foundation, that truth is relative (*that* truth, however, does not appear to be relative). Bloom notes that such a belief is rarely argued by anyone because it need not be; it is simply assumed. Thus, higher education, as he later notes, can be compared to the "barkers" at a fair, each wanting the crowd to step right up to their own particular program and win the big prize. With this, the *uni*versity has become a *multi*versity. It has become so because there no longer remains anything to unify the diversity within a college curriculum. Every program has its own wares to peddle, and may the best salesman win.

2. In the late sixties a "Worldview" conference was called in Europe, consisting of a host of academics and specialists. One of the primary purposes of that conference was for the group to define just exactly what a worldview was. In that goal, the conference failed. When philosopher W. T. Jones was analyzing the failure of the conference to define a worldview, he noted that "the differences of opinion about worldview reflect differences in our own worldviews." In other words, the best minds in the Western world did not have the intellectual equipment necessary to form and define even a generic description of a worldview upon which all could agree.

3. Quoting from a book on worldview and its relationship to postmodernism, David K. Naugle points out the pluralism that postmodernism entails: "Such stark pluralism can no longer be described as a *Streit der Weltanschauungen* [conflict of worldviews], for worldviews can conflict only if they compete as accounts of the same 'world.' In the extreme pluralism of . . . [postmodernity], there is no single 'world'—there are as many worlds as there are worldviews. It is possible . . . that we are now on the threshold of the end of the age of worldviews."[1]

The problem highlighted by this author, some twenty years after the worldview conference, is that the entire notion of a worldview is in danger of dying, given the extreme relativism of the postmodern mind-set.

4. One final example, perhaps more obscure than most, but nevertheless just as cataclysmic: In a recent introduction to the subject of metaphysics (which has to do with the nature of ultimate reality), the author (Peter van

Inwagen of Notre Dame University), who himself wants to promote and set forth a particular view of metaphysics, was compelled, in a refreshing moment of honesty, to note that anyone studying metaphysics—unlike any of the "hard" sciences—needs to be aware of the fact that, though philosophy has been dealing intently with this subject for more than four millennia, there is as yet not one iota of consensus on just exactly what it is that they're dealing with. Van Inwagen confesses his dismay and frustration at this state of affairs, and wonders why it is the case, but he also recognizes that it is. In other words, when it comes to the nature of ultimate reality, the best philosophical minds for the past four thousand years have been unable to establish one truth to which the rest of the philosophical community, and the rest of us, could hold.

Surely these examples, which could no doubt be almost endlessly multiplied and are applied in different contexts, scream for analysis. They *have* been analyzed, but the serious, central, and persistent problems tend to remain. What is needed in such a context is boldness and courage. Relativism, by definition, is weak and insular; it lacks the power to proclaim, since truth is constrained to context, and it hides behind its self-made gate, unable to cross its own boundaries. Such an idea splits society into small, weak fragments and guarantees that all the king's horses and all the king's men will never be able to put it all back together again. Note:

> A fragmented society . . . displays loss of nerve, which means that it cannot summon the will to suppress public obscenity, punish crime, reform welfare, attach stigma to the bearing of illegitimate children, resist the demands of self-proclaimed victim groups for preferential treatment, or maintain standards.[2]

Or, in the words of David Wells:

> It is, therefore, a matter of some poignancy to realize that in the very moment when our culture is plunging into unprecedented darkness, at the very moment in which it is most vulnerable, the evangelical church has lost its nerve. At the very moment when boldness and courage are called for, what we see, all too often is timidity and cowardice.[3]

If it is the case that the church has lost its nerve, it is likely the case that

Christians generally, in whatever endeavor, have lost their nerve as well. Surely this does not bode well for Christians in business.

The "Impossibility of the Contrary"

One way to approach such a problem, and the way I would like for us to approach it here, a way that takes boldness and courage, is to think in terms of (sometimes called) "the impossibility of the contrary." Some have tried to approach the problem in just this way, but have met with little success. The success, or lack thereof, however, is not directly tied to the approach. To simplify, it looks something like this: instead of assuming all truth to be relative, the "impossibility of the contrary" approach takes a stand on a particular view of truth, recognizing that another, contrary, position is unable to come to grips with the problems and difficulties that are real and present before us.

In my view, this is by far the best Christian approach to take—not only with respect to the *truth* of Christianity, but with respect to any applications and implications that stem from that truth (including ethics generally and business ethics more specifically). This is the approach taken, more or less, by Bloom in the book mentioned above. As he analyzes the rampant relativism present in American culture, he goes on to argue for a return to Plato and the Greek understanding of absolutes. This argument, in the end, fails as well since the Greek understanding of absolutes itself has been shown to be seriously deficient. The approach *itself*, however, is not the problem. The problem in Bloom's book is that he proffered the wrong absolute, an absolute that, as it turns out, was just as relative as the relativism he wanted to confront.

From a Christian perspective, "the impossibility of the contrary" approach (I'll just shorten it to the "IC" approach) includes the notion that Christianity, and Christianity alone, is able to address the problems and concerns that happen to be present in any given context (be it "life in general," family, business, etc.). We can put the approach more simply. Christians believe that Christianity is true (John 17:17). They do not believe that it *might be* true, or that it is *only* true "for me," or that its truth is one among many religious truths. More specifically, Christians believe that Christianity *alone* is true.

Whenever we speak of something being "true," we may often, perhaps inadvertently or unconsciously, relegate such a thing to an intellectual category. That is, we may be prone to think that truth is *thought*, but *real* life is *lived*. That is a much too restricted and truncated way to think about truth. Whenever we affirm that something is *true*, we are affirming, at least, that it is inextricably linked to the way the world is and how we live in it. So, to say that Christianity is true is to say that it accurately and really grounds, founds, and articulates what the world is like and how to live in it. More specifically, when we say that Christianity *alone* is true, we are saying that it *alone* accurately describes and defines the world we live in, and that it *alone* describes and defines for us how we are to live in the world.[4] So, when we are thinking of the "impossibility of the contrary," the IC approach, we are arguing for the fact that Christianity *alone* is true, and that anything contrary to it (including business) will inevitably fall short, and will *in principle* be doomed to failure. This has sweeping and vast implications for life, and certainly for the way we think about ethics in the business setting.

That's the positive way to state the IC approach. The negative way to state it is that the IC approach argues for and/or applies the fact that, unless Christianity is true, there is no adequate means available to us to think and live consistently. In the context of business, unless Christian truths and principles are applied, there is no adequate means available consistently to act and live and work.

Included in any IC approach is the fact, well articulated and argued as far back as Aristotle (though only properly incorporated in Christian theology), that any and every thought, along with any and every application of that thought, must itself have a *foundation* or a *ground* on which to stand in order to be what it is, or to do what it is supposed to do. For Aristotle, this foundation or ground was the law of non-contradiction. However, it was soon shown that such a law itself needed a ground in order to be adequately *applied*, and thus the Aristotelian ground crumbled, as all will inevitably do if consistent with their autonomous principles.

It was this IC approach, as a truly Christian approach to thought and life, (i.e., a Christian worldview) that was embedded in the writing of the Westminster Confession of Faith. It seems important for the matter at hand if we first make clear the *theological* rationale for the confession. The question has been asked as to why the confession did not begin with the doctrine of justification, given the central significance of this doctrine during the time of the Reformation, or why it did not begin with Christ, given the centrality of Christology for the Christian faith. We should note here that there was a definite and resolute rationale for beginning this confession with the doctrine of Scripture. In order to understand that rationale, it is necessary for us to remember the deep-seated roots of the theological (and philosophical) notion of *principia* (principles). Because the Latin term is much richer than our English term, "principles," we will use the Latin, which denotes a source, foundation, and ground—that upon which anything else is built.

The term *principia* is one that has its roots in the Greek term *arche*, which means a "beginning point," "a source," or "a first principle." As we noted above, its theoretical roots go back at least as far as Aristotle. Aristotle argued that all *archai*, or first principles, or beginning points, are the "first point from which a thing either is or comes to be or is known"[5] In other words, *archai*, according to Aristotle, provide the bedrock foundation for everything that *is*, or *is known*. This concept of a beginning point, what some have called an *Archimedean point*, is a necessary and crucial aspect of *all* being, thinking, and living. Aristotle understood this, philosophy has continued to articulate this idea (though it has failed to provide the needed starting point), and Christian theology has seen it as basic to its own discipline.

To cite one example in theology, the Dutch theologian Sibrandus Lubbertus argued, in the late sixteenth century, that *all* activities and disciplines, and especially theology, require *principia*, and that such *principia* partake of at least the following properties: (1) they are necessarily and immutably true, and (2) they must be known *per se*, that is, in themselves, as both immediate and indemonstrable.[6] By "immediate here" is meant that the status of a *principium* is not taken from something external to it, but is inherent in the thing itself. It does not mean, strictly speaking, that nothing *mediated* the truth therein, but rather that nothing *external* mediated that truth. By "indemonstrable" here is meant that the *fact* of a *principium* is not proven by way of syllogism or by external means, but is such that it provides the ground upon which any other fact or demonstration depends. In this sense, it entails an IC approach.

For example, *speaking of the discipline of theology*, Philippe du Plessis Mornay, the so-called Hugenot pope, stated, "For if every science has its *principles*, which it is not lawful to remove, be it ever so little: much more reason is it that it should be so with that thing which hath the ground of all *principles* as its *principle*."[7]

Notice what Mornay was saying here. Not only was he saying that theology has its own *principia*, but he was saying much more than that. He was also affirming that, whereas all disciplines have their own *principia*, theology's *principia* must undergird and underlie any and every other *principia*. The *principia* of other disciplines, any other work or activity (e.g., business) are relative to those disciplines or activities; the *principia* of theology are prior to any other *principia* of any and all other disciplines and activities.[8] What this means is that any enterprise that seeks a *ground* for its existence and practice must find that ground in biblical truth.

For Christianity, *principia* can never be located, even if tangentially, in the human self. To do so would lead to the kind of skepticism and relativism that followed in the wake of the rationalism of Cartesian philosophy. Instead, as Richard Muller notes:

> The classical philosophical language of *principia* was appropriated by the Reformed orthodox at a time and in a context where . . . [it] served the needs both of the Reformation sense of the priority of Scripture and the Reformation assumptions concerning the ancillary status of philosophy and the weakness of human reason. By defining both Scripture and God as *principial* in the strictest sense—namely as true, immediate, necessary, and knowable . . . the early orthodox asserted the priority of Scripture over tradition and reason and gave conceptual status to the notion of its self-authenticating character in response to both Roman polemicists and philosophical skeptics of the era.[9]

A couple more points to make with respect to these *principia*: We should make clear here that in standard Reformed thought, including the Westminster Confession, there were two *principia*, and this follows again from philosophical discussions dating at least as far back as Aristotle. In *Metaphysics* IV.3, Aristotle noted that first principles, in order to be *first* principles, must themselves be most certain, indemonstrable, immediately evident, and *never* a postulate or hypothesis. According to Aristotle, first principles are those which anyone must have when he begins to think about anything at all, or to live life based on that thinking. First principles, therefore, cannot be something that someone acquires in the midst of one's reasoning or argument. They must be the ground on which we stand in order to think and live properly.

In this sense, as we just mentioned, the *principia* that form the foundation for everything else are themselves "transcendental" in nature. This means that they transcend the matters and contexts to which they apply. They provide for the *possibility* of anything else, be it in thought or in life (and along with that, the *impossibility* of anything that oppose them); if in a particular discipline or activity, then they provide for the possibility of that discipline or activity. In our context, they provide for the possibility of an ethical foundation for the practice of business. But if in an ultimate sense, as is the case with theological *principia*, then they provide for the possibility of anything else whatsoever. They provide for the possibility of *being* and for the possibility of *knowing*. A particular discipline can be what it is supposed to be, and can know what it is and what it is supposed to be, based only on those ultimate *principia*.

OUR BEDROCK FOUNDATIONS: SCRIPTURE AND GOD

This brings us to a further, general, point concerning *principia* that relates directly to the subject matter of our Confession. In the discussions of *principia*, two categories were central. There was necessarily a *principium* with respect to Being, or existence, and, just as necessarily, a *principium* with respect to knowing. *Principia*, therefore, refer primarily to the *principium essendi*, which is the principle, source, or foundation of something existing and of it being what it is, and the *principium cognoscendi*, which is the principle, source, or foundation of knowledge, or of knowing what one must be and do in a given context.

Given these two concerns, it should be noted here that the two primary doctrines that serve as *principia* for theology are the doctrine of God and the doctrine of Scripture. And while we do not have the time to work out the relationship between these two *principia*, we should note at least the following.

First, the juxtaposition, so familiar in the Reformed confessions, between the doctrine of Scripture and the doctrine of God relates specifically to a particular, Reformed, understanding of who God is and of how He may be known. This is all just another way of saying that the only way in which we can know God, or anything else, is if God graciously chooses to reveal Himself to us. For us as creatures, therefore, and this is the salient point to make with respect to the Reformed confessions, and the Westminster Confession particularly, there is an inextricable link, an inextricable *principial* link, between God and revelation. From the perspective of the creature, you cannot have one without the other. This surely means that for any activity or any endeavor, we must first understand who God is and what He requires of us. We must understand His *design* for such an activity or endeavor.

What we have, therefore, in this most excellent beginning two chapters from the Westminster Confession is something solidly Christian, magnificently creative (in the best sense), and theologically (as well as practically) charged. What we have in these two chapters of the Westminster Confession is an articulation and a true "confession" of what are for Christian folk our bedrock foundations, Scripture and God, apart from which we cannot know anything, without which we cannot have any certainty, and behind which we cannot go.

Now, with respect to our IC approach, what this means is that unless we begin with God and his revelation to us in Scripture, there is no proper way to ground and found anything else that we do, or that we want to do. It is *impossible* consistently to live, to think, to transact business, to organize and maintain a family, etc. without the clear teaching of God in his revelation. This surely means that any view of leadership—civic or otherwise—must come first from what God has said. Let's look a little more carefully at that.

The opening chapters of Genesis are crucial for any worldview, and are a necessary part of a Christian worldview. Not only do these chapters make clear that, prior to creation, there was only God, but they also make clear that anything else that exists is wholly dependent on Him. So, a Christian worldview begins with the God who is self-contained; He did not need anything or anyone else in order to be who He eternally is (Acts 17:25). And then a Christian worldview acknowledges that God freely decided to create. We begin with the fact that God is God—wholly independent and without need of anything—and everything else is created and sustained by Him (cf. Heb. 1:3).

THE FOUNDATIONS OF SOCIETY AND BUSINESS

Yes, Marriage

In the biblical account of creation, God Himself makes a significant distinction between what He created in the first five days, and what He created on the sixth day. God first created the heavens and the earth; after that He created various forms of life, as well as other realities in the universe (including the heavenly bodies), in the first five days.

On the sixth day, however, God took counsel with Himself and determined to create man (meaning, male and female) in His image (Gen. 1:26–27.). This is the only time in the process of creation that God spoke to Himself. In all other creation days, He spoke things *into* existence. On the sixth day, he counseled with Himself in order to affirm the creation of man (male and female) in his own image. This is significant in that, for the first time in creation, and on the last day in which God "worked," one has now been created whose relationship to God is defined in terms of "image." It is this one's responsibility, now, to "image" God in the way he acts and thinks. In that sense, for the first time in creation, that which was created (male and female) is responsible to God—responsible to God to "image" him. This "imaging" begins to define who man is.

When God made man (male and female) in his image, a part of the image included the stewardship of man's dominion over everything else created: "Then God said, 'Let us make man in our image, after our likeness. And let them have dominion over the fish of the sea and over the birds of the heavens and over the livestock and over all the earth and over every creeping thing that creeps on the earth'" (Gen. 1:26 ESV).

This dominion includes the fact that man is responsible to nurture that which God has created in order to bring out its potential, to the glory of God. Creation was not given to man "complete," but was given as a gift to man, in order that we might bring out its latent potential in such a way that God would continue to be glorified in it. It is to be "ruled," in other words, within the confines of his instructions and commands.

So, for example, just as He blessed the fish and the birds and other living creatures, God blessed man and commanded that he be fruitful and multiply. He could have easily created an earth with its entire population intact. Instead, he created Adam and Eve in such a way that they were to populate the earth with more "after their kind" (see Genesis 1:21, 25 KJV).

In keeping with this instruction in Genesis 1, in Genesis 2 the Lord gives us a bit more detail concerning the relationship He established between Adam and Eve. After placing Adam in the garden, which the Lord Himself planted (2:8) so that Adam might "rule" it to the glory of God (2:15), the Lord declares that it is not good that Adam is alone. Everything else the Lord created was seen to be good by Him (Gen. 1:10, 18, 21, 25). The only thing that was "not good" in the garden was that Adam was alone.

> So the LORD God caused a deep sleep to fall upon the man,
> and while he slept took one of his ribs and closed up its place
> with flesh. And the rib that the LORD God had taken from the
> man he made into a woman and brought her to the man. Then
> the man said, "This at last is bone of my bones and flesh of my

flesh; she shall be called Woman, because she was taken out of Man." Therefore a man shall leave his father and his mother and hold fast to his wife, and they shall become one flesh. And the man and his wife were both naked and were not ashamed. (Gen. 2:21–25)

This passage is vital for the establishment, structure, and maintenance of any society. As man (male and female) is created in the image of God, he is responsible, in a way that no other creature is, to "image" God in his relationships. That "image" must necessarily begin with marriage as we have it given to us in this passage.[10]

This means, in the first place, that God is the Creator and Lord of marriage. Marriage is not a social convention; neither is it something that was started or invented by man. God created the institution of marriage because, in a place where there was no sin or evil (yet), it was, nevertheless, *not good* for Adam to be alone. It was not good for man to be alone, in part, because God himself was not alone. He exists as three Persons, each of whom is fully God and together who are the one God. The three, in other words, are One. So also, when God gave Eve to Adam and joined them together, he declared the two to be "one flesh." So, the Three-in-One that is the Godhead is "imaged" in the two-in-one that is marriage.

What this means, in part, is that, in keeping with our IC approach, any attempt, whether conscious or unconscious, willful or not, to undermine or subvert the truth of what marriage is and how it is to be conducted, will inevitably end in failure. It will run headlong into the reality of what marriage *really is*, and therefore will not be able to be sustained in the long run. If marriage is seen, for example, as having its roots and meaning simply in our decision, then it can be too easily overturned with a contrary decision if the going gets difficult. And to rend asunder what God has joined together is to risk incurring some level(s) of God's wrath. Since the family, as created and instituted by God, is the foundational building block of every other relational institution in society (church, school, business, organizations, etc.), those institutions are only as strong as the foundational block on which they rest, and are dependent on it for their "success."[11]

So, leadership (e.g., civic leadership) has to begin with stewardship, and then move from that basic truth to some definite boundaries and principles that must be kept, or else it will fall prey to a mere relativistic approach and practice. This means, then, that marriage must begin as that which is created and ordained by God, and thus practiced according to his principles. To repeat, marriage is neither a social convention, nor something created by the state. So, for example, the practice of abortion not only opposes the principle that God creates and sustains His image from the point of conception on (Ps. 139), but it also violates His "creation command" for marriage to be *fruitful*. *Not* to follow His principles in these areas runs the real risk of destroying and/or perverting that which only God can *truly* prosper, and it runs the risk of incurring God's wrath (cf. Romans 1:24–2:9). More on this below.

But just *how* does one go about incorporating these principles into one's business or corporation? Not only *how*, but *why* should one be concerned to incorporate such principles? What does it really *mean* to say that the family is the building block of all other organizations or groups, including businesses?

With respect to the "why" question, a couple of points are worth noting. First, in a recent study, it was determined that divorce and unwed childbearing cost around $112 billion per year, or $1.1 trillion over a ten-year period. This is perhaps a very conservative number; some estimates are that the costs could be as much as $150 billion per year, or $1.5 trillion over ten years. Even on a conservative basis, it costs more than the annual cost for the war in Iraq. So the actual cost of the decline of marriage is staggering.

But the monetary consequences are not the most important, from a Christian perspective. What might be the consequences on a more personal level—the consequences for the individuals who spend their lives working in these businesses and corporations each day? Social scientists tend to agree that strong marriages more readily lend themselves toward the possibility of greater wealth, great health, longer life, and a happier life. Much of this should not be surprising; it simply confirms what we have said in our IC approach. If God is the Creator and Lord of marriage, then couples who, even if inadvertently, abide by His standards for marriage will reap some of the good consequences that can come in such circumstances. In other words, because the contrary approach is impossible (IC), anyone who ignores or transgresses God's standards for marriage is automatically out of step with God's design and thus will inevitably be, at the deepest level, confused and disenchanted with life. Such a person will have great difficulty being a consistent and productive worker. A business that can support, encourage, and serve marriages that abide by biblical standards will be supporting and encouraging and serving those on whose productivity that business depends. In this way, at least, the family is foundational to a healthy business.

However, there is something much deeper at work for a Christian business.

God's ways in the world are not so formulaic that we can assure anyone who abides by His principles that they will experience health and wealth. Neither is it the case that anyone who flouts God's principles will inevitably fail at everything he attempts. Scripture is clear that oftentimes, perhaps even most of the time, it is *the wicked* who prosper (Ps. 73). So the Christian in business does not succumb to a secular, pragmatic mind-set—a mind-set that thinks that doing things God's way is bound to lead to earthly rewards. Rather, any business that wants to abide by Christian principles will recognize that *everything* in which it is involved is to be conducted for and to the glory of God (Rom. 11:36).[12] If, as the Westminster Shorter Catechism teaches (Q&A 1), man's chief end is to glorify God and to enjoy Him forever, our prime motivation for implementing biblical principles in all that we do is that He would be glorified, *even if it happens that we reap no, or minimal, earthly rewards.*

From a biblical standpoint, then, to "succeed" in any area does *not* mean, first of all, to acquire much wealth or material, but rather it means to practice our activities and disciplines in such a way as to honor and glorify God, even if the going gets rough along the way. It means to function according to the IC approach, i.e., that it is *impossible* for someone, or "someones," (such as groups or businesses) truly to prosper without beginning from the ground and foundation of the triune God's existence and those principles that are embedded in His revelation to us. This does not, of course, mean, in the end, that everyone must *be* a Christian; rather, it means that the principles that must take precedence in any given context must be Christian principles, or the relativism that is self-*destructive* rather than *constructive* will inevitably take hold and undermine, or destroy, that which one attempts to build.

There is another example that shows that the family is the building block of society. In spite of the fact that empirical evidence shows conclusively that babies in the womb are human beings, the sin of abortion, both nationally and internationally, is a blight on the world and a clear betrayal of God's standards. That which He creates in the womb as His image (Ps. 139:13) is destroyed by man, even before it is able to be seen by a watching world. The attack on God and His character could not be more pronounced than the destruction of those children that He has created, even before they have a chance to breathe. This strikes at the heart of what it means to have a right to life.

But there are extreme practical consequences as well. At a recent conference on corporate venturing and corporate innovation, some of the largest global companies, including Procter & Gamble and Citigroup, presented their growth strategies. The question was posed to each of these two companies as to how they are dealing with the fact that there are one hundred countries where the reproduction rate is below the replacement rate. In some countries it is quite serious, such as Japan, where the rate is 1.1, and Italy, where it is 1.3. These rates indicate that in Japan and Italy there will be only half the number there are today in the workplace in the next generation. At the same time, statistics show that there will be two times the people over sixty-five that half the number of today's wage earners will need to support. Even though the population will increase because of people living longer, the overall earning power of the nation will decline dramatically because there are only one-half of the workers in the next generation, and a substantially greater portion of their income will go to supporting retirees.

Clearly, it is crucial for us as individuals, for our families, our churches, our businesses and for society generally that we emphasize the foundational importance of a biblical view of the family. In September 2009, the "Let's Strengthen Marriage Campaign" was launched, beginning with the first National Marriage Week USA, which met with great success. In particular, since only 28 percent of churches have marriage courses, it is important that LSM reach out to the Church. LSM encourages every church to set up a marriage-and-family ministry, along with their ministries of worship, stewardship, outreach and education. Such a ministry could include (1) courses in marriage preparation, dating, and courtship, as well as (2) courses dealing with abstinence in middle school, high school, and college; and (3) marriage enrichment courses for those who are married. In January 2010, LSM held and archived a global webinar for pastors and lay leaders that lays out the critical importance of strengthening marriage.

If, as Christians, we hold to the IC approach—that is, if we hold that any approach to marriage except God's has dire consequences, both in this life and the next, then we need to think creatively about how we might support the biblical standards for marriage in our corporations and our businesses. Not only will we have healthier and happier employees, overall, but we will show the world that, contrary to popular opinion, doing things God's way is not only *not* restrictive, but is the only way for us to be truly *free* to do what God has called us to do in this world.

The Bible

Our discussion of marriage is a more specific example of the IC approach mentioned above. It is a specific area where the practicality and the principle can be seen for what they truly are, i.e., *God's* design. There is also, however, a more general application of the IC approach that has to do with the significance of the Bible itself for all that we are, say, and do—in other words, the significance of the Bible for a *biblical* worldview.

In order to see this example for what it is, we need to emphasize and expand what we were attempting to argue above. The IC approach holds that Christianity is true. The negative way to say this is that anything that is *not* Christianity, or that opposes Christianity, is false. That is, anything opposed to Christianity does not comport with the way the world *really* is. This is basic to any Christian worldview.

When we say that Christianity is *true*, part of what that means is that Christianity *contains* the truth that is needed in order to live in God's world. That truth is now contained in Holy Scripture (John 17:17). In order to see the value of our example below, we need first to get straight just what Scripture *is* as our *principium*, and how we should think about it.

As the Westminster Confession puts it, it is the obligation of every man to believe what Scripture says, because it is the very Word of God (1.5):

> The authority of the holy Scripture, for which it ought to be believed and obeyed, depend[s] not upon the testimony of any man or Church, but wholly upon God (who is truth itself), the Author thereof; and therefore it is to be received, because it is the Word of God. [See 2 Peter 1:19, 21; 2 Timothy 3:16; 1 John 5:9; 1 Thessalonians 2:13]

This section needs a bit of explanation, and a brief look at the Reformer John Calvin can help us here. Holy Scripture is holy because it comes from the mouth of a holy God. It is holy because it is His Word. It is holy because it is God-breathed (*theopneustos* 2 Timothy 3:16). It is not holy simply because it comes from God; it is holy because it is His very Word. Richard Muller's analysis with respect to seventeenth-century Reformed orthodoxy is helpful:

> The definitions of biblical authority offered by the orthodox lead directly to a series of related concepts that further characterize the authority of the text: the specific kind of "authenticity" it bears, yielding its principial status in theology, further defined and qualified by its self-authentication as "worthy of faith" or belief (*autopistos*) in itself. The written Word has authority if it is authentically divine—if it is authentically divine and, therefore, authoritative, it can stand as the *funda-*

mentum [foundation], the sustaining power of Christian faith and life through which the Spirit works, having the authority to adjudicate all theological controversies and all disputes over morals: it is the "authentic norm" (*authentian norma*) which stands above and directs faith and life.[13]

It is because Scripture is the very Word of God, from his mouth, that John Calvin and others defend the character of Scripture in terms of its "self-authentication," or "self-attestation" (*autopistos*). What Calvin means by this needs some explanation. According to Calvin:

It is utterly vain then to pretend that the power of judging Scripture so lies with the church that its certainty depends upon churchly assent. Thus, while the church receives and gives its seal of approval to the Scriptures, it does not thereby render authentic what is otherwise doubtful or controversial . . . But because the church recognizes Scripture to be the truth of its own God, as a pious duty it unhesitatingly venerates Scripture. As to their question—How can we be assured that this has sprung from God unless we have recourse to the decree of the church?—it is as if someone asked: Whence will we learn to distinguish light from darkness, white from black, sweet from bitter? Indeed, Scripture exhibits fully as clear evidence of its own truth as white and black things do of their color, or sweet and bitter things do of their taste.[14]

The point that Calvin is making here might be seen more clearly against the historical, ecclesiastical debates in which he is engaged.

One of the questions that loomed large during the time of the Reformation was the question of ultimate authority. The question was not one of whether or not God was the ultimate authority; that issue was noncontroversial. But then the question that comes most naturally after that was the question of what "vehicle" or "instrument" God uses, ultimately, to communicate Himself and His truth to His people. At the time of the Reformation, the case had been made, and was generally accepted, that God had determined that the church would be the instrument through which His truth was given to His people. This, of course, is true as far as it goes. It is the church of Jesus Christ that is commissioned to spread the gospel, and to proclaim the whole counsel of God to the world.

But the issue ran deeper than that. The issue had to do with just how it could be that one could know what God's truth was, and what He was saying to the church. To oversimplify, the Roman church developed the idea of what was called "implicit faith" in which those in the church were to trust the tradition and officers of the church in matters of faith and life. It was the church that was commissioned by God to determine, propagate, and preserve the truth of God as it is found in Scripture. In other words, for the Roman church, we are to believe that Scripture is God's Word because the church has determined it to be so.

Calvin understood, and set forth clearly, that to think in this way was to put our trust, ultimately, in the church, rather in the Word of God itself. It is, as Calvin notes, the church's "pious duty" to acknowledge Scripture for what it is. This entails, unquestionably, that the church herself is to be subject to Scripture, as the very truth of God, and is not commissioned to *determine* that Scripture is true. The natural question comes, of course, and Calvin anticipates it: If it is the church's responsibility and duty to venerate Scripture (since it is the very Word of God), how, then, are we to know that Scripture is God's own Word?

Calvin's initial answer to this question is with another question—"Whence will we learn to distinguish light from darkness, white from black, sweet from bitter?" The answer to this latter question is simple, on the one hand, but contains within it a profound, Reformed truth with respect to the character of Scripture itself. Simply put, we learn to distinguish light from darkness, white from black, sweet from bitter by the experiencing of those things. All that is needed, therefore, for the attributes of those elements to be known and affirmed is the proper means of experience. Is Calvin saying, then, that the truth of God is itself dependent on something internal to us, something that we have and must utilize?

In order to answer that question, it is important for us to make another distinction, a distinction that was less precise in Calvin's own mind, but which became more precise, and important, as Reformed theology began to develop after Calvin. The distinction has to do with the work of the Holy Spirit, and the relationship of his work to the Word written.

It is the Holy Spirit who Himself is speaking in and through the text of Scripture. "Thus, the highest proof of Scripture derives in general from the fact that God in person speaks in it."[15] This "speaking" to which Calvin refers is not, ever, independent of the words of Scripture themselves. As and when Scripture speaks, God Himself, in the person of the Holy Spirit, speaks. The Spirit does not speak "through" the Word; He does not speak as one who "appropriates" the Word; the Word is not, for Him, an "instrumentality." Rather, the Word is just the Spirit speaking.

It is this speaking of God in Scripture that provides for Calvin the apologetic "punch" that can serve to silence the objector. Scripture needs no other proof to establish it as the Word of God. So, Calvin notes the following:

> True, if we wished to proceed by arguments, we might advance many things that would easily prove—if there is any god in heaven—that the law, the prophets, and the gospel come from him. Indeed, ever so learned men, endowed with the highest judgment, rise up in opposition and bring to bear and display all their mental powers in this debate. Yet, unless they become hardened to the point of hopeless impudence, this confession will be wrested from them: that they see manifest signs of God speaking in Scripture. From this it is clear that the teaching of Scripture is from heaven.[16]

The notion of self-authentication, therefore, is an affirmation that when Scripture speaks, God Himself speaks. The authority of Scripture is not something that only obtains if and when it is affirmed by us. It is an *intrinsic attribute* of Scripture itself, or better, an objective attribute of Scripture, whether or not we affirm it. When Scripture goes out—whether in preaching, in reading, or in evangelizing—it goes out with all the authority of God Himself. It is no "dead letter"; it is the very Word of God Himself, and it never goes out without carrying the authoritative demands of God with it.

This is what the Confession means when it says that God is the author of Scripture. The point is that Scripture is the Word of God because God is its author. We only know that, of course, because Scripture tells us so. But we should not lose sight of the fact that it is God speaking in Scripture that gives it its power, and that defines its identity.[17] This is an important, perhaps *the* important, point to make with respect to Scripture. It attests to its own authority.

As Scripture is God's very Word, it is the Holy Spirit who speaks in Scripture.[18] The words of Scripture are His words. Because these words are God's, they carry His authority. But we need also to remember that, even though the Word of God goes out with the full authority and power of God, no one can be convinced that Scripture is the Word of God apart from the inner testimony of the Holy Spirit.

> Let this point therefore stand: that those whom the Holy Spirit has inwardly taught truly rest upon Scripture, and that Scripture indeed is self-authenticated; hence, it is not right to subject it to proof and reasoning. And the certainty it deserves with us, it attains by the testimony of the Spirit. For even if it wins reverence for itself by its own majesty, it seriously affects us only when it is sealed upon our hearts through the Spirit.[19]

What is needed, therefore, for the full assurance and individual certainty that Scripture is the very Word of God Himself is a necessary "connection" between the Spirit who speaks in Scripture, and that same Spirit who testifies to us and in us, by that very Word, that it is the Word of God.

Given the self-authentication of Scripture—that is, given that the authority of God is given every time Scripture itself goes out, any and every exposure to Scripture is a confrontation with the claims of God, and with His authority. How might this truth be applied?

A few years ago, the George Gallup Organization had been doing polling on the Bible in public schools. According to that polling, 75 percent of Americans wanted to see the Bible taught in public schools, but only 8 percent of public schools actually taught it. This disparity was an evident opportunity. In seeking to take advantage of that opportunity, it was discovered that many people thought that it was illegal to teach the Bible in public schools.

The first task was to address the problem of biblical illiteracy. This illiteracy not only meant that people were ignorant of the gospel, but it also caused young people to have an incomplete understanding of literature, history, music, art, and culture.

The second task was to show, negatively, that there was no legal impediment to teaching the Bible in public schools, and positively, to confirm the notion that students needed to know the Bible, at least, in order to understand English literature and history. Essentials in Education (EIE) proposed and completed its initial research. That research (the first ever national survey) showed that 98 percent of high school English teachers believe that students are disadvantaged in reading English literature if they do not know the Bible, as well.

The third task was to disseminate this research and raise public awareness of the need and of the potential for change in this regard. In its press conference launching the research at the National Press Club in Washington, EIE reached sixty-two million Americans through print and broadcast media, including CNN Headline News.

Public awareness was a relentless effort. It was crucial to keep this issue in front of the press on a weekly basis for nearly two years, generating stories in both national and state newspapers in particular. In addition, largely due to the advocacy provided by Bible Literacy Project, four states have enacted legislation to facilitate the academic study of the Bible.

EIE followed its initial research with a second effort, in order to ascertain what university English professors (from thirty-four universities, including Yale, Harvard, Princeton, Stanford, and the University of California) think incoming freshmen need to know about the Bible. One hundred percent of the professors agreed that part of what it means to be an educated person is knowledge of the Bible. EIE is now in its fourth year, with 356 high schools in forty-three states taking our course. That number will be increased substantially in the near future. Already, we have over 10 percent market share in Georgia's public high schools and over 5 percent in Indiana, Alabama, and South Carolina.

There are widely varying views as to how best to expose our children and our culture to the Word of God. Some opt for home schooling, others for Christian or private schools, and others for public schools. By definition, it is not possible to teach the Bible *as the very Word of God* in a public school. But if the Bible is self-authenticating, if exposure to it exposes us as well to the very character and authority of God, then exposing young people to the Bible in public schools is a worthy calling. Not only so, but it lends further support to the fact that the *principium* of knowledge, the Bible itself, carries with it a confrontation with God and His character. Only such a confrontation can stave off the rapidly rising relativism of our society; only such a confrontation can confirm the truth of Christianity itself, and thus give the lie to all of its cultured despisers.

Notes

1. David K. Naugle, *Worldview: The History of a Concept* (Grand Rapids, MI: William B. Eerdmans Publishing Company, 2002), 174, quoting Paul A. Marshall, Sander Griffioen (authors), and Richard J. Mouw (ed.), *Stained Glass: Worldviews and Social Science* (Lanham, MD: University Press of America, 1989), 12.

2. Robert Bork, *Slouching Towards Gomorrah: Modern Liberalism and American Decline* (New York: ReganBooks, 1997), 11.

3. David Wells, "Our Dying Culture," in *The Formal Papers of the Alliance of Confessing Evangelicals*

Summit (April 17-20, 1996), 18.

4. Note that truth includes *both* principles *and* the applications based on those principles. One topic that deserves much study is the ways in which *pragmatism* (which is the only philosophy invented on American soil) has adversely affected American culture, and, specifically, American (perhaps even Christian) business. Pragmatism holds that you do things *because* they work, whether or not they are right, or the best things to do.

5. Quoted in Richard A. Muller, *Prolegomena to Theology, vol. 1 of Post-Reformation Reformed Dogmatics: The Rise and Development of Reformed Orthodoxy, Ca. 1520 to Ca. 1725* (hereafter *PRRD*) (Grand Rapids, MI.: Baker Books, 1987), 431.

6. Ibid.

7. Philippe du Plessis-Mornay, *A Worke Concerning the Trunesse of Christian Religion, Written in French: Against Atheists, Epicures, Paynims, Iewes, Mahumetists, and Other Infidels. By Philip of Mornay Lord of Plessie Marlie. Begunne to Be Translated into English by That Honourable and Worthy Gentleman, Syr Philip Sidney Knight, and at His Request Finished by Arthur Golding. Since Which Time, It Hath Bene Reviewed, and Is Now the Third Time Published, and Purged from Sundrie Faultes Escaped Heretofore, Thorow Ignorance, Carelesnes, or Other Corruption*, trans. Sir Philip Sidney Knight and Arthur Golding (London: George Eld, 1604), 2.

8. According to Muller, "Divinity alone begins with the absolute first principles of things which depend on no other matters; whereas the basic principles of the other sciences are only first relative to the science for which they provide the foundation, the basic principles of theology are prior to any other 'principle of Being' or 'principle of knowing'" (Muller, *PRRD*, 436).

9. Ibid., 432.

10. This does not mean, as Scripture elsewhere makes clear (e.g., 1 Cor. 7:8), that everyone must marry. It means that if one does marry, their union should be conducted according to the principles in Scripture.

11. This imagery assumes, of course, that Christ Himself is the cornerstone of any and every "building."

12. It should be noted that the Westminster Confession of Faith highlights the glory of God around twenty times as the goal of all that God is doing in the world.

13. Muller, 264.

14. John Calvin, *Institutes*, 1.7.2.

15. Ibid., 1.7.4.

16. Ibid.

17. The inevitable circularity of this affirmation did not escape the Reformed. Without engaging the entire debate, two matters can be mentioned here. First, this understanding of Scripture was consistent with the notion we have discussed above of a ground, or foundation (*principium*), of knowledge (which, it should be noted, is *not* foundationalism). According to Muller:

The Reformers' immediate interest was in the status of Scripture not merely as authoritative but as bound up with the work of salvation: granting their strong emphasis on original sin and on salvation by grace alone, they emphasized the necessity of the biblical Word over against the use of reason and the examination of God's handiwork in the natural order. In addition, the Reformers' clear sense of the self-authenticating character of Scripture—the *a priori* character of Scripture as a self-evidencing norm— flowed directly into the orthodox identification of Scripture as the *principium cognoscendi theologiae* [theological foundation for knowledge]: *principia* [principles], of their very nature, stand prior to and provide the grounds for a form of knowledge. (Richard A. Muller, *Post-Reformation Reformed Dogmatics: The Rise and Development of Reformed Orthodoxy, Ca. 1520 to Ca. 1725: Holy Scripture*, 162.)

Second, and after Calvin, John Owen provided a substantial and penetrating argument for the necessity of this biblical view, over against the circularity of the Roman view. Owen assigns to the church of Rome, not one efficient of belief and one motive of belief; rather, he says, Rome is caught between two different motives of faith, neither of which can prove the other without at the same time contradicting itself as the motive of faith.

And, indeed, they do plainly run into a circle, in their proving the Scripture by the authority of the church and the authority of the church again by the Scripture; for with them the authority of the church is the motive or argument, whereby they prove the divine authority of the Scripture, and that again is the motive or argument, by which they prove the authority of the church. And so both the church and the Scripture are more known than each other, and yet less, too: more known, because they prove each other; and less known, because they are proved by each other. (W. H. Gould, ed. *The Works of John Owen*, vol. 16 [Edinburgh: The Banner of Truth Trust, 1977], 8.527.)

18. As the Westminster Confession of Faith (written after Calvin but surely influenced by him) affirms (1.10) the Holy Spirit is the one who Himself is speaking in Scripture.

19. Calvin, *Institutes*, 1.7.5.

TOTAL DEPRAVITY AND BUSINESS ETHICS

RICHARD GAFFIN

Dr. Richard Gaffin is Professor of Biblical and Systematic Theology, Emeritus at Westminster Theological Seminary, Philadelphia, where he taught from 1965 until 2010. Born of missionary parents in Beijing, China he is a graduate of Calvin College (B.A. in history, 1958) and Westminster Seminary (Th.D., 1969). He is a minister in the Orthodox Presbyterian Church and has been a frequent speaker at conferences and seminars. Among his writings are Resurrection and Redemption; Perspectives on Pentecost *and* By Faith, Not By Sight: Paul and the Order of Salvation.

Originally published in ed. R. C. Chewning, Christians in the Marketplace. Biblical Principles and Business: The Foundations (Colorado Springs: NavPress, 1989), pp. 139-154; *slightly revised and edited, 2010. This chapter originated as a paper presented at a symposium, "Christians in the Marketplace," held at the Hanmaker School of Business, Baylor University, Waco, Texas in March 1988.*

I f the Bible teaches anything clearly, it is the reality of sin. That is the dark side of the clarity of Scripture, confessed by the Protestant Reformers—its unsparing portrayal of human sinfulness. From beginning to end, Genesis 3 through Revelation 22, the Bible documents the full range of sin and its consequences.

Sin is rebellion against God. (1) Specifically, human sin is *lawlessness* (see 1 John 3:4)—violation of God's law, prideful disobedience of the revealed will of God, the Creator, on the part of the creature made in His image and for His service. (2) Sin is *universal* ("There is no one righteous, not even one" and "all have sinned" [Rom. 3:10, 23 NIV; cf. 1:18–3:10]); every human being is born a sinner ("Surely I was sinful at birth, sinful from the time my mother conceived me" [Ps. 51:5 NIV]). (3) Sin is also *intensive* or integral, its corrupting impulse resident at the core of human personality ("For out of the heart come evil thoughts, murder, adultery, sexual immorality, theft, false testimony, slander"

[Matt. 15:19 NIV]). (4) The character of sin as transgression involves *guilt* (e.g. Rom. 5:12ff.) as well as corruption. (5) The ultimate punishment on the condemnation sin deserves from God, in fidelity to His holiness and righteousness, is *death*—eternal death ("The wages of sin is death" [Rom. 6:23 NIV]).

All the historic Christian traditions agree, more or less as stated here, with these points. To deny the reality of sin is to deprive Christianity of any real meaning. There are differences, however, and among these is perennial dispute about the third point above, the depravity or corruption of sin. Briefly stated, the issue is this: Is human depravity total of partial? Is the corruption of human nature complete, or is it limited in some respect? Is there perhaps left in people a remnant unpolluted by sin, some capacity or potential that sin does not govern? I will seek (1) to show that the Bible, in fact, teaches that human depravity is radical and total and (2) to answer, again on a biblical basis, certain apparently formidable objections to this teaching. That, in turn, will provide a necessary framework from which (3) to draw some conclusions, necessarily brief and general, for ethics in business and economics.

TOTAL DEPRAVITY

A good place to begin with biblical teaching on the depth and scope of human sinfulness is 1 Corinthians 2:14: "But the natural man [that is, the person without God's Spirit] does not receive the things of the Spirit of God, for they are foolishness to him; nor can he know them, because they are spiritually discerned" (NKJV).

The larger context is one of those passages where the apostle Paul is concerned with the "big picture," to provide some fundamental perspectives on his gospel ministry as a whole (see 1:18–3:23). In sharp contrast to the false divisions and party spirit present in the church at Corinth (see 1:10–17), he sets out the true nature of division created by the gospel. The result is nothing less than total conflict between God and "the world," "this age" (1:20 ESV), constituted and distinguished by sin and unbelief. In terms of the opposite pairs wisdom-foolishness and power-weakness, this struggle is so unrelieved, the antithesis so absolute, that "Christ the power of God and the wisdom of God" (v. 24 ESV) is rejected as weakness and foolishness. For the unbelieving world, the gospel message of Christ's cross is thoroughly foolish, a "stumbling block" (v. 23 ESV). Conversely, in His "foolishness" and "weakness" God confounds and nullifies human wisdom and power (1:18–29).

Paul goes on to describe this antithesis in individual terms (see 2:14–15 ESV). The unbeliever is "the natural person," the person without the Spirit of God; the believer is "the spiritual person," the person renewed, indwelt, motivated, and directed by God's Spirit. Here, too, the antithesis is total and exclusive. All people fall into one of these categories; there is no middle ground, no third group.

What Paul wrote several verses later is only apparently an exception. When he called Corinthian believers unspiritual and "carnal"/"worldly" (3:1, 3 NKJV; ESV), he was not providing a rationale for two classes of Christians, "spiritual" and "carnal," with unbelievers as the remaining third class of people. Such an understanding would soften and domesticate his intended point. The kind of spiritual immaturity present at Corinth was not merely "low-level" Christian behavior but decidedly un-Christian; their "jealousy and quarreling" (v. 3 NIV), as he made unmistakably plain elsewhere (see Galatians 5:20), was a "work of the flesh,'" totally contradicting the "fruit of the Spirit" (Gal. 5:22 NIV).

There are at least two pertinent comments about unbelievers. First, their sinful condition is such that they do not accept the things of God's Spirit because they are *unable* to do so; they "cannot understand them" (1 Cor. 2:14 NIV). Paul plainly asserts the inability of the unbeliever. Second, what is the extent of this inability? What is the scope of "the things that come from the Spirit of God" that the unbeliever cannot comprehend? Verse 15 points to the answer. The believer, in contrast, comprehends and discerns "all things" (NIV); the things of the Spirit are "all things" (cf. v. 10).

Is there anything that restricts or delimits "all things"? Nothing in the immediate context appears to do so. Further, as already noted, the antithesis in 2:14–15 is part of the mega-conflict between God and the sinful world, that struggle which in scale is nothing less than that between two "aeons," two world orders (see 2:6, 8), between two creations, the old and the new (see 2 Corinthians 5:17). There is no warrant for restricting the inability of the believers to understand; their epistemological inability is comprehensive and total.

First Corinthians 1:18–3:23 is, in effect, a commentary on Jesus' teaching in Matthew 11:25–27 (cf. Luke 10:21–22): "I praise you, Father, Lord of heaven and earth, because you have hidden these things from the wise and learned, and revealed them to little children. Yes, Father, for this was your good pleasure. All things have been committed to me by my Father. No one knows the Son except the Father, and no one knows the Father except the Son and those to whom the Son chooses to reveal him" (NIV).

Present here is the same antithesis, the same countervaluation of human wisdom and understanding, encountered in 1 Corinthians 1–2. Specifically, again, what is negated is the knowledge of unbelievers. What is hidden from them, the "wise and learned" in their own eyes, is revealed to "little children," that is, believers (cf. Matt. 18:3–4; Mark 10:15). Again, too, there is an indication of the comprehensive scope of the knowledge at issue; hidden from unbelievers are nothing less than "all things."

The context defines "all things." "All things" are "these things" (v. 25 NIV). The latter expression, in turn, without an explicit grammatical antecedent in the immediately preceding verses, refers more generally to the account of things that have happened in several towns in Galilee: the rejection of Jesus and His miracles, a rejection that will serve as a basis for the condemnation of those towns at the Final Judgment (see verses 20–24).

Luke, in addition, brackets the passage with Jesus' vision of the eschatological overthrow of Satan and his rule through the mission of the seventy-two (see 10:17–20), and His pronouncement about the blessed advantage of His disciples in view of the new, consummation realities that they were experiencing in contrast to the "many prophets and kings" of the old order (vv. 23–24).

All told, then, "these things"/"all things," hidden from unbelievers are the things of the kingdom of God/heaven brought about by the coming of Christ (cf. esp. Matt. 11:11–13 and Luke 10:9). The mutual self-knowledge of the Father and Son, sovereignly revealed to believers, concerns all that is revealed in the coming of the kingdom.

According to the Synoptic Gospels, the kingdom is at once both the center and the all-encompassing theme of the proclamation of Jesus during His earthly ministry. It is not confined to some restricted ("religious") sector of concerns. Rather, the kingdom is a comprehensive eschatological reality, the consummate realization of the expectations created by God's covenant with his people, the fulfillment of the promises made to the Old Testament fathers (see Luke 10:24). More specifically, the kingdom is a matter of the eschatological lordship of God in Christ, inaugurated and presently being realized through His first coming and to be consummated at His return.

Nothing in the entire creation, then, is irrelevant to this kingdom or falls outside this eschatological rule of Christ. The reality of the kingdom, in the words of Paul's subsequent commentary, is the reality of God's having "placed all things under his feet and appointed him to be head over everything for the church" (Eph. 1:22 NIV), the reality, already begun in his exaltation, of bringing "all things in heaven and on earth together under one head, even Christ" (1:10 NIV).

The kingdom of God—its claim—is totalitarian in the most ultimate sense that the creature made in his image can know and experience. It resists and negates all efforts, be they pre-Kantian dualisms or post-Kantian dimensionalisms, to narrow its scope. All of life, including all knowledge, is "religious." For Jesus, as for Paul after him, we therefore conclude, the cognitive inability of unbelievers is comprehensive and total.

The two passages so far examined express the unbeliever's total inability to know or to understand. Both, however, plainly have in view an inability that while cognitive is not merely or narrowly cognitive. In both instances this inability to understand manifests itself as "wisdom" unable to comprehend the things of God's Spirit and so bound to reject Christ and the gospel. In other words, the cognitive inability in view is immoral—a sinful, culpable inability.

Paul was clear on this point. The ignorance of the Athenians, revealed in their altar to "an unknown God" (Acts 17:23 NIV), is not innocent. Along with their "scientific" sneering at the proclamation of the resurrection of the dead and final judgment (see verse 32), their ignorance is culpable, ignorance that needs to be repented of (see verse 30).

Elsewhere (notably in Romans 1:18ff. and Ephesians 4:17ff.), Paul pictures the depth and magnitude of human sinfulness in the most unsparing fashion, largely, again, with the use of cognitive terms. Sinners, apart from God's saving grace, live "in the futility of their thinking" and are "darkened in their understanding" (Eph. 4:17–18 NIV: cf. Rom. 1:21); supposing themselves to be wise, they have become fools (see Romans 1:22). They are "separated from the life of God because of the ignorance that is in them due to the hardening of their hearts" (Eph. 4:18 NIV). Accordingly, "having lost all sensitivity, they have given themselves over to sensuality so as to indulge in every kind of impurity, with a continual lust for more" (Eph. 4:19 NIV). They "suppress the truth by their wickedness" (Rom. 1:18 NIV); they have "exchanged the truth of God for a lie," the primal, perverse, and perverting lie of idolatrous creature-worship in one form or another (Rom. 1:25 NIV). Consequently, God has abandoned them in their idolatry to the full range of corruption and immorality, some of it of the most degrading, even unimaginable ("unnatural" [Rom. 1:26 NIV]) kind (see Romans 1:24, 26–32).

Plainly, the depravity depicted in these two passages is both radical and total. It is rooted in the human heart, the controlling center of one's being, and nothing there mitigates it or otherwise checks it from completely permeating and dominating the entire person. That makes clear the radical sinfulness of the cognitive incapacity in view above. That total inability to understand is a leading function of radical corruption; total inability is total depravity.

A couple of other facets related to the teaching of these passages need to be highlighted. (1) Total depravity is universal. That is one of Paul's points in Romans 1–3. The Jews, because they may not have committed some of the more conspicuous hard-core sins documented among the non-Jews, are not thereby to suppose that they are better, less depraved. In the matter of God's judgment on everyone "who does evil," too, the regulative principle is "first for the Jew, then for the Gentile" (Rom. 1:16 NIV). (2) Paul closed his indictment of the universality of human sin and depravity with a string of citations from the Old Testament (see Romans 3:10–18). This reflects the pervasive, overall unity of the biblical witness. New Testament teaching on total depravity is fairly seen as an amplification of Jeremiah 17:9, for one: "The heart is deceitful above all things, and desperately corrupt" (RSV).

Romans 8:6–8 can serve to close this brief survey: "The mind of sinful man is death, but the mind controlled by the Spirit is life and peace; the sinful mind is hostile to God. It does not submit to God's law, nor can it do so. Those controlled by the sinful nature cannot please God" (NIV).

The same antithesis between believers and unbelievers found in 1 Corinthians 1–2 comes into view here. All people fall into one of two opposed groups; they are controlled either by their sinful nature ("flesh") or by the Holy Spirit. There is no middle ground, and nothing softens the conflict. It is an absolute, all-inclusive conflict, of nothing less than life-and-death magnitude. On the one side, the disposition ("mind") of sin and death, with its ultimate end, eschatological death (cf. Rom. 6:23), consists in an utter inability to please God or to obey His law and in implacable hostility toward God. The basic dimensions of human depravity are death and enmity—a total inability to be or do anything for God and a total capacity, a radical heart commitment, to being and doing everything against Him.

The Bible never relativizes sin. To do so, it should never be forgotten, relativizes the gospel and gives rise to cooperative schemes in which we presumably contribute, no matter how minimally or covertly, to our own salvation. The Reformers, for one, clearly understood this, that total depravity and *sola gratia,* grace alone, stand or fall together. The sheer graciousness of the gospel is revealed in what from the sinner's side is its incredible, impossible demand: its resurrection-demand. The gospel is God's call to those who are *dead* in transgressions and sins to hear and live (see John 5:25; Ephesians 2:1, 5; 5:14).

We are not sinners because we happen to sin; we sin and cannot do otherwise because we are sinners. Absolutely nothing in sinful human nature alleviates or restrains its corruption. There is in us no remnant of goodness, either actual or potential, no corner or secret recess of human personality, no matter how attenuated we might conceive of it, that remains unpolluted by sin. Human depravity is total.

COMMON GRACE

The doctrine of total depravity has always had its detractors, both outside and within the church. That is so for at least two reasons, apart from inadequate and confusing ways in which the doctrine may sometimes be presented. The deepest reason is our own sinfulness—our native resistance to acknowledging that we are sinners and the full magnitude of our sinfulness. Only the Holy Spirit can produce genuine confession of sin (see John 16:8–11).

But another reason especially warrants our attention here. The doctrine of total depravity seems to contradict reality. To confess radical human corruption, apparently, is in conflict with life as we experience it. Everywhere around us outside the pale of Christianity and among those who make no pretense of being believers are countless and evident instances—in the great as well as the small affairs of life—of kindness and helpfulness to others, of philanthropy and deeds of mercy, of attraction to what is good and right, noble and honorable, of efforts that advance peace and human well-being, of beneficial cultural and artistic accomplishment, of heroism and self-sacrifice, even to the point of death.

Further, we have no difficulty observing a wide spectrum of variations within the general condition of human sinfulness. We see the tireless community volunteer and the hardened criminal; relatively, some people are "good" and others are "bad." A perennially cited example is that of the Roman emperors: the moderation and equity of Titus and Trajan provide a sharp contrast to the cruelty and excesses of Caligula and Nero. In recent times, we think of Hitler and Gandhi.

It is a matter here not only of our experience but also of what Scripture itself recognizes. Abimelech, king of the Philistines, displayed moral restraint and even a certain indignation (see Genesis 20:1–17; 26:8–11). Jehu, who did not abandon the false worship of the golden calves (see 2 Kings 10:29, 31), nonetheless destroyed Baal worship in Israel (v. 28) and is said by the Lord himself to "have done well in accomplishing what is right in my eyes and [to] have done to the house of Ahab all I had in mind to do" (v. 30 NIV). Jesus taught that even corrupt public officials reciprocate love of some sort (see Matthew 5:46) and evident sinners "do good to those who are good to [them]" (Luke 6:33 NIV). The inhabitants of Malta, though pagan (see Acts 28:4), showed Paul and those traveling with him "unusual kindness" (v. 2 NIV) and at their departure generously furnished needed supplies (v. 10).

In view of our undeniable experience and this biblical evidence, then, is it not clear that the doctrine of total depravity exaggerates and distorts human sinfulness? Is not its portrayal of human nature entirely too grim and pessimistic, as its opponents have never tired of insisting? As some even urge, must we not resist this doctrine and its implications for the sake of nothing less than our humanity itself, to preserve what is truly human in human nature? If, after all, we believe that all human beings are made in God's image, must we not maintain that there still remains in them, despite their sin (in some instances, certainly, of the coarsest or most horrifying kind), a remnant of goodness, some smoldering spark of desire for what is right and true that often finds expression?

To conclude that we can continue confessing total depravity only at the expense of our perception of reality and of our own humanity creates a false dilemma. After all, Scripture affirms both—radical human corruption in the face of the full reality of human existence. Paul, for one, does so within the span of a single argument (see Romans 1:18–3:20). He said of the pagan or unbelieving Gentiles that they "do by nature things required by the law" and "show that the requirements of the law are written on their hearts" (2:14–15 NIV). Yet he went on to include them in his unsparing universal indictment, "There is no one righteous, not even one . . . There is no one who does good, not even one" (3:10–12 NIV). Essentially, Paul argued that within the totality of sinful humanity there are some who in a sense do what the law requires, yet, ultimately, they do not do good, nor can they please God (see Romans 8:8). It will simply not suffice, biblically, to shade human sinfulness by entertaining the notion of a somehow uncorrupted remnant within us. Rather, the question is how to account for undeniable gradations and variations within the bounds of total depravity.

The answer, according to the Bible, lies not in us but in God—in His kindness, His graciousness, His patience. From one angle the entire message of the Bible from Genesis 3 on is a message of postponed judgment. The full measure of eschatological death and destruction that the sin of our first parents deserves is delayed. In banishing them from his fellowship-presence in the garden, God did so in hope, with a promise (see Genesis 3:15)—a promise that shows His purpose to have a people ("seed") for himself, that is, to save them from the destruction their sin deserves and eventually to bring the entire creation to a state of consummate blessing and perfection, the "new heavens and a new earth" (cf. Rom. 8:20–21, a Pauline commentary, in effect, on Gen. 3; Isa. 65:17ff.; Rev. 21–22).

Consequently, this promise also entails the delay of the "everlasting destruction" of the unrepentant and disobedient "from the presence of the Lord," a delay that continues until his second coming (2 Thess. 1:9–10). God's rainbow-promise to preserve "all life on the earth" made to Noah and his sons after the flood—itself a grim pointer to eschatological judgment (see 2 Peter 3:3–7)—confirms this delay (see Genesis 9:8–17; cf. 8:21–22). In effect, God's promise of delayed judgment is a promise that the human race will have a *history*. This delay period as a whole is human history in its fullness, unfolding toward its God-ordained consummation.

Ultimately, history (the delay) is for the sake and in the interests of the consummate salvation of the church and the correlative renewal of the cosmos. But the continuation of history also entails postponement of deserved eschatological destruction for those who persist in unbelief. As such, we shall presently see more clearly, it embodies God's favor toward them—not merely negatively as a reprieve period but positively, in a full range of gifts and benefits. Inseparably intertwined and yet distinct from God's special—electing and saving—grace in Christ is His general, nonsaving kindness and forbearance toward every creature, a common grace that embraces the entire creation.

Biblical evidence for common grace is of two sorts—negative and positive. The essence of common grace is divine restraint. The delay of eschatological wrath and judgment, already noted, shows "the riches of [God's] kindness, tolerance and patience" (Rom. 2:4–5 NIV; cf. 2 Peter 3:9). But that delay is bound up with a larger, overall restraint on sin itself and its consequences. God restrains not only his holy and righteous wrath but also the unholy and wicked disposition of the human heart. Sin is a positive, specific evil—not merely privation or limitation. It is lawlessness, rebellion against God and, as such, is inevitably ruinous and chaos-producing. Its inherent tendency, left unchecked, is to destroy everything, including sinners themselves.

God's restraint on sin and its hellish consequences appears already at the time of the Fall. The exclusion of Adam and Eve from the garden—itself a punishment—seems also to have been intended to keep them from the gross, perhaps even eschatological sacrilege of eating from the tree of life (see Genesis 3:21–22). Clear examples are the protective mark put on Cain (see Genesis 4:15) and the explicit declarations of divine restraint present in the cases of Abimelech (see Genesis 20:6) and later, Sennacharib, king of Assyria (see 2 Kings 19:27–28, 32–33). Again, God spares some from the extremes of degrading depravity to which he "gives over" others (see Romans 1:24, 26, 28), extremes to which, without exception, all, left to themselves, are disposed.

The curse on Adam and Eve (Gen. 3:16–19) compounds the futility, decay, and death permeating the entire creation because of sin (see Romans 8:20–21). The environment becomes dangerous. Predatory animals become a threat to human life, and "natural disasters" are a reality. Yet, at the same time, the curse is pronounced in a way that moderates those perils and preserves from their unmitigated consequences. Though Adam's labor becomes frustrating toil, it remains productive; there will be genuine agri-"culture" (cf. Gen. 3:23). Though childbearing becomes agonizing and painful, Eve is "the mother of all the living" (Gen. 3:20 NIV). All told, "Restraint upon sin and its consequences is one of the most outstanding features of God's government of this world— the history of this present world exists within an administration that is one of restraint and forbearance."[1]

There is also a positive side to this restraint and prevention. In his forbearance, God is also genuinely good toward all. His kindness to every creature involves a full range of gifts and benefits. The entire creation, animate and inanimate, is the constant recipient of untold blessing. A number of the psalms, especially, extol this universal generosity (e.g., 65:5–13; 104:13–24; 145:9, 15–16). The whole of humanity, unbelievers as well as believers, enjoys God's bounty and favor. "All nations," including themselves, Paul tells his thoroughly pagan audience at Lystra, have this testimony from God, that "he has shown kindness by giving you rain from heaven and crops in their seasons; he provides you with plenty of food and fills your hearts with joy" (Acts 14:16–17 NIV). The seasonal ordering of crops, God's faithful maintenance of the food-producing capacity of the earth—despite the ravages of famine and drought—is a constant witness to God's goodness, a granting of "creature comforts" calculated to produce joyful contentment. Similarly, Jesus spoke of God's benevolence that (as His disciples' love is to be) is without limits, "He causes his sun to rise on the evil and the good, and sends rain on the righteous and the unrighteous" (Matt. 5:45 NIV). "He is kind to the ungrateful and wicked" (Luke 6:35 NIV).

Within this framework of God's general benevolence, His common grace, belong those phenomena of our experience confirmed in Scripture noted above: the frequent interest of unbelievers in what is right and good, their devotion to expanding the frontiers of knowledge, to developing the arts and sciences in a constructive and worthwhile fashion, to advancing society and promoting the well-being of the human race. In His common grace, God not only bestows good on sinful human beings. He also produces good through them.

Clearly, this aspect of common grace has a direct bearing on economics as a whole and business ethics in particular. Several ramifications are worth further reflection.

(1) We are faced here with what has been called the paradox of common grace, a paradox taught in Scripture itself. In the course of the same argument as we have seen, Paul seems to assert that the unbeliever can do good and cannot do good. No doubt, we encounter here the ultimately impenetrable mystery of the Creator-creature relationship, God's finally incomprehensible dealings with the creature made in His own image. But this apparent contradiction is reduced, if not entirely removed, with the help of a biblically based distinction. That, by the way, is not the distinction between natural or secular good and religious good, the unbeliever presumably being capable of the former but not the latter. Such a distinction, in whatever form, is unbiblical. Its tendency—inevitable, so the history of the Church in the West would seem to teach—is to domesticate and marginalize true religion, to make the worship and service of God increasingly unimportant, peripheral, even irrelevant and so, among other things, to deny total depravity.

Rather, the biblical distinction instructive here is that between conformity and obedience. What God incites in and elicits from unbelievers is a degree of conformity but not genuine obedience to Himself and delight in His will. Ultimately, this conformity to his law, though beneficial to themselves and others, is such that it does not please God but is compatible with hostility toward him (see Romans 8:7–8). Yet to neglect it would be "more sinful and displeasing unto God."[2]

This conformity is not merely "external." Common grace is not, at least usually, an outward, mechanical-like constraint. It does not force the unbeliever to do something unwillingly. There is an inward dynamism to common grace, a positive restraint that engages the person—will, desires, emotions as well as intellect. As such, common grace is genuine kindness; it restrains and ameliorates sin and its effects in unbelievers and so makes them a means of blessing and good to themselves and others.

But—and this is critical—common grace, no matter how positive its effects, is *restraint*, not renewal. It is not a matter of the heart; it does not restore unbelievers at the core, in the integrity of their persons. It does not destroy the disposition of the "flesh." Nor does it create the mind-set of the Spirit, that renewing of the mind, that living sacrifice of praise without which God cannot be acceptably worshiped and served (see Romans 8:6; 12:1–2). Its movement to good, in other words, is not a removal of total depravity. Only one "restraint" can accomplish that, only one limiting factor on our radical corruption: the saving, resurrecting grace of God in Christ.

(2) In a real sense "common" grace is a misnomer; it is anything but indiscriminate. God's gracious restraint differentiates. It, not some self-determining capacity in ourselves, explains the wide, varied spectrum of attitudes and behavior in sinful humanity—virtue here and vice there, the conscientious law-conformity of some and the vicious unscrupulousness of others, why one is "given over" (see Romans 1:24, 26, 28) to gross sinning and suffers its degrading consequences, while another is spared and enjoys a prosperous, happy life. In a real sense, in comparison with others, some unbelievers ought to acknowledge, "There, but for the grace of God, go I."

God's restraining and preserving grace is hardly predictable; it sustains anything but a static relationship to sinful human existence. It sovereignly cuts across all sorts of motives and many different lifestyles, and no one is in a position to bring all the factors involved under one denominator.

(3) Common grace also explains the "grayness"—the disconcerting and sobering ambiguity—that frequently results from comparing believers and unbelievers. As it has been put, too often the world exceeds, and the Church fails to meet, expectations. Unbelievers, we must admit, sometimes put believers to shame. Seldom in life do we encounter an antithesis between full-blown wickedness and undeviating holiness. Similarly, unrenewed human existence can display unmistakable parallels with the sanctified living of Christians. There can be a striking likeness between actions of unbelievers and the good works of believers.

(4) It bears repeating that the variations and ambiguity noted in (2) and (3) do not point to limitations on human depravity. These are not based on presumably uncorrupted remnants in unbelievers. A remnant notion if applicable is so only in terms of the constant activity of God's restraining grace. The unchecked tendency of sin is to self-destruction, to efface the divine image in which we are made. So, to the extent that the functions and capacities constitutive of that image are preserved, we may speak of remnants of God's image in our fallen nature.

But—and this once more is the point—the existence of these remnants does not alleviate our depravity. To the contrary, human sinfulness finds its expression just in terms of these remnants. Sin has not destroyed God's image but has redirected its capacities totally, from the heart, in total hostility toward

God. Those endowments from God, incomparable in the entire creation because they are functions of His image, have been turned against Him. Sin has not annihilated our humanity; *man*, male and female, is a sinner. That is the appalling awfulness, the desperate culpability, of our sin.

(5) Among the remnants graciously preserved by God are the capacity to reason, volition, and the power of discrimination. One other factor, usually overlooked, deserves attention because it is especially pertinent to our topic: our sense of community, of common humanity.[3] God's restraining gifts are not only individual but corporate. The social side of sin's self-destructive tendency is alienation and eventual isolation from others; self-murder/hatred involves the murder/hatred of others as does the reverse.

God preserves humanity from destruction and chaotic self-isolation; he maintains in sinners, through a complex web of relationships, a need and desire to be with others, a concern, at various levels, to preserve community. But neither is this corporate, social dimension of the divine image to be thought of as an uncorrupted remnant; it is not "like the Sphinx in the desert sands of Egypt."[4] Racism and ever-present varieties of national aggression, covert or open, make it all too evident that there is solidarity in sinning ("They not only continue to do these . . . things [that deserve death] but also approve of those who practice them" [Rom 1:32 NIV]).

(6) What can/does the unbeliever know? The answer to this much-mooted question, also relevant to our topic, eludes easy formulation. In view of earlier discussion, we can be brief here. Scripture recognizes that unbelievers have knowledge and sees that as a gift from God (e.g., Isa. 28:26). Technology apparently began (see Genesis 4:17, 20–22) and has certainly continued to develop impressively in the line of unbelief.

However, Jesus and Paul were emphatic that unbelievers understand nothing truly (see Matthew 11; Luke 10; and 1 Corinthians 1–2, discussed above). They "suppress the truth by their wickedness" (Rom. 1:18 NIV). As the religious center of all human knowledge more and more comes into view, it becomes increasingly apparent that their knowledge is "ignorance" (Eph. 4:18 NIV). The most that can be said is that theirs is "futile" thinking and "darkened" understanding (Rom. 1:21; Eph. 4:18 NIV). The knowledge of unbelief, at best and in its undeniably impressive manifestations, is fragmented and ambiguous; its integrity is illusory.

Unbelievers, to use Calvin's evocative analogy, are like travelers at night after a momentary lightning flash;[5] for an instant the terrain around them has been illumined far and wide, but before they can take even a step, they are plunged back into darkness and left groping about aimlessly. To vary the figure, unbelievers exist and function perpetually in the split second after the firing of a flash attachment in a darkroom—left with a blurred and fading, still indelible impression of everything just illumined and yet now no longer seeing anything, knowing and yet not knowing.

Business Ethics

The conclusions reached so far may be summed up in two controlling perspectives on business and economic life.

(1) Balance needs to be maintained between common grace and total depravity as two correlative, mutually qualifying poles. To ignore either or emphasize one without the other results in distortions.

(2) Until Christ's return for final judgment—despite catastrophes, periodic disruptions, and ever-present, often widespread pockets of poverty—we can count on the maintenance of at least some measure of economic stability, on the continuation of available resources and structures for production, distribution, and exchange that ensure throughout the world conditions of economic viability and, on occasion, well-being and even prosperity.

But for all that we rely on God, not man—not on presumed remnants of goodwill or common sense or conscience, or "enlightened" self-interest, or the social impulse in human nature, or even our instinct for survival—but on God's covenanted fidelity to sinful humanity and the creation (e.g., Gen. 8:21–22; 9:8–17; Acts 14:17). Left to themselves, sinners can reckon only on economic chaos and disaster. But thanks to God's preserving, restraining mercy, there will be a minimum at least, sometimes more, of economic order. Ultimately that order eludes calculation and control, even of what is deemed the best economic theory and its implementations. If nothing else, the widespread economic debacle of recent years to the present makes that unmistakably clear—at least to those with eyes to see it. Under the ubiquitous pressure of human corruption, economic order constantly threatens to disintegrate.

These two general perspectives can be amplified by brief answers to several questions that could be posed.

(1) What can be derived for business ethics from general (natural) revelation? Strictly speaking, the answer is nothing. Taken by itself, general revelation will never provide the basis for a stable natural theology or natural law business ethics. Romans 1:18–25 makes that point. The world around us is plain

enough; it clearly evidences God's eternal power and who He is as God (see verse 20). The world in its entirety is His creation. It depends on Him and exists for Him. The problem, however, is that all unbelievers are inveterate truth-suppressors (see verse 18). The most to be said for their comprehension of the environment is that ultimately it is "futile" and "darkened" (v. 21 NIV). Apart from the acceptance, in faith, of God's special saving revelation in Christ and his inscripturated Word, a true and reliable understanding of general revelation is permanently excluded. Neither can there be genuine ethical conduct, business or otherwise, that is not living in Christ, *coram Deo*.

Of course, various codes of business conduct are based on the conviction, more or less strong, that self-interest and the interests of others, at whatever level (individual, regional, national, international), need not conflict but ought to serve each other economically. Where such ethical codes function, they will, apart from the adverse effect of other factors, no doubt produce economic benefits, for a shorter or longer time and to a greater or lesser extent. But that will happen, despite human depravity, by God's common grace. And under the impact of that depravity, even these codes of conduct, and the theorizing supporting them, will constantly tend to be implemented in ways that result in economic injustice and exploitation.

(2) Is business conduct based on biblical revelation ethically superior to that based on general revelation? Here, in addition to the answer to the previous question, the comprehensive epistemological-ethical antithesis between belief and unbelief of 1 Corinthians 1–2 and Matthew 11:25–27/Luke 10:21–22 comes into play.

For unbelievers, special revelation functions much as does general revelation. As revelation from the true and living God, it is suppressed and rejected as foolishness. Nonetheless, when the "wisdom" of the world, in effect, takes over biblical principles (e.g., the eighth, ninth, and tenth commandments or aspects of the Sermon on the Mount) as unacknowledged "borrowed capital" (C. Van Til), that is likely to have more beneficial economic consequences than if those principles are neglected. But such *de facto* conformity to God's law is not true obedience. To think of this conduct as somehow ethically superior is risky at best.

For believers, the problem with an ethics supposedly based on general revelation alone is not merely that it is inferior. It is an unbiblical abstraction, having no more promise than the efforts of unbelievers. The Christian has experienced the only limit there is to human depravity—God's resurrecting, regenerating grace in Christ, the renewing presence of the Holy Spirit. The only legitimate access to general revelation is, by faith, in the light of biblical revelation. The Scriptures are the indispensable "spectacles"[6] for rightly examining and perceiving the world about us, essential, among other things, for formulating sound business ethics.

Expanding on this last sentence would take us beyond the scope of this article. But perhaps one observation may be permitted here, especially pertinent where human depravity and the curse on sin continue. Writing to the Church in the "shortened time" between the resurrection and the return of Christ, Paul exhorted his readers, "Those who buy [should do so] as though they had no goods, and those who deal with the world as though they had no dealings with it" (1 Cor. 7:30–31 esv). Paradoxical as it may at first seem, where this eschatological reserve, this "as if not," controls the economic life and outlook of Christians, the potential is there for some among them to be useful, both in theory and practice, as economic guides for "the present form of this world" that is "passing away."

(3) Does capitalism cater to human depravity? Any economic system, including capitalism, is subject to exploitation by the deceit and perversity of the human heart. No system is immune to or a protection against that corruption. There ought to be no doubting that reality, even on the assumption that private ownership and a free market economy are compatible with or even demanded by biblical principles. Individual or corporate possession of the means of production and distribution, geared to the acquisition of profit, carries an almost irresistible temptation to all sorts of economic manipulation and intimidation—sometimes blatant but often refined, veiled even to the perpetrators themselves.

It is not simply as an afterthought that the Bible warns against "the love of money" (1 Tim. 6:10 esv; cf.3:3; 2 Tim. 3:2) and "dishonest gain" (1 Tim. 3:8 esv; 1 Peter 5:2 nkjv), especially in those who would be leaders in the church. It also teaches that the desire to be rich usually coexists with other vices in a snarled web, working harm for others as well as one's own destruction (e.g., Eccl.. 5:8ff.; 1 Tim. 6:9–10).

However else it is evaluated, capitalism abets the perverse inclination to secure ourselves rather than serve others. Like any other economic system, it will remain an instrument of misery and confusion until it functions under the transforming power of the Holy Spirit in that three-stage program of economic renewal announced, for instance, in Ephesians 4:28: "[1] He who has been stealing must steal no longer, [2] but must work, doing something useful with his own hands, [3] that he may have something to share with those in need" (ESV).

To close this article on a somber but appropriate note, we are bound to acknowledge the inescapable, simply devastating biblical basis for the position taken at Summit III of the International Council on Biblical Inerrancy in Article XIII of *The Chicago Statement on Biblical Application*: "We affirm that human depravity, greed, and the will to power foster economic injustice and subvert concern for the poor."

Notes

1. J. Murray, "Common Grace," *Collected Writings* (Edinburgh: Banner of Truth, 1977), 2: 102.
2. Westminster Confession of Faith, 16: 7.
3. This facet is thoughtfully developed by G. C. Berkouwer in *Man: The Image of God*, trans. D. W. Jellema (Grand Rapids: Eerdmans, 1962), 179–84.
4. Ibid., 184.
5. John Calvin, *Institutes of the Christian Religion*, trans. F. L. Battles (Philadelphia: Westminster, 1960), 1:277 [2:2:18].
6. Calvin, *Institutes of the Christian Religion*, 1: 70, 160 [1:6:1; 1:14:1].

DEVALUING THE SCHOLASTICS: CALVIN'S ETHICS OF USURY

MICHAEL WYKES

Dr Michael Wykes joined the University of Exeter in 2004 following a research council funded D.Phil. at the University of Oxford, where he also studied at undergraduate and master's levels. His D.Phil., supervised by Professor Oliver O'Donovan, investigated the ethical aspects of Intellectual Property Rights with reference to global access to Essential Medicines, and he has acted as an external PhD examiner in this field. In between his academic studies, Michael has also worked for the pharmaceutical industry, in public sector executive search, and spent a year working for L'Arche in France.

A diachronic reading of usury theory perceives a linear progression from an economically suffocating and naïve prohibition of lending money at interest, which characterized the medieval scholastic theologians, toward an invigorating and transforming defence of usury that heralded the dawning of the capitalist era sometime in the sixteenth century. On the one hand, we hear repeated the view of eminent scholars in this field, such as Raymond de Roover, who says "the great weakness of scholastic economics was the usury doctrine . . . As time went by it became a source of increasing embarrassment." [1] On the other hand, even despite the criticisms of Weber's seminal thesis *The Protestant Ethic and the Spirit of Capitalism*, we are told that of the many shackles that the Reformation loosed, those imprisoning economic freedom and capitalist practice were among the most significant. In particular, we associate the name of John Calvin first and foremost with the liberation of usury from medieval economic thought.

Such a reading would of course be a gross oversimplification. The diversity of scholastic usury theory resists such a narrative, and the question of the socioeconomic circumstances that attended or have been claimed to be the result of Calvin's teaching in particular are relevant only at the fringes of a theological discussion. Therefore, in order to focus on core theological and ethical arguments in this debate, this article examines Calvin's usury theory in relation to a key exponent of the medieval scholastic position—Thomas Aquinas. While no clear dependence can be established between Calvin and Aquinas on this topic, both theologians have made a distinct and valuable contribution to the field of usury theory. Choosing Aquinas as the exponent of scholastic usury theory may have the side effect of boosting his status as the representative "voice of scholasticism." One should be cautious, however, and acknowledge both the limitations of his economic thought and the subsequent development of scholastic usury theory. Indeed, it has been recently argued that the Franciscans Peter Olivi and John Duns Scotus, "combined evangelical spiritual and moral rigour with an unrivalled level of analytical sophistication, and so may plausibly be regarded as the high-water mark of scholastic economic ethics." [2] Our comparison of Calvin and Aquinas, however, is motivated by different reasons. First, the scholastic usury theory that Calvin devalues is represented admirably by Aquinas. Second, he makes groundbreaking use of Grosseteste's newly available Latin translations of Aristotle. Third, Aquinas coins a significant and enduring argument from the "consumptibility" of money in his attack against usury. Their comparison is therefore both interesting and illuminating.

This article begins by contextualizing this conversation with a presentation of some of the key theoretical prolegomena to Aquinas' usury theory. These are found in Aristotle and in the medieval discussions of property, natural law, and the just price. This provides a backdrop to the central task of describing and evaluating Aquinas' and Calvin's usury ethics from a close reading of primary texts. The underlying intention is to apprehend Calvin's "devaluation" of scholastic usury theory at three key stages; namely, through his biblical exegesis; his reconceptualization of key terminology; and his distinctive focus upon charity, social welfare, and equity. [3] Finally, to introduce Calvin's innovation in the sixteenth century, we include a brief assessment of the salient features of Luther's teaching on usury. This presentation highlights Luther's specific attack on riskless investment together with his conservative treatment of usury as being sinful. Luther's caution sets the scene for Calvin's groundbreaking insights.

A Background to Aquinas' Usury Theory

The apogee of ethical reflection about usury is arguably the cliché and somewhat misrepresentative detail of Aristotle's so-called doctrine of the *barrenness* of money. [4] In stark contrast, and much closer to contemporary thought, is Benjamin Franklin's *Advice to a Young Tradesman*, in which he urges: "remember that money is of a prolific and generating nature. Money can beget money, and its offspring can beget more." [5] A selection of Aquinas and Calvin for a comparative discussion thus provides a sharp focus to strategic theological developments that took place in the key centuries between these two poles. These advances shadow the transition from an agrarian, market-based, feudal economy to one of international discovery and trade. This transition lies at the bottom of mainstream economic analysis of this period. Sauer supports this interpretation by showing that "standard treatments of economic history argue that the dominant factor in the capitalistic evolution, which started in the twelfth and thirteenth centuries but which came to full force in the fifteenth and sixteenth centuries was with the change from a natural to a money economy." [6] It may therefore seem important to set the early scholastic denunciation of usury under natural, agrarian economic conditions. However, the relevance of this socioeconomic background to a primarily theological discussion is by no means to link Aquinas' condemnation of usury with the fact that the majority of loans were required for subsistence. Rather, it is merely intended to suggest that by Calvin's era the accelerated nature of commercial and capitalist practice was such that loans were more often required for investment and innovation. Calvin therefore might have found the scholastic inflexibility over usury theory all the more difficult to relate to his own situation.

Of prior importance in this article, however, is the intellectual prehistory to this debate: the cross-fertilization of ideas that nurtured, framed, and informed the development of usury theory. Out first staging post in such an account is Aristotle. First of all, we note the development of his argument from the *Nicomachean Ethics to The Politics*. This impressive sequence of economic thought is cast under the auspices of Justice—the title to book 5 of the *Ethics*. In a central economic discussion in book 5:v 1132b, we find Aristotle's guiding principle: "It is proportional requital that holds the state together." [7] This principle must be evident in the fundamental exchange of goods, produce, or services that constitute the fabric of society and thereby conform these exchanges to justice. In order to facilitate this exchange of goods such as he describes between a builder and a shoemaker, Aristotle posits an aetiology whereby "all products that are exchanged must in some ways be comparable." He declares that "it is this that has led to the introduction of money, which serves as a sort of mean (or medium of exchange), since it is a measure of everything, and so a measure of the excess and deficiency of value, informing us, for example, how many shoes are equivalent to a house or so much food." [8]

Aristotle refines this statement by proposing that the standard by which all commodities are measured is in fact demand. Yet, he argues, "by convention demand has come to be represented by money. This is why money is so called, because it exists not by nature but by custom"—thus illustrating the etymological link between the Greek word for custom or law, *nomos*, and that for currency or money, *nomisma*.[9] Value is therefore intimately related to demand; exchange must be ordered toward just reciprocity—Aristotle's guiding principle. "There will be reciprocity, then," he expounds, "when the products have been equated, so that as the farmer is to the shoemaker, so is the product of the shoemaker to the product of the farmer."[10] Aristotle presented a flowing image of interdependent concepts in his conceptualization of justice-in-exchange. This highlights his understanding of the basic fabric of society and how it is to be regulated. Money is quite literally the facilitator of *movement* within society: "so money acts as a measure which, by making things commensurable, enables us to equate them. Without exchange there would be no association, without equality there would be no exchange, without commensurability there would be no equality."[11]

In the *Nicomachean Ethics*, we find a passing but condemnatory reference to usury in book 4 during an extended discussion of the "right attitude" to money. Here, the moneylender is grouped with others engaged in "illiberal occupations" who receive "more than is right, and not from the right sources."[12] Yet, Aristotle's criticism at this stage seems to be one of "social comment," rather than a philosophical reflection upon the essence of lending at interest. It is later, amidst his polarization of economics and chrematistics, that the singular reference to the famed "argument from sterility" can be discovered. This occurs during his discussion of the "Natural and Unnatural Methods of Acquiring Goods" in *The Politics* 1.9. Aristotle frames his argument by the contrast between "economics," literally "household management," and "chrematistics," the "acquisition of goods/wealth."[13] The passage in question is worth citing in full as it contains several important issues that would have lasting significance in the thought of both Aquinas and Calvin:

> The acquisition of goods is then, as we have said, of two kinds;
> one, which is necessary and approved of, is to do with house-
> hold management; the other, which is to do with trade and
> depends on exchange, is justly regarded with disapproval, since

it arises not from nature but from men's gaining from each other. Very much disliked also is the practice of charging interest; and the dislike is fully justified, for the gain arises out of currency itself, not as a product of that for which currency was provided. Currency was intended to be a means of exchange, whereas interest represents an increase in the currency itself. Hence its name, for each animal produces of its like, and interest is currency born of currency. And so of all types of business this is the most contrary to nature."[14]

Of several points raised by this extract—such as the contempt for trade when it is beyond the satisfaction of needs and the reiteration of the purpose of money—the argument against usury claims special status because Aristotle supports his earlier social condemnation with recourse to nature. The etymology of *tokos*—"offspring"—gives weight to Aristotle's resolute association of money as part of the inanimate, unproductive order. Money by itself can be exchanged for other goods, but it cannot of itself produce anything in excess of its principal. Langholm has rightly focused on this aspect of Aristotle's account, arguing, "I would suggest that this is perhaps the single most important thing to realise in order to grasp the Aristotelian theory of usury: it was a theory based on the conception of money as coin."[15]

This last point is significant. Money as a symbolic, physical, and inert reality had purpose only as the medium for exchange and the measure of demand for other goods. In many senses, money is valueless in itself and therefore unable to create value by itself. Aristotelian economic thought was the product of a contemplative consideration of certain aspects of justice that were cashed out in the day-to-day transactions of the *polis*, transactions that were necessary for the proper functioning of a household. Such a virtuous social theory did not include practices that were unnecessary, such as the art of chrematistics, or "unnatural," making usurious a substance intended to facilitate the smooth operations of exchange.

In conjunction with Aristotle, it is possible to identify further three clusters of thought that are intimately related to usury theory. These provide more detail to the background of Aquinas' thought on the subject; although each section commands a separate literature in its own right. These clusters are property rights, natural law, and the "just price," and we discuss them only briefly here. Initially, and perhaps chiefly, an understanding of property rights informs two separate aspects of Aquinas' usury theory. First, property rights underpin the motivation and intention of individuals in commerce: You can- not take advantage of a circumstance that does not belong to you. Second, they prompt his reflection about how the ownership of money ceases in its exchange. Indeed, as Langholm argued,

> the connection between property theory and economic theory was a very close and important one in scholastic thought . . . in some of their more central economic texts the two subjects are virtually inseparable. There is nothing remarkable about this relationship. On the contrary, the remarkable thing is the subsequent separation of property theory and economic theory."[16]

It is not astonishing, therefore, that a discussion of property peppers Aristotle's treatment of economics in *The Politics* 1.8; less still that the whole issue of property defined one of the major scholastic schools—the Franciscans—for whom property ownership necessitated the development of economic circumlocutions by the papacy in order to separate the ownership from the use of their property. Such periphrasis was an example of how scholastic usury theory became a "source of increasing embarrassment" that the Reformers would attack. At the same time, Aquinas overlooked the Stoic model of common ownership, a theme that was strongly present in the Fathers' vehement condemnation of private property. Lockwood O'Donovan has argued that Aquinas' treatment of usury "moves more entirely within the ambit of Aristotle's economic ethic, at the expense of the patristic Stoic-Platonic legacy."[17] We may therefore note the elevation of individual property rights to a far more prominent place in Aquinas' system. By contrast, we will note the genesis of the separation of property theory from economic theory in Calvin.

A second important theoretical background to usury theory is natural law. Arguably, this reflection was far more of a guiding principle for Aquinas than for Calvin because Aquinas would assert ontologically that usury is sinful *secundum se* (according to itself).[18] This assertion is an extrapolation of familiar precepts in earlier condemnations of usury, such as the selling of time, that were informed by natural law principles. However, Aquinas does not repeat this older criticism of usury, preferring to develop a new attack of his own. Finally, and directly related to the principle of justice in exchange, is the third issue— the "just price"—*justum pretium*. Caution should be exercised with regard to this last concept because it is a moot point whether one confuses an older sib- ling of usury theory with its parent, natural justice. Sauer argued that the prohibition of interest-bearing loans was derived from the scholastic principle of the just price. However, it may well be the case that both are children of the same concept.[19]

Finally, and to complete a background to the main discussion, we find specific biblical texts in the tradition. These are of fundamental importance to all of our theologians' problematization of usury. Calvin was arguably the most conscious of these conditional, if not negative, statements. The Old Testament usury (*nesek*) references that are relevant to this paper are Exodus 22:25, Leviticus 25:35-8, Deuteronomy 23:19-12, Psalms 15:5, and Ecclesiasticus 29:1-20. Divine offered a useful categorization of these texts into three groups, distinguishing different emphases upon the limits to Jewish usury practice amongst brethren and strangers and more general condemnations of avarice and greed.[20] Insofar as the New Testament is concerned, Luke 6:35, "love your enemies, and do good, and lend, expecting nothing in return," is an uncomfortably isolated reference. It was repeatedly claimed to prohibit the practice of usury by the scholastics and was radically reinterpreted by Calvin.

Usury theory has therefore both an impressive ancestry and interdisciplinary concerns. To divorce usury theory from its Greek, Hebrew, and, as we will soon observe, Roman intellectual heritage would be as ill advised as discussing it without reference to property rights, natural law, or the just price. The importance of these clusters of thought to all of our theologians' understanding of usury is undeniable. As such, these indicate the wealth of interdisciplinary issues that are at stake in any devaluation of scholastic usury theory.

AQUINAS

While Aristotle's influence upon the mind of Aquinas was both instant and profound, the absorption of his economic thought was not completed smoothly and in one movement. Having studied the *Nicomachean Ethics* under Albert the Great in Cologne, Thomas would have to wait for Grosseteste's Latin translation of *The Politics* until his arrival in Paris in the 1250s.[21] From this point onward, we discover his distinctive argument against usury. Important groundwork had, of course, been laid in advance of Aquinas, not least in the *Summa Aurea*[22] of William of Auxerre (d.1231) who was probably the first of the Paris theologians to reap the benefits of Aristotle through Latin extracts from Averroist sources. The bishop of Lincoln, however, furnished Aquinas with the seminal translation. This translation would become notorious due to a crucial error of Greek to Latin translation: Grosseteste translated *chrematistics*, meaning "trade" as opposed to "household management" in *The Politics* 1.9, as *campsoria* meaning "money-changing." Grosseteste thus inadvertently presented Aristotle's dislike for unnecessary trade as a mere aversion to money changing. Aristotle's critique would thus be bypassed and a considered embrace of trade by Aquinas and others put in its place.

Aquinas' innovative attack against usury lies in his argument about the *consumptibility* of money. This thesis has three key movements: first, that money is a token of value that is intended to act as a measure of exchange to facilitate the trade of goods; second, that money is "sunk in exchange" or is consumed in the act of exchange; and third, that the use of money cannot be separated from its substance. In order to grasp a key conceptual premise to this argument, we note one final element in the background to Aquinas' thought. This lies in the Roman legal contract of *mutuum* or "loan." The spurious derivation of the word *mutuum* from the passage of ownership from something that is mine (*meum*) to something that is yours (*tuum*) of course reveals the importance of *property rights* as the substructure to a theory of loans. Ownership of the article being loaned is seen to be the fulcrum of the exchange. The *mutuum* contract concerned itself with the legal category of "fungibles"—goods that can serve for or be replaced by goods of a similar description because they are consumed in their use.[23] These goods also imply exclusive ownership and provide the legal back-ground to Aquinas' usury theory. It is also worth noting how the *mutuum* contract is to be distinguished from various other Roman legal contracts. These distinctions mark careful differences between types of commercial engagement, such as the *locatio*, a lease contract, or a *societas*, a business partnership. Aquinas displays acute commercial acumen as he clearly differentiates these categories in his discussion of commerce and usury in the *Summa* (2a2ae qq. 77-78). However, by the time that Calvin examines the practice of loaning money at interest, elisions among *mutuum*, *locatio*, and *societas* are arguably rife.

From this basis and context of the *mutuum* contract, we perceive Langholm's insight that "what lies at the bottom of the consumptibility argument is the sterility of money, or, to be more precise, the sterility of all those things which can be the objects of a *mutuum*."[24] Langholm argued incisively that Aquinas had distanced himself from the somewhat intellectually questionable Aristotelian argument (about the sterility of money as coin) by this move to focus upon the consumptibility of the objects in question.[25] By exposing the fine detail of Aquinas' usury theory, it is intended to clarify and evaluate Aquinas' association between the ownership of a fungible good and the consumptibility of money.

As Langholm put it with great clarity: "the point of the ownership argument is that money is consumed in use. As Thomas Aquinas put it originally, money and other objects of a *mutuum* have no use separate from their substance hence to pay for their substance and their use as well, is to pay twice."[26]

One of the substantial primary texts where usury is explicitly examined is the *De Malo* (On Evil).[27] The context of the discussion is question thirteen, *De Avaritia* (On Greed), in the lengthy fourth article "whether to lend at usury is a mortal sin." The fact that Thomas discusses usury within the context of greed highlights his continuity with the patristic approach. However, Aquinas marks key differences with this tradition by focusing the discussion with Aristotelian concepts. In his detailed reply, Aquinas makes clear his argument against the selling of both the use *and* the substance of money in a loan. He explores those things that are consumed in their use, such as wine or bread, and those that are not, such as a house; thereby delineating the indistinguishability of ownership and use in the case of fungibles and a legitimate separation of ownership and use in the *locatio* of a house. The argument builds toward his assertion, "now the use of money, as it has been said, is nothing other than its substance, therefore either the lender sells something which doesn't exist, or he sells the same thing twice, namely the money itself whose use is its consumption, and this is manifestly against the principles of natural justice."[28] The reply closes with a recapitulation of a remark made at its beginning: to lend money at usury is *secundum se*—a mortal sin because it contravenes natural justice. This argument also applies to other goods whose substance is consumed in their use, such as wine and wheat.

In addition to his extended discussion in *De Malo*, Aquinas devotes two questions to economic matters in the *Summa Theologiae* (2a2ae qq. 77, 78), where he remains faithful to Aristotle's architectonic of discussing economics as part of justice. The content of his instruction on economic matters reveals that the "angelic doctor" had a reasonably coherent and sophisticated understanding of medieval business practice. The key to unlocking Aquinas' discussion in these two questions is to read question 77 "of cheating which is committed in buying and selling" as a conceptual preamble to the discussion of "the sin of usury which is committed in loans." Aquinas' argument revolves around the dual concepts of the *intention* of the actors in exchange and the *right* of each actor to make use of the circumstances that affect either party; thereby adjusting the price of goods or withholding details of certain faults or damage. In his reply to question 77, Aquinas faithfully recites Aristotle's aphorism that money was invented for the purpose of measuring the value of an object before he pro- ceeds to the main debate concerning a transaction that may tend to benefit one party or another and how, if at all, this should affect the price of the goods.

Two questions are fundamental to his resolution of this issue as well as to usury: first, what *actually* as opposed to *potentially* exists, and second, to whom does an advantage *belong*? In other words, what are the quantifiable, tangible factors in an exchange, and who owns the intangible factors? The second question is answered by Aquinas' argument:

> If one man derive a great advantage by becoming possessor of another man's property, and the seller be not at a loss through being without that thing, the latter ought not to raise the price, because the advantage accruing to the buyer, is not due to the seller, but to a circumstance affecting the buyer. Now no man should sell what is not his, though he may charge for the loss he suffers.

Property rights, here relating to nontangible goods, i.e., the circumstances affecting parties involved in a transaction, impose restrictions on the pricing of goods and ensure that the exchange remains within the bounds of the equality of justice. When this argument is transferred into a discussion of usury in his *Commentary on the Sentences* (3.37.6 ad 4), we note how Aquinas refutes the charge that should a borrower make more money from his loan, he would be obliged to repay greater than the original principal. The logic is the same: Circumstances affecting one member of an exchange, in this case the borrower's industry or financial acumen, have no bearing upon the other party. Property rights are therefore a positive notion for Aquinas, although he refocuses our attention on a different type of fungible: money.

To conclude this evaluation of Aquinas' usury theory, we return to the contribution of the *Summa Theologiae*. Specifically, we dwell upon the important and delicate question concerning the loss sustained by a creditor in the act of lending. While this is not technically part of Aquinas' usury theory, we contend that it is an essential feature of the scholastic position that Calvin will devalue. The prehistory of economic reflection by the Roman civil lawyers had produced a fine distinction regarding extrinsic entitlements to compensation. This is indicated by two separate legal categories. The central concern of usury has less to do with *damnum emergens*—the case for compensation occasioned by late repayment of a loan—than with *lucrum cessans*—the case for compensation for a lost opportunity for profit. This implies that the lender had alternative investment opportunities that would have returned a profit. Aquinas' teaching on this subject is indicative of refined scholastic opinion witnessed by his ready acceptance of the former entitlement to compensation and stubborn rejection of the latter title.

The basis for his argument answers the first of the two questions that we raised earlier: What are the actual factors of trade, and what are potential and subject to the vagaries of commerce? He argues in 2a2ae 78.2.ad 1:

> A lender may without sin enter an agreement with the bor-
> rower for compensation for the loss he incurs of something he
> ought to have . . . . But the lender cannot enter an agreement
> for compensation, through the fact that he makes no profit out
> of his money: because he must not sell that which he has not
> yet and may be prevented in many ways from having.

The first part of the reply details the contractual obligation that is understood in the case of *damnum emergens*, and the latter half is a resolute rejection of *lucrum cessans*. There is to be no compensation for missing out on an alternative investment opportunity because any profits from that venture, quite simply, may never have come about. Aquinas' argument would perhaps apply most legitimately to an agrarian economy whereby agriculture remained a common investment opportunity and one that was very much subject to uncontrollable factors. This socioeconomic consideration will have radically altered by Calvin's time when return on investment either through financial support of international trading or the expansion of retail activities were prospects that carried less and less risk and promised greater and greater returns. Recent events in the global economy, however, serve to emphasise the wisdom and continued relevance of Aquinas' argument.

Aquinas' does not, of course, rule out the prospect of "ethical" profit as is shown by his description of the *societas* in 78.2 ad 5. Here, he outlines the implications of investing money with a craftsman and yet retaining the ownership of the money. This differs from the more usual practice in which ownership passes unconditionally:

> he that entrusts his money to a merchant or craftsman so
> as to form a kind of society, does not transfer ownership of
> his money to them, for it remains his, so that at his risk the

merchant speculates with it, or the craftsman uses it for his craft, and consequently he may lawfully demand as something belonging to him, part of the profits derived from his money.

Risk and the retention of ownership are therefore the distinguishing features of the *societas*. These justify the possibility of receiving more than the original sum invested. Finally, should you be concerned about the loss of potential profit upon your capital, Aquinas contends in *De Malo* 13.4 ad. 14 that you should not have entered into the loan situation, "for he who lends money ought to protect himself lest he incur a loss, nor ought he who takes a loan incur loss through the stupidity of the lender."[29]

The resounding image of many features that distinguish Aquinas' critique of usury in the late thirteenth century is his sustained presentation of the argument about the consumptibility of money: the coidentification of its substance and use coupled with the unconditional transfer of ownership (both actual and potential). Upon this substructure, Aquinas set his related condemnation of the practice of *lucrum cessans*, while showing himself to be sensitive to the practice of *societas* by acknowledging the role that risk must play in investment. Further, it is important to note his happy acceptance of an Aristotelian frame- work to economic discussion under the umbrella of "justice in exchange." More significantly, it is important to be clear about his extension of the Aristotelian concept of the sterility of money into the consumptibility of money in exchange and the sterility of fungible goods. Finally, through the progress of his arrangement in the *Summa Theologica* from trade to usury, we note the importance of the intention of the actors in commercial transactions and their obligations to one another informed by the principle of justice. The critique of unjust sale and the practice of usury are intimately related. This discussion, however, has not been uncritical of Aquinas' arguments: His intellectual creditors have been acknowledged, and his successors signaled. Further, the peripheral question of Aquinas' *Sitz* has been exposed to address the relation- ship of his innovative usury theory to the root innovation of a time of predominantly agrarian concerns.

LUTHER

Calvin's devaluation of scholastic usury theory is brought into focus by illustrating how Luther, responding innovatively to the theological inadequacy of scholastic thought in so many other important ways, failed to reach the conclusions about usury that Calvin himself would expound. The German Reformer adheres to an uncompromising critique of usury; thus, Luther's conservatism serves to highlight Calvin's innovation.

A brief survey of secondary commentators' opinions of Luther's economic competency reveals an almost unnerving consensus that is far from favorable.[30] Some are perhaps guilty of certain historical anachronisms in their assessment of Luther. Consequently, they are arguably accountable for the inflation of Calvin's economic ability to an almost precious level. For example, McGrath maintained that "[T]he fact that Luther's economic thought—if one can dignify it with such a title—was hostile to any form of capitalism largely reflects his unfamiliarity with the sophisticated world of finance then emerging in the great free cities."[31] Luther's economic ability was thus jejune and uncritical of centuries-old scholastic and canonical teaching. No doubt these opinions are by and large correct, although Luther's own socioeconomic background and audience are perhaps not taken into consideration more often. The primary intention in this brief presentation of Luther's thought is to give Calvin center stage by illustrating how Luther adhered to a longstanding critique of usury that was about to be radically revised. Nelson captured this assessment in rather more apocalyptic language::

> within less than three decades after the day when Luther stood before the boy Emperor at Worms, there occurred a fateful desertion of a principle which had claimed the allegiance of men in the Judaeo-Christian tradition for more than two millennia, the principle that the taking of interest from a co-religionist was utterly antithetical to the spirit of brotherhood.[32]

The vast majority of our record of Luther's teaching on usury dates from the beginning of his public career. He delivered a *Short Sermon on Usury* in November 1519 that was published in 1520. This was reprinted with his treatise on trade and published in 1524 as the complete treatise, *On Trade and Usury*.[33] The distinctive feature of Luther's understanding of usury and his ethical critique lies in his concentration upon the factor of risk and his utter contempt for those who become rich without any effort of their own. Scholastic arguments, however, permeate his 1524 treatise. The Fathers' and Aquinas' voices are almost audible as Luther condemns those who "consider not the value of the goods or what his own efforts and risk have deserved, but only the others man's want or need."[34] There is also no doubt that Luther tailored this treatise to the predominantly rural economies of his day as his advice on how to determine how much profit one ought to take is egalitarian: "there is no better way to reckon it than by comparing the amount of time and labour you have put into it, and comparing that with the effort of a day labourer who works at some other occupation and seeing how much he works in a day."[35] This advice is characteristic of Luther's social ethic whereby "borrowing would be a fine thing if it were practised between Christians, for every borrower would then willingly return what had been lent him and the lender would willingly forgo repayment if the borrower were unable to pay."[36]

In the earlier *Long Sermon on Usury*, Luther anticipates a key exegetical step—that Calvin will announce clearly—through his interpretation of the isolated reference to usury in the New Testament in Luke 6:35. Luther maintains that what Jesus intended was "that we should lend not only to friends, to the rich, and to those we like, who can repay us again by returning the loan, or by lending to us, or some other favour; but that we lend also to those who are unable or unwilling to repay us, such as the needy and our enemies."[37] Luther has not, however, loosed himself from the traditional scholastic criticisms as he details three reasons to censure usury including the charge that charging for a loan is contrary to natural law: "it is clear that such lenders are acting contrary to nature, are guilty of mortal sin, are usurers, and are seeking in their own profit their neighbour's loss."[38] However, Luther's last point reflects a concern with avarice, which Calvin will certainly amplify.

The resounding tone of Luther's homily is struck out of his marked reaction against the historical practice of *zinss kauff*—literally "the purchase of rent." This was a supposedly nonusurious arrangement whereby a creditor purchased an income by giving money to an individual who would effectively repay the loan plus interest. Luther argued: "This practice involves a pretty pretence by which a man can seemingly without sin—burden others and get rich without worry or effort . . . this slippery and newly-invented business very frequently makes itself an upright and loyal protector of damnable greed and usury."[39] Luther seethed against this practice whereby not only were you able to get rich without worry or effort, but also he maintained, "in a transaction of this sort, the buyer finds goods always on hand; he can do business if he is sitting down or is sick . . . you cannot make money just with money."[40] His tirade against the idle enrichment of practitioners of *zinss kauff* is supported by an ethical argument about risk that Lockwood O'Donovan has argued "occupies the pivotal place in Luther's usury theory that the arguments about selling time and the consumptibility of money occupy in the early scholastic and Thomist theories."[41] Luther's final move is to differentiate investment and the purchase of a *zinss kauff* in a thoroughly Thomist way. Luther contended,

> money engaged in business and money put out at zinss are two different things, and the one cannot be compared with the other. The latter has a base which is constantly growing and producing profit out of the earth without any fear of capital losses; while there is nothing certain about the former, and the only interest it yields is accidental and cannot be counted on.[42]

By all accounts, Luther lacks a sophisticated macroeconomic knowledge of European finance, but this was probably irrelevant to his own socioeconomic situation. His raw intelligence nevertheless pierced the soft underbelly of avaricious economic practice through a social critique of unearned income and an economic attack against riskless investment. Luther's conservative stance on usury is relevant to the comparison of Aquinas and Calvin, for it provides a snap- shot of sixteenth century thought that bears a close similarity to medieval scholastic teaching. Calvin's treatment of usury is, therefore, all the more significant.

CALVIN

So much has been attributed to Calvin's—and more importantly to Calvinism's—influence over the course of Western economic thought that it is hard to approach an evaluation of his work without a sense of great expectation. Indeed, with regard to our present concern, the reality of the matter is certainly sophisticated and innovative, although perhaps less voluminous than one would expect. However, a close reading of Calvin's limited references to usury reveals the wealth of his understanding and his innovative approach to an issue that had stigmatised medieval economics, eluded Luther, and remained at loggerheads with the burgeoning economic expansion of this period.

A discussion of how Calvin addressed the theological and ethical content of scholastic usury theory is not primarily concerned with the detail or implications of the Weber-Tawney thesis. However, any treatment of this kind cannot fail to acknowledge the relationship of the socioeconomic situation to Calvin's social ethic and, in particular, to his usury ethics. At the same time, it is important to bear in mind this article's underlying concern to describe and assess Calvin's devaluation of the scholastic treatment of usury, as represented in particular by Aquinas, through his biblical exegesis; through his reconceptualization of key terms; and through his distinctive focus upon charity, social welfare, and equity. Yet, to do justice to the attendant socioeconomic discussion, the following comments intend to put his theological and ethical justification of a previously forbidden practice into a certain historical perspective.

In stark contrast to the popular opinion that Luther's economics were intellectually unsatisfying, Calvin is readily presented as a veritable "old hand" in financial matters. This financial acumen is present in a key primary text *De Usuris* (On Usury) of 1545. In this era, McGrath maintains,

> Calvin's willingness to allow a variable rate of interest shows an awareness of the pressures upon capital in a more or less free market. The ethical interests served by such a prohibition could in any case be safeguarded by other means. Furthermore, he was aware of the importance of generating new industries through injection of capital, as is evident from his lobbying for a state sponsored cloth industry in the 1540s.[43]

It is also recorded that in 1543 Calvin chaired a committee that investigated interest rates, which recommended to the Little Council an upper limit of 5 percent.[44] This historical detail provides a good background to Calvin's writings on usury. Yet, it is important to acknowledge the seminal research of André Biéler who warned both against the anachronistic nomenclature of Calvin's "economic thought" and an undue emphasis upon what was not the most developed aspect of his theology. Above all else, as Biéler urged: "it was not possible to speak of the economic and social thought of Calvin without linking it to the theological premises upon which it rests. To uproot it from its foundations would have been quite simply to betray its author."[45]

To conclude this brief statement of the peripheral socioeconomic question together with Biéler's argument, the conclusion reached by Divine serves excellently to keep a proper focus upon the ethical and theological debate. Divine has captured the relevance of the historical issues nicely by suggesting, "Calvin's approach to the problem of interest was that of the father of an urban movement writing in the environment not of a self-sufficing economy of peasant farmers and small craftsmen and traders but of large and prosperous cities that knew the advantages of large scale commercial enterprise."[46] This pertinent observation suitably captures Calvin's *Sitz*—and by a polarized contrast, Luther's—in order for this discussion to move toward its theological essence. Whether or not economic prosperity was the midwife of Calvin's teaching on usury or vice versa is both a very interesting but ultimately misleading diversion from the central tenor and quality of Calvin's arguments.

Calvin wrote explicitly on the subject of usury in his 1545 letter to "one of his friends" known to be a certain Claude de Sachin. This letter constitutes, along with a few references in his commentaries, the sum total of his "interest in interest." Clearly, this issue remained urgent and topical. Rapid economic growth exposed the need for either a restatement of the church's official position, subtle modification and reinterpretation of it (in favor of capitalist activity), or, as in Calvin's case, a genuinely *theologically* informed revision. At the same time, it was a relatively minor ethical debate compared to weightier maters of theology and the absence of any comment on usury, it would seem, in the *Institutes of the Christian Religion.*

One of the most striking aspects of De Usuris is his cautious introduction.[47] He begins: "I have not yet experimented but I have learnt by the example of others how perilous it is give a reply to the question about which you ask my advice: because if we so completely forbid usuries we bind consciences with a tie more strictly than God himself." Calvin is fully aware of opening the floodgates to usurious practice on the one hand, but the reason why his initial caution is striking is in order to emphasise his first substantial and unambiguous point that "there is no witness of scripture by which all usury is totally forbidden." Man has no business in deciding matters that God himself has not revealed though Scripture. This argument is characteristic of a common Reformation concern to found theological doctrine and ethical practice *evangelically* and thereby avoid the danger of creating an over-scrupulous conscience that is misinformed and believes in salvation by works. Calvin therefore proceeds swiftly to tackle the *locus classicus* of scriptural prohibition in Luke 6:35 by an appeal to the immediate context of the passage and indeed the broader setting in Luke; for example, regarding inviting the poor, the maimed, the lame, and the blind to a banquet in Luke 14:13-14 simply because they are unable to "return the same."[48] In a matter of a few words therefore Calvin sweeps aside centuries of standard interpretation through an exegesis informed by considerations that reveal his socioeconomic agenda of welfare provision: "but moreover," Calvin urges, "we must help the poor for whom money is at risk."

What then of the Old Testament prohibition in Deuteronomy 23:19, "you shall not lend upon interest to your brother"? This law, Calvin states, "is political and has no more bearing upon us now than equity and human reason carry. Of course it would be good to desire that usurers were expelled from the entire world and that the name became unknown. But since that is impossible we must submit to a common utility." This argument is quite extraordinary in some respects because Calvin appears to state an admonition that is contrary to the permission that he has just granted. Why should it be good to desire the expulsion of usurers if their activities are not against the Word of God, and who is Calvin to pronounce upon what God has not? It certainly seems as if Calvin is somehow exposed here in an attempt to please all parties concerned, by permitting usury on the one hand and yet wishing it did not exist on the other due to the greed and exploitation that invariably accompanies the practice. What is also striking is how Calvin seems to relegate usury to a secular field as he takes recourse to "common utility"—an arguably nontheological justification—in his defence. Further on, Calvin creates a more sophisticated philological argument, displaying his knowledge of Hebrew, to attack erroneous interpretations of Psalm 55:12, which tries to suggest that usury is intended by the psalmist. Ultimately, his central argument against the seemingly robust testimony of the Old Testament is due to the radically different political situation that the Jews experienced, which compared to Calvin's own time "has no point of similarity." For this reason, Calvin does not see why usury should be condemned unless it is contrary to "equity or charity." This last statement, as we will make clear below, captures the heart of Calvin's theological defence of usury that rests upon the golden rule of Matthew 7:12.[49] This fact refutes the charge that he has made usury a secular matter.

The devaluation of the arguments from the Old Testament suggests a historical critical hermeneutic that succeeds in liberating consciences from being unduly oppressed by an absolute ban upon a practice that Calvin acknowledges has a certain "common utility"—even if there is some tension in his argument. In any case, Calvin is confident that there is no evangelical ban upon the practice of usury as he uncovers the root concern of the Lucan narrative: charity. In so doing, Calvin has devalued a second and fundamental scholastic teaching that usury was sinful *secundum se*—an important feature of Aquinas' position. There is more to this argument than simply the lack of a divine prohibition because Calvin constructs his understanding of the sinfulness of usury upon the concepts of equity and charity. These two concepts have a strong continuity with the scholastic approach when they are taken together as a pair. Calvin, however, brings out the independence of the two concepts as he builds his argument toward the core of his innovative approach in the theme of mutual benefit.

Yet, before Calvin details the social policy of this letter, he engages with Ambrose and Chrysostom, who are representative for Calvin of the Aristotelian argument against usury from the sterility of money. This paragraph is marked by Calvin's impatience with what he considers to be childish arguments: "The reason that Ambrose and Chrysostom suppose is too frivolous in my opinion: to realise that money does not father money." Later, in similar fashion, he will repeat his distaste for this argument by stressing, "Indeed, I concede that *children* perceive that if you shut money up in a box it will be sterile."[50] The scholastic argument being of course that money even outside of a box was sterile. Calvin is by no means blind to the reasoning that the value of money is not to be found in itself but through its yield or use. Therefore, he bangs the drum of rational arguments in classic humanist rhetorical style: "one would be at liberty to rent out a field imposing a charge, and yet it would be illegal to take some fruit from money? What? When does one ever buy a field thinking that money does not father money?" At this point Calvin's dismissal of scholastic arguments is seen to be somewhat cavalier and possibly detrimental to the central tenor of his own argument. His conflation of the scholastic distinction between a locatio and *mutuum* is such that he seems to bypass the importance of property rights, which underpin the scholastic system. Calvin asserts a moral equivalence between an entitlement to rent from leasing a field and an entitlement to interest from lending money. In the place of ownership, Calvin has made the issue of the productivity of money central as he moves the debate away from a complicated legal sphere to a more transparent moral sphere. Insofar as Calvin is concerned, because the value of money comes from its employment and human industry, if someone is prepared to borrow, they ought to be prepared to repay more than the principal.

The neglect of property rights is evident in the fact that for Calvin the lender continues to own his money after it has been lent out. Furthermore, the criterion of risk in legitimate profit-making, which was made pivotal by Luther, is entirely absent from the discussion. As for the Thomist argument about the consumptibility of money, it would appear that a wedge has been driven between the substance and use of money and the understanding that money as a token of exchange, which is consumed in the very act of exchange, is an understanding that no longer holds currency. Calvin has given money a certain independence as he equates the economic equivalence of lending or investing that ensures the perpetual motion of money in an economy.

Calvin's innovation in usury theory however is clearly visible not only in his exegesis of the key texts but also in his announcement that the rule of mutual reciprocity or benefit should be the litmus test for any ethical judgment of usury. In *De Usuris*, Calvin ends his discussion of the biblical evidence and the traditional arguments by stating: "I now conclude that one must not judge usuries according to some certain and particular pronouncement of God but only according to the rule of equity." To clarify this emphasis, which is dependent upon Matthew 7:12 for its theological content, it may well be useful to bear in mind the secular concept of proportional reciprocity that is interestingly somewhat reminiscent of Aristotle's framework in book 5 of the *Nicomachean Ethics*. Calvin hypothesises a situation where two individuals are able to mutually benefit each other through usury.[51] In so doing, he highlights the economic similarities between buying land for the purpose of gaining an income through renting it out, and lending money for the purpose of receiving interest. According to Sauer:

> Calvin moves the issue from the level of common sense, which sees these as two fundamentally different operations from the horizon of the observer . . . to a theoretical differentiation where the two operations are fundamentally identical to each other. The theoretical horizon is the horizon of money in use for producing an income. . . . The distinction that Calvin has made is between transactions for consumption and transactions for production. This is a profound theoretical differentiation.[52]

Unfortunately, it is perhaps not quite so obvious to appreciate the sense of profundity that Sauer experiences in his outline of Calvin's theory. This is due to the weakness of Calvin's hypothetical situation where the exchange is uniquely empowered by good-natured and mutually advantageous economic incentive. In other words, his theory would only work in rare "win-win" propositions. Calvin has moved the debate away from both theology and law and toward the economic equivalence of operations in the market. Money is no longer sunk in exchange; it is active and fertile, perpetually in use. It earns a return either in lending at interest or through investing and leasing. The situation that Calvin describes is more akin to the *societas*, albeit without the scholastic requirement of risk, and yet he makes it relevant to usury. However, one of the chief achievements of Calvin's account is to distance a justification of mutual benefit through usury or commerce from a proper focus upon *charity*. This captures the meaning of Luke 6:35, thereby giving this virtue its own powerful voice.

The consistency of Calvin's thought on this topic is impressive. The other main references to usury, found in his commentaries upon various books of the Bible, illustrate the clarity of his understanding on this delicate matter. Regarding the contentious verse in Luke 6:35, Calvin's *Harmony of the Gospels* reiterates his unambiguous position: "This utterance has been wrongly attribute to usury . . . the phrase 'hoping for nothing again' is wrongly taken as a reference to interest."[53] His fifty-fourth lecture on Ezekiel 18:5-9, in which he comments on Deuteronomy 23:19, repeats the exegetical stance of *De Usuris* to highlight the political nature of the prohibition.[54] This enables him to mark a more fundamental theological argument that usury is in fact not against God's law. Calvin argued, "If then we wish to determine whether interest is unlawful we must come to the rule of the law, which cannot deceive us: but we shall not find all interest contrary to the law, and hence it follows that interest is not always to be condemned."[55] One can almost hear Calvin drawing his breath after such a statement; perhaps conscious that his teaching could be interpreted in a licentious manner. Therefore, he is quick to remind his audience that "the usurer is certainly an illiberal trade, and unworthy of a pious and honourable man."[56] Again, as in *De Usuris* above, this seems to reflect a certain undermining of his argument as Calvin seeks to be "all things to all men."

This tension is resolved in our final primary text. Calvin addresses another *locus classicus* of usury condemnation, Psalm 15:5, where he must deal with the fact in his own words, "David seems to condemn all kinds of usury in general and without exception."[57] His answer to this seemingly unequivocal statement centers on the rule of equity in exchange: "there is no worse species of usury than an unjust way of making bargains, where equity is disregarded on both sides. Let us then remember that all bargains in which the one party unrighteously strives to make gain by the loss of the other party, whatever name may be given to them, are here condemned."[58] Ultimately, Calvin's final word on the subject relates to neighbourly love. This arguably reveals that his account of usury is only a by-product of his primary concern to implement and enforce justice in exchange. Citing Leviticus 25:35-7, Calvin concludes,

> we see that the end for which the law was framed was that men should not cruelly oppress the poor, who ought rather to receive sympathy and compassion. This was, indeed, a part of the judicial law which God appointed for the Jews in particular, but it is a common principle of justice which extends to

all nations and to all ages, that we should keep ourselves from plundering and devouring the poor who are in distress and want. Whence it follows that the gain which he who lends his money upon interest acquires, without doing injury to anyone, is not to be included under the head of unlawful usury.[59]

His final word on the subject, for which he is often remembered, is an appeal to Matthew 7:12, the so-called golden rule according to which *modus vivendi* Calvin says "it would not be necessary to enter into lengthened disputes concerning usury."[60] Of course the golden rule, as the summary of the natural law, was far from absent in the work of both Aquinas and Luther in relation to just practice in exchange. Calvin has given this timeless principle an important and specific application through his creative perspective on usury.

To frame this assessment of Calvin's devaluation of the scholastic theory of usury it is of benefit to return to his most distilled treatment in the treatise *De Usuris*. The earlier exposition and analysis stopped short of the closing section of the text to allow for the incorporation of material from his biblical commentaries. The letter closes by listing seven exceptions to the practice of usury. However, it is not necessary to list them all to understand the thoroughgoing concern that he has for the equitable treatment of the poor in accordance with the "rule of Christ." Calvin states that the practice must be biblically informed and conscious of its impact upon the public benefit and with respect to the law of the land. Calvin therefore seems to chart an almost pragmatic approach to usury. Perhaps it was more in the interests of social welfare that Calvin transferred what could be seen already as a "double standard" of the Deuteronomic prohibition of Deuteronomy 23:19-20 (whereby Jews could lend at interest to foreigners but not among themselves), into one of his own time, whereby it was ethical for the rich and the shrewd to lend amongst themselves at usury but not between the rich and the poor. However, this double standard is a front to the thoroughgoing exhortation to justice in exchange and to charity that Calvin insisted upon. Here, it is possible to understand the tensions in his thought, which were highlighted above, between his legitimating usury and his desire to banish usurers from the land, for Calvin is acutely aware of the sinful proclivity of humankind to exploit and gain through the loss of others. The medieval concern to fight against avarice is thus very much present in Calvin.

CONCLUSION

Calvin's brief but sustained approach to usury theory is constructed on a close biblical exegesis that owes much to philological discipline and a historical-critical method, which is characterized by an internal consistency. He faces up to stark condemnations of usury in the Old Testament, and marks a clear distinction between the political circumstances of the Jews and those of sixteenth-century Geneva. The two situations have no similarity he contends, and therefore the ancient usury laws no longer apply. Calvin's exegesis is also distinguished by powerful movements away from seemingly unequivocal Old Testament texts and toward the golden rule. At times, his interpretation appears to be of a radical nature as he skillfully cuts the Gordian knot of scholastic adherence to Luke 6:35 to reveal a call to charity and social welfare that underlies the passage and is faithful to the tone of Luke's gospel as a whole. In this respect, the Reformers' concern to liberate salvation from the demands of an over-scrupulous conscience that believes in justification by works is brought to the fore. Through his biblical exegesis, Calvin has shown that God has not required a complete prohibition of usury, and that he of all people is not about to bind someone's conscience more tightly than God himself has done.

As a result of the distinctive nature of his exegesis, Calvin is able to focus upon charity. The presentation of Luther's thought served to convey the Reformation concern to combat avarice, which for Luther was exemplified by making money without any effort and even when ill. Calvin expands this concern and transforms it into an extensive welfare issue that would become a key feature of Genevan life. Indeed, as Olson has argued, "Calvinism is characterised more by a struggle against poverty than by a justification of lending money at interest or of keeping ones profits to oneself."[61] This central axis not only serves to move the question of lending to the poor toward one of unconditional giving but also to differentiate trade and investment where lending at interest may be permitted. By distinguishing different types of usury, Calvin removes lending to the poor from the realm of usury and places it firmly in the unconditional giving of charity. This is an important step in Calvin's justification of lending at interest: He acknowledges the common utility that it can serve when practiced according to the rules of mutual benefit and equitable reciprocity.

In his dissatisfaction with scholastic arguments, it is important to recall Calvin's impatient and at times condescending analysis of standard arguments.

This feature can be argued to be a weakness of his presentation. In *De Usuris* in particular, Calvin seems to have made a distinctly rash conflation of the *locatio* and *mutuum*—two essential aspects of usury theory—by divorcing usury from its proper association with property rights. Calvin has made this move, however, by assuming the continued ownership of lent money and thereby ignoring the whole issue of ownership and theft. The sole instance where property rights are an issue for Calvin is when an *unconditional* transfer of the ownership of money is made. This is the case of a charitable donation to the poor. The fundamental exclusion of property rights from usury theory, together with the conceptual separation of the use and substance of money, may arguably be identified as the decisive moments in the development of Calvin's argument for the toleration of lending at interest in situations where the principle of equity was unchallenged. What is more, it is upon an understanding of the *independence* of money, that is neither owned, static, nor, above all else, *sterile* within an economy, that we might see behind Calvin's economic thought. By equating the economics of leasing and lending, Calvin honed an argument for the moral equivalence of an income from either. The conflation of *mutuum* and *locatio* was a logical impossibility for Aquinas and the scholastics due to the quintessential importance of ownership. Rightly or wrongly, Calvin distanced usury theory from property rights and thus removed what had been a lynchpin of the scholastic position. Even if his theoretical example of a mutually beneficial but not culpable usurious loan in *De Usuris* serves better as an example of good business practice than one of everyday money lending, it clearly outlines the sophistication of his economic insight.

The theological and ethical issues at stake in this evaluation are of primary importance, yet this discussion points toward the question of the nature of the relationship between Calvin's understanding of usury and the "invisible hand" of economic progress. For McGrath, the issue is clear-cut: "Genevan capitalism arose and developed in response to factors which were primarily *indirectly* due to the religious ideas of Calvin."[62] This typically brief, albeit accurate, assessment is fleshed out superbly by the authoritative work of Biéler:

> Calvin, as we know, is the first of the Christian theologians to free the loan at interest from the moral and theological shame which the Church had weighed upon it until then; it is not however just to attribute to him the complete justification of liberal capitalism. His views on riches and their social ends led him to insist upon a very strict control over lending at interest;

he had prophetically sensed the social ravages to which pure liberalism would lead.[63]

It is in the spirit of this assessment that we are able to qualify the excitement occasioned by Calvin's economic ethics as we recall not only those seven binding conditions at the end of *De Usuris*, but also the ever-present call to charity in the face of avarice. It is here that we set the apparent tension in Calvin's argument between legitimating usury and desiring its eradication.

How may we compare and evaluate Aquinas' core argument from the consumptibility of money in the face of such significant advances in terms of exegesis and differences of emphasis? To base an answer entirely upon the radically different historical situations in which Aquinas and Calvin wrote would fail to give sufficient acknowledgement to their respective theological achievements. Aquinas succeeded in distancing his usury theory from the antiquated Aristotelian argument, from the sterility of money, by penetrating to the bottom of the *mutuum* contract and reconceiving the sterility of money in his presentation of the consumptibility of money. His theory demonstrated the intimate relation of property rights to usury discussion, and the indistinguishability of the use and substance of money. As a theory of usury set within an agrarian-intensive society, Aquinas' argument is reasoned and well placed. The rapid pace with which economic expansion coursed through Europe, however, outgrew the economics of Aquinas within a number of years of his death, and it was left to the Franciscan scholastics to cope with the demands that commerce placed upon the church. This was a task that they met as the scholastic analysis of usury developed, although never quite to the satisfaction of the Reformers.

In an acknowledgement of profitable activity through usury as not inconsistent with the word of God, Calvinism was able to reap the benefits of an association with commerce that would only continue to grow in importance throughout Europe. Crucial, however, for the perseverance of ethical economic teaching, was a focus upon the social impact of commerce. It is this aspect of Calvin's economic theory that assumes precedence in his discussion of usury, and it does so through a thorough devaluation of the scholastic school. In a single bound, Calvin hurdled the seemingly mountainous logical obstacle of allowing just usury by neutralising the objection from ownership and insisting upon the moral parity between the return on investment in both a *locatio* and a *mutuum*. In so doing, Calvin gave money its independence and its fertility. He set new parameters for the debate by clarifying business agreements where usury could legitimately be practiced and disassociating these from the theological call to charity. His resounding ethical appeal for economic welfare, and the reduction of economic oppression, can still be heard strongly today in calls for the relief of Third World debt.[64] Furthermore, Calvin's restraint in setting an upper limit to usury that Biéler notes was initially 5 percent, rising only to "one in fifteen,"[65] had the effect of retaining the merchant class and therefore fostering a healthy economy of trade and innovation.[66] In the final analysis, Calvin's almost disinterested argument was clear: "in short, provided we had engraven on our hearts the rule of equity which Christ prescribes in Matt. 7:12, 'therefore, all things whatsoever ye would that men should do to you, do ye even to them,' it would not be necessary to enter into lengthened disputes concerning usury."[67]

Notes

*I would like to express my sincere thanks to Dr. Joan Lockwood O'Donovan, who supervised my writing of this article. I would also like to thank the United Kingdom Arts and Humanities Research Board for their support of this research as well as the editor and anonymous reviewers of the Calvin Theological Journal for their insightful suggestions of ways to improve this article.

1. See R. De Roover, "Scholastic Economics," Quarterly Journal of Economics 69 (1955): 173, where he also provides a standard definition of usury as "any increment demanded beyond the principal of a loan."
2. J. Lockwood O'Donovan, "The Theological Economics of Medieval Usury Theory" in Studies in Christian Ethics, vol. 14, no.1 (Edinburgh: T. & T. Clark, 2001), 58.
3. With regard to equity, Guenther Haas has made an important contribution to usury studies in Calvin in a brief chapter in The Concept of Equity in Calvin's Ethics (Carlise: Paternoster, 1997), 117-121.
4. Aristotle, The Politics 1258a38, trans. T. A. Sinclair, rev. T. J. Saunders (London: Penguin Books, 1981), 87.
5. From B. Franklin, "Advice to a Young Tradesman," cited by G. Harkness in John Calvin: The Man and his Ethics (Oxford: Abingdon Press, 1931), 179.
6. J. B. Sauer, Faithful Ethics according to John Calvin, Toronto Studies in Theology, vol. 74 (Lewiston: Edwin Mellen Press, 1997), 209.
7. Aristotle, Nicomachean Ethics, trans. J. A. K. Thomson, rev. H. Tredenick (London: Penguin, 1976), 183.
8. NICOMACHEAN ETHICS, 184.
9. Ibid., 184.
10. Nicomachean Ethics, 185.
11. Ibid., 185.
12. Nicomachean Ethics, 148.
13. Aristotle, The Politics, 1.9 1256b40-1258a14.
14. Ibid., 87.

15. O. Langholm, The Aristotelian Analysis of Usury (Norway: Universitetsforlaget AS, 1984), 60.

16. O. Langholm, Economics in the Medieval Schools (New York: E. J. Brill, 1992), 20.

17. Ibid., 55.

18. Aquinas, De Malo, 13.4 reply. For a fuller discussion, see the discussion of Aquinas.

19. J. B. Sauer, Faithful Ethics, 198.

20. T. F. Divine, Interest: An historical and Analytical Study in Economics and Modern Ethics (Milwaukee: Marquette University Press, 1959), 5.

21. Langholm considers this to be fundamental to understanding Aquinas' economics because he espoused an immature argument based upon the Ethics that usury "diversified the measure" in his Commentary on the Sentences, 3:37, which following the incorporation of The Politics would disap- pear from scholastic usury theory. See The Aristotelian Analysis of Usury, 82.

22. Langholm certainly views the Summa Aurea as "the single most influential contribution to economics prior to the Summa Theologica of Thomas Aquinas" in Economics in the Medieval Schools, 64.

23. See Gratian's Institutes, 1.3., tit. 15, a translation of which is provided by A. Beck in "Usury and the Theologians," The Dublin Review, vol. 203 (London: Burns Oates & Washbourne, 1938), 81.

24. Langholm, Economics in the Medieval Schools, 244.

25. Ibid., 248.

26. Ibid., 588.

27. Sancti Thomae De Aquino Opera Omnia, vol. 23 (Rome: Commissio Leonina, 1982).

28. "usus autem pecunie ut dictum est non est aliquid quam eius substantia, unde vendit id quod non est vel vendit idem bis, ipsam scilicet pecuniam cuius usu est consumptio eius, et hoc est manifeste contra rationem iusti- tie naturalis."

29. "debet enim ille qui pecuniam mutuavit sibi cavisse ne detrimentum incurreret, nec ille qui mutuo accepit debet damnum incurrere de stultitia mutuantis."

30. See, for example, R. Gill, ed., A Textbook of Christian Ethics, 2d (Edinburgh: T. & T. Clark, 1995), 176; Divine, Interest, 68; R. H. Tawney, Religion and the Rise of Capitalism (Penguin, 1990), 112.

31. A. E. McGrath, A Life of John Calvin (Oxford: Basil Blackwell, 1990), 231. McGrath also paraphrases the opinion of C. M. Jacobs and W. I. Brandt, translator and reviser respectively of Luther's Works, vol. 45 (Philadelphia: Fortress Press, 1962), 233.

32. B. Nelson, The Idea of Usury: From Tribal Brotherhood to Universal Otherhood (Chicago: University of Chicago Press, 1969), 29. Nelson's distinctive thesis is that Calvin's rejection of the Deuteronomic usury prohibitions "charted the path to the world of 'Universal Otherhood' where all become brothers in being equally others," 73.

33. All quotations are taken from Luther's Works, vol. 45.

34. Luther's Works, vol. 45, 248.

35. Ibid., 251.

36. Ibid., 258.

37. Ibid., 291.

38. Ibid., 292.

39. Ibid., 295. The zinss kauff or "rent sale" as Brandt explains on pp. 235-36 concerned the technical sale of a piece of land in return for a guaranteed income in such a manner as to avoid usury prohibitions.

40. Luther's Works, vol. 45, 299.

41. O'Donovan, "The Theological Economics of Medieval Usury Theory," 63.

42. Luther's Works, vol. 45, 301.

43. McGrath, A Life of John Calvin, 231.

44. Sauer, Faithful Ethics, 176

45. "Il n'était pas possible de parler de la pensée économique et sociale de Calvin sans la rattacher aux prémisses théologiques sur lesquelles elle repose. La détacher de ses fondements eût été tout simplement trahir son auteur." A. Biéler, La Pensée Économique et Sociale de Calvin (Geneva: University of Geneva 1959), xiii.

46. Divine, Interest, 87.

47. All quotations are my own translations from the sixteenth-century French text provided by J. B. Sauer, "Appendix Two," in Faithful Ethics according to John Calvin, 255-58.

48. In this respect, the above presentation of Luther's theory highlights certain similarities to his exposition of Luke 6:35 as he was also concerned by the humbling appeal of this verse. See above.

49. I am grateful to one of the anonymous readers for drawing my attention to Haas, in particu- lar, on this point. His argument is, "it is the principle of equity that allows Calvin to analyse the social and economic realities of his day, that transcends a rigid biblical literalism and that liberates the Christian conscience," at 121.

50. Langholm, The Aristotelian Analysis of Usury, 105.

51. The scholastics, of course, were far from unaware of the idea of mutual reciprocity, but Calvin marks new ground in applying this argument to usury theory.

52. J. B. Sauer, Faithful Ethics, 188 n.100.

53. John Calvin, A Harmony of the Gospels: Matthew, Mark and Luke, vol. 1, trans. A. W. Morrison (Edinburgh: Saint Andrew Press, 1972), 197.

54. John Calvin, Commentaries on the Prophet Ezekiel, vol. 2 (Edinburgh: T. Constable, 1850), 226.

55. Ibid., 226.

56. Ibid., 227.

57. John Calvin, Commentary on the Book of Psalms, vol. 1 (Edinburgh: Edinburgh Printing Com- pany, 1845), 212.

58. Ibid., 212.

59. Ibid., 213-4; my italics.

60. Ibid., 214.

61. J. E. Olson, Calvin and Social Welfare: Deacons and the Bourse Française (n.p.: Associated Uni- versity Press, 1989), 167.

62. McGrath, A Life of John Calvin, 229.

63. "Calvin, on le sait, est le premier des théologiens chrétiens qui ait libéré le prêt à intérêt de l'opprobre moral et théologique que l'Eglise avait fait peser sur lui jusqu'alors; il n'est toutefois pas juste de lui attribuer la justi- fication intégrale du capitalisme libéral. Ses conceptions sur les richesses et leurs fins sociales le portent à exiger une réglementation très stricte du prêt à intérêt; il avait prophétiquement pressenti les ravages sociaux auxquels le libéralisme pur devait conduire." Biéler, La Pensée Économique et Sociale de Calvin, 168.

64. S. L. Buckley notes in Usury Friendly? The Ethics of Moneylending: A Biblical Interpretation (Cambridge: Grove Books Ltd., 1998), 5, that one third of Tanzania's budget every year is con- sumed by the interest repayment upon foreign debt. See more recently, "Dicing with Debt," The Economist (January 26, 2002): 23-25.

65. Biéler, La Pensée Économique et Sociale de Calvin, 168.

66. This point is nicely illustrated by an early seventeenth-century tract by Sir Thomas Culpepper. His argument against usury was that it actually damaged trade as: "generally all merchants when they have gotten any great wealth, leave trading and fall to usury, the gain whereof is so easy, cer-

tain and great" in his 1621 Tract Against Usurie, facsimile (Amsterdam: W. J. Johnson, 1974), 3.

67. Calvin, Commentary on the Book of Psalms, 214.

ARE PROFITS MORAL?

Answers from a Comparison of Adam Smith, Max Weber, Karl Marx, and the Westminster Larger Catechism

PHIL CLEMENTS

Philip J. Clements is the managing director of the Center for Christian Business Ethics Today, LLC. Clements has been a leader in the business community for over thirty years. He has held the position of Executive Vice President of Standard & Poor's Corporate Value Consulting ("CVC") division. He led the transition of CVC to S&P, after S&P acquired CVC from PricewaterhouseCoopers LLP (PwC). Prior to joining Standard & Poor's, Clements was the Global Leader of the CVC practice of PwC. He also served on the U.S. boards of Coopers & Lybrand and Pricewaterhouse Coopers and the global board of PwC. He was a member of the Finance Committees of both firms. Clements was Chairman of the Board of Trustees of the National Bible Association. Seattle University School of Law Board of Visitors, International Leadership Board of Advisors, and HOPE Bible Mission board are others boards that Clements has served or is serving on. In addition to founder and CEO of the Center, Philip J. Clements is also Managing Direcotor at Cathedral Consulting Firm.

PETER LILLBACK

Doctor Peter A. Lillback is President and Professor of Historical Theology at Westminster Theological Seminary. Lillback also serves as the President of The Providence Forum, the nonprofit organization that is committed to preserving and promoting America's spiritual roots of religious and civil liberties.

Living between Philadelphia and Valley Forge for many years, Dr. Lillback has pursued an avid interest in the history of the Judeo-Christian heritage of the United States. He has done much research and study on the founding and Founders of our nation through examination of original source documents in numerous libraries and archives. His books Freedom's Holy Light *and* Proclaim Liberty *are outgrowths of his research. In 2006, Dr. Lillback's bestseller on the Christian faith of George Washington was released.* George Washington's Sacred Fire *represents the culmination of over twenty years of original research and scholarship. In May 2010, the paperback reached #1 on Amazon.com.*

WAYNE GRUDEM

Wayne Grudem is Research Professor of Theology and Biblical Studies at Phoenix Seminary in

Phoenix, Arizona. Prior to Phoenix Seminary he taught for twenty years at Trinity Evangelical Divinity School, Deerfield, Illinois, where he was chairman of the department of Biblical and Systematic Theology. He received a BA from Harvard University, an MDiv from Westminster Seminary, Philadelphia, and a PhD (in New Testament) from the University of Cambridge, England. He has published sixteen books, including Systematic Theology, Recovering Biblical Manhood and Womanhood (co-edited with John Piper), The TNIV and the Gender-Neutral Bible Controversy (co-authored with Vern Poythress), The First Epistle of Peter (Tyndale NT commentary), *and* Business for the Glory of God. *He was also the General Editor for the* ESV Study Bible (published October 2008).

He is a past president of the Evangelical Theological Society, a co-founder and past president of the Council on Biblical Manhood and Womanhood, and a member of the Translation Oversight Committee for the English Standard Version *of the Bible.*

JOHN WEISER

John Weiser spent his first twenty-one years in Bloomington, Indiana, as the son of a professor of music at Indiana University. There he graduated from IU in business administration and began his business career with National City Bank in Cleveland, Ohio, where he was first exposed to the realm of institutional investments and has never left that path. With several intermediate stops, he has spent the last twenty-three of thirty-five years in this field and continues to work in his specialty of global fixed income investments with a private "hedge fund" in Texas.

John was a founder and Elder at Fort Worth Presbyterian Church, PCA, until his recent move to Charlottesville, Virginia. He has served on the Board of Trustees at Westminster Theological Seminary for fourteen years and currently serves on the board of In Medias Res, a support foundation for the Institute for Advanced Studies in Culture at the University of Virginia.

INTRODUCTION

We live in a time when business and business profits are routinely challenged as to morality. The Middle Ages had similar perspectives. Part of the outcome of the Reformation was a new respect for business and its appropriateness for all members of a community.

Why does society struggle with the question, "Are profits moral?" As with so many things, a review of the past sheds real light on both the reasons and implications. This paper presents a collection of material from the past to show the perspectives that lead up to the current views. Please read on; the message will shock you.

The paper starts with a brief look at the Westminster Larger Catechism (hereinafter called Catechism)[1] questions and answers surrounding the Ten Commandments. We start with the Catechism because it articulates well the Reformed Christian perspectives on business and profits. This perspective lays the foundation for the following authors' material, which supports and contrasts the Christian worldview. There is much more richness in the Catechism than papers such as this one, can fully explore; so, we encourage the reader to study the Catechism for the wisdom it contains.

The first author is Adam Smith and *The Wealth of Nations*.[2] Smith framed the essence of business and how business contributes to the progress in a society. Smith, a professor of moral philosophy at Glasgow, studied the business activities of his day, which were done in a culture that was essentially Christian. Space does not allow an exploration of the distinctives of the Christianity of his time. However, we will touch on the connection to the Catechism. Next up is Max Weber and *The Protestant Ethic and the Spirit of Capitalism*.[3] Weber was a social scientist and not a Christian. However, Weber's thesis was that Reformed Christianity did indeed change the way in which business was engaged and how it was viewed in the period following the Reformation. Weber cited the Westminster Confession of Faith as the theology of Reformed Christianity, but he decidedly rejected its application later. Many protest Weber's findings, but they are most useful in comparing them to the next author, Karl Marx and *Communist Manifesto*.[4] Marx can be said to have turned the world upside down in his writings. Marx rejected religion, particularly Christianity, and the capitalism that underlies the Reformed orientation to commerce. This paper quotes extensively Marx's writings because they speak quite clearly and are decidedly reflected in the rhetoric we see today about business and profits.

Before jumping into the topic, we would call to remembrance that the Bible is God's revealed Word. It is God's provision of redemption for mankind and the history of that provision. The Bible is not a book on economics. Yet, even in its role, the Bible provides insights into the realities of human existence. Part of man's existence is commercial activity; therefore it is reasonable to anticipate that the Bible contains principles and illustrations of man's commercial activities, pursuit of wealth, and the rights of individual private property.[5]

Westminster Larger Catechism

The Catechism contains 196 questions and answers designed to lead the believer into a deeper and fuller understanding of Christian faith and its blessings, duties, and practices. Each question and answer contains Bible verses that tie the principles to Scripture so that the studious Christian can know for himself the Word of God on the matter. It is in this spirit that we pride here a selection of the Catechism questions and answers that related to the first, fifth, eighth, and tenth commandments. These commandments and questions have been selected because these most crisply highlight the Bible's view on private property, business, and profits. Of particular significance is Question 141. Especially note the italicized text at the end of the answer where it is declared to be a moral duty before God to "further the wealth and outward estate of others, as well as our own." We have highlighted works and phrases to draw your attention to the portions most applicable to this topic.[6]

> *Question 99:* What rules are to be observed for the right understanding of the ten commandments?
>
> *Answer:* For the right understanding of the ten commandments, these rules are to be observed: That *the law is perfect*, and binds everyone to full conformity in the whole man unto the righteousness thereof, and unto entire obedience forever; so as to require the utmost perfection of every duty, and to forbid the least degree of every sin. That *it is spiritual*, and so reaches the understanding, will, affections, and all other powers of the soul; as well as words, works, and gestures. That one and the same thing, in divers respects, is required or forbidden in several commandments. That as, where a duty is commanded, the contrary sin is forbidden; and, *where a sin is forbidden, the contrary duty is commanded*: so, where a promise is annexed, the contrary threatening is included; and, where a threatening is annexed, the contrary promise is included. That: What God forbids, is at no time to be done; What he commands, is always our duty; and yet every particular duty is not to be done at all times. *That under one sin or duty, all of the same kind are forbidden or commanded; together with all the causes, means, occasions, and appearances thereof, and provocations thereunto.* That: What is forbidden or commanded to ourselves, we are bound,

according to our places, to endeavor that it may be avoided or performed by others, according to the duty of their places. That in: What is commanded to others, we are bound, according to our places and callings, to be helpful to them; and to take heed of partaking with others in: What is forbidden them.

Question 99 has been included to set the stage for the specifics of those commandments, questions, and answers that most bear upon the question of profits and business.

Question 103: Which is the first commandment?
Answer: The first commandment is, Thou shall have no other gods before me.

Question 104: What are the duties required in the first commandment?
Answer: The duties required in the first commandment are, the knowing and acknowledging of God to be the only true God, and our God; and to worship and glorify him accordingly, by thinking, meditating, remembering, highly esteeming, honoring, adoring, choosing, loving, desiring, fearing of him; believing him; trusting, hoping, delighting, rejoicing in him; being zealous for him; calling upon him, giving all praise and thanks, and yielding all obedience and submission to him with the whole man; *being careful in all things to please him, and sorrowful when in anything he is offended;* and walking humbly with him.

Question 105: What are the sins forbidden in the first commandment?
Answer: The sins forbidden in the first commandment are, atheism, in denying or not having a God; idolatry, in having or worshiping more gods than one, or any with or instead of the true God; the not having and avouching him for God, and our God; the omission or neglect of anything due to him, required in this commandment; ignorance, forgetfulness, misapprehensions, false opinions, unworthy and wicked thoughts of him; bold and curious searching into his secrets; all profaneness, hatred of God; *self-love, self-seeking, and all*

other inordinate and immoderate setting of our mind, will, or affections upon other things, and taking them off from him in whole or in part; vain credulity, unbelief, heresy, misbelief, distrust, despair, incorrigibleness, and insensibleness under judgments, hardness of heart, pride, presumption, *carnal security*, tempting of God; using unlawful means, and *trusting in lawful means; carnal delights and joys*; corrupt, blind, and indiscreet zeal; lukewarmness, and deadness in the things of God; estranging ourselves, and apostatizing from God; praying, or giving any religious worship, to saints, angels, or any other creatures; all compacts and consulting with the devil, and hearkening to his suggestions; making men the lords of our faith and conscience; *slighting and despising God and his commands*; resisting and grieving of his Spirit, *discontent and impatience at his dispensations*, charging him foolishly for the evils he inflicts on us; and *ascribing the praise of any good we either are, have, or can do, to fortune, idols, ourselves, or any other creature.*

Question 106: What are we specially taught by these words before me in the first commandment?

Answer: These words before me, or before my face, in the first commandment, teach us, that God, *who sees all things*, takes special notice of, and is much displeased with, the sin of having any other God: that so it may be an argument to dissuade from it, and to aggravate it as a most impudent provocation: *as also to persuade us to do as in his sight, Whatever we do in his service.*

The first commandment lays a foundation for man's relationship to his God. Question 106 captures the implications of this first commandment for those engaged in business: God "*sees all things*" and "*persuade[s] us to do as in his sight, whatever we do in his service.*" All bosses know that being present changes behavior. Christian behavior should be grounded in the knowledge of the ever presence of our Creator God. This directly affects the importance of understanding His charge and expectation of engaging in business and making a profit. The fifth, eighth, and tenth commandments bear directly on the commercial activity.

Question 122: What is the sum of the six commandments

which contain our duty to man?

Answer: The sum of the six commandments which contain our duty to man is, *to love our neighbor as ourselves, and to do to others: What we would have them to do to us.*

Here we find stated the "golden rule." John Maxwell's book *There's No Such Thing as "Business" Ethics: There's Only One Rule for Decision Making*[7] adopts this golden rule as the rule for business.[8] But as will be seen below, the commandments have a richness in application that needs the separate analysis and consideration given by those who assembled the Catechism.

Question 126: What is the general scope of the fifth commandment?

Answer: The general scope of the fifth commandment is, the performance of those duties which we mutually owe in our several relations, as inferiors, superiors, or equals.

Question 127: What is the honor that inferiors owe to their superiors?

Answer: The honor which inferiors owe to their superiors is, all due reverence in heart, word, and behavior; prayer and thanksgiving for them; imitation of their virtues and graces; willing obedience to their lawful commands and counsels; due submission to their corrections; fidelity to, *defense and maintenance of their persons and authority,* according to their several ranks, and the nature of their places; bearing with their infirmities, and covering them in love, that so they may be an honor to them and to their government.

Question 128: What are the sins of inferiors against their superiors?

Answer: The sins of inferiors against their superiors are, all neglect of the duties required toward them; *envying* at, contempt of, and rebellion against, their persons and places, in their lawful counsels, commands, and corrections; cursing, mocking, and all such refractory and scandalous carriage, as proves a shame and dishonor to them and their government.

Question 129: What is required of superiors towards their inferiors?

Answer: It is required of superiors, according to that power they receive from God, and that relation wherein they stand, to love, pray for, and bless their inferiors; to instruct, counsel, and admonish them; countenancing, commending, and *rewarding such as do well*; and discountenancing, reproving, and chastising such as do ill; *protecting, and providing for them all things necessary for soul and body*: and by grave, wise, holy, and exemplary carriage, to procure glory to God, honor to themselves, and so to preserve that authority which God has put upon them.

Question 130: What are the sins of superiors?

Answer: The sins of superiors are, besides the neglect of the duties required of them, an *inordinate seeking of themselves, their own glory, ease, profit, or pleasure; commanding things unlawful, or not in the power of inferiors to perform; counseling, encouraging, or favoring them in that which is evil; dissuading, discouraging, or discountenancing them in that which is good*; correcting them unduly; careless exposing, or leaving them to wrong, temptation, and danger; provoking them to wrath; or any way dishonoring themselves, or lessening their authority, by an unjust, indiscreet, rigorous, or remiss behavior.

Question 131: What are the duties of equals?

Answer: The duties of equals are, to regard the dignity and worth of each other, in *giving honor to go one before another; and to rejoice in each other's gifts and advancement, as their own.*

Question 132: What are the sins of equals?

Answer: The sins of equals are, besides the neglect of the duties required, *the undervaluing of the worth, envying the gifts, grieving at the advancement of prosperity one of another; and usurping preeminence one over another.*

Not all of the questions related to the fifth commandment have been included, but we see here great guidance and affirmation of the roles of superiors and their reports in a business context.

Questions 131 and 132 are very telling in today's world, that we should celebrate success, not envy or usurp preeminence one over another. Such a contrast to what we will see below.

Question 140: Which is the eighth commandment?
Answer: The eighth commandment is, Thou shalt not steal.

Question 141: What are the duties required in the eighth commandment?
Answer: The duties required in the eighth commandment are, *truth, faithfulness, and justice in contracts and commerce between man and man; rendering to everyone his due; restitution of goods unlawfully detained from the right owners thereof; giving and lending freely, according to our abilities, and the necessities of others; moderation of our judgments, wills, and affections concerning worldly goods; a provident care and study to get, keep, use, and dispose these things which are necessary and convenient for the sustentation of our nature, and suitable to our condition; a lawful calling, and diligence in it; frugality; avoiding unnecessary lawsuits and suretyship, or other like engagements; and an endeavor, by all just and lawful means, to procure, preserve, and further the wealth and outward estate of others, as well as our own.*

Question 142: What are the sins forbidden in the eighth commandment?
Answer: The sins forbidden in the eighth commandment, besides the neglect of the duties required, are, *theft, robbery, man stealing, and receiving anything that is stolen; fraudulent dealing, false weights and measures, removing land marks, injustice and unfaithfulness in contracts between man and man, or in matters of trust; oppression, extortion, usury, bribery, vexatious lawsuits, unjust enclosures and depopulations; engrossing commodities to enhance the price; unlawful callings, and all other unjust or sinful ways of taking or withholding from our neighbor: What belongs to him, or of enriching ourselves; covetousness; inordinate prizing and affecting worldly goods; distrustful and distracting cares and studies in getting, keeping, and using them; envying at the prosperity of others; as likewise idleness, prodigality, wasteful*

> *gaming; and all other ways whereby we do unduly prejudice our*
> *own outward estate, and defrauding ourselves of the due use and*
> *comfort of that estate which God has given us.*

Clearly the eighth commandment is a centerpiece for understanding God's perspective on commercial relations. Throughout modern history and across the globe, the role of private property in commercial development of a society or country affirms that the principles in the eighth commandment on the respect for private property are universal and essential. In the discussions on alienation of poverty through economic activity, Hernando De Soto noted that there is plenty of capital in the developing world; it is just trapped in poor ownership/legal structures.[9] De Soto's point is that where private property is respected and ownership is clear, the values created in building businesses or enhancing property become transferable or form collateral for loans to increase economic activity. In short, private property creates the framework for profits that create the economic activity that create blessed communities. But where private property is not respected or ownership is not clear, the enhancements or businesses have no value, because they cannot be transferred or become collateral for financing. While this seems a simple set of statements, De Soto properly highlights what the Bible had addressed thousands of years before. It is essential to economic development and the profitability of a community, that property rights be clear and respected. The eight commandment questions of the Catechism capture the richness of this respect and the comfort that following this commandment brings to individuals and communities.

The contrasts of the obligations set forth in these questions and answers with the views of Marx could not be more graphic. Clearly there are simply different and irreconcilable worldviews between the Catechism and the *Communist Manifesto*.[10]

> *Question 146:* Which is the tenth commandment?
> *Answer:* The tenth commandment is, Thou shalt not covet thy neighbor's house, thou shalt not covet thy neighbor's wife, nor his manservant, nor his maidservant, nor his ox, nor his ass, nor any thing that is thy neighbor's.
>
> *Question 147:* What are the duties required in the tenth commandment?
> *Answer:* The duties required in the tenth commandment are,

such a full contentment with our own condition, and such a chari-
table frame of the whole soul toward our neighbor, as that all our
inward motions and affections touching him, tend unto, and fur-
ther all that good which is his.

Question 148: What are the sins forbidden in the tenth commandment?
Answer: The sins forbidden in the tenth commandment are,
discontentment with our own estate; envying and grieving at the
good of our neighbor, together with all inordinate motions and
affections to anything that is his.

Question 149: Is any man able perfectly to keep the commandments of God?
Answer: No man is able, either of himself, or by any grace received
in this life, perfectly to keep the commandments of God; but does
daily break them in thought, word, and deed.

The tenth commandment gets somewhat short attention in the *Catechism*. In part, much of its charge seems to be covered elsewhere. But in today's
business world the specifics of this commandment should challenge us to the
same depth of thinking on behavior and duties as those of the other commandments. Space in this paper limits our ability to cover the application of
contentment in our business as we operate in the competitive marketplace, but
the reader is encouraged to meditation on this commandment with the spirit
of the Catechism.

We would summarize these passages as to the question of the morality
of profits by noting that profits and wealth creation cannot become an idol,
to displace God. Nowhere in these questions and answers are profits treated as
an error or immoral. Rather, instruction and caution are given as to both the
pursuit and the treatment of our and others' assets and wealth accumulations.
We should be content with what we have been given by God. But we have a
responsibility to make it productive, which generally means creating increase,
or more profits.

Adam Smith, The Wealth of Nations, and the Basis of Profits

We leave the Catechism and look to the work of Adam Smith. The classic capitalistic insights of labor, profits, and supply and demand were stated by Adam Smith in his seminal work, *The Wealth of Nations*. Smith's work shows that man is by nature of necessity, a businessman. The following excerpts are provided from book 1, chapter 2, and chapter 3. These show the basics of the need for barter and the benefits, he found, from division of labor or making labor more productive.[11] An added concept embedded in Smith's findings are the effects of the economic law of supply and demand. Highlights have been provided to draw the reader's attention to portions that provide contrasts with other material in this paper:

> [Chapter 2] In civilized society he stands at all times in need of the cooperation and assistance of great multitudes, while his whole life is scarce sufficient to gain the friendship of a few persons. In almost every other race of animals each individual, when it is grown up to maturity, is entirely independent, and in its natural state has occasion for the assistance of no other living creature. *But man has almost constant occasion for the help of his brethren, and it is in vain for him to expect it from their benevolence only. He will be more likely to prevail if he can interest their self-love in his favour, and show them that it is for their own advantage to do for him what he requires of them.* Whoever offers to another a bargain of any kind, proposes to do this. *Give me that which I want, and you shall have this which you want, is the meaning of every such offer; and it is in this manner that we obtain from one another the far greater part of those good offices which we stand in need of.* It is not from the benevolence of the butcher, the brewer, or the baker, that we expect our dinner, but from their regard to their own interest. We address ourselves, not to their humanity but to their self-love, and never talk to them of our own necessities but of their advantages. Nobody but a beggar chuses to depend chiefly upon the benevolence of his fellow-citizens. Even a beggar does not depend upon it entirely. The charity of well-disposed people, indeed, supplies him with

the whole fund of his subsistence. But though this principle ultimately provides him with all the necessaries of life which he has occasion for, it neither does nor can provide him with them as he has occasion for them. The greater part of his occasional wants are supplied in the same manner as those of other people, by treaty, by barter, and by purchase. With the money which one man gives him he purchases food. The old cloaths which another bestows upon him he exchanges for other old cloaths which suit him better, or for lodging, or for food, or for money, with which he can buy either food, cloaths, or lodging, as he has occasion.

As it is by treaty, by barter, and by purchase, that we obtain from one another the greater part of those mutual good offices which we stand in need of, so it is this same trucking disposition which originally gives occasion to the division of labour. In a tribe of hunters or shepherds a particular person makes bows and arrows, for example, with more readiness and dexterity than any other. He frequently exchanges them for cattle or for venison with his companions; and he finds at last that he can in this manner get more cattle and venison, than if he himself went to the field to catch them. From a regard to his own interest, therefore, the making of bows and arrows grows to be his chief business, and he becomes a sort of armourer. Another excels in making the frames and covers of their little huts or moveable houses. He is accustomed to be of use in this way to his neighbours, who reward him in the same manner with cattle and with venison, till at last he finds it his interest to dedicate himself entirely to this employment, and to become a sort of house-carpenter. In the same manner a third becomes a smith or a brazier; a fourth a tanner or dresser of hides or skins, the principal part of the clothing of savages. And thus the certainty of being able to exchange all that surplus part of the produce of his own labour, which is over and above his own consumption, for such parts of the produce of other men's labour as he may have occasion for, encourages every man to apply himself to a particular occupation, and to cultivate and bring to perfection whatever talent or genius he may possess for that particular species of business.

The difference of natural talents in different men is, in reality, much less than we are aware of; and the very different genius which appears to distinguish men of different professions, when grown up to maturity, is not upon many occasions so much the cause, as the effect of the division of labour. *The difference between the most dissimilar characters, between a philosopher and a common street porter, for example, seems to arise not so much from nature, as from habit, custom, and education.* When they came into the world, and for the first six or eight years of their existence, they were perhaps, very much alike, and neither their parents nor playfellows could perceive any remarkable difference. About that age, or soon after, they come to be employed in very different occupations. The difference of talents comes then to be taken notice of, and widens by degrees, till at last the vanity of the philosopher is willing to acknowledge scarce any resemblance. But without the disposition to truck, barter, and exchange, every man must have procured to himself every necessary and conveniency of life which he wanted. All must have had the same duties to perform, and the same work to do, and there could have been no such difference of employment as could alone give occasion to any great difference of talents.

[Chapter 3] As it is the power of exchanging that gives occasion to the division of labour, *so the extent of this division must always be limited by the extent of that power, or, in other words, by the extent of the market.* When the market is very small, no person can have any encouragement to dedicate himself entirely to one employment, for want of the power to exchange all that surplus part of the produce of his own labour, which is over and above his own consumption, for such parts of the produce of other men's labour as he has occasion for.

There are some sorts of industry, even of the lowest kind, which can be carried on no where but in a great town. A porter, for example, can find employment and subsistence in no other place. A village is by much too narrow a sphere for him; even an ordinary market town is scarce large enough to afford him constant occupation. In the lone houses and very small villages which are scattered about in so desert a country as the Highlands of Scotland, every farmer must be butcher, baker and brewer for his own family. In such situations we can scarce expect to find even a smith, a carpenter, or a mason, within less than twenty miles of another of the same trade. The scattered families that live at eight or ten miles distance from the nearest of them, must learn to perform themselves a great number of little pieces of work, for which, in more populous countries, they would call in the assistance of those workmen. Country workmen are almost every where obliged to apply themselves to all the different branches of industry that have so much affinity to one another as to be employed about the same sort of materials. A country carpenter deals in every sort of work that is made of wood: a country smith in every sort of work that is made of iron. The former is not only a carpenter, but a joiner, a cabinet maker, and even a carver in wood, as well as a wheelwright, a ploughwright, a cart and waggon maker. The employments of the latter are still more various. It is impossible there should be such a trade as even that of a nailer in the remote and inland parts of the Highlands of Scotland. Such a workman at the rate of a thousand nails a day, and three hundred working days in the year, will make three hundred thousand nails in the year. But in such a situation it would be impossible to dispose of one thousand, that is, of one day's work in the year.

This division of labor that is inherent in human commerce which is coupled with the law of supply and demand, also ultimately creates human profits. For example, in book 1, chapter 9, he declares:

It is not easy, it has already been observed, to ascertain what are the average wages of labour even in a particular place, and at a particular time. We can, even in this case, seldom determine more than what are the most usual wages. But even this can seldom be done with regard to the profits of stock. *Profit is so very fluctuating, that the person who carries on a particular trade cannot always tell you himself what is the average of his annual profit.* It is affected, not only by every variation of price in the commodities which he deals in, but by the good or bad fortune both of his rivals and of his customers, and by a thousand other accidents to which goods when carried either by sea or by land, or even when stored in a warehouse, are liable. It varies, therefore, not only from year to year, but from day to day, and almost from hour to hour. To ascertain what is the average profit of all the different trades carried on in a great kingdom, must be much more difficult; and to judge of what it may have been formerly, or in remote periods of time, with any degree of precision, must be altogether impossible.

But though it may be impossible to determine with any degree of precision, what are or were the average profits of stock, either in the present, or in ancient times, some notion may be formed of them from the interest of money. It may be laid down as a maxim, that wherever a great deal can be made by the use of money, a great deal will commonly be given for the use of it; and that wherever little can be made by it, less will commonly be given for it. *According, therefore, as the usual market rate of interest varies in any country, we may be assured that the ordinary profits of stock must vary with it, must sink as it sinks, and rise as it rises. The progress of interest, therefore, may lead us to form some notion of the progress of profit.*

Thus profits and labor go hand in hand, when the actual forces of the market itself determine their activities. Competition, supply and demand, and the inherent instinct of the human soul to engage in commerce are bread-and-butter concepts for Western modern and postmodern civilization. But are such profits in themselves moral? Are profits a good thing, or just a necessary evil that must be controlled by competition, government intervention, or even revolution? Note that Smith did not answer these questions. Rather he recorded his observations as a scientist of the functioning of the world around him.

Max Weber and the Development of the Ethics of Capitalism

The American principle of the propriety of the economic pursuit of profits is well captured by Max Weber's *The Protestant Ethic and the Spirit of Capitalism.*

Interestingly, his assessment focuses on the great American Founding Father, Ben Franklin, and argues that there is a direct connection between Franklin's capitalism that sees profits as a moral pursuit, and the Puritan tradition as represented by Richard Baxter. Weber wrote:

> [Chapter 2] In the title of this study is used the somewhat pretentious phrase, the spirit of capitalism. What is to be understood by it? The attempt to give anything like a definition of it brings out certain difficulties which are in the very nature of this type of investigation. . . .
>
> We turn to a document of that spirit which contains what we are looking for in almost classical purity, and at the same time has the advantage of being free from all direct relationship to religion, being thus for our purposes, free of preconceptions.
>
> *"Remember, that time is money. He that can earn ten shillings a day by his labor, and goes abroad, or sits idle, one half of that day, though he spends but sixpence during his diversion or idleness, ought not to reckon that the only expense; he has really spent, rather thrown away, five shillings,* besides.
>
> "Remember, that credit is money. If a man lets his money lie in my hands after it is due, he gives me interest, or so much as I can make of it during that time. This amounts to a considerable sum where a man has good and large credit, and makes good use of it.
>
> "Remember, that money is of the prolific, generating nature. *Money can beget money, and its offspring can beget more, and so on.* Five shillings turned is six, turned again it is seven and three pence, and so on, till it becomes a hundred pounds. The more there is of it, the more it produces every turning, so that the profits rise quicker and quicker. He that kills a breeding sow, destroys all her offspring to the thousandth generation. He that murders a crown, destroys all that it might have produced, even scores of pounds."
>
> "Remember this saying, *The good paymaster is lord of another man's purse. He that is known to pay punctually and exactly to the time he, promises, may at any time, and on any occasion, raise all the money his friends can spare.* This is sometimes of great use. After industry and frugality, nothing contributes more to the

raising of a young man in the world than punctuality and justice in all his dealings; therefore never keep borrowed money
an hour beyond the time you promised, lest a disappointment
shut up your friend's purse for ever.

"The most trifling actions that affect a man's credit are to
be regarded. The sound of your hammer at five in the morning, or eight at night, heard by a creditor, makes him easy six
months longer; but if he sees you at a billiard table, or hears
your voice at a tavern, when you should be at work, he sends
for his money the next day; demands it, before he can receive
it, in a lump. *'It shows, besides, that you are mindful of what you
owe; it makes you appear a careful as well as an honest man, and
that still increases your credit.'*

"Beware of thinking all your own that you possess, and of
living accordingly. It is a mistake that many people who have
credit fall into. *To prevent this, keep an exact account for some
time both of your expenses and your income.* If you take the pains
at first to mention particulars, it will have this good effect: you
will discover how wonderfully small, trifling expenses mount
up to large sums, and will discern what might have been, and
may for the future be saved, without occasioning any great
inconvenience.

"For six pounds a year you may have the use of one hundred pounds, provided you are a man of known prudence and
honesty.

"He that spends a groat a day idly, spends idly above six
pounds a year, which is the price for the use of one hundred
pounds.

"He that wastes idly a groat's worth of his time per day, one
day with another, wastes the privilege of using one hundred
pounds each day.

"He that idly loses five shillings' worth of time, loses five shillings, and might as prudently throw five shillings into the sea.

"He that loses five shillings, not only loses that sum, but
all the advantage that might be made by turning it in dealing, which by the time that a young man becomes old, will
amount to a considerable sum of money."

It is Benjamin Franklin who preaches to us in these sentences. .

. . Let us pause a moment to consider this passage, the philosophy of which Kurnberger sums up in the words, "They make tallow out of cattle and money out of men." The peculiarity of this philosophy of avarice appears to be the ideal of the honest man of recognized credit, and above all the idea of a duty of the individual toward the increase of his capital, which is assumed as an end in itself. *Truly what is here preached is not simply a means of making one's way in the world, but a peculiar ethic.* The infraction of its rules is treated not as foolishness but as *forgetfulness of duty.* That is the essence of the matter. It is not mere business astuteness, that sort of thing is common enough, it is an ethos. This is the quality which interests us. . . .

The concept spirit of capitalism is here used in this specific sense, it is the spirit of modern capitalism. For that we are here dealing only with Western European and American capitalism is obvious from the way in which the problem was stated. Capitalism existed in China, India, Babylon, in the classic world, and in the Middle Ages. But in all these cases, as we shall see, this particular ethos was lacking . . .

In fact, the *summum bonum* of his ethic, the earning of more and more money, combined with the strict avoidance of all spontaneous enjoyment of life, is above all completely devoid of any eudaemonistic, not to say hedonistic, admixture. It is thought of so purely as an end in itself, that from the point of view of the happiness of, or utility to, the single individual, it appears entirely transcendental and absolutely irrational. Man is dominated by the making of money, by acquisition as the ultimate purpose of his life. Economic acquisition is no longer subordinated to man as the means for the satisfaction of his material needs. This reversal of what we should call the natural relationship, so irrational from a naive point of view, is evidently as definitely a leading principle of capitalism as it is foreign to all peoples not under capitalistic influence. At the same time it expresses a type of feeling which is closely connected with certain religious ideas. If we thus ask, *why* should "money be made out of men," Benjamin Franklin himself, although he was a colorless deist, answers in his autobiography with a quotation from the Bible, which his strict Calvinistic father drummed into him again and again in his youth: "Seest thou a man diligent in his business? He shall stand before kings" (Prov. xxii. 29). The earning of money within the modern economic order is, so long as it is done legally, the result and the expression of virtue and proficiency in a calling; and this virtue and proficiency are, as it is now not difficult to see, the real Alpha and Omega of Franklin's ethic . . .

For the purposes of this chapter, though by no means for all purposes, we can treat ascetic Protestantism as a single whole. *But since that side of English Puritanism which was derived from Calvinism gives the most consistent religious basis for the idea of the calling, we shall, following our previous method, place one of its representatives at the centre of the discussion.* Richard Baxter stands out above many other writers on Puritan ethics, both because of his eminently practical and realistic attitude, and, at the same time, because of the universal recognition accorded to his works, which have gone through many new editions and translations. . . . His Christian Directory is the most compendium of Puritan ethics, and is adjusted to the practical experiences of his own ministerial activity . . .

Now, in glancing at Baxter's Saints' Everlasting Rest, or his Christian Directory, or similar works of others,' *one is struck at first glance by the emphasis placed, in the discussion of wealth and its acquisition,* on the ebionitic elements of the New [T]estament. Wealth as such is a great danger; its temptations never end and its pursuit is not only senseless as compared with the dominating importance of the Kingdom of God, but it-is morally suspect. Here asceticism seems to have turned much more sharply against the acquisition of earthly goods than it did in Calvin, who saw no hindrance to the effectiveness of the clergy in their wealth, but rather a thoroughly desirable enhancement of their prestige. Hence he permitted them to employ their means profitably. Examples of the condemnation of the pursuit of money and goods may be gathered without end from Puritan writings, and may be contrasted with the late mediaeval ethical literature, which was much more open-minded on this point. Moreover, these doubts were meant with perfect seriousness; only it is necessary to examine them somewhat more closely in order to understand their true ethical significance and implications. *The real moral objection is to relaxation in the security of possession, the enjoyment of wealth with the consequence of idleness and the temptations of the flesh, above all of distraction from the pursuit of a righteous life. In fact, it is only because possession involves this danger of relaxation that it is objectionable at all.* For the saints' everlasting rest is in the next world; on earth man must, to be certain of his state of grace, "do the works of him who sent him, as long as it is yet day." Not leisure and enjoyment, but only activity serves to increase the glory of God, according to the definite manifestations of His will.

Waste of time is thus the first and in principle the deadliest of sins. The span of human life is infinitely short and precious to make sure of one's own election. Loss of time through sociability, idle talk, luxury, even more sleep than is necessary for health, six to at most eight hours, is worthy of absolute moral condemnation. It does not yet hold, with Franklin, that time is money, but the proposition is true in a certain spiritual sense. It is infinitely valuable because every hour lost is lost to labour for the glory of God. Thus inactive contemplation is also valueless, or even directly reprehensible if it is at the expense of one's daily work. For it is less pleasing to God than the active performance of His will in a calling. Besides, Sunday is provided for that, and, according to Baxter, it is always those who are not diligent in their callings who have no time for God when the occasion demands it.

Accordingly, Baxter's principal work is dominated by the continually repeated, often almost passionate preaching of hard, continuous bodily or mental labour. . . . "Work hard in your calling." *But the most important thing was that even beyond that labour came to be considered in itself the end of life, ordained as such by God. St. Paul's "He who will not work shall not eat" holds unconditionally for every-one. Unwillingness to work is symptomatic of the lack of grace.*

Here the difference from the *medieval view-point* becomes quite evident. Thomas Aquinas also gave an interpretation of that statement of St. Paul. But for him labour is only necessary *naturali ratione* for *the maintenance of individual and commu-*

nity. Where this end is achieved, the precept ceases to have any meaning. Moreover, it holds only for the race, not for every individual. It does not apply to anyone who can live without labour on his possessions, and of course contemplation, as a spiritual form of action in the Kingdom of God, takes precedence over the commandment in its literal sense. *Moreover, for the popular theology of the time, the highest form of monastic productivity lay in the increase of the Thesaurus ecclesie through prayer and chant.*

Now only do these exceptions to the duty to labour naturally no longer hold for Baxter, but he holds most emphatically that wealth does not exempt anyone from the unconditional command. Even the wealthy shall not eat without working, for even though they do not need to labour to support their own needs, there is God's commandment which they, like the poor, must obey. *For everyone without exception God's Providence has prepared a calling, which he should profess and in which he should labour.* And this calling is not, as it was for the Lutheran, a fate to which he must submit and which he must make the best of, but God's commandment to the individual to work for the divine glory. This seemingly subtle difference had far-reaching psychological consequences, and became connected with a further development of the providential interpretation of the economic order which had begun in scholasticism.

The phenomenon of the division of labour and occupations in society had, among others, been interpreted by Thomas Aquinas, to whom we may most conveniently refer, as a direct consequence of the divine scheme of things. But the places assigned to each man in this cosmos follow ex causis naturalibus and are fortuitous (contingent in the Scholastic terminology). The differentiation of men into the classes and occupations established through historical development became for Luther, as we have seen, a direct result of the divine will. The perseverance of the individual in the place and within the limits which God had assigned to him was a religious duty. This was the more certainly the consequence since the relations of Lutheranism to the world were in general uncertain from the beginning and remained so. Ethical principles for the reform of the world could not be found in Luther's realm of ideas; in fact it never quite freed itself from Pauline indifference. Hence the world had to be accepted as it was, and this alone could be made a religious duty—But in the Puritan view, the providential character of the play of private economic interests takes on a somewhat different emphasis. True to the Puritan tendency to pragmatic interpretations, the *providential purpose of the division of labour is to be known by its fruits. On this point Baxter expresses himself in terms which more than once directly recall Adam Smith's well-known apotheosis of the division of labour. The specialization of occupations leads, since it makes the development of skill possible, to a quantitative and qualitative improvement in production, and thus serves the common good, which is identical with the good of the greatest possible number.* So far, the motivation is purely utilitarian, and is closely related to the customary view-point of much of the secular literature of the time.

But the characteristic Puritan element appears when Baxter sets at the head of his discussion the statement that "*outside of a well-marked calling the accomplishments of a man are only casual and irregular, and he spends more time in idleness than at work,*" and when he concludes it as follows: "*and he [the specialized worker) will carry out his work in order while another remains in constant confusion, and his business knows neither time nor place . . . therefore is a certain calling the best for everyone.*" Irregular work, which the ordinary labourer is often forced to accept, is often unavoidable, but always an unwelcome state of transition. A man without a calling thus lacks the systematic, methodical character which is, as we have seen, demanded by worldly asceticism.

The Quaker ethic also holds that a man's life in his calling is an exercise in ascetic virtue, a proof of his state of grace through his conscientiousness, which is expressed in the care and method with which he pursues his calling. What God demands is not labour in itself, but rational labour in a calling. In the *Puritan concept of the calling the emphasis is always placed on this methodical character of worldly asceticism, not, as with*

Luther, on the acceptance of the lot which God has irretrievably assigned to man.

Hence the question whether anyone may combine several callings is answered in the affirmative, if it is useful for the common good or one's own, and not injurious to anyone, and if it does not lead to unfaithfulness in one of the callings. Even a change of calling is by no means regarded as objectionable, if it is not thoughtless and is made for the purpose of pursuing a calling more pleasing to God, which means, on general principles, one more useful.

It is true that the usefulness of a calling, and thus its favour in the sight of God, is measured primarily in moral terms, and thus in terms of the importance of the goods produced in it for the community. But a further, and, above all, in practice the most important, criterion is found in private profitableness. For if that God, whose hand the Puritan sees in all the occurrences of life, shows one of His elect a chance of profit, he must do it with a purpose. Hence the faithful Christian must follow the call by taking advantage of the opportunity. *"If God show you a way in which you may lawfully get more than in another way (without wrong to your soul or to any other), if you refuse this, and choose the less gainful way, you cross one of the ends of your calling, and you refuse to be God's steward, and to accept His gifts and use them for Him, when He requireth it: you may labour to be rich for God, though not for the flesh and sin."*

Wealth is thus bad ethically only in so far as it is a temptation to idleness and sinful enjoyment of life, and its acquisition is bad only when it is with the purpose of later living merrily and without care. But as a performance of duty in a calling it is not only morally permissible, but actually enjoined. The parable of the servant who was rejected because he did not increase the talent which was entrusted to him seemed to say so directly. To wish to be poor was, it was often argued, the same as wishing to be unhealthy; it is objectionable as a glorification of works and derogatory to the glory of God. Especially begging, on the part of one able to work, is not only the sin of slothfulness, but a violation of the duty of brotherly love according to the Apostle's own word. The emphasis on the ascetic importance of a fixed calling provided an ethical justification of the modern specialized division of labour. In a similar way the providential interpretation of profitmaking justified the activities of the business man. The superior indulgence of the seigneur and the parvenu ostentation of the nouveau riche are equally detestable to asceticism.

But, on the other hand, it has the highest ethical appreciation of the sober, middle-class, self-made Man. "God blesseth His trade" is a stock remark about those good men who had successfully followed the divine hints. The whole power of the God of the Old Testament, who rewards His people for their obedience in this life, necessarily exercised a similar influence on the Puritan who, following Baxter's advice, compared his own state of grace with that of the heroes of the Bible, and in the process interpreted the statements of the Scriptures as the articles of a book of statutes. . . .

The idea of a man's duty to his possessions, to which he subordinates himself as an obedient steward, or even as an acquisitive machine, bears with chilling weight on his life. The greater the possessions the heavier, if the ascetic attitude toward life stands the test, the feeling of responsibility for them, for holding them undiminished for the glory of God and increasing them by restless effort. The origin of this type of life also extends in certain roots, like so many aspects of the spirit of capitalism, back into the Middle Ages. *But it was in the ethic of ascetic Protestantism that it first found a consistent ethical foundation. Its significance for the development of capitalism is obvious. This worldly Protestant asceticism, as we may recapitulate up to this point, acted powerfully against the spontaneous enjoyment of possessions; it restricted consumption, especially of luxuries. On the other hand, it had the psychological effect of freeing the acquisition of goods from the inhibitions of traditionalistic ethics.* It broke the bonds of the impulse of acquisition in that it not only legalized it, but (in the sense discussed) looked upon it as directly willed by God. The campaign against the temptations of the flesh, and the dependence on external things, was, as besides the Puritans the great Quaker apologist Barclay expressly says, not a struggle against the rational acquisition, but against the irrational use of wealth.

But this irrational use was exemplified in the outward forms of luxury which their code condemned as idolatry of the flesh, however natural they had appeared to the feudal mind. On the other hand, they approved the rational and utilitarian uses of wealth which were willed by God for the needs of the individual and the community. They did not wish to impose mortification on the man of wealth, but the use of his means for necessary and practical things. The idea of comfort characteristically limits the extent of ethically permissible expenditures. It is naturally no accident that the development of a manner of living consistent with that idea may be observed earliest and most clearly among the most consistent representatives of this whole attitude toward life. Over against the glitter and ostentation of feudal magnificence which, resting on an unsound economic basis, prefers a sordid elegance to a sober simplicity, they set the clean and solid comfort of the middle-class home as an ideal. . . .

When the limitation of consumption is combined with this release of acquisitive activity, the inevitable practical result is obvious: accumulation of capital through ascetic compulsion to save. The restraints which were imposed upon the consumption of wealth naturally served to increase it by making possible the productive investment of capital. How strong this influence was is not, unfortunately, susceptible to exact statistical demonstration. In New England the connection is so evident that it did not escape the eye of so discerning a historian as Doyle. But also in Holland, which was really only dominated by strict Calvinism for seven years, the greater simplicity of life in the more seriously religious circles, in combination with great wealth, led to an excessive propensity to accumulation. . .

We may hence quote here a passage from John Wesley himself which might well serve as a motto for everything which has been said above. For it shows that the leaders of these ascetic movements understood the seemingly paradoxical relationships which we have here analysed perfectly well, and in the same sense that we have given them. He wrote:

I fear, wherever riches have increased, the essence of religion has decreased in the same proportion. Therefore I do not see how it is possible, in the nature of things, for any revival of true religion to continue long. For religion must necessarily produce both industry and frugality, and these cannot but produce riches. But as riches increase, so will pride, anger, and love of the world in all its branches. How then is it possible that Methodism, that is, a religion of the heart, though it flourishes now as a green bay tree, should continue in this state? For the Methodists in every place grow diligent and frugal; consequently they increase in goods. Hence they proportionately increase in pride, in anger, in the desire of the flesh, the desire of the eyes, and the pride of life. So, although the form of religion remains, the spirit is swiftly vanishing away. Is there no way to prevent this— this continual decay of pure religion? We ought not to prevent people from being diligent and frugal; we must exhort all Christians to gain all they can, and to save all they can; that is, in effect, to grow rich.

There follows the advice that those who gain all they can and save all they can should also give all they can, so that they will grow in grace and lay up a treasure in heaven. It is clear that Wesley here expresses, even in detail, just what we have been trying to point out. As Wesley here says, the full economic effect of those great religious movements, whose significance for economic development lay above all in their ascetic educative influence, generally came only after the peak of the purely religious enthusiasm was past. Then the intensity of the search for the Kingdom of God commenced gradually to pass over into sober economic virtue; the religious roots died out slowly, giving way to utilitarian worldliness. . . .

One of the fundamental elements of the spirit of modern capitalism, and not only of that but of all modern culture: rational conduct on the basis of the idea of the calling, was born—that is what this discussion has sought to demonstrate from the *spirit of Christian asceticism.* One has only to reread the passage from Franklin, quoted at the beginning of this essay, in order to see that *the essential elements of the attitude which was there called the spirit of capitalism are the same as what we have just shown to be the content of the Puritan worldly asceticism, only without the religious basis, which by Franklin's time had died away. . . .*

The Puritan wanted to work in a calling; we are forced to do so. For when asceticism was carried out of monastic cells into everyday life, and began to dominate worldly morality, it did its part in building the tremendous cosmos of the modern economic order. This order is now bound to the technical and economic conditions of machine production which today determine the lives of all the individuals who are born into this mechanism, not only those directly concerned with economic acquisition, with irresistible force. Perhaps it will so determine them until the last ton of fossilized coal is burnt. In Baxter's view the care for external goods should only lie on the shoulders of the "saint like a light cloak, which can be thrown aside at any moment." But fate decreed that the cloak should become an iron cage.

While the above is a long and full citation of Weber's thinking, it omits the citation of the other chapter in his work of the Westminster Confession of Faith. Some observations are useful here. First, the action and attitude findings of asceticism and stewardship of time, talent, and goods is consistent with the questions and answers in the Ten Commandments cited above. Weber finds these as the grounding for modern capitalism and modern business. Second, Weber finds that profits form a fundamental moral dimension to the Protestant belief. He does not find it immoral, but does note that before the Reformation, profits were consumed, not reinvested, which then creates more profits. Third, we should see that Weber misses the essential reason for why the Protestant is hardworking and a bit ascetic—he serves his Creator God, question 106. It is the love of God, found in the magnificence of our salvation and the assurance that we will spend eternity with our Savior that compels the Protestant. Unfortunately, Weber did not see this; rather, he applied humanistic interpretations to actions in order to explain the Protestant's motive as a self-interest action as found in the Smith quotation.

So Weber affirms profits are moral and fundamental and derived from an ethic that is grounded in hard work and thriftiness. It is useful to note that these principles remain valid today. So we turn to the last author to get a complete contrast.

KARL MARX'S REPUDIATION OF CAPITALISM AND PROFITS

The Communist agenda is clearly defined in Marx's *Communist Manifesto*.[12] To gain a sense of Communism's hostility to private property and therefore to the whole notion of capitalism and private property, consider this selection from *The Communist Manifesto*. The italicized portions are added to aid the reader in the points being made:

> In this sense, the theory of the Communists may be summed up in the single sentence: *Abolition of private property*.
>
> We Communists have been reproached with the desire of abolishing the right of personally acquiring property as the fruit of a man's own labor, which property is alleged to be the groundwork of all personal freedom, activity and independence.
>
> Hard-won, self-acquired, self-earned property! Do you mean the property of petty artisan and of the small peasant, a form of property that preceded the bourgeois form? There is no need to abolish that; the development of industry has to a great extent already destroyed it, and is still destroying it daily.
>
> Or do you mean the modern bourgeois private property?
>
> *But does wage labor create any property for the laborer? Not a bit. It creates capital, i.e., that kind of property which exploits wage labor*, and which cannot increase except upon conditions of begetting a new supply of wage labor for fresh exploitation. Property, in its present form, is based on the antagonism of capital and wage labor. Let us examine both sides of this antagonism.
>
> To be a capitalist, is to have not only a purely personal, but a social STATUS in production. Capital is a collective product, and only by the united action of many members, nay, in the last resort, only by the united action of all members of society, can it be set in motion.

Capital is therefore not only personal; it is a social power.

When, therefore, capital is converted into common property, into the property of all members of society, personal property is not thereby transformed into social property. It is only the social character of the property that is changed. It loses its class character.

Let us now take wage labor.

The average price of wage labor is the minimum wage, i.e., that quantum of the means of subsistence which is absolutely requisite to keep the laborer in bare existence as a laborer. What, therefore, the wage laborer appropriates by means of his labor merely suffices to prolong and reproduce a bare existence. We by no means intend to abolish this personal appropriation of the products of labor, an appropriation that is made for the maintenance and reproduction of human life, and that leaves no surplus wherewith to command the labor of others. *All that we want to do away with is the miserable character of this appropriation, under which the laborer lives merely to increase capital, and is allowed to live only in so far as the interest of the ruling class requires it.*

In bourgeois society, living labor is but a means to increase accumulated labor. In communist society, accumulated labor is but a means to widen, to enrich, to promote the existence of the laborer.

In bourgeois society, therefore, the past dominates the present; in communist society, the present dominates the past. In bourgeois society, capital is independent and has individuality, while the living person is dependent and has no individuality.

And the abolition of this state of things is called by the bourgeois, abolition of individuality and freedom! And rightly so. The abolition of bourgeois individuality, bourgeois independence, and bourgeois freedom is undoubtedly aimed at.

By freedom is meant, under the present bourgeois conditions of production, free trade, free selling and buying.

But if selling and buying disappears, free selling and buying disappears also. This talk about free selling and buying, and all the other "brave words" of our bourgeois about freedom in general, have a meaning, if any, only in contrast with restricted selling and buying, with the fettered traders of the Middle Ages, but have no meaning when opposed to the communist abolition of buying and selling, or the bourgeois conditions of production, and of the bourgeoisie itself.

You are horrified at our intending to do away with private property. But in your existing society, private property is already done away with for nine-tenths of the population; *its existence for the few is solely due to its non-existence in the hands of those nine-tenths.* You reproach us, therefore, with intending to do away with a form of property, the necessary condition for whose existence is the non-existence of any property for the immense majority of society.

In one word, you reproach us with intending to do away with your property. Precisely so; that is just what we intend.

From the moment when labor can no longer be converted into capital, money, or rent, into a social power capable of being monopolized, i.e., from the moment when individual property can no longer be transformed into bourgeois property, into capital, from that moment, you say, *individuality vanishes.*

You must, therefore, confess that by "individual" you mean no other person than the bourgeois, than the middle-class owner of property. This person must, indeed, be swept out of the way, and made impossible.

Communism deprives no man of the power to appropriate the products of society; all that it does is to deprive him of the power to subjugate the labor of others by means of such appropriations.

It has been objected that upon the abolition of private property, all work will cease, and universal laziness will overtake us.

According to this, bourgeois society ought long ago to have gone to the dogs through sheer idleness; *for those who acquire anything, do not work.* The whole of this objection is but another expression of the tautology: There can no longer be any wage labor when there is no longer any capital.

All objections urged against the communistic mode of producing and appropriating material products, have, in the same way, been urged against the communistic mode of producing and appropriating intellectual products. Just as to the bourgeois, the disappearance of class property is the disappearance of production itself, so the disappearance of class culture is to him identical with the disappearance of all culture.

That culture, the loss of which he laments, is, for the enormous majority, a mere training to act as a machine.

But don't wrangle with us so long as you apply, to our intended abolition of bourgeois property, the standard of your bourgeois notions of freedom, culture, law, etc. Your very ideas are but the outgrowth of the conditions of your bourgeois production and bourgeois property, just as your jurisprudence is but the will of your class made into a law for all, a will whose essential character and direction are determined by the economical conditions of existence of your class.

The selfish misconception that induces you to transform into eternal laws of nature and of reason the social forms stringing from your present mode of production and form of property—historical relations that rise and disappear in the progress of production—this misconception you share with every ruling class that has preceded you. What you see clearly in the case of ancient property, what you admit in the case of feudal property, you are of course forbidden to admit in the case of your own bourgeois form of property. . . .

[Omitted are precepts on family, marriage, and nations.]

"Undoubtedly," it will be said, "religious, moral, philosophical, and juridicial ideas have been modified in the course of historical development. But religion, morality, philosophy, political science, and law, constantly survived this change.

"*There are, besides, eternal truths, such as Freedom, Justice, etc.*, that are common to all states of society. But communism abolishes eternal truths, it abolishes all religion, and all morality, instead of constituting them on a new basis; it therefore acts in contradiction to all past historical experience."

What does this accusation reduce itself to? The history of *all past society has consisted in the development of class antagonisms,* antagonisms that assumed different forms at different epochs.

But whatever form they may have taken, one fact is common to all past ages, viz., *the exploitation of one part of society by the other.* No wonder, then, that the social consciousness of past ages, despite all the multiplicity and variety it displays, moves within certain common forms, or general ideas, which cannot completely vanish except with the total disappearance of class antagonisms.

The communist revolution is the most radical rupture with traditional relations; no wonder that its development involved the most radical rupture with traditional ideas.

But let us have done with the bourgeois objections to communism.

We have seen above that the first step in the revolution by the working class is to raise the proletariat to the position of ruling class to win the battle of democracy.

The proletariat will use its political supremacy to wrest, by degree, all capital from the bourgeoisie, to centralize all instruments of production in the hands of the state, i.e., of the proletariat organized as the ruling class; and to increase the total productive forces as rapidly as possible.

Of course, in the beginning, this cannot be effected except by means of despotic inroads on the rights of property, and on the conditions of bourgeois production; by means of measures, therefore, which appear economically insufficient and untenable, but which, in the course of the movement, outstrip themselves, necessitate further inroads upon the old social order, and are unavoidable as a means of entirely revolutionizing the mode of production.

These measures will, of course, be different in different countries.

Nevertheless, in most advanced countries, the following will be pretty generally applicable:

- *Abolition of property in land and application of all rents of land to public purposes.*
- *A heavy progressive or graduated income tax.*
- *Abolition of all rights of inheritance.*
- *Confiscation of the property of all emigrants and rebels.*
- *Centralization of credit in the banks of the state, by means of a national bank with state capital and an exclusive monopoly.*
- *Centralization of the means of communication and*

> *transport in the hands of the state.*
> - *Extension of factories and instruments of production owned by the state; the bringing into cultivation of waste lands, and the improvement of the soil generally in accordance with a common plan.*
> - *Equal obligation of all to work. Establishment of industrial armies, especially for agriculture.*
> - *Combination of agriculture with manufacturing industries; gradual abolition of all the distinction between town and country by a more equable distribution of the populace over the country.*
> - *Free education for all children in public schools. Abolition of children's factory labor in its present form. Combination of education with industrial production, etc.*

When, in the course of development, class distinctions have disappeared, and all production has been concentrated in the hands of a vast association of the whole nation, the public power will lose its political character. Political power, properly so called, is merely the organized power of one class for oppressing another. If the proletariat during its contest with the bourgeoisie is compelled, by the force of circumstances, to organize itself as a class; if, by means of a revolution, it makes itself the ruling class, and, as such, sweeps away by force the old conditions of production, then it will, along with these conditions, have swept away the conditions for the existence of class antagonisms and of classes generally, and will thereby have abolished its own supremacy as a class.

In place of the old bourgeois society, with its classes and class antagonisms, we shall have an association in which the free development of each is the condition for the free development of all.

CONCLUSION

Clearly, in the biblical system of ethics, profit is godly if it is gained in God's way. And surprisingly, this means that *not* making a profit may also be a sin against God, one's neighbor and oneself!

Adam Smith established by rational evaluation that profit making was an inherent part of human conduct as it worked itself out in the social environment of human culture. What Adam Smith described was actually a traditional perspective of the Reformed tradition as evidenced by Max Weber. This is not only evident in Weber's analysis, however. It is in fact established by a careful reading of the Reformed tradition's classic ethical treatise, the Westminster Larger Catechism. And this serves to underscore how an inherent hostility to profits gained in a just manner is actually an expression of the socialistic spirit that emanates from Marx's *Communist Manifesto*.

While there clearly can be "obscene profits" under the Calvinistic system, that is, a violation of one's duty to God and man in acquiring profits, it must also be maintained that profit making itself is not inherently obscene. If such were not the case, the parable of the talents given by our Lord could not righteously include the words to the unfaithful steward in Matthew 25:26–27, "His master replied, 'You wicked, lazy servant! So you knew that I harvest where I have not sown and gather where I have not scattered seed? Well then, you should have put my money on deposit with the bankers, so that when I returned I would have received it back with interest'" (NIV).

We trust that this study has been a *profitable* undertaking for all who have engaged the business themes of this article!

Notes

1. *Westminster Confession* (Glasgow: Bell and Bain first published 1646, repr. 2001 containing the *Westminster Larger Catechism* approved 1648).

2. Adam Smith, *The Wealth of Nations,* (New York: Bantam Classic, first published 1776, repr. 2003).

3. Max Weber, *The Protestant Ethic and the Spirit of Capitalism* (New York: Scribner, 1958). *The Protestant Ethic and the Spirit of Capitalism* was first published in German in 1904.

4. Karl Marx and Friedrich Engels, *Communist Manifesto,* public domain, first published in German in1848.

5. The following Bible passages illustrate such principles:
   - Second Kings 6:24–7:20 manifests the laws of supply and demand, profits, and just war.
   - Acts 5:1–11 emphasizes the rights of private property and stands as an apostolic indictment against Christian communitarian or communistic economic ethics.
   - Exodus 20:15 commands man not to steal from his neighbor, thus emphasizing, when expressed positively, the right to private property. The story of Naboth's vineyard in 1 Kings 21 stands as a condemnation of the greed of the state over against the property rights of the individual.
   - Paul's teaching in 1 Timothy 6:3–19 shows that wealth is a gift of God and that compassion is a choice of the believer, not a mandate of the church or the state.

6. Because of the use of the Internet to find material such as the Catechism and the number format of the questions, no page references to the published book are given in footnote 1.

7. John C. Maxwell, *There's No Such Thing as "Business" Ethics: There's Only One Rule for Making Decisions* (New York: Warner Books, 2003).

8. A number of other books endeavor to take similar use of the Ten Commandments as a model for business ethics, such as Wes Cantrell and James R. Lucas, *High-Performance Ethics: 10 Timeless Principles for Next-Generation Leadership* (Carol Stream: Tyndale, 2007).

9. Hernando De Soto, *The Mystery of Capital: Why Capitalism Triumphs in the West and Fails Everywhere Else* (New York: Basic, 2003).

10. The ninth commandment questions and answers are included here due to space limitations. But the reader is encouraged to see the depth of care we are to take in our dealings with our business colleagues.

Question 143: Which is the ninth commandment?

Answer: The ninth commandment is, Thou shalt not bear false witness against thy neighbor.

Question 144: What are the duties required in the ninth commandment?

Answer: The duties required in the ninth commandment are, the preserving and promoting of truth between man and man, and the good name of our neighbor, as well as our own; appearing and standing for the truth; and from the heart, sincerely, freely, clearly, and fully, *speaking the truth, and only the truth, in matters of judgment and justice, and in all other things: Whatsoever; a charitable esteem of our neighbors; loving, desiring, and rejoicing in their good name; sorrowing for, and covering of their infirmities; freely acknowledging of their gifts and graces, defending their innocency; a ready receiving of a good report, and unwillingness to admit of an evil report, concerning them; discouraging talebearers, flatterers, and slanderers; love and care of our own good name, and defending it when need requires; keeping of lawful promises; studying and practicing of: Whatsoever things are true, honest, lovely, and of good report.*

Question 145: What are the sins forbidden in the ninth commandment?

Answer: The sins forbidden in the ninth commandment are, *all prejudicing the truth, and the good name of our neighbors, as well as our own, especially in public judicature; giving false evidence, suborning false witnesses, wittingly appearing and pleading for an evil cause, outfacing and overbearing the truth; passing unjust sentence, calling evil good, and good evil; rewarding the wicked according to the work of the righteous, and the righteous according to the work of the wicked; forgery, concealing the truth, undue silence in a just cause, and holding our peace when iniquity calls for either a reproof from ourselves, or complaint to others; speaking the truth unseasonably, or maliciously to a wrong end, or perverting it to a wrong meaning, or in doubtful and equivocal expressions, to the prejudice of truth or justice; speaking untruth, lying, slandering, backbiting, detracting, tale bearing, whispering, scoffing, reviling, rash, harsh, and partial censuring; misconstructing intentions, words, and actions; flattering, vainglorious boasting, thinking or speaking too highly or too meanly of ourselves or others; denying the gifts and graces of God; aggravating smaller faults; hiding, excusing, or extenuating of sins, when called to a free confession; unnecessary discovering of infirmities; raising false rumors, receiving and countenancing evil reports, and stopping our ears against just defense; evil suspicion; envying or grieving at the deserved credit of any, endeavoring or desiring to impair it, rejoicing in their disgrace and infamy; scornful contempt, fond admiration; breach of lawful promises; neglecting such things as are of good report, and practicing, or not avoiding ourselves, or not hindering: What we can in others, such things as procure an ill name.*

11. A Christian worldview discussion of the implications of the concepts underlying division of labor are beyond the scope of this paper. However, the concept of increasing the productivity of labor is indeed consistent with the Catechism and is noted in Weber's material.

12. Although lesser-known communist movements have existed, the type we know of today is best explained by Karl Marx in his treatise *The Communist Manifesto* (in Karl Marx, *Selected Writings*, ed. David McLellan [Oxford, UK: Oxford University Press, 1977], 221–47) The Communist league

was started largely under the leadership of Marx and Engels in June 1847. It linked the main centers of Communist activities in Paris, London, Brussels, and Cologne. At the request of this League, Marx wrote the Manifesto, which was first published in Brussels in February 1848. Marx wrote: "I. Communism is already acknowledged by all European Powers to be itself a Power. II. It is high time that Communists should openly, in the efface of the whole world, publish their views, their aims, their tendencies, and meet this nursery tale of the Spectre of Communism with a Manifesto of the party itself" (222). With the Bolshevik Revolution in 1917, seventy years after the Communist League was formed, the czar of Russia was toppled and the world experienced the first Communist nation in history.

The fact that Christianity has been open to the allure of Communism under the cloaks of "Christian Communism" or "Liberation Theology" or "Christian Socialism" is anticipated by Marx's remarks in the *Manifesto*: "Nothing is easier than to give Christian asceticism a socialist tinge. Has not Christianity declaimed against private property, against marriage, against the state? Has it not preached in the place of these, charity and poverty, celibacy and mortification of the flesh, monastic life and Mother Church? Christian socialism is but the holy water with which the priest consecrates the heart-burnings of the aristocrat."

What Is at Risk for
Business If We Lose
a Christian
Worldview?

BARRY ASMUS

Barry Asmus is a Senior Economist with the prestigious National Center for Policy Analysis. Doctor Asmus has been named by USA Today *as one of the five most requested speakers in the United States. He has spoken to thirty world bankers at the home of Harvard's President, three thousand farmers in Des Moines, and seven thousand members of the Million Dollar Round Table at Radio City Music Hall.*

He has testified before the House Ways and Means Committee regarding our income tax system; was a featured speaker in a privatizing Social Security conference for Western European leaders; and has addressed the faculty of the Young Presidents Organization in Cape Town, South Africa. His appearance at the Forbes Chateau de Balleroy in France with former Czech Prime Minister Vaclav Klaus, members of British Parliament, and other Western European leaders focused on the importance of public policy decision in Europe.

Doctor Asmus is the author of nine books. His latest is Bulls Don't Blush, Bears Don't Die *(2006), which explores the limitless opportunities emerging from a borderless and knowledge-driven society, sharing the international economic and political trends shaping business and investment strategy in today's global economy. As a Professor of Economics, he was twice voted University Professor of the Year and was honored with the Freedom Foundation Award at Valley Forge for Private Enterprise Education.*

WAYNE GRUDEM

Wayne Grudem is Research Professor of Theology and Biblical Studies at Phoenix Seminary in Phoenix, Arizona. Prior to Phoenix Seminary he taught for twenty years at Trinity Evangelical Divinity School, Deerfield, Illinois, where he was chairman of the department of Biblical and Systematic Theology. He received a BA from Harvard University, an MDiv from Westminster Seminary, Philadelphia, and a PhD (in New Testament) from the University of Cambridge, England. He has published sixteen books, including Systematic Theology, Recovering Biblical Manhood and Womanhood *(co-edited with John Piper),* The TNIV and the Gender-Neutral Bible Controversy *(co-authored with Vern Poythress),* The First Epistle of

Peter (Tyndale NT commentary), *and* Business for the Glory of God. *He was also the General Editor for the* ESV Study Bible (published October 2008).

He is a past president of the Evangelical Theological Society, a co-founder and past president of the Council on Biblical Manhood and Womanhood, and a member of the Translation Oversight Committee for the English Standard Version *of the Bible.*

Not everyone in America professed to be a Christian in previous generations, but a Christian worldview generally prevailed in our culture and was taught in our schools. Beginning in early colonial times, generations of children learned to read from *The New England Primer,* where the letter *a* was taught with the rhyme "In Adam's fall / We sinned all," and the letter *b* was taught with a picture of the "Holy Bible" accompanied by the rhyme "Thy life to mend,/ This Book attend." *The McGuffey Readers* later became the most widely used textbooks in the nation (after their publication in 1836–37), and they similarly taught an explicitly Christian worldview and Christian moral standards.

Even people who disavowed many Christian beliefs still believed in moral principles and standards of business conduct that reflected a Christian worldview. This is why German sociologist Max Weber could use the deist Benjamin Franklin as an example of the influence of Calvinistic Protestant moral standards on an entire culture, even on those who no longer professed Christian religious beliefs. Weber claimed, I think correctly, that the "Protestant ethic" still expressed itself in "the spirit of capitalism" in the lives of Americans who, like Benjamin Franklin, no longer held to Christian religious beliefs.[1] But hard work, honesty, diligence, frugality, and a sense of duty to one's vocation or "calling" in life still remained, passed on from generation to generation.

One modern example of approximations to biblical ethics finding expression in a secular business organization is the widely quoted "Rotarian four-way test" of the Rotary Clubs:

1. Is it the truth?
2. Is it fair to all concerned?
3. Will it build goodwill and better friendships?
4. Will it be beneficial to all concerned?

Biblical standards of truth and justice are echoed in the first two questions, and the need to love one's neighbor as oneself are echoed in the last two.

And so, whether we agree with all the details of Max Weber's analysis of American society or not, it is certainly true that the most influential worldview in American culture from the landing of the Pilgrims in 1620 to at least the 1960s or 1970s was one that included the basic components of biblical moral standards—honor your father and your mother, do not murder, do not commit adultery, do not steal, and do not lie—as well as large elements of the biblical meta-narrative, the overarching story that explains all of life—namely, that human beings were created by the God described in the Bible; we are accountable to Him for our actions in this life; history will end in a final judgment; and people will spend eternity in heaven or in hell.

These elements of a Christian worldview had a significant influence on people's conduct, so that the pattern of life that was *honored* and *rewarded* in society was one of productive work, honesty, generosity, fairness, personal responsibility for one's actions, financial reward according to the value of one's work, and personal integrity in business dealings.

Because many people in American society sought to follow this Christian worldview, I think it is fair to say that *American society received many blessings from God, due to God's common grace.* In theology, "common grace" is the grace or favor God gives to people in the world in general, not solely to Christians. In God's providential oversight of peoples and nations, *more* common grace usually comes to nations and societies that seek to live according to biblical moral standards than to those that flagrantly abandon them. "Righteousness exalts a nation, but sin is a reproach to any people" (Prov. 14:34 ESV). In the book of Proverbs alone, dozens of verses speak of the positive consequences that come from good and wise dealings, and the negative consequences that follow evil and foolish actions.

This is not to say, of course, that eternal salvation or a present-day relationship with God can ever be earned by good works. "For by grace you have been saved through faith. And this is not your own doing; it is the gift of God, not a result of works, so that no one may boast" (Eph. 2:8–9 ESV). But it is to say that God sovereignly governs the world in such a way that, *as a general pattern,* good or bad deeds receive fitting rewards or punishments even in this lifetime. There are surely exceptions, and the exceptions are more numerous when governments become oppressive and corrupt, and those exceptions cause us to long for a future divine settling of all accounts that will be truly just. But the overall pattern of reward for good deeds and punishment for evil ones is itself one means by which God teaches the entire world that a future day of greater judgment is still coming. Such a pattern of warnings found in the ordinary consequences of events in life is itself another expression of common grace.

Now the question is this: *What is at risk if we abandon this Christian worldview as a society?* I suggest that at least five things are at risk.

We Risk Losing Belief in Moral Accountability to God

God Is Watching

The Christian worldview teaches that God is watching human activity and will hold everyone accountable, whether in this life or in the life to come. Paul tells servants (employees), "Work heartily, as for the Lord and not for men, knowing that from the Lord you will receive the inheritance as your reward" (Col. 3:23–24 ESV). Then he adds that there are certain consequences to good and evil deeds: "The wrongdoer will be paid back for the wrong he has done, and there is no partiality" (v. 25 ESV). In the next sentence, he warns masters with a similar hint of judgment: "Treat your slaves justly and fairly, knowing that you also have a Master in heaven" (Col. 4:1 ESV).

James warns that employers who fail to pay their employees as they have promised are accountable to God: "Behold, the wages of the laborers who mowed your fields, which you kept back by fraud, are crying out against you, and the cries of the harvesters have reached the ears of the Lord of Hosts" (James 5:4 ESV).

The Old Testament also contains similar statements. For example, the wisdom teachings in Proverbs speak more generally of God's continual watching of human activity, with the implication that he will hold everyone to account:

> For a man's ways are before the eyes of the Lord, and he ponders all his paths. (Prov. 5:21 ESV).

> The eyes of the Lord are in every place, keeping watch on the evil and the good. (Prov. 15:3 ESV)

And Jeremiah says the Lord is "great in counsel and mighty in deed, whose eyes are open to all the ways of the children of man, *rewarding each one according to his ways and according to the fruit of his deeds* (Jeremiah 32:19 ESV;

emphasis added).

Without this sense of accountability to God, life loses meaning and business loses any ultimate sense of fulfillment. This is because God is supreme, and we are not. We worship and serve because we were created to worship and serve. Without a sense of something bigger than ourselves, the pursuit of possessions becomes a tedious and empty struggle. In the end, it becomes a "joyless quest for joy."[2]

PEOPLE ARE MORALLY ACCOUNTABLE FOR THEIR ACTIONS

A Christian worldview also teaches that there are both good and evil tendencies in every person's heart, and that people are morally accountable for the choices they make. The tendency toward good comes from God's common grace, by which God writes "the work of the law" on every person's heart, and also gives them a conscience that "bears witness" (Rom. 2:15 ESV). But the tendency toward evil is seen in the fact that "all have sinned and fall short of the glory of God" (Rom. 3:23 ESV). James says that people do evil when they give in to the temptations of their own evil desires (James 1:14–15).

Such a Christian perspective of moral accountability to God leads to higher personal integrity in business, because people realize that God is watching their conduct, and they expect that He will hold them accountable. Such a perspective will tend toward honesty, reliability, quality in one's work, and care for others as well as oneself—all of which have immense value in the business world. In addition, this idea of personal moral accountability supports an economic system in which people are rightly rewarded for the value of their work, and people who make wrong choices are held responsible for them and suffer the consequences of those choices.

Any economic system devised by man, then, will perform better if supported by moral values such as mutual respect, honesty, and love. Personal well-being and property are best protected when others act in love toward their neighbors, for "love is the fulfilling of the law" (Rom. 13:10 ESV). When morality and markets reinforce each other, the best of a worldly world is realized— not perfect nor our final home, of course, but the best we can do in this age in terms of business and economics.

Loss of a Sense of Moral Accountability

But if we lose a Christian worldview, we lose this sense of moral accountability to God. When no one else is looking, it will lead to shoddy work and theft. When no one else is listening who knows the truth, it will lead to dishonesty. Loss of a Christian worldview will lead to selfishness and greed rather than genuine care for others. It will lead to laziness rather than diligence, and faithlessness rather than reliability.

Once the idea of moral accountability to God is abandoned, what does secular American culture use as a substitute motive for ethical behavior? Often merely the threat, "You will get caught!" And then, in order to make good on that threat, massive regulatory mechanisms have to be imposed to try to catch the wrongdoers, and endless accountability reports must be submitted to those who watch the watchers. Does it work? Not very well. People planning to do wrong simply calculate that the chance of getting caught seems small and the rewards look great, and they go ahead and lie about their product, or falsify a report, or pilfer from their company, or claim more hours than they actually worked. Unless people really believe that God is watching, and therefore police themselves, the mere threat of getting caught rings hollow, moral standards disintegrate, and the cost of everything increases.

Loss of the Idea That People Are Responsible for Their Own Financial Situations

Another consequence of the loss of belief in personal moral accountability is the idea that people who make wrong or foolish choices should not be held responsible, for they are seen as merely *victims* of external influences that they have experienced in society. While I certainly agree that it is right to help the poor (Matt. 19:21; Gal. 2:10), we must also remember that God expects people to care for their own financial situations, to seek to work with their hands "and be dependent on no one" (1 Thess. 4:12).

An economic system that emphasizes personal responsibility does not distribute its rewards equally to everyone. Capitalism offers nothing but frustrations and rebuffs to those who want to get without giving, who want to take without risking, who want to profit without sacrifice, and who want to exalt themselves without first humbling themselves. The value of society's goods ultimately derives from the values of its people.

When a sense of personal responsibility is lost, the alternative is to think that somehow "society" is responsible for everyone's financial mistakes, so individuals should not have to suffer the consequences. For example, it is argued that homeowners should be able to keep their homes whether they can afford them or not, and companies that are "too big to fail" should get billions of dollars of everybody else's money (that was paid in taxes), and unemployment benefits should be extended as long as people want to get them, and every single member of society deserves a "Cadillac" health insurance plan, no matter whether people have earned these things or not. When a Christian worldview and sense of accountability are lost, people are no longer thought responsible for their own financial situations, for it is "society" as a whole that is more and more thought to be responsible for everyone's financial well-being.

No society can lose belief in moral accountability to God for very long without destroying itself.

WE RISK LOSING BELIEF IN THE MORAL GOODNESS OF BUSINESS

The Goodness of Making Products from the Earth That Benefit Mankind

The Christian worldview understands that God put human beings on the earth to "subdue it" (Gen. 1:28 ESV), which means taking earth's resources and developing them into products useful for the lives of other people and themselves. Therefore it is *morally good* to produce products from the earth for the benefit of other people, whether food or clothing or housing, or automobiles or computers or airplanes. When such productivity from the earth is valued and encouraged, societies can bring great benefit to everyone in them.

But many forces today seek to block such economic development. For example, there are some who say that "drilling for oil alone cannot come close to meeting our energy needs." Really? A recent study by Daniel Yergins's Cambridge Associates (as well as the National Association of Regulatory Utility Commissioners) finds that the U.S. has more than 200 billion barrels of oil and 2,000 trillion cubic feet of natural gas that are recoverable with today's technology. When fully developed, we could eliminate completely our 10 million barrels' daily import of foreign oil for half a century. But if such development is blocked, the alternative is to keep importing oil from Venezuela and the Middle East.

The Goodness of Selling Products for a Profit

The godly woman of Proverbs 31 is one who "perceives that her merchandise is *profitable*" (v. 18 ESV; emphasis added), and so she earns a profit from selling what she has produced. The good and faithful servant in Jesus' parable is the one whose five talents (approximately two million dollars in modern terms), through wise investment and development, "made five talents more" (Matt. 25:20 ESV). He made a substantial profit.

If a baker today can take two dollars of ingredients and bake a loaf of bread that sells for four dollars, that profit margin simply measures the amount of *added value* that the baker has contributed to the society. The ingredients were worth two dollars. The loaf of bread is worth four dollars. Therefore, when the baker baked the loaf, he added two dollars of value to the economy as a whole. Therefore *profit* is a measure of the *value* that one has contributed to the economy. Now someone may object, "How do you know that the loaf of bread is really worth four dollars?" I know because many people have bought such a loaf for four dollars. Individual buyers in the free market assigned the value of four dollars to it when they bought it. Therefore, that is a fair measure of its value—at least to people in that society at that time.

Business Transactions as a Way of Loving Your Neighbor as Yourself

A Christian view of business also understands that a voluntary business transaction ordinarily brings benefit to both buyer and seller. When I voluntarily buy that baker's loaf of bread for four dollars, I am using my money to say that the bread is more valuable to me than four dollars, so I will make the purchase. I genuinely believe that *I am better off* walking home with that loaf of bread, because I wanted the bread more than I wanted the four dollars. And so *the baker has done good for me.*

But the baker wanted my money more than he wanted the loaf of bread. He is happy to put the four dollars in his cash register. So he believes that *I have done good for him.* In this way a voluntary business transaction *does good* for both parties. It is "win-win." Therefore, a Christian worldview understands buying and selling to be a way of fulfilling Jesus' command "You shall love your neighbor as yourself" (Matt. 22:39 ESV).

When this process is understood, a free market economy can be described in four words: *serve others, serve yourself.* Mutual benefits come from voluntary exchange. Free markets merge altruism and man's flawed nature in a way that no system has ever done. I must help you before I help myself. The only way I benefit is if you benefit. Successful, highly productive businesses understand this: the needs of customers are first.

The free market system is a dynamic process. Self-interested producers interact, bargain, and trade with self-interested consumers. Behaviors and prices are continually modified until a *mutually beneficial* exchange is agreed upon. The key components of these remarkable actions are *property, prices, profits,* and *losses.* The market takes account of these factors and becomes a miraculous instrument of communication and a stupendous transmitter of opinions, while in the process determining value. Millions of people, even billions, determine supply and demand, which in turn produce the signaling system of prices. Though markets need some basic oversight by governments to prevent fraud and criminal activity, in general we can say that markets are neither designed nor planned; they just happen. And from a Christian perspective we can see such amazing market activity as a wonderful gift of God, an ability that He has given to the human race that sets us apart from the animal kingdom and in fact from all the rest of God's creation. The free market system of mutual gains from voluntary exchange is evidence of the infinite wisdom and goodness of God, shown through the abilities to own, plan, evaluate, communicate, and trade, with which He created the entire human race.

We can say similar things about employment arrangements. Employers and employees both "win" when one works for the other. For example, one of the two authors of this paper (Wayne Grudem) works as a professor at Phoenix Seminary. He truly believes that Phoenix Seminary is doing "good" for him when it pays his salary, so he happily works to receive that salary. But Phoenix Seminary apparently thinks that he is doing "good" for the seminary when he teaches there, so they continue to employ him year after year. He is doing good for them, and they are doing good for him. Every time he completes a month of teaching and is paid for it, he and Phoenix Seminary are both better off. It is "win-win." And therefore the situation of one person working for another is, in the business world, another way of fulfilling Jesus' command, "You should love your neighbor as yourself" (Matt. 22:39 ESV).

Business, Therefore, Is Morally Good in Itself

These verses and many others show that God views ordinary business activity not as something *morally evil,* or even as something *morally neutral,* but as something *morally good* in itself. Of course, business activities can be done in immoral ways, and for immoral purposes, but surely that is not true of most business activities. In fact, God told the people of Israel, "If you make a sale to your neighbor or buy from your neighbor, you shall not wrong one another" (Lev. 25:14 ESV), which implied that ordinarily buying and selling could be carried out without wronging each other. A Christian worldview recognizes that business activities *in themselves* are morally good and should receive our approval and praise.

Governments Should Leave Businesses Free to Be Productive

When a society views business as morally good in this way, then it will have low levels of taxation and low levels of regulation. It will unleash business so that it might do as much good as possible in the society, subject only to laws that prevent fraud, enforce the keeping of contracts, prohibit the production of harmful products, and so forth. Good laws will prevent crime, but they will not regulate and tax to death.

Government burdens on businesses should be small because the basic ideology that makes possible the growth of the wealth of nations is a system of property, contracts, and consent, which allows freedom of trade and social cooperation. It works best when government is constrained and limited. Ambition must be made to counter ambition with checks and balances, and government power needs to be limited with constitutional delegations and enumerations, or else government will begin to expand its control relentlessly. James Madison, author of much of the U.S. Constitution, said it best: "In forming a government which is to be administered by man, the great difficulty lies in this: you must first enable the government to control the governed and in the next place oblige it to control itself."

Viewing Business as Evil

But when society loses the Christian view of the moral goodness of business, then business can easily be viewed as evil. In such a hostile climate, rightful business activities in developing and subduing the earth are opposed as "exploiting" the earth by environmentalists for whom Mother Earth is their new god, a god that must be left untouched and unused. Employers are thought of as evil bourgeois capitalists who exploit the laborers (the proletariat, according to Marxist theory) and wrongfully derive profit from their labor.

If we lose the Christian belief in the moral goodness of business activity, then business will increasingly be viewed with suspicion. It will be subject to higher and higher rates of taxation and more and more government regulation. Government with take over more and more businesses so as to save society from the supposed "evil" of business activity. And society as a whole will be suspicious of business. As one of us wrote elsewhere:

> If people think business is evil, they will hesitate to start businesses, and they will never feel real freedom to enjoy working in business, because it will always be tainted with the faint cloud of false guilt. Who can enjoy being an evil materialist who works with evil money to earn evil profits by exploiting laborers and producing material goods that feed people's evil greed and enhance their evil pride and sustain their evil inequality of possessions and feed their evil competitiveness? Who wants to devote his life to such an evil pursuit as business? What government would ever want to establish laws and policies that would encourage such an evil thing as business? If business is evil, then why not tax it and regulate it until it can barely survive? And so with the attitude that business is fundamentally evil in all its parts, business activity is hindered at every point, and poverty remains. (In fact, if the devil himself wanted to keep people created by God in the wretched bondage of lifelong poverty, it is hard to think of a better way he could do it than to make people think that business is fundamentally evil, so they would avoid entering it or would oppose it at every turn. And so I suspect that a profoundly negative attitude toward business in itself—not toward distortions and abuses, but toward business activity in itself—is ultimately a lie of the enemy who wants to keep God's people from fulfilling his purposes.)[3]

No society can lose belief in the moral goodness of business for very long without destroying itself.

We Risk Losing Belief in the Moral Goodness of Holding Private Property

Property Belongs to Individuals, Not Government

According to a Christian view of property, ownership of property is entrusted to individuals, and they should use that property as God's stewards, ones who are accountable to Him. But nowhere does the Bible support the idea that government should be the primary property owner in a nation, or that government is the "default" owner of property after a person dies.

Embedded in the Ten Commandments is this command: "You shall not steal" (Ex. 20:15 ESV). And two verses later God explained the heart attitudes that were also prohibited: "You shall not covet your neighbor's house . . . or his ox, or his donkey, or anything that is your neighbor's" (v. 17 ESV). Why should I not steal my neighbor's ox? Because it belongs to my neighbor. It is his ox, not mine. And it is his house, not mine, and not society's.

Therefore God assumed the idea of ownership of private property in the Ten Commandments. And this idea of ownership of property was enforced at several places elsewhere in the Bible, where there were laws for stealing and restitution for damage of another person's farm animals or agricultural fields (see Exodus 21:28–36; 22:1–15; Deuteronomy 22:1–4; 23:24–45). God prohibited moving a "neighbor's landmark, which the men of old have set" (Deut. 19:14 ESV), which would be to steal the land that belonged to one's neighbor.

The laws concerning the year of Jubilee provided that "each of you shall return to his property" (Lev. 25:10 ESV), showing that the right to the ownership to at least some productive land was guaranteed to all the families in Israel. When King Ahab, with the help of wicked Queen Jezebel, seized Naboth's vineyard of (see 1 Kings 21:1–29), it vividly illustrated the tendency of government to seize more and more land and thus abuse its power. In fact, Samuel the prophet warned the people about the evils of a king who would take and take and take from the people. "He will *take* the best of your fields and vineyards and olive orchards and give them to his servants" (1 Sam. 8:14 ESV; emphasis added). Even the remarkable generosity of the early church, where they had "all things in common" (Acts 2:44 ESV), was entirely *voluntary*, and did not abolish private ownership of property, as Peter himself affirmed to Ananias (Acts 5:4).

This is also evident from the frequent references after Acts 2 to Christians still meeting in homes that some of them *owned* (see Acts 2:46; 12:12; 17:5; 18:7; 20:20; 21:8, 16; Romans 16:5; etc.).

The Right to Accumulate Personal Wealth

A Christian view of the moral goodness of ownership of private property implies that in an economic system, people should be free to accumulate wealth according to the value of their work. Even in the Old Testament laws for the year of Jubilee, while family farmland returned to the family that had owned it, the houses that people had built within walled cities did not return to anyone, but were owned forever (Lev. 25:30), until they were sold or traded. In the Jubilee, there was no mention of any requirement to equalize money or jewelry or livestock that people had accumulated. People could retain the fruit of their labor.

Therefore, the biblical idea of ownership of private property also lends support to the idea that people should be able to acquire ownership of factories and businesses, and should be free to accumulate wealth as their business prospers. If a society has private ownership of property, factories, and businesses, and if it has relatively low taxation and regulation of business, then it will function as a free market society, not as a socialist or communist society. But in a free market economy, the market assigns reward according to the value of the product that is produced (or at least according to the way the buyers in the market evaluate the value of that product, whether it is goods or services).

We can read again Jesus' parable of the talents in Matthew 25:14–30 and see anew that an ethic where profit is suspect and entrepreneurship is frowned upon is not the Bible's lesson for economic affairs. It is not immoral to profit from your resources. Hard work constitutes good stewardship. Burying your talents is condemned. Being enterprising is rewarded. Looking to the future with a courageous sense of opportunity and hope is a distinctive Christian view. Even the command "Give, and it will be given to you" (Luke 6:38 ESV) assumes private ownership of property. You cannot give what you do not own.

A Step Away from Government Confiscation

If this Christian worldview is lost, however, then there is a tendency for government either to place more and more regulations and restrictions on the use of one's property, or to confiscate the property altogether. Karl Marx said, "The theory of the Communists may be summed up in the single sentence: Abolition of private property."[4]

But when *government* regulates or owns private property, it harms business, because government is never an efficient producer of economic goods. Therefore, socialist and communist economies can never come close to the economic productivity, inventiveness, and quality of products that are produced by a free market economy. Increasing government control means decreasing freedom and productivity for business. The ultimate result is a society where people are trapped in an equality of poverty, with privilege and reward going only to those who hold the reins of government power. The impoverishment of Russia, of Eastern Europe under Communism, of Cuba, and of North Korea, is the ultimate result of losing belief in the moral goodness of private ownership of property.

No society can lose belief in the moral goodness of private property for very long without destroying itself.

We Risk Losing Belief in the Moral Goodness of Productive Work

The Moral Goodness of Productive Work

Even before there was sin in the world, God put man in the garden of Eden "to work it and keep it" (Gen. 2:15 ESV), thus demonstrating the moral goodness of productive work and its necessity for fulfilling God's purpose for us here on earth. Paul told the Thessalonian church, "With toil and labor we *worked* night and day," and this was "to give you in ourselves an example to imitate" (2 Thess. 3:8–9 ESV; emphasis added). Then he added, "If anyone is not willing to *work*, let him not eat" (v. 10 ESV; emphasis added). A Christian worldview holds that work should be rewarded, for Jesus teaches that "the laborer deserves his wages" (Luke 10:7 ESV).

Therefore the Bible views productive work as morally good and even commands that Christians should "work heartily, for the Lord and not for men" (Col. 3:23 ESV). In the Old Testament, the book of Ecclesiastes speaks often about joy in one's work: "There is nothing better for a person than that he should eat and drink and find enjoyment in his toil. This also, I saw, is from the hand of God, for apart from him who can eat or who can have enjoyment?" (2:24–25 ESV).

When this Christian viewpoint is affirmed by a society, working at a regular job is seen as a rightful source of personal fulfillment and dignity, and the culture in general assumes that honorable people will strive to become diligent, faithful, cheerful workers who willingly do a bit more than what is required because they view productive work as a moral good, and they really believe that God will be pleased if they strive for excellence in their work.

Work Should Be Balanced with Times of Rest

A Christian worldview also recognizes that God built times of periodic rest into the structure of His people's lives. The fourth commandment proclaimed, "Six days you shall labor, and do all your work, but the seventh day is a Sabbath to the LORD your God. On it you shall not do any work, you, or your son, or your daughter, your male servant, or your female servant, or your livestock, or the sojourner who is within your gates" (Ex. 20:9–10).

Christians today differ over the exact way this command applies to believers who live under the new covenant in Christ (see Colossians 2:16–17; Acts 20:7; Rev. 1:10), but I think all Christians would agree that it is still *wise* for us to take regular times of rest from work, times to enjoy the fruit of our labor. In doing this, we rightly imitate God Himself, who saw that "everything that he had made" was "very good" (Gen. 1:31 ESV), and then God "rested on the seventh day from all his work that he had done" (Gen. 2:2 ESV)—surely on that day enjoying and taking delight in the work of His hands.

It is also necessary for to rest from work in order to be able to enjoy the fruit of our labor: "Everyone also to whom God has given wealth and possessions and power to enjoy them, and to accept his lot and rejoice in his toil—this is the gift of God" (Eccl. 5:19 ESV).

Rest from work is also a time to demonstrate our trust in God to prosper the times that we do work. For "unless the LORD builds the house, those who build it labor in vain. Unless the LORD watches over the city, the watchman stays awake in vain," so "it is in vain that you rise up early and go late to rest, eating the bread of anxious toil; for he gives to his beloved sleep" (Ps. 127:1–2 ESV).

People Becoming Lazy and Shoddy in Their Work

If a Christian view of work is lost, a secular worldview will tend toward various harmful consequences. A failure to view productive work in a positive way will lead many in society to lead lives of laziness and poor work habits. People will place more of their hope for becoming wealthy not on hard work of good quality by rather on getting something for nothing (such as in the lottery). There will be more of a tendency to think that those who do well economically are just "lucky," and those who do not do well are just the victims of bad luck. There will be more of a tendency to view economically productive people with envy, thinking that they do not deserve what they have earned, but that they should rather feel guilt and shame. And there will be a tendency to argue that economic reward in the workplace should not be based on merit or the quality of one's work, but should be allocated only according to seniority (as in the pay scale of public schoolteachers today, for example).

In addition, the goal of life will not be seen as having an economically productive life that finds fulfillment in doing work that brings value to others, but rather in leisure pursuits, longer weekends and vacations, and then complete retirement that results in little if any productivity even though one may still have twenty or more years of health and strength. People become consumers and no longer producers.

Others Are Driven to Become Workaholics

On the other hand, the desire for material prosperity can become a different kind of idol, with people working incessantly, driving themselves day and night to accumulate more and more, but never having enough. Modern Japan is an economic miracle, a small nation that still has the second largest economy in the world, but the nation lacks a Christian worldview and has basically adopted a form of Buddhism that has made work into a religion. Suicide and divorce rates are high, and wealth has not led to true fulfillment or happiness. But Japan is not alone in this, for many businesspeople in the United States have followed the same pattern of life, and after thirty years the result is large homes and fancy cars but destroyed marriages, alienated children, and broken health.

> There is an evil that I have seen under the sun, and it lies heavy on mankind: a man to whom God gives wealth, possessions, and honor, so that he lacks nothing of all that he desires, yet God does not give him power to enjoy them, but a stranger enjoys them. This is vanity; it is a grievous evil. (Eccl. 6:1–2)

Conflict Between Two Groups of Workers

But what will happen to a society that bifurcates into two groups: the lazy, careless, selfish consumers, who produce less and less of value for society; and the workaholics, who produce more and more, and gain immense wealth, but leave trails of broken families and lost children? The "have-nots" will pull the economy down, and the "haves" will pull it up, and there will be increasing conflict between the two groups as they pull apart. Nobody will find joy and fulfillment in work.

No society can lose belief in the moral goodness of productive work, and endure such conflict and disillusionment, for very long without destroying itself.

We Risk Losing a Hopeful View of Time and History

Moving Toward a Goal

A Christian worldview sees that time is moving forward toward a goal. Time began with the creation in Genesis 1, and it is moving toward a final judgment that is described in the book of Revelation. Therefore, history is linear and goal oriented.

In addition, God entrusts us every day with time that we are to use wisely as good stewards: "Look carefully then how you walk, not as unwise but as wise, *making the best use of the time*, because the days are evil" (Eph. 5:15–16 ESV; emphasis added). Time is therefore valuable, according to a Christian worldview, and is to be used in ways that are honoring to God.

In addition, a Christian view of history includes belief in God's sovereignty over history and the fact that He brings reward and success to work carried out faithfully, in obedience to Him. "And let us not grow weary of doing good, for in due season we will reap, if we do not give up" (Gal. 6:9 ESV). And Paul told the Corinthian church, "Therefore, my beloved brothers, be steadfast, immovable, always abounding in the work of the Lord, knowing that in the Lord your labor is not in vain" (1 Cor. 15:58 ESV). In this context he shows that Christ's resurrection guarantees that there will be eternal consequences for our actions in this life, and the good results of our work will endure forever.

Hope That Work Can Bring Positive Change

Therefore, a Christian worldview encourages attempts to improve our lives, to bring change and improvement to the human situation. That is because we can have confidence that the good that we do will receive God's blessing and will endure.

This Christian worldview leads to a willingness to take risks, to start businesses and invest, and to build for the future. It leads to a hopeful view of time and history and contributes to innovation and development in the business world. In a passage that uses poetic metaphor to speak of investing time or resources in various ways in the hope that at least some of them will prosper, Ecclesiastes tells us: "Cast your bread upon the waters, for you will find it after many days. Give a portion to seven, or even to eight, for you know not what disaster may happen on earth" (11:1–2 ESV).

One economic area of great concern today is energy, and yet it is in the energy field that innovation and risk taking are showing signs of bringing great reward. Energy production today provides countless examples of entrepreneurs at work. Dr. Stanley Ovshinsky, with his hundreds of chemical engineers, works on amorphous silicon or anhydrous silicon, or CIGS (photovoltaic) cells made from copper, indium, gallium, and selenium, which one day will be placed in roofing material to generate electricity from the sun. Another example is Vinod Khosla, who can produce a fuel cell that can turn natural gas or natural grass into electricity. Or Stanford professor Brent Constants, who has developed a process that takes CO_2 emissions from a coal-fired generating plant and naturally converts it into calcium carbonate, which is then sprayed and dried into cement to build buildings and highways. Thus the elusive idea of clean coal becomes a reality. Coal-fired power with this system would be 100 percent clean, and no CO_2 would be released into the atmosphere.

Wasted Time and Fear

But if this Christian view of time and hope is lost, a society will tend toward wasting time and focusing on immediate gratification. People will not work as hard but will give in to a natural human tendency to laziness. They will retire early rather than realizing that they can still do good for society. And they will tend to fear innovation and change, because of a loss of hope that change can be made for the better.

A society where people seek only immediate gratification will not invest in long-term projects; neither will people seek the long-term good of society. And a society that views the future with fear instead of hope will resist change, oppose plans for long-term progress, and seek only to protect the *status quo*. Business cannot survive for long once these views become dominant.

No society can lose a hopeful view of time and history, and come to be dominated by seeking immediate gratification and fearing every change, without soon decaying from within and destroying itself.

Too Much at Stake If We Lose a Christian Worldview

In conclusion, we can see that much is at stake for business and for the entire society if we lose a Christian worldview and the need to conduct business according to the principles of the Bible.

But should we as Christians care about whether *society* functions according to these elements of a biblical worldview? Yes, certainly we should. To care for the economic well-being of society is also to be obedient to Jesus' command "You shall love your neighbor as yourself" (Matt. 22:39 ESV). As the apostle Paul said, "as we have opportunity, let us do good to everyone, and especially to those who are of the household of faith" (Gal. 6:10 ESV).

Notes

1. Max Weber (1864–1920), *The Protestant Ethic and the Spirit of Capitalism*, transl. Talcott Parsons (Los Angeles: Roxbury, 1996; first English publication, 1930), 47–78.
2. Leo Strauss, *Natural Right and History* (Chicago: The University of Chicago Press, 1953) p. 251.
3. Wayne Grudem, *Business for the Glory of God* (Wheaton, IL: Crossway, 2003), 82–83.
4. Karl Marx, *Communist Manifesto* (New York: International Publishers, 1948), 23.

SECTION 2

WORKPLACE ETHICS

SECTION 2: WORKPLACE ETHICS

PHILIP J. CLEMENTS

Section 2 includes six papers that describe different components of the workplace and the Christian's ethics while engaged in the workplace. The first three consider the nature of work in God's world and our calling to work. The second three wrestle with implications of behavior in the business and work environment. All of the papers have a blend of principles and application. Each offers fresh insights into the role of the Christian in his or her calling in God's world.

As we consider work in God's world, there are several critical changes in thinking that occurred during the Reformation. The first was the notion that all work is worthy. The papers in this section cover this perspective nicely. However, it bears repeating that God created each of us for a calling to contribute in His world. Our work is part of that contribution. Therefore, we do not need to seek what is often called full time Christian ministry to be in God's full time ministry. The priest and the laundry maid were of equal importance in God's eyes and their work was also. Chapter 14 in Section 3 has a particularly nice summary of the Reformation notion of dual calling, a calling to faith and a calling to work.

Our attitude toward work has been shown to be a critical Reformation distinctive. In the Introduction to this text, there is an extensive discussion of modern social science exploration of the contribution of Christianity to the attitude toward work and its implications on business. Here, the source of this attitude is touched upon. Colossians 3:22-25 lays down the ethic for work:

> Servants, obey in all things your masters according to the flesh; not with eyeservice, as menpleasers; but in singleness of heart, fearing God: and whatsoever ye do, do it heartily, as unto the Lord, and not as unto men: knowing that of the Lord ye shall receive the reward of the inheritance: for ye serve the Lord Christ. But he that doeth wrong shall receive for

the wrong which he hath done: and there is no respect of persons.

This powerful passage presents the work ethic challenge to every Christian — who are you working for? If it is for yourself, or for money, or for promotion, you are not work with the right ethic. All work is unto the Lord; for God Almighty. God deserves perfect; perfect all of the time. Pay is not the requirement for perfect all of the time. What is in it for me, is not a consideration for perfect all of the time. I am not paid to do this, is not a factor in perfect all of the time. It was these kinds of messages that resonated throughout Reformation Christendom. These messages changed the world. In 1904, Weber[1] records this change based on his research in the changes in the business community in the 1600s. For modern business people, understanding what Weber found can be quite shocking, because too many modern Christians do not model the behavior required in this passage.

To Colossians 3 we need to add 1 Thess 4:9-12 that says we are to work quietly, with our own hands, and be a model to our community; 2 Thess 3:10-14 where Paul says that since you did not get the message in 1 Thess 4, he wants to be clear — anyone who will not work, should not eat; Eph 4:28 where Paul says stop stealing and start working so that you can give to those who have needs, and 1 Tim 5:8, if we do not provide for our own families, we are worse than an infidel. While there are other passages, these capture the work ethic message. It was this message, combined with the status of a worker's calling that enabled the Reformation Christian to have a different work ethic.

The papers in this section expand on this basic framework of God's work ethic.

WORK AND REST: GOD'S PERSPECTIVE

William Edgar in "Work and Rest: God's Perspective" opens this series by framing the work problem with an illustration of the frustration that comes from purposeless work. As a result, today work is bad and leisure is good. It is God's world, so Edgar takes the reader to the Bible to understand God's view of work and rest. Using the concept of vocation, Edgar shows us that work is a creation ordinance. Work "is grounded in the divine pattern." God created for six days, then rested. "When done diligently, [work] brings a sense of accomplishment,[...] even though everything is of the Lord."

Next the paper considers the curse of work and the hope of redemption. John Murray is cited in explaining that the curse is not on work itself. Murray's work referred to is *Principles of Conduct: Aspects of Biblical Ethics, 1957*. This is a particularly good book on Reformation thinking regarding work. Redemption delivers us from sense that hard work is meaningless. Redemption removes us from being under the curse of sin, and our work has meaning, since it is now done for the One who saved us. Edgar reminds us that God is working in us, creating a new creation, while we work in His world in our vocation, serving and being of service to others.

Two additional facets of work in God's world should be touched on here. The papers in this section did not have the space or topics to address them. But both topics fit nicely with Edgar's "Work and Rest: God's Perspective." The first is the notion of rest. In God's world there are several uses of rest: rest from work, Edgar covers this nicely; rest from sin's effect on our lives and the world, Heb 4:1-10, Rom 8:23, and rest of seeking God, Jesus' declaration of peace such as in Matt 11:29-30 and John 14:27. Reformation principles of assurance directly relate to this rest. This rest gives peace, regardless of what is happening the believer knows that is relationship with God is sure and his future will be in heaven. Why is this important to business? In the 1990s the concept of *the only constant is change* was used as the mantra for how to properly run a company. This mantra meant that companies should project the image that nothing could be counted upon. The effect of this principle on companies and their workers was a complete loss of the stability for the worker. The worker did not know if he would have a job from day to day. Loss was the sense of company and worker loyalty or mutual commitment. Loss was the peace of working well in a well managed firm. As Christian business people, we need to see the blessing of our salvation and assurance. Where possible we need to build this same blessing and assurance into our companies. This not the "company man" of the 1950s, but it is a mutual commitment.

The second aspect of rest is the balance between vacation, holidays, and vocation. *Society & Puritanism: in Pre-Revolutionary England* [2] captures this issue nicely in the Puritan times as regards the Sabbath. Modern man does not appreciate that religions can create productivity burdens and in Christendom the Catholic Church had created many holy days in addition to weekly observances and key days such as Christmas. Society records that there were as many as 100 holy saints days, which were required, in addition to Sundays. Reformers read the Bible as showing God rest was on the seventh day and He worked six and so instructed Moses. The Sabbath movement was about only having Sunday as a day of worship and rest rather than all of the saints' days. This freed believers up to do productive work a hundred additional days, which is economically huge.

This comment is not to develop the principles of the Sabbath; it is to point out that modern business people need to understand God's perspective on rest. God gave the Sabbath as a rhythm of work and rest. Modern man is pushing for work 24/7 or work all of the time. Such a view is not consistent to God's perspective. The other view is the French view, where work is limited to 35 hours a week. This is equivalent to the 100 saints' days: a limitation on productivity. As France tries to change the 35 hour rule, union members are protesting. Reformers would attribute that protest to fallen man's failure to appreciate God's calling.

Add to this discussion cultures such as Asian and Latin American and the work week, work day, and timeliness aspects of work are all very relevant to the Christian business person. The reader is reminded that the Introduction covers some of the implications of Christianity on this topic. Landes found that a key contribution of Reformation Christianity is the value of time. The balance of rest and work in God's world is part of the blessing of Christianity and part of Christianity's distinctiveness.

DOING BUSINESS IN GOD'S WORLD: BUSINESS IS A CALLING

"Doing Business in God's World: Business Is a Calling," frames the concept of calling with a citation of John Calvin's *Institutes*, III.10.6. Calvin's passage expands the concept of vocation that Edgar cites in his paper. Chapter 14 also contains a series of comments on the Reformation concept of vocation. The Reformers viewed all of life, including vocation, to be lived by faith in Jesus Christ.

"Doing Business" then explores some key issues that arise to the business person from the question of being obedient to the Call. How does one know if he or she is called? Four indicators are explored: The Bible, prayer, circumstances, and counsel. Cases within the Bible and recent situations are used to illustrate these points. The next question considered is, "What if you do not answer the Call?" The answer to this question looks to the blessings of both the called and the community or business being served. Part of the answer to a Call is courage. God's instruction to Joshua in his call is cited as an example of the need for courage, because God is with the called.

Three cases are used to show the importance of proper Christian ethics in responding to our calling in business. The first addresses the problem of the bribe. The second is addressing the pressures of values and the bottom line. The third looks at cross-cultural problems in business behavior and where to draw the line.

THREE OFFICES AND THE ENTREPRENEUR

Julius J. Kim and Phillip H. Kim, no relation to each other, present a challenging discussion of how the call to business reflects our call to serve the community. In "Three Offices and the Entrepreneur: How the Church Community helps the Business Leader do well by Doing Good," the three offices of the believer are evaluated in the business role. This paper's concepts are truly innovative and should provide the reader with material for constant reflection. The use of the office concept gives the role of running or building a company a fresh spiritual importance, without distorting the spiritual role.

The three offices are prophet, priest and king. Jesus fulfills these three offices in his role of Redeemer. "Prophetic entrepreneurship involves knowing and revealing God's truth, goodness and beauty, preeminently revealed in the person and work of Jesus Christ." Entrepreneurship involves creating products and services that meet unmet needs in the marketplace, with resources beyond oneself. Therefore in the process of meeting these market needs, the entrepreneur can apply his God given skills and talents to proclaim His message and His goodness. "Priestly entrepreneurship involves sacrificial service to the church and the world, following the pattern set by Christ." The entrepreneur services both Christians and non-Christians with his God given time, talent, and treasure. "Kingly entrepreneurship involves a life characterized by the peace and order of God's perfect authority and rule." In the business endeavor, the entrepreneur should seek to uphold peace and justice to show God is in control of his life.

The paper nicely considers the different stages of life and the potential for entrepreneurship. In every situation real-life examples and Scripture citations aid the reader in understanding the principles and their application.

To help churches consider how they can aid the entrepreneur in the congregation the work of Redeemer Presbyterian Church in New York City is cited. The paper closes with a series of questions the reader can use to apply the principles to his own church.

SOME BIBLICAL CONTRIBUTIONS TO BUSINESS ETHICS

The next series of papers probes three different sets of issues in running or participating in business. Galen Radebaugh and Vern S. Poythress look at how the Bible could guide us in the midst of business decisions. "Some Biblical Contributions to Business Ethics" contains three cases from the pharmaceutical industry. Each case is fully documented with public information. The paper sets the stage by noting that companies are trying to aid their people in making the right decision with company value statements or codes of conduct. The cases illustrate that these do not work as well as companies would like.

With the stage set, the paper considers Bible principles for ethics and how these principles would provide useful guidance. John Frame's work, *Perspectives on the Word of God: An Introduction to Christian Ethics*, is used as a tool to develop answers. Frame articulates "three main perspectives, ..., normative, existential (personal) and situational." In developing the framework for ethical analysis, the authors explore both the theories underlying these perspectives and the need for divine resources. The importance of Jesus being fully man and fully God gives us comfort that He understands the pressures we face and can help us through. The problem of the pluralism of the world is reviewed with counsel given for the Christian business leader. The universal Lordship of Christ is part of the answer to the pluralism in the world – Jesus is lord and judge of people and business.

Having explored theology and theory, the authors then tackle the cases. The discussion and analysis is rich and specific. A particularly nice aspect is the blending of the theological with the practical. Business aspects are continually analyzed from a perspective of how business works and what those pressures were that created the situations. Yet, good Biblical analysis is brought to bear as well. This paper shows nicely the blending of good theology and business practices.

COURAGE AND CONVICTION IN THE PUBLIC COMPANY

"Courage and Conviction in the Public Company" analyzes the Jeffrey Conway situation. Conway was the chief financial officer and interim president of a public company. During his tenure, the SEC asserted that the company had filed misleading financial statements. Conway settled the case by pleading guilty and serving eighteen months in federal prison. Many Christians look at the risk and consequences of being an officer in a public company after Conway's situation and resist the Call. This is exactly what the paper "Doing Business In God's World" was addressing. In this paper, a real life case sets the stage for Jeffrey A. Conway and Andrew J. Peterson's discussion of the courage Christians should have in serving God in the leading of a public company.

This paper opens with a review of the development and social benefits of the public company. The authors set forth a number of Biblical principles, including the need for courage and the comfort of God's presence. The Conway story is revealed in an unvarnished fashion that should prove useful reading for all business people. The pressures are real and the outcomes, including the rebuilding of Conway's life are important. The paper closes with a look at hope, assurance, and help that the Christian can bring to the public company. What is particularly constructive in the paper is the authors' continual stress on business as well as theory and Bible. The real life story of Conway keeps the reality of business in the center of the discussion.

THE IMPORTANCE OF A BUSINESS LEADER'S CONTRIBUTION TO COMMUNITY LEADERSHIP

The final paper in this section, "The Importance of the Business Leader's Contribution to Community Leadership," looks at leadership and the impact good leadership can have on communities. While leadership is overly covered in the business literature, this paper brings Christian perspectives and some illustrations not often seen. The key perspective is the contribution leaders make to society. Citing William Wilberforce, Chuck Stetson notes that one individual can make a difference in a matter such as slavery. In our world, business leaders have the talent and resources, although not necessarily the time, to aid in the building of better communities. In case the reader is wondering what aspects of our communities need help, Stetson highlights a number: Government, Education, Demographics. The reader can add to this list his own pet projects.

This paper is included in this text because it adds to the richness of the Call that God gives to the business leader. Proverbs 31 talks of the husband of the bountiful wife who sites in the gates; he is part of the civic leadership. Boaz, in Ruth, is part of the civic leadership, knowing and being known by the leaders in his community. America needs godly business people to step up to building great companies and these business leaders need to step up to help their communities as well.

Notes

1. Max Weber, *The Protestant Ethic and the Spirit of Capitalism*, New York: Scribner, 1958. The Protestant Ethic was first published in German in 1904.
2. Christopher Hill, *Society & Puritanism: in Pre-Revolutionary England*, New York: Schocken, 1964, p145-160.

Work and Rest: God's Perspective

WILLIAM EDGAR

Dr. William Edgar was born in Wilmington, North Carolina, in 1944 and grew up in Paris, France. He studied at St. George's School (secondary), Harvard University (Honors, BA in Music), Westminster Theological Seminary (MDiv), and the University of Geneva (DTh). He has been at Westminster since 1989 and is currently Professor of Apologetics, Coordinator of the Apologetics Department, and Chairman of the Faculty.

Doctor Edgar belongs to a number of learned societies, including the American Musicological Society, the Evangelical Theological Society, the American Historical Association, and the Society for Ethnomusicology. He serves on several boards, including the Huguenot Fellowship (President). Edgar is an ordained minister in the Presbyterian Church in America and has served on several denominational committees. His books include Taking Note of Music (London: SPCK, 1986), Reasons of the Heart (Baker/Hourglass, 1996; P & R, 2003), La carte protestante (Labor et Fides, 1997), The Face of Truth: Lifting the Veil (P & R, 2001), *and* Truth in All Its Glory: Commending the Reformed Faith (P & R, 2004).

Confusion with Work

The following blues lyrics from the legendary Henry Gray & Cousin Joe express a sentiment many people today would share about the drudgery of work.

> Fifty years ago
> Me and hard work fell out
> Yes, fifty years ago, me and hard work fell out
> Now hard work don't talk to me,
> And I don't speak to hard work no more.

Why is it we so often feel that work, hard work, is not a pleasure, but an enslaving necessity? Surely there are many reasons. But perhaps the central one is that we have divorced work from hope.

A number of years ago, there was a gang of laborers digging holes in the street. They had to blast through six inches of asphalt and concrete with an air hammer, then shovel out rocks and sand to get down five feet deep. It took about forty-five minutes. After the first hole was dug, the foreman looked down, nodded his head, and yelled, "OK, fill 'er back up." Again, moving a little bit away, the men blasted through six inches of asphalt and concrete with an air hammer, then shoveled out rocks and sand to get down five feet deep. The foreman came over, nodded, and told them to fill it up and move on. They did this several more times, and each time they dug, the foreman would tell them to fill it back up.

At the lunch break they all came to the boss and said they quit. "Just pay us and we'll go." When the astonished foreman asked why, one of them said, "No one's going to make a fool of me, digging up holes and filling them in." The foreman laughed and then explained that this was an older section of the city; they had lost the records, and were looking for the water mains. This is the only method they could think of to find them. So, of course, the men went back to work.[1]

We need to have meaning, some sort of purpose, or our work soon becomes *de*meaning. Centuries ago, the author of Ecclesiastes wrote, "What do mortals get from all the toil and strain with which they toil under the sun? For all their days are full of pain, and their work is a vexation; even at night their minds do not rest. This also is vanity" (2:22–23 nrsv).

Work without purpose is simply humiliating. For high school I attended a small New England boys' boarding school. It afforded a marvelous education. But there were lots of rules and restrictions. If caught in violation one of the most dreaded punishments was called "rock pile." This consisted of moving large rocks from one place to another. When the task was done, and if we had been bad enough, we had to move the rocks right back to the original pile. Of course, the purpose of this punishment was to make us do meaningless, hard work. It was very effective.

On a far more serious level, the powers controlling prison camps understand this full well. Few accounts tell of the wretchedness of working for no purpose (other than humiliation) better than the story of Viktor Frankl (1905–97). But few give more hope. The young psychiatrist and his family were deported in 1942 to a concentration camp in Bohemia. Then they were moved to Auschwitz. Only Victor survived. Finally, he went to another camp. Everything was stripped from him, including the manuscript of his life's work, *The Doctor and the Soul*, which he later spent hours and hours trying to reconstruct on bits of paper. The Nazis were grim specialists in degrading the prisoners by giving them meaningless work in unspeakable conditions.

Frankl found that people came to counsel with him, not only prisoners, but guards as well. In hours of conversation he discovered a fact that would later define his life's work. He began to discover a pattern among those who survived the camps, that is, among those given the chance to survive. The most likely to make it psychologically were not the well-born, nor the physically strong, but those who nurtured some sort of hope. While certainly not a Nietzschean, he found that there was something to the philosopher's dictum, "He who has a *why* to live for can bear with almost any *how*."[2] He saw that people who had hope, various kinds of hope, such as being reunited with loved ones, or projects they felt a need to complete, or, especially, those who had great faith, tended to have better chances than those who had lost all hope.

After his liberation Frankl developed an approach to psychiatry known as *Logotherapy*, from the idea of meaning, or purpose. At the heart of it, he stressed, was the necessity of love. Whatever his understanding of biblical religion might have been, he is certainly here expressing one of the central tenets of a Scriptural outlook.

Human work must be grounded in purpose. But not just any purpose. Biblically, what matters is that our work be grounded in the divine purpose for our lives. Indeed, human work, as the Bible teaches, is a microcosm of God's own work. We are speaking here of vocation, in the deepest sense.

Such a purpose for work is far from clear today. In his marvelous s book *The Call*, Os Guinness reflects on the confusion between work, leisure, and worship:

> Today we tend to talk of "work" and "leisure" as opposites. Work is serious, leisure is play, it is said. Work is drudgery, leisure is fun. Work is for pay, leisure is free. Work is what we do for someone else, leisure is for ourselves—and so on. But a moment's thought shows this is not so. Far closer to the mark is the observations that the modern world has scrambled things so badly that today we worship our work, we work at our play, and we play at our worship.[3]

THIS IS GOD'S WORLD

Calling, though, requires the deeper backdrop of a setting in which God is in control and gives meaning to our world. Unfortunately, this big-picture background where God is the ultimate environment for our work, has become largely secularized. Vocation is often simply thought of as going into the priesthood. The economic theories most often put forth are those which have little or no reference to this setting where God is acknowledged.

So we have government policies to try to regulate the economy and provide jobs, but they do not take into account the fact that we are in God's world. Even laypersons are familiar with some of the broad strokes of modern economic policy. Most of us know something about fiscal policies based on Keynesian economics. John Maynard Keynes famously argued that classical theory was wrong. It thought, erroneously, that "supply creates its own demand." During times of crisis this is not so, argued Keynes, and therefore we need government involvement to increase aggregate demand.[4] Only when such stimuli exist can we hope for a return to stability and full employment.

Keynes no doubt brought some needed correctives to an unbridled capitalism. And he was no socialist. And yet, as Bob Goudzwaard has forcefully argued, he ended up treating economics as a machine.[5] With a few adjustments, balancing out savings and investment levels, and the like, full employment could be regained. Keynes's model comes from the Enlightenment idea that the end of prosperity justifies the means of avarice, as we wait. To use an interesting metaphor, Keynes advocated a large-scale market economy that resembles a greenhouse plant, which only works when there are enough artificial protectors around it, as opposed to a plant out in nature, subject to the Providence of God.[6]

In a subtle way, government has begun to replace Providence in the Keynesian scheme. Not that all of it is bad. Some government regulation is important in order to maintain justice and reward good behavior in God's world (Rom. 13:1–7) But neither government nor institutions, nor individuals, are meant to operate in a mechanical model. Economics to be authentic require the larger setting of God's world. Norms for economic life will need to be derived from biblical revelation if we are to hope for any significant advancement. This is very difficult in a world that has become so highly secularized that everything is reduced to a system, rather than an open universe with God in control.

THE GLORY OF WORK

"If we are to recover the power of vocation to infuse all of life with religious meaning, and extend its range into all relational fields, then we must return to the expansive, religiously rich understanding of vocation in the Bible and the Reformation."[7]

Vocation is not simply a matter of going into the priesthood, as we have said. That line of work is of course most legitimate. But vocation is a much broader notion in Scripture. It was a reality even before the fall. It was meant to characterize human life throughout. But we have lost this sense that work has purpose. Indeed, we have lost the very sense of what work is meant to be.

If we are going to recover a rich, full-orbed notion of work, we will first have to look at it in its original design. For that we go back to the creation. Work may be problematic today, but the fall is not the proper point of departure for understanding it. Work is a creation ordinance.

Not only does this calling go back to the creation; it is grounded in the divine pattern. This is one of the most astonishing emphases to come out of the biblical worldview. God worked for six days to create the heavens and the earth and all their hosts. And He rested from that work on the seventh day, which is why that day is blessed and hallowed (Gen. 2:1–2). This pattern is the rationale given for the human rhythm of work and rest, according to the Ten Commandments. (Ex. 20:11) We often forget that the fourth commandment is not only about the Sabbath, but is a directive to work for six days.

The pattern of working in six units was comprehensive in the Old Testament. Not only were there literally six days to work, followed by rest, but there were to be six years of sowing the land and harvesting, followed by a rest for the field, and a time for the poor especially to be fed. (Ex. 23:10; Lev. 25:1–8) God works, and each work day brings morning and evening, and so man works, going out to labor until the evening. (Ps. 104:23–24)

Working as an imitation of the divine prototype stands in stark contrast to the mythologies of the ancient Near East. For example, according to the Babylonian accounts, human beings were created in order to bear the burdens the gods were not willing to carry. But in the Genesis account man is made after the image of God, in order to function as his vice gerent here on earth.

Twice, following the structure of Hebrew poetry, the text tells us about the special nature of humankind, being created after God's image. And twice this is followed by the divine call to work. (Gen. 1:26, 27–30) What is the connection? Among other things, imaging God means we are kings. Just as God is the King of kings, pronouncing infallibly that everything He had made was good and very good, so we are to rule the world in God's stead, lesser kings, judging between good and evil, working the soil to good purpose, going into all the world and subduing it.

Indeed, the earth doesn't function right until man is there to work the soil (Gen. 2:5, 15). Even after the Fall, our purpose is still to cultivate the ground (Gen. 3:23; Matt. 21:28). What we sometimes call the cultural mandate is a call to work in the wonderful world God has made. Our work needs to be done with honesty and integrity (Jer. 48:10). It should be done with skill and craft (Jer.10:9). This work is the great privilege of life. There is no work in hades (Eccl. 9:10)!

There was to be development in work. The skill mentioned above is not learned in an instant, but in laboring week after week, generation after generation. John Murray notes that there was marvelous development. Abel kept sheep, and Cain tilled the ground. Commenting on the cultural mandate, he says, "Every indication is that toil was a pervasive feature of life in this world, that such toil had a variety of forms from the outset, and took on increasing multiformity with the development of the race." Thus, by the time of Noah, people knew how to build a ship. During the Patriarchs, we have wealth, which in itself carries no dishonor.[8]

Proper work is rewarding. When done diligently, it brings a sense of accomplishment. Even though everything is of the Lord, there is a proper sense in which we can be rewarded according to the work of our hands (Eccl. 5:19; Prov. 12:14). Anyone who has come home after a hard day's work in which he or she has accomplished something good knows the feeling.

Work is not just an individual endeavor. It has a communal aspect. One of the obvious fruits of our labor is provision for the family (2 Thess. 3:10). How many fathers want to know, when their daughters' hands are asked in marriage, will you provide for her?
Proverbs 31 is not put in the Bible to make housewives feel guilty. It is the final chapter of God's training manual in the art of wisdom. The fully wise sage will rise early, work hard, provide for the family, reflect well on her relatives. Labor was done in ancient Israel for the benefit of the entire community (Neh. 10:37).

THE CURSE OF WORK

Work is a creation ordinance. It is not a necessity from the Fall. Nevertheless, the Fall has deeply infected our labors. Surely it is significant that God's judgment upon our first parents was tailored to their characteristic callings. Eve, the mother of all living persons, was cursed in childbearing. Adam, tiller of the ground, was told that everything would be hard. The ground over which he was to have been lord would itself yield only with difficulty what was meant to come easily, and eventually would swallow him up in death (Gen. 3:17–19).

Again, John Murray is helpful here. He notes that the curse is not a curse on work itself. The ground is cursed. So there is still fruit from labor. But everything is hard. Work easily becomes drudgery. Worse, there is no real rest from this accursed work: "What has a man from all the toil and striving of heart with which he toils beneath the sun? For all his days are full of sorrow, and his work is a vexation. Even in the night his heart does not rest. This also is vanity" (Eccl. 2:22–23 ESV). Those of us who do not sleep very well often are plagued by worries about what needs to be done, what was not done well, what needs to be done over again.

If good work brings reward, work done under the curse receives "evil" as a recompense. So often now the work of our hands is to build idols and put a name for ourselves in the heavens (Gen. 11:1–9). This brings displeasure to God Himself (Jer. 25:6). It is, in every sense of the term, futile.

No wonder, then, that a pervasive image for our sinful condition is slavery. Slavery was all too real in the ancient world, even as it still is. Israel labored hard under captivity until God emancipated his people. But slavery is also an apt metaphor of the human condition. Even at our best, we are captives, wretched people serving the law of sin (Rom. 7:23–25).

The entire creation groans as it longs for freedom from decay and bondage. Few literary images surpass that of the land of Mordor in J. R. R. Tolkien's *Lord of the Rings*, ruled by Sauron, portraying the hellishness of work under the curse of God.

WORK AND REDEMPTION

Finally, though, we are not left with a groaning world of drudgery. We are given hope. Meaning is restored and even enhanced. When Israel groaned under their bondage in Egypt, God heard their cry and came down and delivered them. He set them free in the promised land, free to worship, free to celebrate, and of course, free to work, but for a very different master. Like His great Son's yoke, the Father's yoke is easy, and His burden is light.

Salvation is called, over and over again, the great work of God. What our first parents failed to do, what Israel failed to do in the desert, Jesus Christ, God's beloved Son, triumphed in doing. He came to do the work of the Father, and in so doing to relieve a dying world of its slavery. Jesus' work is sometimes known as his "active obedience." Not only did He die to take upon Himself the sins of the world, but He positively fulfilled the entire will of God.

Because of this, His work is reproduced in us, so that we may be saved. "He who began a good work in [us] will bring it to completion at the day of Jesus Christ" (Phil. 1:6 esv) In one of the most beautiful statements of God's plan in the entire Bible, Paul contrasts the futility of good works for getting us to God with the gift of God: "Not a result of works, so that no one may boast. For we are his workmanship, created in Christ Jesus for good works, which God prepared beforehand, that we should walk in them" (Eph. 2:9–10 esv).

This changes everything! Now that we are no longer under a curse, our work can have meaning once again. Not only meaning, but power. We may be builders. Working on an edifice is an image often used in the New Testament to signify the wonderful work in progress that we are, and that we construct. We are, amazingly, being built into a holy structure for God's dwelling (Eph. 2:22). Because of this we build each other up ("edify") when we can (Rom. 15:2; 1 Cor. 10:23). Again, our work has a social function. The Hebrew word for work (*melakah*) literally means "to serve." We serve God, and we serve our neighbor.

Thus, work plays a social role. It helps develop the world. Consider that what we do here and now is an investment in the world to come. Is this counterintuitive? Only to the American mentality of "sola-bootstrapsa."[9] Citing Isaiah 60, Revelation 21:24 tells us the kings of the earth will bring their glory into the new Jerusalem. What is this glory? It is the accumulated wealth of the nations (Isa. 60:5–7). In other words, it is the fruit of much labor.

Salvation is not simply wrenching a Platonic soul from each of our bodies to bring it safely to heaven. It is the transformation of our entire selves, the new creature, to serve the earth that is being renewed. In the end what will be destroyed is not the world as world, but the sinful cancer of corruption. And so the work of the scientist, the farmer, the citizen, the parent, the minister, the artist, and indeed, any of the legitimate callings addressed to us in this fallen world, all of it is a worthwhile investment in the age to come. "Whatever you do . . . , do it unto the Lord" (1 Cor. 10:31; Col. 3:23, paraphrased).

And of course in our work, we serve the needy. But notice how even the relief of the poor is not purely functional. Paul tells the thief he may no longer steal, but do honest work with his own hands. Note the contrast between theft, which is a shortcut to possessions gained by someone else's hard work, and the integrity of work with one's own hands. But then he goes on to give work an even higher purpose: "so that he may have something to share with anyone in need" (Eph. 4:28 ESV). And that process is redemptive in the highest order.

Work now takes on new meaning, a significance it did not have even before the Fall. We labor for the sake of the One who labored for our salvation, the One who made Himself poor that we might become rich in Him (2 Cor. 8:9). We labor so that we may rest. Yes, to enjoy the rest of the Sabbath. But far more, to enjoy the "heavenly rest" of eternal fellowship with Jesus, in the unity of the Father and the Spirit.

What does all this have to do with business? Much in every way! If we had this grand perspective on work, everything could change. But for this to happen we need a new reformation. A reformation of work. A reformation of everything!

Let me close with this quote from the Puritan preacher Thomas Case:

> Reformation must be universal . . . reform all places, all persons and callings; reform the benches of judgment, the inferior magistrates... Reform the universities, reform the cities, reform the countries, reform inferior schools of learning, reform the Sabbath, reform the ordinances, the worship of God . . . you have more work to do than I can speak . . . Every plant which my heavenly father hath not planted shall be rooted up.[10]

Notes

1. From John A. Bernbaum and Simon M. Steer, *Why Work? Careers and Employment in Biblical Perspective* (Grand Rapids: Baker, 1986).
2. Friedrich Nietzsche, quoted in Victor E. Frankl, *Man's Search for Meaning*, rev. upd. ed. (New York, Pocket Books, 1997), 126
3. Os Guinness: *The Call: Finding and Fulfilling the Central Purpose of Your Life* (Nashville: Word, 1998), 160.
4. See John Maynard Keynes: *Treatise on Money* (London: MacMillan, 1930), 90.
5. Bob Goudzwaard: *Capitalism and Progress* (Grand Rapids: Eerdmans, 1979), 139.
6. Ibid., 105.
7. Douglas J. Schuurman, *Vocation: Discerning Our Callings in Life* (Grand Rapids: Eerdmans, 2004), 4.
8. John Murray: *Principles of Conduct* (Grand Rapids: Eerdmans, 1955), 82.
9. An expression I learned from Bryan Chappel, president of Covenant Theological Seminary.
10. Michael Walzer:, *The Revolution of the Saints* (Cambridge, MA: Harvard University Press, 1965), 10–11.

DOING BUSINESS IN GOD'S WORLD: BUSINESS IS A CALLING

PHILIP J. CLEMENTS

Philip J. Clements is the managing director of the Center for Christian Business Ethics Today, LLC. Clements has been a leader in the business community for over thirty years. He has held the position of Executive Vice President of Standard & Poor's Corporate Value Consulting ("CVC") division. He led the transition of CVC to S&P, after S&P acquired CVC from PricewaterhouseCoopers LLP (PwC). Prior to joining Standard & Poor's, Clements was the Global Leader of the CVC practice of PwC. He also served on the U.S. boards of Coopers & Lybrand and Pricewaterhouse Coopers and the global board of PwC. He was a member of the Finance Committees of both firms. Clements was Chairman of the Board of Trustees of the National Bible Association. Seattle University School of Law Board of Visitors, International Leadership Board of Advisors, and HOPE Bible Mission board are others boards that Clements has served or is serving on. In addition to founder and CEO of the Center, Philip J. Clements is also Managing Direcotor at Cathedral Consulting Firm..

PETER LILLBACK

Doctor Peter A. Lillback is President and Professor of Historical Theology at Westminster Theological Seminary. Lillback also serves as the President of The Providence Forum, the nonprofit organization that is committed to preserving and promoting America's spiritual roots of religious and civil liberties.

Living between Philadelphia and Valley Forge for many years, Dr. Lillback has pursued an avid interest in the history of the Judeo-Christian heritage of the United States. He has done much research and study on the founding and Founders of our nation through examination of original source documents in numerous libraries and archives. His books Freedom's Holy Light *and* Proclaim Liberty *are outgrowths of his research. In 2006, Dr. Lillback's bestseller on the Christian faith of George Washington was released.* George Washington's Sacred Fire *represents the culmination of over twenty years of original research and scholarship. In May 2010, the paperback reached #1 on Amazon.com.*

MAC MCQUISTON

Mac McQuiston's career in Christian leadership spans forty-five years and encompasses key roles in some of America's most recognizable and influential Christian ministries. After graduating from Indiana Wesleyan University, Mac went to work for World Wide Pictures in association with the Billy Graham Organization. He then served as Senior Vice President for Chuck Swindoll's Insight for Living ministry. And in 1977, he joined Focus on the Family as one of the original Board members and a signatory of Focus' incorporation. He became Vice President of Administration and Development and helped launch Dr. Dobson's City Wide Seminars in 1977 and Dobson's first film series in 1978.

When the CEO Forum began in Focus on the Family in 1995, Mac was appointed its President/CEO, a role he has filled for almost fifteen years. In 2005, the CEO Forum became an independent organization headquartered in Colorado Springs. The mission of the CEO Forum is to develop spiritual statesmen among senior executives of major corporations and, through them, advance the kingdom of God and impact the business and social cultures of America. Forum members include CEOs of Fortune 1,000 companies.

LOU GIULIANO

Mr. Giuliano retired as Chairman, President, and Chief Executive Officer of ITT Corporation at the end of 2004. During his sixteen-year tenure at ITT, Mr. Giuliano focused on leadership development and an overarching strategy of continuous improvement. Initiation of a corporate-wide Lean Six Sigma implementation allowed ITT's leadership team to significantly improve its competitive position and operating performance. He also oversaw a rapid expansion of ITT's activities in China.

Prior to being named President and Chief Operating Officer of ITT Corporation in 1998, Mr. Giuliano was President and Chief Executive of ITT Corporation's Defense and Electronics businesses and Senior Vice President of ITT Corporation for eight years. During that time, the businesses entered new, rapidly growing markets and achieved consistent sales and income growth, despite dramatic reductions in the defense budget.

He is a graduate of Syracuse University with a BA in chemistry and an MBA. He is Chairman of the Board of Governors of the United States Postal Service. He is also on the Board of Directors of the John Maneely Company, a Senior Advisor to The Carlyle Group, a member of the CEO Forum, and on the Advisory Board for the Princeton University Faith and Work Initiative.

The question is, "Are you going to be obedient to the Call?" The "Call" is the call to business, be it a nurse or a doctor or a hospital CEO. Everyone is created by God with a purpose. To put it another way, God had a purpose for creating each person. That purpose is His purpose and fits into His plan for His world. Whether an individual fulfills his purpose is up to him. If he chooses not to walk with God and undertake those things that He purposes, then those things may not get done. In short, everyone is called by God to do the work he does, regardless of his belief. Whether he sweeps the floor or manages the company, he fulfills God's call. But if there is a business vocation, then there are divine blessings to be enjoyed by the Christian businessperson as well as moral responsibilities incumbent on the believer.

Theologians of various persuasions would pose a variety of issues with this statement, but as a practical matter this statement proves to be the experience of many business colleagues. Perhaps the following quote from John Calvin, *Institutes*, III.10.6, provides a good framework [emphasis added]:

> The last thing to be observed is, that the Lord enjoins every one of us, in all the actions of life, to have *respect to our own calling*. He knows the boiling restlessness of the human mind, the fickleness with which it is borne hither and thither, its eagerness to hold opposites at one time in its grasp, its ambition. Therefore, lest all things should be thrown into confusion by our folly and rashness, he has assigned distinct duties to each in the different modes of life. And that no one may presume to overstep his proper limits, he has distinguished the different modes of life by the name of callings. *Every man's mode of life, therefore, is a kind of station assigned him by the Lord,* that he may not be always driven about at random. So necessary is this distinction, that all our actions are thereby estimated in his sight, and often in a very different way from that in which human reason or philosophy would estimate them. There is no more illustrious deed even among philosophers than to free one's country from tyranny, and yet the private individual who stabs the tyrant is openly condemned by the voice of the heavenly Judge. But I am unwilling to dwell on particular examples; it is enough to know that in every thing *the call of the Lord is the foundation and beginning of right action. He who does not act with reference to it will never, in the discharge of duty, keep the right path.* He will sometimes be able, perhaps, to give the semblance of something laudable, but whatever it may be in the sight of man, it will be rejected before the throne of God; and besides, there will be no harmony in the different parts of his life. Hence, he only who directs his life to this end will have it properly framed; because free from the impulse of rashness,

he will not attempt more than his calling justifies, knowing that it is unlawful to overleap the prescribed bounds. He who is obscure will not decline to cultivate a private life, that he may not desert the post at which God has placed him. *Again, in all our cares, toils, annoyances, and other burdens, it will be no small alleviation to know that all these are under the superintendence of God.* The magistrate will more willingly perform his office, and the father of a family confine himself to his proper sphere. *Every one in his particular mode of life will, without repining, suffer its inconveniences, cares, uneasiness, and anxiety, persuaded that God has laid on the burden. This, too, will afford admirable consolation, that in following your proper calling, no work will be so mean and sordid as not to have a splendour and value in the eye of God.*

The following will be a brief look at some key issues that arise from the question of being obedient to the Call. Where possible, descriptions of real-life situations are presented, with names changed for proper confidentiality.

How does one know if he or she is called? For everyone this is a most challenging question. It fits into that great study of knowing God's will. Much has been written on this topic, so a practical summary is offered here. The starting place should be the Bible. The Westminster Confession of Faith, chapter 1, "Of the Holy Scripture," says that "it pleased the Lord . . . to reveal Himself and declare His will to the Church." Second Timothy 3:16 gives us the comfort that in Scripture there is guidance for "training in righteousness" (NIV). A strong knowledge of the Bible and a diligent search of the Bible on each point of life, including business decisions, allow God to give guidance through His Word. God instructed Joshua to take care to study His Word, meditate on it day and night, and not to deviate to the right or left, that Joshua would prosper wherever he went.[1] So we learn God's Word, and then we follow it with care.

The second indicator is prayer. But prayer starts with a strong relationship with God. The blessing of Christianity is that we have direct access to God, the Father. We have a relationship with Him, and this relationship allows Him to hear our prayers, and He answers our prayers. How God answers our prayers tends to differ by individual, but it is often described as an inner peace.[2] But the reader is challenged to realize that not all prayers are answered with inner peace, yet the Call is clear. For example, Gideon knew he was called, but still struggled with the inner peace. Jesus knew the Call, but still wrestled with the burden the cross meant when He prayed in the Garden of Gethsemane.[3] But in both cases, the prayers were heard and the Call affirmed and executed.

The third indicator of a call is circumstances. Often it is clear that a situation is ripe for the individual to respond. Sometimes it is skills, sometimes contacts, sometimes character, sometimes for no reason but that he is there; all of these create situations where the individual can assume the leadership or action role. Joshua is an excellent example of one for whom the Call to lead the people into the promised land was a natural extension of his life. Esther is an example of a more problematic situation that cried for action. Esther was queen, but under the law of the land could not go into the court of the king without his call or his permission, signaled at the time of a non-called entry, otherwise she would die. But the king had issued a decree allowing the death of all the Jews in the kingdom. Esther's uncle, Mordecai, informed Esther and challenged her with these words: "For if you remain completely silent at this time, relief and deliverance will arise for the Jews from another place . . . Yet, who knows whether you have come to the kingdom for such a time as this?"[4] Esther, in preparing to act, requested that Mordecai call the Jews together for fasting and prayer for her, while she did likewise.[5] Esther acted, and the result is a blessing for the Jews and the kingdom.

A fourth indicator of a call is counsel. Trusted colleagues give great advice. Their response to the sense of call can be affirming or challenging. In either case, further Bible study and prayer on such counsel can aid in giving guidance. Two verses give strong encouragement to develop a good network of counselors: Proverbs 15:22, "Plans fail for lack of counsel, but with many advisers they succeed" (NIV), and Proverbs 27:17, "As iron sharpens iron, so one man sharpens another" (NIV). In looking at the question of calling, it is important to remember that it is not the counselor that is called, but the individual. Therefore, the counselor will tend to be a sounding board and an inquisitor on the basis for the sense of calling. In the end, it is for the individual to determine the Call.

A recent example of this playing out in modern business was the case of Henry, who was ready to leave his company, feeling that it was time to move on. During a call to his prayer counselor, the counselor raised the question, what was God saying? Henry responded that he felt the Lord suggesting that he stay. The counselor then raised the question of whether Henry was open to staying. Initially, Henry was not, but as he prayed and meditated on the situation, he became open to the possibility of staying at the company. In their regular discussions the counselor continued to ask the same question, eventually receiving Henry's affirmation of his openness to staying. The next day a board member challenged Henry to stay in the company because change was afoot. Shortly thereafter, Henry was asked to become CEO. As it turned out, the company was in severe stress, resulting in a dozen weeks of tough decisions and actions. Today Henry looks back and declares that he was indeed called, and that had prepared him for the task. Henry has no question that his service in this company is all about bringing God glory, for He set Henry in the role.

But what if you do not answer the Call? What happens? Does God's work not get done? These are hard questions, theologically. Perhaps an answer focused on the positive outcomes of answering the Call would start to address these questions. When we answer the Call to business, God's people are blessed. Two passages outline this kind of thinking.   Solomon had become king of Israel and had begun to build the temple. Solomon needed a skilled worker "to work in gold and silver, in bronze and iron, in purple and crimson and blue, who ha[d] skill to engrave with the skillful men . . . in Judah and Jerusalem"[6] So Solomon sent the job description to Hiram, king of Tyre. Hiram's response is most telling: "Because the LORD loves His people, He has made you king over them"[7] Note that it is not because the Lord loved Solomon, but Israel, that Solomon was given to be a leader. The king of Tyre is affirming the blessing that great leadership is to a people. This fully applies to a company. Those called to lead a company have the privilege of being a blessing to the customers, suppliers, employees, and investors.

The second situation was also with Solomon. The queen of Sheba heard of Solomon's wisdom and visited him. At the end of the visit, the queen declared, "Because your God has loved Israel . . . , He made you king over them, to do justice and righteousness."[8] The theme of the king of Tyre is repeated: that God loves a people by providing good leadership. The queen then added that the outcome of good leadership is doing justice and righteousness.

Today we have very large companies, as well as modest and small companies. The need for justice and righteousness in the leadership of companies in order to be a blessing to the people is a great challenge. God cares about the people in a company, and God will provide a leader that can lead righteously.

An example of this may be the case of Ben. Ben was a division leader who was prepared to retire. The law was changing so that Ben's division could no longer be a part of the company. There were more than five hundred people in the division. If it could not be sold, most of the people would have to be terminated, creating great emotional stress on the various families as the employees searched for new employment. But it was clear to all that only Ben could lead a sale and transition. The company CEO asked Ben to defer retirement to do the sale and transition. A transition such as this takes three years and the sale another year, so Ben's commitment was somewhere in the four- to five-year period. The sale was successful, and at the closing the buyer spoke to the senior members of Ben's group and expressed his view that Ben had played the role of Moses and that the buyer hoped that Ben's team would find the buying company to be the promised land. All employees kept their jobs. Ten years later over 70 percent of the senior employees remain at the company. The important part of this story was that throughout the sale process, both the buyer and Ben's team acknowledged that God had provided Ben for this time and that no one else could have gotten the task done.

So the question of, "If I do not answer the Call, will God's work get done?" has not been answered. But we do see that answering the Call is participating in the blessing God has for others. Esther's situation, noted above, suggests that, indeed, God would find another way to get what He needs done, if we do not answer the Call. The concern is that indeed we cannot assert that God's will requires Him to find another to take our place. Rather, the Call is clearly ours to answer, but we do not necessarily get to delegate it to another. The concern is that the people or company will suffer because the Call was ignored. Proverbs 29:2 suggests this outcome: "When the righteous thrive, the people rejoice; when the wicked rule, the people groan"(NIV). Similarly, Proverbs 29:18: "Where there is no vision, the people perish: but he that keepeth the law, happy is he" (KJV).

Calling and courage go together. Running companies is tough, hard work. Today leaders face the added stress of competition, recessions, regulations, Senate hearing abuse, lawsuits, and fickle employees. But is that so different from what Moses or Joshua faced? When God charged Joshua with the leadership of Israel, there were approximately two million Israelites to be led.[9] The Israelites were going into the promised land, but it was hostile. The people had been grumbling and acting badly for forty years in the wilderness. So God gave Joshua a command and a word of encouragement, "Have I not commanded you? Be strong and of good courage; do not be afraid, nor be dismayed, for the Lord your God is with you wherever you go."[10]

A word of encouragement about the next generation and business. Young people today are passionate and energized about their faith and about making a change in the world. This passion, coupled with a strong understanding of Christian principles, gives hope that companies will have leaders who execute justice and righteousness.

The following three cases from the business life experience of Lou Giuliano illustrate some of the critical applications of how God calls us into positions, and how these positions will challenge our ethical framework. The endurance of these trials does indeed develop character, but also is critical to the company. The names of the other parties have been changed for proper confidentiality.

As we consider these challenges, let us be conscious of the time frames within which the business person must act. Often business issues must be decided immediately. While many a good management book or counseling recommendation says take time to fully deliberate, Lou's experiences are illustrative of the real-life action business requires. Deadlines, filings, buy-sell decisions all are done in real time. It requires a proper foundation in order to run business in real time. For this foundation, we are led directly to the principles contained in the Scriptures and the theological insights of the Westminster Standards.

As a panel, we are convinced that Lou did the right thing in each of these three instances. But why? Is it because he acted in accord with an international code of business ethics? Was it because he was wisely reflecting well-established business culture or corporate tradition? While these may in fact be true, the reality is that Lou was following the historic wisdom of Scripture. To demonstrate this, let's take a brief look at the biblical and theological matters that are engaged by these cases.

Case One: What Is a Bribe?

As a young businessman Lou was working at a large multinational company, EFG, that was proposing on an international contract worth millions of dollars. It was clear that EFG had a strong chance to secure the deal. The leader of the contracting team privately approached Lou and gave him an empty briefcase. "Twenty-five thousand dollars from you in this case will guarantee that you will get the contract," he said. Some of the questions Lou faced were: Is this the normal way of doing business in this country? Is this a cultural way of doing business? Is this a bribe? Where can I get this kind of money? He sent the briefcase back empty. Today, at this stage in his career, it is much clearer that this was the right step than it was at the time. What would the impact have been if they still got the contract? What would the impact have been if they had not gotten the multimillion-dollar contract? (EFG did, however, get the contract.)

Scripture and Theological Observations

First, what do the Scriptures teach us about a bribe? The Bible is realistic. The

Proverbs recognize that a gift/bribe may in fact have a powerful impact on its recipient. (All passages hereafter are from the King James Version.) Proverbs 18:16 declares, "A man's gift maketh room for him, and bringeth him before great men." Proverbs 17:8 says, "A gift is as a precious stone in the eyes of him that hath it: whithersoever it turneth, it prospereth." So a gift is a blessing to the recipient and the giver. Paul noted this spirit in his parting words to the Ephesians in Acts 20:35, citing Jesus who said, "It is more blessed to give than to receive."

But does that make the giving of all gifts right? Clearly, there is a point when one has crossed the line between a gift and a bribe. Custom and circumstance can make gifts to business acquaintances appropriate. Yet, somewhere the line can be crossed between giving proper honor, duties and taxes, fear and respect to whom these are due as taught by Romans 13:7, and the giving or asking for a bribe. Proverbs 17:23 states, "A wicked man taketh a gift out of the bosom to pervert the ways of judgment." In this verse, the gift influences the decision, thereby making it evil or a bribe. In the above-referenced case, the request was to turn over money so that winning the contract would be "guaranteed." A bribe was requested.

A bribe is a form of oppression. Oppression is one of the sins forbidden in the eighth commandment as taught by the Westminster Larger Catechism (hereinafter called simply Catechism), question and answer 142. Oppression directly violates Scripture. For example, Ezekiel 22:29 and Leviticus 25:17 declare, "The people of the land have used oppression, and exercised robbery, and have vexed the poor and needy: yea, they have oppressed the stranger wrongfully" and "Ye shall not therefore oppress one another; but thou shalt fear thy God: For I am the LORD your God."

The Bible has more instruction on the problems caused by bribery. Consider Job 15:34, "For the congregation of hypocrites shall be desolate, and fire shall consume the tabernacles of bribery." A fair reading of this text argues that hypocrisy and bribery are intimately linked. Moreover, the outcome of these activities is not success but devastation. The words "desolate, and fire shall consume" give little hope of enduring profits for the "congregation of hypocrites" and the "tabernacles of bribery."

The course of wisdom is well taught in Proverbs 15:27, "He that is greedy of gain troubleth his own house; but he that hateth gifts shall live." Here see the link between greed, or aggressive wealth gathering, that leads to accepting or giving inappropriate gifts or bribes, and the outcome of trouble. Rather, it is better to neither give or receive gifts in the business context, because of this risk.

Today this standard remains just as important as what Lou found in his early days. Governments and companies legislate limits on gifts such that the gift will not be sufficient to influence business decisions. While these rules provide good guidelines, we need to recognize that such rules only try to enact what wisdom recommends from the outset. Similarly, Proverbs 16:16 declares, "How much better is it to get wisdom than gold! and to get understanding rather to be chosen than silver!"

Case Two: Between High Values and the Bottom Line

The tension many business leaders feel is one between doing the right thing and meeting business objectives, specifically, the tension between *timing* and *sales*. Several years later, Lou was part of a large multinational company, LMN, and his division had won a $150,000,000 government bid at a time when the company desperately needed work to keep its large industrial plants in operation without facing massive layoffs. But Friday before the weekend when the contract was to be signed and returned, the LMN business office called Lou and explained that a major mistake had been made in the cost estimate in the bid, which is why their bid was so extraordinarily competitive. Under the bid amount the company would make no profit, but could possibly break even. Given the factory situation, LMN would accept the bid as given, but was there more to be done? Lou immediately called his superior to inform him of the error in the bid and to inquire as to whether the government agency needed to be informed. In speaking with his superior, Lou was simply told, "You know what to do!" What did he know to do? Should he wait over the weekend to think it over before he responded, which would be too late, since the contract would have been signed? Should he just keep quiet, accept the contract, and try to work potential scope changes in the contract or cost management to get more profits? Should he immediately inform the agency of the problem and ask them to permit LMN to offer another bid? Should he simply tell the agency his circumstances and ask them if they would reconsider the matter? The principle that Lou developed here was "No order was wanted if LMN had to go into the gray zone to secure it. All orders had to be within the 'bright light.' An order in the gray zone was already off to a wrong start and therefore off-limits." Lou called that day, explained the error and its implications, and asked the agency if they would reconsider the bid.

The agency responded that they would accept the deal as bid, if LMN wanted it, but LMN had to live with the contract pricing. LMN took the contract under these terms and kept its workforce gainfully employed.

What Is Full Disclosure in Business Dealings?

What do the Scriptures teach about truthfulness and timely reporting in business matters? The Catechism in question and answer 140 defines the duties required in the eighth commandment. The answer calls for "truth, faithfulness, and justice in contracts and commerce between man and man." This duty of the eighth commandment's "Thou shalt not steal" is supported by explicit scriptural texts. Consider the following:

> Psalm 15:2, 4: "He that walketh uprightly, and worketh righteousness, and speaketh the truth in his heart . . . He that sweareth to his own hurt, and changeth not."

> Zechariah 7:4, 10: "Then came the word of the Lord of hosts unto me, saying, . . . Oppress not the widow, nor the fatherless, the stranger, nor the poor; and let none of you imagine evil against his brother in your heart."

> Zechariah 8:16, 17: "These are the things that ye shall do; speak ye every man the truth to his neighbour; execute the judgment of truth and peace in your gates: And let none of you imagine evil in your hearts against his neighbour; and love no false oath: for all these are things that I hate, saith the Lord."

In question and answer 142, we are told that among the sins forbidden in the eighth commandment are "false weights and measures" and "injustice and unfaithfulness in contracts between man and man." Biblical texts that affirm this understanding include several. Amos 8:5: "Saying, When will the new moon be gone, that we may sell corn? and the sabbath, that we may set forth wheat, making the ephah small, and the shekel great, and falsifying the balances by deceit?" The concern is the manipulation of the relationship to gain advantage. Lou's disclosure put the relationship in a state where the risk and temptation for manipulation was minimized. Proverbs 11:1: "A false balance is abomination to the Lord; but a just weight is his delight." And Proverbs 20:10, "Divers weights, and divers measures, both of them are alike abomination to the LORD." These passages are clear instructions against secret dealings that the other party may not catch. God is watching, and He knows. In business the temptation to let things slide or cover them up or "work the contract" such that one gets a gain beyond that agreed by the other party is always there. These passages express both the error and that God knows the error. Clearly, Lou's full, truthful, and timely report of the bid error and its benefit to the agency, while a burden to LMN, put the agency and LMN on a better footing in working through the production in the contract because each party had a greater sense of their capacity to trust the other. The outcome was in fact in accord with biblical and confessional wisdom.

CASE THREE: THE PROBLEMS OF CROSS-CULTURAL BUSINESS

As Western business moved into the emerging markets of China, not only were there vast barriers to overcome to do international business, but also vast cultural differences. To the RST company business leaders' surprise, it was explained that Chinese custom calls for a red envelope, filled with a great deal of cash, to be given to the Chinese businesses with which RST was working. It was said that this was the Chinese custom of celebrating the New Year and a standard way of doing business. However, this was not the typical American way of business and seemed to run counter to the "bright light" policy Lou brought to RST. But to reject making the gift had the appearance of causing offense and declaring a moral superiority of the Western business leaders over their Chinese partners. Was it proper to make the gifts? What if by not taking the gifts such offense would be given that the business relationships were ended, resulting in harm to investors and workers? At a meeting of the various RST business leaders, a young businessman declared he could not make the gifts because it was not the RST way of doing business and, in his view, was wrong. After a major discussion, no red envelopes were distributed. The business projects continued unaffected between the Chinese and RST.

What Is Influencing Purchasing?
The third case study from Lou's career has to do with the red envelopes designed to keep customers interested. They were a form of keeping business partner-

ships in place. But were they actually a form of influence purchasing? Because this is in the context of existing business relationships and in a cross-cultural setting, it is possible to view this differently than as an overt bribe. Instead the red envelope problem falls in a slightly different category. The general category is in Catechism question and answer 141 to the eighth commandment, where the Catechism speaks of "an endeavor, by all just and lawful means, to procure, preserve, and further the wealth and outward estate of others, as well as our own." Is this a lawful means to further the wealth of both parties in the business partnership? Or could this fall under the rubrics of Catechism question and answer 142, where the sins forbidden by the eighth commandment include "covetousness; inordinate prizing and affecting worldly goods; distrustful and distracting cares and studies in getting, keeping and using them; . . . prodigality, wasteful gaming; and all other ways whereby we do unduly prejudice our own outward estate, and defrauding ourselves of the due use and comfort of that estate which God hath given us"? Numerous scriptural texts address these kinds of economic sins. Consider the following:

> Luke 12:15: "And he said unto them, Take heed, and beware of covetousness: for a man's life consisteth not in the abundance of the things which he possesseth."

> 1 Timothy 6:5: "Perverse disputings of men of corrupt minds, and destitute of the truth, supposing that gain is godliness: from such withdraw thyself."

> Colossians 3:2: "Set your affection on things above, not on things on the earth."

> Proverbs 23:5: "Wilt thou set thine eyes upon that which is not? For riches certainly make themselves wings; they fly away as an eagle toward heaven."

> Psalm 62:10: "If riches increase, set not your heart upon them."

> Matthew 6:25, 31, 34: "Therefore I say unto you, Take no thought for your life, what ye shall eat, or what ye shall drink; nor yet for your body, what ye shall put on. Is not the life more than meat, and the body than raiment? . . . Therefore take

no thought, saying, What shall we eat? . . . Take therefore no thought for the morrow: for the morrow shall take thought for the things of itself. Sufficient unto the day is the evil thereof."

Ecclesiastes 5:12: "The sleep of a labouring man is sweet, whether he eat little or much: but the abundance of the rich will not suffer him to sleep."

Psalm 73:3: "For I was envious at the foolish, when I saw the prosperity of the wicked."

Psalm 37:1, 7: "Fret not thyself because of evil doers, neither be thou envious

against the workers of iniquity. . . . Rest in the LORD, and wait patiently for him: fret not thyself because of him who prospereth in his way, because of the man who bringeth wicked devices to pass."

2 Thessalonians 3:11: "For we hear that there are some which walk among you disorderly, working not at all, but are busybodies."

Proverbs 18:9: "He also that is slothful in his work is brother to him that is a great waster."

Proverbs 21:17: "He that loveth pleasure shall be a poor man; he that loveth wine and oil shall not be rich."

Proverbs 23:20–21: "Be not among wine bibbers; among riotous eaters of flesh: For the drunkard and the glutton shall come to poverty: and drowsiness shall clothe a man with rags."

Proverbs 28:19: "He that tilleth his land shall have plenty of bread; but he that followeth after vain persons shall have poverty enough."

Ecclesiastes 4:8: "There is one alone, and there is not a second;

yea, he hath neither child nor brother: yet is there no end of all his labour; neither is his eye satisfied with riches; neither saith he, For whom do I labour, and bereave my soul of good? This is also vanity, yea, it is a sore travail."

Ecclesiastes 6:2: "A man to whom God hath given riches, wealth, and honour, so that he wanteth nothing for his soul of all that he desireth, yet God giveth him not power to eat thereof, but a stranger eateth it: this is vanity, and it is an evil disease."

1 Timothy 5:8: "But if any provide not for his own, and specially for those of his own house, he hath denied the faith, and is worse than an infidel."

Clearly in view of such biblical teaching, the need to use monetary gifts to buy influence with customers is less-than-ideal business! Lou's team wrestled with the question of this need and its implications. One of the key outcomes of deciding to do the right thing is accepting the consequences. The risk of losing business was real. By not passing out the envelopes, RST would break a cultural barrier. But these verses articulate the true standard: trust in what is right, not in riches or business that can fly away.

This paper opens with a discussion of the call to engage in business. In this third case we see the blessing of a young person that stood up to the Call. Not only was he at RST, but he was engaged enough to stand up and challenge the company relative to what was the right thing to do. The result was the company adopting a practice of higher standards. In the Call discussion we noted that God calls us to be a blessing to a company and its customers, employees, and investors. This young man was such a blessing.

CONCLUSION

Proverbs 11:3 gives us the conclusion that a well-developed biblical ethic gives to a leader in business matters. It asserts, "The integrity of the upright shall guide them: but the perverseness of transgressors shall destroy them." May we answer God's call to business with integrity and be a blessing!

Notes

1. Josh. 1:1–9.
2. John 14:27.
3. Luke 22:39–46.
4. Est. 4:13–14 NKJV.
5. Est. 4:15–17.
6. 2 Chron. 2:7 NKJV.
7. 2 Chron. 2:11 NKJV.
8. 2 Chron. 9:8 NKJV.
9. Num. 26:51 (scholars estimate between 2 and 2.5 million people based on the more than six hundred thousand men mentioned in this verse).
10. Josh. 1:9 NKJV. It is worth noting that in verses 1 to 9 God, commanded Joshua to have courage four times.

THREE OFFICES AND THE ENTREPRENEUR

HOW THE CHUCH COMMUNITY HELPS THE BUSINESS LEADER DO WELL BY DOING GOOD

JULIUS KIM

Prior to taking his current position at Westminster Seminary California (WSC), Dr. Kim ministered in a variety of ecclesiastical and academic settings. He has served in Presbyterian Church in America churches in California and Illinois. His current church calling is as Associate Pastor of New Life Presbyterian Church in Escondido, California. While in Illinois, he taught undergraduate communications at Trinity International University and church history at Trinity Evangelical Divinity School. Following a brief tenure as Visiting Scholar with the Faculty of Divinity at Cambridge University, Dr. Kim returned to Southern California to serve as Dean of Students and to teach Practical Theology at WSC.

Dr. Kim also continues to serve the broader Christian community as a preacher, speaker, and ministry consultantHis goals are to contribute both to the church and the academy through his teaching, preaching, and writing. He is the author of The Religion of Reason and the Reason for Religion: John Tillotson and the Latitudinarian Defense of Christianity, 1630–1694 and a contributor to Covenant, Justification, *and* Pastoral Ministry: Essays by the Faculty of Westminster Seminary California and Heralds of the King: Christ-centered Sermons in the Tradition of Edmund P. Clowney.

PHILLIP KIM

Phillip H. Kim is an Assistant Professor of Management and Human Resources at the University of Wisconsin–Madison School of Business. He earned his MA and PhD in Sociology at the University of North Carolina at Chapel Hill and his BS (Economics) and BAS (Materials Sciences) at the University of Pennsylvania. His research and teaching interests focus on the topic of entrepreneurship.

Professor Kim is also a faculty member of the Weinert Center for Entrepreneurship at the Wisconsin School of Business. Through the Center, he advises entrepreneurs on issues related to launching and establishing their businesses, coaches student entrepreneurs as they start their businesses, and teaches service-based entrepreneurship classes. He has also worked as a management consultant advising businesses in the manufacturing, agriculture, professional services, retail, and non-profit sectors. His research has been published in Strategic Entrepreneurship Journal, Small Business Economics, *and* American Behavioral Scientist. *He has received a Best Reviewer Award from the* Journal of Business Venturing.

In a business world beset by greed and dishonesty and a society plagued by brokenness and injustice, can the church of Jesus Christ help the business leader glorify God and promote good? More specifically, what biblical paradigms and practices can pastors and leaders in churches offer to entrepreneurs in order to foster ventures that honor God and benefit their communities? As part of their shepherding task, the leaders of the church have both the privilege and the responsibility to help business leaders of the congregation pursue the practice of truth, goodness, and beauty in their businesses, especially in the context of entrepreneurial opportunities. One way for leaders to do this is by utilizing the biblical paradigm of the prophet, priest and king to aid their members in evaluating and executing their business plans.

This chapter will first present the theological presuppositions that will govern both the analysis of the issues and the implementation of practices; specifically, the biblical paradigm of prophet, priest and king. Second, we will examine entrepreneurship issues with this paradigm. Finally, the chapter will conclude by proposing some practical steps of evaluation and implementation of this paradigm for the church community. It is the hope that this chapter will provide church leaders with more wisdom to shepherd their members for the glory of God and for the good of neighbor.

PRESUPPOSITIONS AND THE THREE OFFICE PARADIGM

In his seminal work on economic sociology, Max Weber argued that the Protestant Reformation of the 16th century influenced the growth and development of capitalism. [1] This proposal, also called the "Weber Thesis," stated that the impulses of a Calvinistic worldview led to the emergence of a society that promoted the accrual of wealth through individual enterprise and investment. He based his argument on what he believed was the influence of a Puritan ethic, which stated that God commands economic stewardship and advancement. This is pictured in the following verses:

Proverbs 22:29, "Do you see a man skilled in his work? He will serve before kings."

Colossians 3:23, "Whatever you do, work at it with all your heart, as working for the Lord, not for men."

History has demonstrated that the Protestant worldview has changed the way people have engaged in business. In fact, it may be argued that the Protestant faith has been a positive influence in the world of business as Christians attempt to integrate their faith with their work. For the purposes of this chapter, we argue that the Protestant Christian worldview, best articulated in the 17th century document, the *Westminster Confession of Faith* (hereafter WCF) and its Larger (WLC) and Shorter (WSC) Catechisms, provides not only a helpful summary of the Protestant Christian worldview as presented in the Bible, but also insightful concepts from which wise and ethical business principles and practices may be extracted.

What then are some of the key truths of a Protestant Christian worldview that positively influence good business practices? While many theological themes can be offered, this chapter will utilize the three-fold designation of prophet, priest and king to describe the fundamental paradigm that presuppose principles for good business practices—especially as it relates to entrepreneurial opportunities.

The Prophet, Priest, and King Paradigm

Christ's redemptive work in his three offices of prophet, priest, and king provides a helpful paradigm in assessing the value and worth of various entrepreneurial opportunities. While not exhaustive, the insights that these three offices and their implications provide will aid church leaders in their discipleship and counseling of those involved in starting and running new business ventures that reveal God's truth, goodness and beauty.

What is Christ's threefold office? Question 23 of the Westminster Shorter Catechism asks, "What offices doth Christ execute as our Redeemer?" The answer states:

Christ, as our Redeemer, executeth the offices of a prophet, of a priest, and of a king, both in his estate of humiliation and exaltation. [2]

From the Old Testament to the New, these three offices have shaped the way God has related to his people, be it Israel or the Church. In fact, without an understanding of these three offices, one cannot fully grasp man's original state, Christ's saving work, and the Church's ministry.[3] This in turn provides a new Gospel-centered paradigm useful for helping members of our congregations who are evaluating, creating, and developing entrepreneurial opportunities.

The Three-fold Office and Man's Original State

Scriptures teach that man as originally created in the image of God (Gen 1:26; cf. WCF 4.2) had true knowledge, holiness, and righteousness. Adam, prior to the Fall, was created in *knowledge* (Col 3:10). That is, he was able to understand God's revelation of himself. When Adam engaged in the naming of the animals, he revealed that he was able to grasp in his mind their true nature and reveal it. As such, he functioned as a *prophet* who was able to <u>discern</u> God's truth, goodness and beauty and <u>testify</u> to it.

Second, Scripture teaches that God originally created Adam in *holiness* (Eph 4:24). Prior to sin entering his heart, man was truly devoted to God, delighting only in him. Though this idea of holiness becomes more pronounced in the Old Testament through the system of worship that God would reveal to Moses, here at the Garden, Adam serves God with a pure heart, wholly consecrated, finding perfect peace and contentment in his creator alone. So he functioned as a *priest*, <u>loving</u> and <u>serving</u> God and his will.

Third and last, Adam was created in the image of God in *righteousness* (Eph 4:24). As a righteous man, he was able to obey God perfectly, doing the perfect will of God without sinning. God gave him the authority and responsibility to rule over everything God had created. Thus, as God's vice-regent, Adam received and exercised dominion over all the earth. In this way he functioned as a *king*, providing <u>peace</u> and <u>order</u> to God's world.

Thus, man, as originally created in the image of God, was to function as a true prophet, true priest and true king over the earth, under the reign and rule of God. In his mind, heart and will (cognition, emotion and volition), man was endowed with the knowledge, holiness, and righteousness to know God and care perfectly for God's world. This was God's intention in the creation of man in his own image. Man, as originally created, was to go about his work within this framework, as a prophet, priest and king. Williamson helpfully summarizes it this way:

Because he knew the Lord's will (as a prophet), and desired to serve Him only (as a priest), he was also able to do works of righteousness as king of creation. Thus we see that it is not really accurate to speak of the image of God in man. It is rather proper to speak of man himself as the very image of God. The image of God was not something in man, or some part of man (the soul). No, man himself—thinking as a prophet, feeling as a priest, and acting as a king—was the image of God.[4]

The Three-fold Office and Christ's Saving Work

Understanding this three-fold designation of man's original state not only helps us understand God's intention at creation, but also the necessity of Christ's work of redemption as the true prophet, priest and king. Scriptures teach that though man was created in this original three-fold state of knowledge, holiness, and righteousness, he fell from that lofty position. WSC Question and Answer 13 states:

> Did our first parents continue in the estate wherein they were created? Our first parents, being left to the freedom of their own will, fell from the estate wherein they were created, by sinning against God (Gen 3:6; cf. WCF 6.1).

As a result of their sin, every aspect of man, his mind, heart and will, became corrupt (Rom 3:10; Gen 6:5; Matt 15:19; cf. WCF 6.2). This corruption, the Bible teaches us, affected all mankind since Adam represented all of humanity (Rom 5:12; Rom 3:23; WCF 6.3). And now, all mankind is justly under the wrath and curse of the Holy God, deserving death for their sin (Rom 6:23; WCF 6.6). But God did not "leave all mankind to perish in the estate of sin and misery" (WSC 20).

> God having, out of His mere good pleasure, from all eternity, elected some to everlasting life, did enter into a covenant of grace, to deliver them out of the estate of sin and misery, and to bring them into an estate of salvation by a Redeemer (WSC 20).

In his great mercy, God chose from the mass of sinful humanity some to be saved from their peril through the work of Jesus Christ the Redeemer—not because of anything they merited, but solely through the unconditional grace of God (Eph 1:4; Rom 3:21-22; WCF 7.3). Christ's work as Redeemer could only be accomplished because Jesus, as the sinless God-man, became the perfect prophet, priest and king, not only fulfilling all of the promises of the Old Testament, but also sacrificing himself for his elect who lost their original knowledge, righteousness and holiness becoming ignorant, guilty and sinful (WCF 7.1).

Christ has become the Savior of the elect through these three offices. Sinful man must *know* through Christ, via his Word and Spirit, that only he can save him. Sinful man must *feel* his need for the cleansing work of Christ's blood. Sinful man must then *live* a life worthy of Christ through the power of Christ. Williamson states it succinctly when he says, "In other words, a man is saved only if, and when, Christ alone becomes his prophet, priest and king." [5]

This is the story of the entire Bible. The New Testament book of Hebrews reveals how Christ united this three-fold designation found within Old Testament people, history and events through his perfect life and ministry. He became a greater prophet than Moses, a greater priest than Aaron, and a greater king than David. And while there is no one clear-cut passage that describes these three offices as relating to Jesus Christ, there nonetheless exists numerous texts that reveal Christ's work through these functions. In Hebrews 1:1-3 Jesus is seen as the final word spoken by God to man superseding the work of the prophets of old. In Hebrews 5:6-10 Jesus is regarded as the high priest par excellence in the line of Melchizedek (c.f., Heb 6:20-10:18). Finally, in passages like 1 Corinthians 15:12-28 and Ephesians 1:19-23 we read of Christ's reign as king over the kingdom God the Father gave to him (c.f., 1 Pet 3:18-22; Rev 1:5, 17-18).

In his book, *The Church*, Edmund Clowney argues persuasively that the three offices of Christ bring together the way in which God himself worked with his covenant people Israel. Regarding the passing of the Old Testament institution of the temple he writes,

> The function of the temple ended with his death. Jesus rose and ascended; our great High Priest entered the Holy of Holies, heaven itself, for us. Hebrews warns us there can be no going back. One final sacrifice for sin has paid the debt forever; once at the end of the ages, Jesus put away sin by the sacrifice of himself. Jesus, the same yesterday, today and forever, is the final Prophet, Priest and King.[6]

Robert Letham echoes the idea that Christ's work cannot be fully understood without the backdrop of the Old Testament institutions: "The structures of

Israel were themselves God-given and revelatory. The priesthood and the sacrificial ritual, prophetism and the word of the Lord, the kingdom and the theocracy were, or had been, integral to the life and experience of Israel." [7]

Thus, the entire Bible and its central story line of God's redeeming work in Christ, cannot be understood apart from the three-fold paradigm of prophet, priest and king. So while it is true that Christ never ascribed to himself any of these offices, seeing Christ's work among humanity through these offices is not only biblical, but also insightful for our task as we attempt to discern the implications of these three offices for business practices that honor God and promote good to neighbor.

When Jesus ministered on earth he revealed some of these implications. As the true and final prophet, he embodied and spoke the truth as no one had ever done before. He himself was the truth and he always spoke the truth. As the true and final priest, he offered himself as the once-for-all sacrifice on the cross though he was holy and blameless. As the true and final king, he possessed all authority and rule with order over men and creation. Dead men were raised to life and the winds and waves obeyed him. And now, from heaven, Christ continues his ministry not only through his Word and Spirit, but especially through his bride, the Church. We now turn to examine these three offices in the life and work of the Church.

The Three-fold Office and Church Ministry

This three-fold designation of man's original state and Christ's redemptive work also illuminates the marks of the true Church as a body of believers converted and transformed in knowledge, holiness and righteousness. We see this as the Church faithfully preaches God's word (prophet), rightly administers the sacraments (priest), and properly exercises discipline (king), fulfilling Christ's three-fold ministry. But the ministry of the church at present is one that exemplifies the cross, that is, redemption that comes through weakness and suffering. Glory will come, but for now, we follow "in his steps" by experiencing suffering and then glory.

Under the headship of Christ, these ministries of word, sacrament and nurture are not only advanced through the special offices of the Church (i.e., the ministers, elders, and deacons), but also through the general office of all believers who share in the redemptive work of Christ alone received by the grace of God alone through the instrumentality of faith alone. Thus, believers by virtue of their union with Christ are now redeemed and transformed by Christ to serve God's church and world as prophets, priests and kings.

How do believers exercise their roles as prophets, priests, and kings? Edmund Clowney argues that the New Testament Church continues the work and ministry of Jesus as those who learn from him and ultimately follow him. He states, "Gentiles become full members of God's people because they are joined to Christ, whose death is the only atoning sacrifice for Jew or Gentile. As Adam represented old humanity, bringing death to all, so a new humanity is created in Christ (Rom 5:12ff.)."[8] So, individual believers carry on the three-fold ministry of Christ because of what Christ has done through his sinless life and vindicating resurrection, recreating them in God's original image that was lost at the Fall. They follow "in his steps" in promoting the truth, goodness and beauty of God, preeminently revealed in the Gospel.

In other words, a more robust understanding of the Gospel of Jesus Christ and its implications equips and empowers Christian entrepreneurs to create and operate business ventures that glorify God and promote the common good in our culture. Entrepreneurs thus continue the work of the perfect prophet, priest and king in ministering to God, the Church, and the world. They do so as those redeemed and transformed by the good news of Jesus. They do so as those who believe that this Gospel impacts every aspect of life—even entrepreneurship. They do so as Christ-centered prophets, priests and kings. With these themes in mind, we now turn to evaluating entrepreneurial opportunities within a Gospel three-fold office framework.

THE ENTREPRENEURSHIP AND THE THREE OFFICES

What is Entrepreneurship?

In this section, we define entrepreneurship and provide an approach for thinking about engaging in this type of work from a three-fold office perspective. Entrepreneurship is "the pursuit of opportunity beyond the resources you currently control." [9] This definition implies that entrepreneurship is not only a conceptual exercise; it also is about taking action to transform potential opportunities into viable and sustainable organizations.[10] Organizations exist so that certain goals can be achieved collectively based on efforts of multiple individuals.[11] New organizations may provide the structure for people to tackle challenges bigger than themselves. Starting such organizations also likely requires people to rely on assistance from others.

Entrepreneurship can occur in many forms. For most people, starting and operating a business is simply a way to make a living. Thus, entrepreneurship is a form of work and as one's work, it is tied to their calling. These entrepreneurs are not necessarily aiming to grow their businesses or seek investors nor are they planning for an eventual financial exit (e.g., selling the business for financial gain). Rather than working for someone else, they are starting and running businesses to work for themselves. Some people might pursue entrepreneurship because it is a way to create new products or services or recombine existing ideas into a new way of doing things. As a result, entrepreneurship is a vehicle for creative expression or pursuing a personal passion or hobby.

Evaluating Entrepreneurial Opportunities

People considering entrepreneurship can evaluate potential opportunties along three dimensions. First, promising entrepreneurial opportunities provide attractive solutions to potential users and customers whose needs are unmet by existing options. Entrepreneurs are more likely to attract customers if they are able to resolve their customers' problems in ways that existing solutions are unable to do so. Second, promising entrepreneurial opportunities have qualities in them that contribute broadly to the common good. For Christians, solving problems that address the frailty of the human condition is one way that entrepreneurship aligns their professional and spiritual domains. Third, promising opportunities can be personally rewarding for entrepreneurs to pursue. Entrepreneurs may be captivated by the prospects of developing a business around a specific interest they have. Whether the business opportunity is related to a personal hobby or has formed as a result of certain work experiences, entrepreneurs require a measure of passion to transform their ideas into fruition. At the same time, entrepreneurs need to be authentic and honest about their own abilities and skills so that they pursue opportunities for which they are qualified to tackle or to collaborate with others who are.

Evaluating opportunities is both an art and a science. Of course, not all opportunities are valid ones, and simply having an idea that seems promising to the entrepreneur does not necessarily ensure its success. We argue that for

Christians, evaluating opportunities ought to be more than rational calcula-
tions about financial returns and thwarting competitive threats. Instead, it
should spur deeper reflections. For example, should financial metrics, such
as profitability, income, and return on investment, be the primary criteria
for evaluating opportunities? To what extent should entrepreneurs weigh the
potential societal benefits that result from their ventures? What if there are
no discernable societal benefits – are these opportunities still worth pursuing
for other reasons, such as having the right skills or experience? Should people
be encouraged to seek opportunities that improve the human condition, even
if the returns are not as significant or require a longer investment horizon?
How should entrepreneurs (and those who advise them) evaluate potential
business opportunities and decide which ones to pursue? And what principles should help govern those decisions?

We begin to tackle these questions by presenting some general observations of how the three-fold paradigm of prophet, priest and king may influence the entrepreneur in any stage of life. We then provide some practical
wisdom and encouragement to the church community as they seek to disciple, counsel, and guide three groups of people who are considering a new
business venture: a recent college graduate, a mid-career businessperson, and
a recent retiree.

Prophetic, Priestly and Kingly Entrepreneurship?

Prophetic entrepreneurship involves knowing and revealing God's truth,
goodness and beauty, preeminently revealed in the person and work of Jesus
Christ. This includes such components as hearing and knowing God's will
in his Word, teaching others God's way found in his Word, and speaking
God's truths to the world through the business venture. This requires, of
course, being committed to a life of prayer where God's will and way are
received. By examining the prophetic roles of Adam, Christ and the Church,
we have seen that the Christian entrepreneur was created and redeemed to
discern and testify to God's truth, beauty and goodness, both in word and
deed. The Apostle Paul told the Church in Philippi, "Whatever is true,
whatever is noble, whatever is right, whatever is pure, whatever is lovely,
whatever is admirable—if anything is excellent or praiseworthy—think
about such things (Phil 4:8). Likewise, the Christians in Ephesus were told,
"Therefore, each of you must put off falsehood and speak truthfully to his
neighbor, for we are all members of one body" (Eph 4:25).

Thinking prophetically about entrepreneurship requires Christians to apply their skills and talents creatively to producing excellent products and services that can solve unresolved customer problems or address their unmet needs. An entrepreneurial surgeon, for example, could create and manufacture a medical device that helps alleviate the suffering of many people. A health-conscious parent may partner with local farmers to develop ways to make fresh produce more widely available to low-income neighborhoods so that children living in these areas can eat healthier foods and learn about sustainable growing practices. An engineer can design and market a trendy new electronic device for students to learn math and improve their reading skills. Thus, these prophetic business leaders are pursuing entrepreneurial ventures that provide both the knowledge and disclosure of the truth, goodness and beauty of God. By seeking to know these attributes of God, prophetic entrepreneurs can also align more closely their understanding of God's calling for them with the way they pursue their careers. These entrepreneurs are able to authentically apply their skills and talents in producing high quality products and services that address specific needs or problems experienced by their customers.

Priestly entrepreneurship involves sacrificial service to church and world, following the pattern set by Christ. This includes serving Christians and non-Christians with their time, talent and treasure, both in word and deed ministry. By examining the priestly roles of Adam, Christ and the Church, we have seen that the Christian entrepreneur was created and redeemed to <u>love</u> and <u>serve</u> others sacrificially and mercifully. As the Apostle Paul reminded the Church in Galatia, "Let us not become weary in doing good, for at the proper time we will reap a harvest if we do not give up. Therefore, as we have opportunity, let us do good to all people, especially to those who belong to the family of believers" (Gal 6:9-10). The entrepreneur pursues the way of the cross—allowing the paradigm of serving the 'other' to be a priority in the decision-making process—whoever the 'other' may be in the circle of relationships that the Lord providentially places in our journey, be it local, national, or international.

The business leader thus pursues in the venture the benefits that can come to the 'outsider', the 'stranger' and the 'alien', providing solutions of mercy to those in need, both body and soul. This could happen, for example, when Christ-followers start businesses that engage their local communities for the common good—especially in being a blessing to those segments of the community that are underrepresented and marginalized by other businesses and services. Priestly entrepreneurship requires people to consider opportunities for more than the prospects of financial returns. Priestly entrepreneurs may also want to contribute and become active in local causes, civic groups, and other voluntary associations that are consistent with Kingdom values.

Kingly entrepreneurship involves a life characterized by the <u>peace</u> and <u>order</u> of God's perfect authority and rule. For the believer, this first involves worshipping God regularly according to the structures God has established, that is, the church, and being subject to the accountability and discipline of the church. By examining the kingly role of Adam, Christ and the Church, the Christian entrepreneur seeks to exhibit an active presence and witness of Gospel peace and order through one's life and work. As God told the exiled Israelites in Babylon to "seek the peace and prosperity of the city" (Jer 29:7), the entrepreneur should seek to pursue the peace and justice of God through his venture. The business leader also pursues order and excellence: "Make it your ambition to lead a quiet life, to mind your own business and to work with your hands, just as we told you, so that your daily life may win the respect of outsiders and so that you will not be dependent upon anybody" (1 Thess 4:11-12). Paul here is talking about the "inauspicious yet crucial task of loving and serving our neighbors with excellence." [12]

Thus, entrepreneurs who desire to exhibit kingly qualities in their ventures may be recognized by their peers for characteristics such as excellent customer service, effective human resource practices, and environmentally sustainable operating principles. Kingly entrepreneurs should strive to provide glimpses of the Garden of Eden as they lead their business and become known throughout their communities for doing so. Producing high quality products and services, honoring warranties and assurances, creating jobs, and paying taxes are all ways that kingly entrepreneurship can occur.

It must be noted that all of these goals and pursuits, while admirable, cannot be attained apart from the work of Christ in the life of the believing business leader. The Scriptures teach the undeniable truth that without Christ's work of transforming the believer, inside and out, the business leader lacks both the power and the motivation to be a prophet, priest and king in all of his worship and work. Ultimately, Christians who seek to pursue an entrepreneurial career should do it for the right reasons. The Gospel not only transforms the establishing and execution of entrepreneurial ventures, but it also transforms the entrepreneur, whether a recent graduate, in mid-career, or a recent retiree. Here are some practical words of advice that can be offered to entrepreneurs in these three different stages of life.

The Recent Graduate

Encourage them to be bold in Christ. Encourage them to take risks. Recent graduates are full of energy and often think that they are somewhat invincible. They should use this to their advantage. Help them try out different opportunities and not be afraid to fail because they have less to lose than they realize. They must learn from these experiences, however. As such, they should also seek wise mentors and gain from their knowledge.

As for possible ventures they may pursue, they ought to challenge themselves to develop their life calling around a pressing social problem so that they can devote their career finding ways to address it. This may require travel to other regions worldwide and immersing in different cultures. So challenge young people to dream imaginatively about their careers. Remind them about pressing social problems that are bigger than what they might have experienced personally and how their efforts can help improve the human condition. Show linkages from their personal ambitions to Kingdom values and how their career aspirations tie in. Encourage them to gain relevant experience by working for established businesses or for other young companies. Keep them accountable to their plans by making them informally commit to milestones and personally follow up on their progress. But most of all encourage them to be persistent about their mission of being a prophet, priest and king in their ventures that honors God and provides good for their neighbors.

Mid-Career

Studies show that about 2/3 of working adults in the United States have some ambition to run their own business, but only 40 percent actually experience this during their careers.[13] Mid-career people who harbor such ambitions but have yet to act upon them are in a difficult position. They may have invested significant time, energy, and financial resources into their education and early career development and so may be reluctant to pursue a potentially risky entrepreneurial endeavor that would derail their efforts at achieving certain professional accomplishments. At the same time, they may be juggling family demands (such as caring for young children, negotiating through their children's adolescent years, or tending to their aging parents) with their own professional aspirations. Moreover, financial resources may not be sufficiently available to be deployed towards an entrepreneurial pursuit. Complicating matters even more are the prospects that entrepreneurs are likely to earn substantially less than those who work for someone else, especially over the long-term. [14]

One way to reconcile these conflicting factors is to evaluate one's entrepreneurial interests with one's calling. Tackling an entrepreneurial project might be most meaningful if it is aligned with one's calling. If an alignment exists, one could justify more easily the decision to start a business and leverage his extensive work and life experience and professional relationships to deal with challenges associated with starting and running businesses. As such, help mid-career entrepreneurs process their gifts and experiences so as to maximize their unique prophetic, priestly and kingly calling to glorify God and benefit their communities.

Retiree

The most appealing pathway to entrepreneurship for this life stage may not necessarily be personally starting a business but to serve as a mentor or advisor to younger entrepreneurs. This could be done informally when people seek wisdom or advice on matters of vision or calling or formally by serving as an advisor or director on corporate boards to deal with strategic matters. For concepts that align with their personal calling or mission, those in this life stage can be encouraged to consider providing seed funding or joining investor networks that provide early-stage funding, especially if they have adequate financial resources.

If they decide to start their own business, however, it may be beneficial to bring on board younger talent. These people may harbor entrepreneurial ambitions, but may be reluctant to pursue them on their own. Working with a seasoned leader may provide them with sufficient assurances and wisdom to venture into a start-up situation that is financially viable, God-centered, and beneficial to society. At the same time, the experienced business leader will benefit from the energy and insight of younger leaders.

Evaluation & Implementation of the Three Offices

How can the church community evaluate and implement some of these ideas and practices? Church leadership can accomplish these goals in two ways: ask and act.

Ask

1. What is your church's vision and strategy of discipling business leaders?
2. What is your church's curriculum in preaching, teaching and counseling the three-fold office of prophet, priest and king?
3. What is your church doing to help entrepreneurs connect thinking, feeling, and living out their calling?
4. What are the unique characteristics and needs of your community that would benefit from God-honoring, good-promoting businesses?
5. Who in your church can serve as teachers and mentors of this entrepreneurship program?
6. Who in your church are entrepreneurs that need support and resourcing?

Act

1. Develop and train church leaders as mentors in a biblical theology of entrepreneurship using the three-fold office paradigm.
2. Identify the needs of the community.
3. Identify, train, support and resource entrepreneurs.
4. Network and partner with other like-minded organizations.
5. Pray regularly for the Spirit of Christ to bless the ministry of entrepreneurs.

One organization that has already begun to tackle this challenging yet rewarding work is Redeemer Presbyterian Church of New York City. As part of their *Center for Faith and Work*, the *Entrepreneurship Initiative* was established to "encourage and support entrepreneurs within our congregation who have a bold vision to start a new arts, for-profit, or not-for-profit venture that fosters shalom and brings about gospel-centered renewal to New York City and beyond." [15] Their website lists five different services to church members who seek to become entrepreneurs:

1. The Ei Network: A network of people with skills and experience to mentor, partner, and consult with new ventures and their entrepreneurs.
2. Theological Foundations: A solid Biblical foundation for our role in cultural renewal and God-glorifying approaches to leadership, serving customers, and benefiting society.

3. The Entrepreneurs Fellowship: A monthly meeting aimed at connecting entrepreneurs, new and experienced, in a community.

4. The Business Plan Competition: An annual offering to draw out the best ideas and entrepreneurs from our midst and provide them with visibility, connections, and resources.

5. The Forum: Our gathering of investors and entrepreneurs committed to building a movement of innovative, gospel-centered, culture-renewing institutions and ventures.

Admittedly, most churches will not have the resources to launch a program of this scale. Nonetheless, the ideas presented here can be scaled according to the unique resources and personnel of each church. It is our hope that Redeemer's model will stimulate and encourage the growth of church communities that will glorify God and do good to neighbor as they help Christian business leaders pursue ventures that know, love, and practice the truth, goodness and beauty of God.

CONCLUSION

Several years ago, Christianity Today asked several leading scholars, pastors, and leaders to answer this question: *How can followers of Christ be a counterculture for the common good?* In her essay entitled "Loving the Storm-Drenched," Frederica Mathewes-Green argued that attempting to change the culture would be tantamount to trying to change the weather: while it's possible to influence culture to some degree, it is pointless to try and take over culture and control it. Rather, she states, "God has not called us to change the weather. Our primary task as believers, and our best hope for lasting success, is to care for individuals caught up in the pounding storm."[16]

The best advice you can give to Christian business leaders seeking to start new ventures that promote glory to God and good to neighbor is to utilize the paradigm of prophet, priest and king so that they may discern and testify to the truth, goodness and beauty of God, sacrificially loving and serving God and neighbor, providing peace and order to an otherwise storm-filled existence. And when they do this, Christian entrepreneurs will point weary pilgrim people to a heavenly home where there will be no more greed and dishonesty, brokenness and injustice, tears and sorrow, but only everlasting joy and peace.

Notes

1. *Max Weber, The Protestant Ethic and the Spirit of Capitalism (New York: Scriber & Sons, 1958).*

2. All references to the Westminster Confession, Larger Catechism, and Shorter Catechism are taken from *The Confession of Faith, Together with The Larger Catechism and Shorter Catechism*, 3rd ed. (Atlanta, GA: Committee for Christian Education & Publications, 1990).

3. This section adapted from G. I. Williamson, *The Shorter Catechism: For Study Classes*, vol. 1 (Phillipsburg, NJ: P & R, 1970).

4. Williamson, *The Shorter Catechism*, 38.

5. Williamson, 87.

6. E. Clowney, *The Church* (Downers Grove, IL: InterVarsity Press, 1995), 45.

7. R. Letham, *The Work of Christ* (Downers Grove, IL: InterVarsity Press, 1993), 20.

8. E. Clowney, *The Church*, 43.

9. H. Stevenson, "*The Heart of Entrepreneurship*," Harvard Business Review (March-April 1985), 85-94.

10. W. Gartner. "A Conceptual Framework for Describing the Phenomenon of New Venture Creation," *Academy of Management Review* (October 1985), 696-706.

11. H. Aldrich, *Organizations and Environments* (Stanford, CA: Stanford Business Books, 2007).

12. Michael S. Horton, "How the Kingdom Comes," *Christian Vision Project*, http://www.christianvisionproject.com/2006/01/how_the_kingdom_comes.html.

13. H. Aldrich and M. Ruef, *Organizations Evolving* (London: Sage Publications, 2006); G. Steinmetz and E. Wright. "The Fall and Rise of the Petty Bourgeoisie: Changing Patterns of Self-Employment in the Postwar United States," *American Journal of Sociology* 94(5): 973-1018, 1989.

14. B. Hamilton, "Does Entrepreneurship Pay? An Empirical Analysis of the Returns of Self-Employment," *Journal of Political Economy* 108(3): 604-631, 2000.

15. www.faithandwork.org/ei

16. F. Mathewes-Green, "Loving the Storm Drenched," *Christian Vision Project*, http://www.christianvisionproject.com/2006/03/loving_the_stormdrenched_1.html.

SOME BIBLICAL
CONTRIBUTIONS TO
BUSINESS ETHICS

GALEN RADEBAUGH

Galen Radebaugh recently retired as Vice President, Pharmaceutical Sciences, of Pfizer Research. With over thirty-two years of international R&D experience in several major pharmaceutical companies, he has helped develop and commercialize over twenty-five new products that have improved people's lives, including: Asmanex, Clarinex, Lipitor, Nasonex, Neurontin, PEG Intron, Protonix, Relistor, Tylenol Extended Release, and Zetia. He has managed multicultural organizations on three continents and worked with government regulatory authorities across the globe.

Doctor Radebaugh obtained his PhD in Pharmaceutics from the University of Connecticut and his BS in Pharmacy from the University of Michigan. He is an inventor on fourteen primary patents for novel drug delivery systems, has authored or coauthored over seventy technical publications and book chapters, and has been a frequent invited speaker at national and international pharmaceutical conferences.

VERN POYTHRESS

Vern S. Poythress earned a BS in mathematics from California Institute of Technology (1966) and a PhD in mathematics from Harvard University (1970). After teaching mathematics for a year at Fresno State College (now California State University at Fresno), he became a student at Westminster Theological Seminary, where he earned an MDiv (1974) and a ThM in apologetics (1974). He received an MLitt in New Testament from University of Cambridge (1977) and a ThD in New Testament from the University of Stellenbosch, Stellenbosch, South Africa (1981).

He has been teaching in New Testament at Westminster Theological Seminary in Philadelphia since 1976. In 1981 he was ordained as a teaching elder in the Reformed Presbyterian Church Evangelical Synod, which has now merged with the Presbyterian Church in America. Doctor Poythress studied linguistics and Bible translation at the Summer Institute of Linguistics in Norman Oklahoma in 1971 and 1972, and taught linguistics at the Summer Institute of Linguistics in the summers of 1974, 1975, and 1977. He has published books on Christian philosophy of science, theological method, dispensationalism, biblical law, hermeneutics, Bible translation, and Revelation.

Ow does the Bible guide us in the midst of business decisions? We have provided three case studies from the pharmaceutical industry that illustrate the consequences of decisions and actions by the company and government regulators. The cases studies are:

1. Eisai Medical Research, Inc., and decisions and actions surrounding the marketing of a popular medicine for treatment of the symptoms of Alzheimer's disease in late 2009
2. McNeil Consumer Products Company (a division of Johnson & Johnson) and the decisions and actions surrounding tampering with Extra Strength Tylenol Capsules in 1982 and 1984
3. McNeil Consumer Healthcare (a division of Johnson & Johnson) and decisions and actions surrounding the manufacture of OTC drug products in 2008 and 2009

These case studies were selected because they are: current (Cases 1 and 3); well documented in public government records (Cases 1 and 3); in the press and widely known (Case 2); and in a state where decisions were made with defined consequences. They were also selected because the pharmaceutical industry operates within a framework of governmental laws, regulations, and guidance documents that are often subject to interpretation. Because the laws, regulations, and guidance documents are not always black and white, the industry must often make decisions about the "gray" areas. It is usually the gray areas that present the most difficult decisions, and where companies spend significant effort "managing risk."

To help companies and their employees make decisions about the gray areas of the law and better manage risk, companies have created many internal statements and policies to aid employees in making the right decisions. Typically, they fall into one of two categories—*Company Values* or *Codes of Conduct.*

COMPANY VALUES

1. quality
2. integrity
3. respect for people
4. community
5. collaboration/teamwork

6. leadership
7. performance
8. innovation

Codes of Conduct

1. accuracy of public disclosures
2. advertising and promotional standards
3. antitrust and competition
4. business records and internal controls
5. conflicts of interest
6. environmental, health, and safety laws
7. false reporting to government agencies
8. food, drug, and medical device laws
9. gifts and entertainment policy
10. improper payments in the public and private sectors
11. standards on relationships with medical professionals
12. intellectual property and confidential information
13. international trade controls
14. discrimination in employment and unlawful harassment
15. money laundering
16. political contributions
17. privacy laws
18. securities transactions

But even with all these policies and procedures, poor decisions are still made and companies suffer the legal, public, and financial consequences.

In all fairness to the companies listed above, it must be noted that the FDA also issues dozens of Warning Letters every year to other companies for similar circumstances. Our intent is not to criticize or commend these particular companies, but to use them as examples of the decision making that occurs in the pharmaceutical industry. Reference materials for cases are presented in the appendix to this paper.

The presentation of the cases in Part I comes primarily from Dr. Radebaugh, while reflections on biblical principles in Part II come primarily from Dr. Poythress.

Part I: Cases

Case Study 1

This case study is based on a Warning Letter from the U.S. FDA, which is posted on the FDA Web site and is reproduced in the appendix at the end of this article. The company's response to the letter is classified as confidential.

Setting: A prescription pharmaceutical company, Eisai Medical Research, Inc., received a Warning Letter from the FDA in early 2010 for misleading advertising for a drug product (Aricept) to treat mild to moderate Alzheimer's disease.

General findings: The company was accused by the U.S. FDA of violating the Federal Food, Drug, and Cosmetic Act and the 21 CFR 202.1 by overstating the efficacy of the drug, thereby misbranding the drug.

Specific findings: The company created TV ads that depicted patients with Alzheimer's symptoms, before and after use of Aricept. The FDA accused the company of presenting drastic improvements in the patient's cognitive abilities that were not supported by the clinical data.

Requesting Action: The company was requested to immediately cease disseminating promotional materials that violate the law.

Possible Ethical Questions: (1) Did the company knowingly violate the law by overstating efficacy, or did the company in good faith interpret the clinical data differently than the FDA did? (2) Did the company knowingly violate the law on the assumption that the temporary use of the TV ads would give financial benefits that would outweigh the potential penalties? (3) What policies did the company have in place to guide employees in their decision making, and were they adequate? (4) What is the moral authority for the policies? (5) What reward system was in place for the employees, and did it provide incentive to make the decisions that were made? (6) If the ads were the result of a good faith difference of opinion, how will the company learn from this experience so that the violation does not occur again?

Biblical Questions: (1) Does the Bible provide clear guidance such that, if known and followed, it would have prevented this violation of the law? (2) How would the Bible help navigate the "gray" areas of the law that are subject to interpretation? (3) How can biblical principles be built into company policies?

Case Study 2

This case study is based on many press reports. Even today, this case study is taught in business schools as a model for effective crisis management.

Setting: In 1982, several bottles of Tylenol Extra Strength Capsules were tampered with through the addition of cyanide, and placed on pharmacy shelves in the Chicago area. Seven people died from ingesting the cyanide-laced capsules from the tampered-with bottles. In 1984, a second round of tamperings occurred, but there were no known deaths as a result of these tamperings.

General findings: The major product of a leading consumer health care company, McNeil Consumer Products of Johnson & Johnson, was a victim of external tampering that caused death to unsuspecting customers. The company was faced with the dilemma of resolving the problem without damaging/destroying the reputation of the company and its most profitable product. Based on the principles of the J&J Credo, putting public safety first as opposed to the company, the company reacted to the tamperings in such a way that public trust in the product and the company was restored.

Company Actions: In the first round of tamperings, bottles of Tylenol Extra Strength Capsules were purchased from Chicago area pharmacies and tampered with by replacing the contents of the hard gelatin capsules with cyanide. The bottles were then placed back on pharmacy shelves and purchased by unsuspecting customers. Some customers who did not notice the tampering died from ingesting capsules laced with cyanide. The perpetrator of the crime was not apprehended and convicted. Even though the company was not responsible for the tamperings, it assumed responsibility for public safety. As a remedy, the company recalled all products that had left the factory (31 million bottles) and replaced them at no cost to the public (in excess of $100 million cost to the company). In addition, it began selling the capsules in tamper-evident packaging. In the second round of tamperings (viewed by some as copycat tamperings), there were no deaths, but a crisis of confidence in the product was rekindled in the public. Again the product was recalled and replaced at company expense. Because the company could not develop technology that could prevent the hard gelatin capsules from being emptied and refilled with poisons, it withdrew the hard gelatin capsule from the market and replaced it with caplet-shaped solid tablets. Due to company decisions and actions (senior management embracing the J&J Credo), confidence in the product and the company was restored. The Tylenol tamperings have become a textbook business example of how a company successfully managed a crisis, using the ethical principles of its credo, and prevented irreparable damage to the company and a major product.

Ethical Questions: (1) Could the company have made the same business decisions without the Credo? (2) What is it about the Credo that guided the senior executives in their decision making?

Biblical Questions: (1) Does the J&J Credo embrace biblical principles, and if so, which ones? (2) How could the Bible help guide decision making and enhance the principles of the Credo?

Case Study 3

This case study is based on documents posted on the FDA Web site, namely, an FDA Warning Letter and the company's response to the Warning Letter. The documents are reproduced in the appendix at the end of this article.

Setting: On January 15, 2010, McNeil Consumer Healthcare received a Warning Letter from the FDA for violation of quality regulations in the manufacture of various OTC drug products. Multiple products were recalled from the marketplace as a result of violations.

General findings: In 2008 and 2009, the company became aware of product contamination (via complaints from consumers of "uncharacteristic odors" and gastrointestinal distress) that led to the recall of several lots of Tylenol Arthritis Relief Caplets. The company determined that the odor was due to the presence of TBA, which is a degradant of TBP, a pesticide used to treat wooden pallets for transporting packaging materials. The FDA expressed concern about the company's response to the problem, based on timeliness, thoroughness, and resolution of the issues. FDA deemed that management at J&J and McNeil Consumer did not take appropriate action to ensure the quality, safety, and integrity of its products. Additional consequences are that FDA may withhold approval of export certificates, or approval of new products until the violations are corrected, and quality management systems are put in place that ensure compliance with FDA regulations.

Requested Actions: The company was requested to recall additional products, and put quality management systems in place to ensure compliance with FDA regulations. The product could not be manufactured until the TBA problem was resolved.

Ethical Questions: (1) Given that the J&J Credo that existed in 1982, still existed in 2009, why was the response to this crisis handled differently than the Tylenol tampering crisis in 1982 and 1984? (2) Did the Credo cover this situation? What is needed besides written credos and policies? (3) In addition to the Credo, were there written compliance policies that should have covered this situation? Why were they not followed? (4) Were these issues the result of poor management and/or a deficiency in moral judgment?

Biblical Questions: (1) Did the company violate or compromise biblical principles? (2) What guidance could the Bible have provided that might have remediated the situation sooner or prevented it from happening?

Part II: Reflection on Biblical Principles

Let us begin with Case Study 1, which involved Eisai. The FDA accused Eisai of misleading advertising for a drug product, Aricept, which is used in treating Alzheimer's disease.

The Eisai case at first glance may appear to be one-dimensional. The advertising by overreaching violated specific federal statutes, namely the FD&C Act and 21 CFR 202. The most obvious ethical issue, then, is the principle of obedience to the authority of civil government, which is expounded most fully in the Bible in Romans 13:1–10, but also comes up for discussion elsewhere (1 Peter 2:13–17) and is one aspect of a larger issue of submission to authorities of various kinds (Eph. 5:21–6:9; 1 Peter 2:18–3:6; Ex. 20:12; Deut. 17:8–20).

Several Dimensions in Ethical Responsibility

This case contains greater complexity than what appears on the surface. A closer inspection reveals several dimensions. To begin with, we must deal with the issue of truth. The Bible stresses the importance of telling the truth (Ex. 20:16; Ps. 101:7; Prov. 6:19; 8:7; 12:17, 19; 14:5, 25; 19:5, 9; Eph.4:25). Did the advertising do that? Moreover, TV advertising includes a visual element, and the visual accompaniment of words can suggest much more than the words convey in themselves. What did the visual accompaniment suggest? Did it suggest more than the product could deliver?

Because of the power of visual imagery, we need also to ask about the potential for manipulation. Viewers may be enticed and lured into interest in the product not because of the virtues of the product but because of the humorous mood or the pleasant smiles or scenes of happy family activity. The advertiser needs a larger biblical view of the world and of fellow human beings, a view that would remind him that he should regard the client with respect as a human being, and not as a virtually subhuman object to be trapped into a commitment against his better judgment.

On the other hand, we should take into account the larger context of modern advertising. Decades of TV advertising have created a cultural context in which most viewers are sophisticated. Many viewers, one might suggest, know some of the aims and techniques of advertising, and have developed a distant attitude that makes them resistant to manipulation. They may have a kind of tacit bargain with the advertiser: If you the advertiser present something humorous, clever, or engaging, I in return will consent to devote a little attention to what you have to say about your product. I know beforehand that you are going to present your product in the most favorable light, and not introduce all possible qualifications or drawbacks. That is part of the "game" that I the viewer and you the advertiser play. Given that context, the advertiser has considerable freedom.

We can also explore the aspect of promising that belongs to many advertisements. Some advertising may make direct promises: "We promise that if you buy our product, you will see improvement within three days, and you will be satisfied with your purchase." Much advertising is less direct, but still contains an implicit element of promise. Promises are a specific kind of commitment that has ties with the broader area of personal responsibility and commitment making. The Bible expresses this commitment making through its discussion of "covenants." God makes covenants with various human beings. God is a person who can make commitments. We as human beings made in His image can also make commitments. We are responsible for those commitments, by analogy with the central commitments that come to expression in God's covenants. What implicit commitments did the advertising make, and were these commitments that the product could realistically fulfill? (The FDA letter to Eisai notes that the Eisai ads include "the superimposed text, 'Individual results may vary,'" but states that this inclusion "does not mitigate these misleading presentations" [p. 4].)

The joint presence of many dimensions in advertising makes moral evaluation more complex. In this case study, Dr. Radebaugh legitimately raises the question of whether someone in Eisai was deliberately violating the statutory rules, or whether the advertisement fell in a "gray" area and was not clearly in violation. Was the conflict due to two distinct interpretations of the statutes, one by the FDA and one by Eisai? If so, did the FDA allow any discussion or appeal of its initial ruling? If it did allow discussion, officials within Eisai would have to employ wisdom to decide whether to pursue further discussion or just concede the case.

The case also contains many challenges about the internal processes at Eisai. What procedures and relationships among the employees at Eisai led to the initial decision to go forward with the advertising? If we are seeking to be guided by biblical principles, we should try not only to find ways to express elements of biblical ethics in company procedures and guidelines, but also to help the individual employees and clusters of employees to grow in discernment when confronted with similar issues in the future. We must be concerned for the people (the principle of love) as well as the rules (moral standards).

In particular, Dr. Radebaugh asks, "What was the reward system that was in place, and did it provide incentive to violate the law?" The Bible is realistic about sin. The Lord's Prayer includes the petition, "Lead us not into temptation" (Matt. 6:13 KJV), partly because sin does root itself in people's hearts. Whether we are Christians or not, we are prone to temptation (James 1:14–15). Companies need to be realistic about fallen human nature. If company policies promise rewards for concrete accomplishments, such as advertising, but provide no specific incentives with respect to the issues of violating the law or lying or dealing underhandedly, the reward system may end up undermining any verbal policies that have nice-sounding moral phraseology but no "teeth," no "bite" within the company's system of rewards.

The concern for people also comes to the surface in Dr. Radebaugh's question, "How will the company learn from this experience so that the violation does not occur again?" If patterns of policy and behavior have become systematically entrenched, it may not be enough simply to say to the guilty party, "Don't do it again!" Taking more time to understand how things go wrong is not only the kind thing to do for the people involved, but may also be the wise thing to do for the long-term benefit of the company as a whole, since it may uncover ways in which the broader atmosphere and morale of the employees can be influenced for the better.

Such efforts are particular important when we deal with "gray" areas in which civil laws leave room for interpretation. Companies and employees have a natural tendency to interpret any gray areas in their favor. Up to a point, this latitude in interpretation may be legitimate. Those who make the laws are reasonable, and want to allow space for legitimate advertising that stresses a product's positive features. But employees under pressure may easily slide into unreasonable "bending" of the law, or even deliberate violation. Internal company discussion needs to address these temptations frankly and realistically.

Perspectives

A complex, multidimensional situation like this one demands not only attention to biblical standards for ethics, but creativity in discerning how standards come to bear on a particular business situation. Creativity can be enhanced if we use multiple perspectives on a situation. John Frame's work on biblical ethics presents a biblical basis for three main perspectives, which he has termed the *normative* perspective, the *existential* (or *personal*) perspective, and the *situational* perspective.[1]

The *normative* perspective asks about the norms, the ethical rules that bear on human living. The Ten Commandments are a summary of God's norms. In the Eisai case, norms include obedience to civil authority, coming to focus in the fifth commandment (Ex. 20:12), and telling the truth, coming to focus in the ninth commandment (Ex. 20:16).

The *personal* perspective focuses on the persons in the situation and their motives. In the Eisai case, we ask whether an employee deliberately violated a statute, and whether the reward system unwittingly encouraged the pursuit of unethical motives.

The *situational* perspective focuses on the situation: Eisai is a prescription drug company working in U.S. territory, subject to particular statutes with respect to drug advertising. The situation includes the "culture" of advertising and viewer expectations, as well as the "culture" of Eisai, including policies it may have in place specifying ethical standards, the answerability of employees to superiors, and the responsibility of the company as a whole to its board and stockholders.

These three perspectives do not come out of thin air. Biblical ethics gives us norms, in the Ten Commandments. It tells us to pay attention to persons (the principle of love), including God, who is the most important Person in our lives. It tells us to pay attention to our situation when it commands us to bless others, to do good, and to promote the glory of God (Rom. 12:14; 1 Peter 3:9; 4:19; 1 Cor. 10:31). These three aspects—norms, persons, and situation—fit together, because God gives us the norms, He created us as persons, and He providentially controls our situations. He has promised that we will never be in a situation where we have no good alternative, where we are "compelled" to sin (see 1 Corinthians 10:13). But situations may be difficult. It may sometimes look as if we have no alternatives.

Each of the three perspectives is actually a perspective on the whole of ethics. The norms tell us to pay attention to persons and to motives, and therefore they implicitly include the personal perspective. The norms also tell us to pay attention to our situations, and to exercise discernment (Phil. 1:9). Thus the normative perspective points to the situational perspective. Similarly, the situational perspective points to the normative perspective. God is the most important person in our situation, so a robust consideration of the situation includes God. It therefore includes God's norms (His evaluations) as well. The same holds for all three perspectives. It is nevertheless useful to have all three, because we may then be encouraged to notice what we may have previously overlooked. The personal perspective tells us to pay attention to employees' motives, their temptations to sin, and the way in which a reward system may unwittingly encourage improper behavior.

Divine Resources

The intersection of moral standards (norms) with situations leads to pressure on people, and people need the resources of Christ. Jesus Christ Himself was fully man, and He did not ever sin. He faced the uniquely difficult situation of his crucifixion and death. Hebrews reminds us that "we do not have a high priest who is unable to sympathize with our weaknesses, but one who in every respect has been tempted as we are, yet without sin" (Heb. 4:15 ESV). It also exhorts us to pray: "Let us then with confidence draw near to the throne of grace, that we may receive mercy and find grace to help in time of need" (Heb. 4:16 ESV). We have access to God through Christ our high priest, and through Him we "may receive mercy and find grace to help." Specifically, it is "help in time of need." These promises hold for a person in Eisai dealing with a tempting opportunity to advertise Aricept, or people in McNeil Consumer Products dealing with contaminated products.

The "help" can take the form of sustenance when we are tempted to do something that is clearly wrong (as might have been the case with the Eisai example). It can also take the form of sustenance emotionally and spiritually when company executives must face a crisis that is not at all their fault (McNeil, 1982 and 1984), when perhaps they feel that it is all "unfair" and may be tempted to despair. And it can take the form of a renewed creativity and boldness that fellowship with God supplies. God the Creator is the source of creativity, and we are meant to be bold in following his ways even when we cannot see how it will turn out for good ("We walk by faith, not by sight" [2 Cor. 5:7 ESV]).

This boldness in doing good has particular relevance in addressing business temptations to cut corners, morally speaking, for the sake of short-term gains in money, power, or prestige. In 1982 and 1984 the officials at McNeil could easily have argued to themselves that money was all-important and that it was too expensive (more than $100 million in 1982) to recall all the Tylenol. Instead, they followed the hard course of recalling the bottles. But in the long run, this hard course helped the company by restoring public confidence.

Or consider the Eisai case. Dr. Radebaugh asked, "Did the company knowingly violate the law on the assumption that the temporary use of the TV ads would give financial benefits that would outweigh the potential penalties?" The situation becomes even more tempting if no clear violation of law is at stake. For example, it appears that in 2008 and 2009 McNeil made at least a minimal effort to solve the problem of contamination with TBA. Presumably key officials within McNeil thought that they had solved the problem through minimal investigations and minimal changes, and this minimum would have been justified as monetarily the best solution. But it proved inadequate.

We can see the same issue rise again when we consider the importance of looking at employee motives, employee relationships, and employee morale. The personal perspective invites us to pay attention to these dimensions. In the long run, paying attention to these dimensions helps a company. But in the short run it may look like an unnecessary bother. The one-dimensional businessperson may tell himself that he needs to go full steam ahead, caring only about profit, not about the employees.

The temptations also increase when business employees tell themselves, "No one will ever know." Or at least "no one will ever know until I am long out of the picture." They may tell themselves, "No harm will come to the public, and in the meantime I increase the company's profit and enhance my own career prospects." It is a useful antidote to remind oneself in response, "God knows. Christ knows." And also God controls situations. He controls monetary success and company reputation as well as having authority over ethical standards. In many instances doing the right thing ethically, as McNeil attempted in 1982 and 1984, issues eventually in situational changes that are a blessing to the company. Proverbs is full of examples reminding us that following God's way can lead to blessing, often in this life as well as in the next. But we cannot guarantee company success by some kind of ironclad mechanics of the marketplace. The company employee in a tight spot must believe God, even when he cannot by sheer calculation of future consequences assure himself that the outcome will be prosperous.

The Universal Claims of Christ

I have framed the discussion in Christian terms. I believe that only in this way can we fully appreciate the resources found in the Bible. Let me further expand the horizons by reflecting on the larger salvific context given by the Bible, within which we carry on ethical decision making.

The Bible is not designed by God merely to be a moral handbook, to give us some boundaries for ethics. It does indeed give us moral norms. It also shows that the norms lead to personal and situational perspectives on ethics.

But in addition, it is a book communicating salvation. The gospel is "the power of God for salvation to everyone who believes" (Rom. 1:16 ESV). At its center is the salvation accomplished by Jesus Christ, the great high priest (Heb. 4:15). This salvation is an exclusive salvation, found only in Christ (John 14:6; Acts 4:12). Only in Christ are we going to find the "mercy" and "grace" we need (Heb. 4:15–16), in the sphere of business as well as in every other area of life. Ethics cannot be detached from God. And God is the God who opens access to Himself only through Christ. Through Him we receive power that transforms our hearts, that clarifies our moral compass, that enables us to do what is right, and that stimulates us to find ways to bless others around us.

Furthermore, we learn from the Bible that Christ is Lord of all of life, not merely a narrowly "religious sphere": "All authority in heaven and on earth has been given to me" (Matt. 28:18 ESV; see also Ephesians 1:20–22). All of life should be in service to Christ. The person who is a disciple of Christ has committed everything to Him (Luke 14:26–27, 33). We are never "off duty." Leisure, rest, and family activities as well as work belong to Him. Every aspect of business rightly belongs to Him. Today we have popular language about "full-time Christian service," but in actuality every Christian is supposed to be serving Christ all the time. The issue of who is paying for our service is secondary. Loving God with all our hearts implies that we are to be loving Him all the time. Thus, the Bible challenges us not merely with respect to a few ethical principles, which might apply only in a few scattered situations, but all the time, in all activities. Our motives and our actions always have an ethical dimension. And God the Judge of all evaluates all human motives and actions. The goal for life is not merely individualistic or private, but universal allegiance to Christ throughout the world, "so that at the name of Jesus every knee should bow, in heaven and on earth and under the earth, and every tongue confess that Jesus Christ is Lord, to the glory of God the Father" (Phil. 2:10–11 ESV). This universal allegiance includes in principle the transformation of the whole world of business, to bring it to display the glory of Christ.[2]

The Pluralistic Challenge

The exclusiveness of salvation in Christ and the absoluteness of His claims create real challenges in a pluralistic world. How do we negotiate these challenges? The obvious answer is the one that Hebrews 4:15–16 already gives: God in Christ must provide power, wisdom, creativity, humility, and boldness, to invigorate us to face the challenges. There is a way through, even if we do not yet see it.

We also have examples in Scripture of people who lived in pluralistic situations or lived in faith to God in situations of idolatry. We can look at Joseph in Egypt (Gen. 39–50), Daniel and his three friends in Babylon (Dan. 1–6), Jeremiah's and Ezekiel's messages to exiles in Babylon, Esther in Persia, Paul in the Roman Empire, and the instructions in the New Testament letters, which are directed to Christians, who were a minority. Throughout history, exemplary disciples did not compromise their faith, and at the same time they became a testimony and a blessing to pagans around them.

Bridge Building with Pluralism

The Bible provides resources for navigating modern pluralism. But in our own thinking we should assess realistically the deep differences that stem from religious commitments rather than paper them over. Christ is Lord over all, whether non-Christians are aware of it or not. They owe allegiance to Him as universal Lord, and they are guilty of rebellion whether they are aware of it or not. The Bible tells us that people are either in rebellion against God or in submission to Him. The world of people is divided by this great divide. The transition from rebellion to submission comes from God's work of salvation, which takes place through Christ. There is no other way.

Much of modern pluralism does not like these truths. It likes neither the exclusiveness of Christ's claims, nor His universal Lordship, nor the separation between followers and opponents of Christ. But in principle Christians are in a better position than anyone else to live in pluralistic situations, because they know the actual situation. They know that Christ is Lord and Judge (Acts 17:31). They recognize that the need for salvation extends into the specific of the business world and every other sphere of life. They can look with honesty at the depth of the difficulties that come with human disagreements. Moreover, the Christian message tells us to love our enemies, and to be agents of reconciliation in the midst of painful differences (2 Cor. 5:18–21). The opportunities are great.

Many dimensions go into the foundations for bridge building:

1. All people are made in the image of God (Gen. 1:26–28). We have a foundation for sympathy and understanding.
2. All people, even people who are deeply wrong in their ideas or in their actions, can still be respected for what they were created to be (James 3:9).

3. All people except Christ in His human nature have been caught in the tangle of sin. They are guilty before God (Rom. 3:23; 6:23). The effects of sin are radical, and influence us in every aspect of life. Followers of Christ should not present themselves as morally superior or proud, but as those who themselves still confront temptations and need forgiveness. And we should demonstrate the reality of the forgiveness we receive by our readiness to forgive others (Matt. 6:12, 14–15).

4. All people know God, though in rebellion they try to suppress the truth about God (Rom. 1:18–25).

5. All people have a sense of right and wrong, though that sense can be twisted by sin (Rom. 1:32; 2:14–15).

6. All people have longings that can only be fulfilled in communion with God, but which people vainly try to fulfill with idolatrous substitutes (Rom. 1:21–25). These substitutes can include not only the worship of images (physical idols) that took place in the ancient world, but heart commitments to false religions or to secular goals that are made into ultimate commitments, goals such as money, power, fame, sex, pleasure, or even the goal of being a morally admirable, "good" person.[3] These idolatrous goals crop up in the business world as well as all other areas of life.

7. God is gracious to both good and evil people. People get better than they deserve. And this graciousness of God includes restraint of sin. People are not as bad in practice as their sinful rebellion could lead them to be. Non-Christians, as well as Christians, accomplish good things in the world. This graciousness of God to people outside Christ has been called "common grace."

8. Christ is universal Lord, and is Savior of all who place their trust in Him. The offer of salvation goes out to all.

These various commonalities can serve as bridges for communication and encouragement of others in the workplace, even when opportunity does not arise for Christians to explain all the dimensions of their own understanding of God and the world.

Discussion of the Eisai Case

We may take the Eisai case as an example. Suppose Sue is a Christian employee of Eisai and participates in the internal discussion within Eisai responding to the FDA. She employs the three perspectives on ethics: normative, personal, and situational. From the normative perspective, she brings into the discussion the principles of obedience to civil government, truth-telling, fulfilling promises, and endeavoring to serve customers (customers being one form of "neighbor" in biblical terminology). All of these principles are found in the Bible. All of these principles come from God, who is sovereign Creator and who created each individual with a moral sense (conscience).

Sue knows these things more clearly and more accurately because she has instruction from the Bible. But even people with no contact with the Bible know these truths dimly. God has given to each human being a conscience, a moral sense, and some knowledge of God and His character. Moral principles have probably been written into some of the specific policy statements that Eisai already has in place. Sue can at many points agree with both general policy statements and the individual convictions of fellow employees about what is the right thing for the company to do, even if the individual employees and the authors of the policy statements are not Christians. The policy statement from Johnson & Johnson, "Our Credo," is a good example of the operation of common grace. The policies formulated there are in accord with biblical principles, though no direct appeal is made to the Bible.

But Sue may also find points of sensitivity and potential conflict. Individuals will not always agree about what is right, even on the level of more general principles. Even if people have a measure of agreement on a general principle, their views on the implementation of the principle may differ. For example, just how does the principle of truth-telling intersect the principle of serving the company by maximizing its success? And under what circumstances is it permissible to "shade" the truth without falling into a blatant lie? The company policy statements may be morally flawed; or they may be so general that their implications for advertising Aricept are not clear.

Sue should recognize, on the basis of the teaching of the Bible about her own imperfections and the possibility of self-deceit (Jer. 17:9), that she herself is not perfect in moral discernment. When her judgment differs from someone else's, she needs to listen respectfully, not merely assume that she is superior because she is a Christian. Christian grace includes humility. On the other hand, Sue should recognize that the direct instruction of the Bible, and the work of the Holy Spirit in purifying her conscience, gives her potentially an advantage in the clarity of her moral discernment. She can in many situations become a moral leader. On occasion, she may have to stand for obedience to God even when everyone else opposes her.

Sue's interaction with other people in Eisai must also use the personal perspective. People matter. Eventually some decision has to be made, one way or the other. But Sue should be eager to express respect to others with whom she disagrees ("speaking the truth in love" [Eph. 4:15 ESV]), no matter whose opinions win out in one particular case. Building bridges to people, and not merely narrowly "getting the job done," form part of her responsibility. Sue can find a foundation for bridge building in the commonality of human nature, made in the image of God, and in the biblical principle of respecting human beings with whom she disagrees.

Sue also looks at the situation. She wants to take into account the limitations that exist because a company like Eisai is a public company set up with guidelines and specifications. She wants to consider the situation involved in the process leading to the production of the advertising, and consider possible alterations that will head off a repetition of the same mistake in the future. For her as a Christian, knowing the reality of temptation, it should be natural to ask, "What reward system was in place, and did it provide incentive to violate the law?" Others can join with her in this discussion because considerations of this kind make good practical sense, even if the others do not consciously operate from a biblically grounded framework.

The Inescapability of God and of Christian Redemption

But the reality of deep differences ought also to be faced. Sue knows that Christ as Lord makes universal claims, not merely on her but even on non-Christians. Those claims are normative, and they are also part of the situation. Sue has to reckon with these realities, even though others do not accept them. Sue does not merely fit in. She has a different knowledge of the total "situation." In addition, things that are going on in her mind and her spirit do not match "the world," that is, the world in rebellion against God (1 John 2:15–17; John 15:18–21).

Moral standards go back to God. Persons and their value go back to God, who created them. If Sue is following the Bible's instruction, she learns to think about the world in personal terms, with God as a person at the center. Moral standards are not just abstract principles sitting in the air, but reflect the character of a personal God. Knowing God the infinite person helps in discerning the meaning and applicability of His standards to difficult cases and so-called gray areas where the implications of a particular federal statute may not be crystal clear. Non-Christians also, as we have observed, know God inescapably (Rom. 1:21). But their knowledge is clouded and problematic. That will have effects on their understanding of moral principles, including principles of obeying authority and principles of truth-telling. The effects may be very subtle; but at times they may also be dramatic. Sue needs to be instructed by the Bible at this point, and not to be naive about the reality of differences.

Sue's personal perspective also includes her communion with God. She should be devoting herself to God in body and in spirit throughout the day's activities (Rom. 12:1–2). She can offer up praises and petitions. She may be praying for God-honoring decisions within Eisai, for God-honoring ethical principles, and for God to work in the people in Eisai. She prays for people to come to know Christ as Savior, because that is the foundational remedy not only for individuals but for the world, including the "world" of business. At the same time, short of that fundamental change, she prays for incremental changes that are in line with biblical principles.

Significance of Differences

We may wonder about the reasons for the differences in the earlier and later cases that confronted McNeil Consumer Products. As Dr. Radebaugh points out, McNeil had the same policy, "Our Credo," in 1982–84 and in 2008–2010. What made the difference? It might be the case that in 1982–84 key officials were more personally in tune with the depth motivations of the "Credo," which according to a Christian view go back to God in his personal character. At a later point, in 2008–2010, it is possible that officials, whether Christian or non-Christian in name, suppressed this depth dimension in the "Credo" and treated it as little more than wishful verbiage, with little personal depth and little situational relevance. Norms have meaning in interaction with persons and situations (using the three perspectives)—they are not rightly treated as impersonal abstractions.

The differences between human viewpoints impinge even more painfully when we consider redemption. Suppose that at Eisai someone deliberately violated the law. What is the remedy? Does he get fired? Does he get a slap on the wrist? Does he merely get sympathy? If we listen to the Bible, we realize that the deliberate violation was a sin, not merely a human violation against a human rule. Christ is the only remedy for sin. But we cannot force redemption on anyone. People are saved only by the power of God. As a minimum, we can pray for the person at fault. But depending on the situation, a Christian might or might not have opportunity to share with the person at fault the deeper recesses of the problem.

In a typical public company, or even in an explicitly Christian company, Christians have to weigh the situation and the personal dimension, which may include specific resistance, on the part of some people, to any overt Christian message. Many situations are difficult, and require us to seek creativity from God.

Fundamental Loyalties

Within these situations, we should recognize that our loyalty to Christ rises above all other loyalties. And this loyalty includes as one aspect the importance of announcing Christ's claims. Peter and the apostles said, "We must obey God rather than men" (Acts 5:29 ESV). The apostles disobeyed recognized human authorities who had been put in place through God's providence. Normally we must obey the authorities over us. Why did the apostles do otherwise? Their loyalty to God and to Christ trumped the claims of human authorities.

The same principles apply today. If human authorities within a company tell us to sin, whether by way of lying or fraud or disobedience to civil government, we cannot consent. Neither do we consent when human authorities tell us to keep quiet about the realities of Christ. That was the issue to which the apostles more than once responded by pointing to the ultimacy of divine authority (Acts 4:19–20; 4:29–33; 5:29).

Christians confront resistance in this area for several reasons. First, human authorities are tempted to imagine that their authority is absolute. Second, they do not like people who upset the apple cart by going against "standard policy." Third, people are incited both by sin and by the devil to try to suppress the Christian message and its effects. Sometimes they use as an excuse the disruptive character of the Christian message (Acts 16:20–21; 19:26–27; 24:5), which of course is partly related to its exclusiveness, but also to its absoluteness. Businesses or civil governments or other authorities may put in place rules against "proselytism" or religious "insults" or "offensive [religious] language" or other specifications that have as one effect the suppression of free propagation of the gospel. We should recognize that all such suppression is at root rebellion against God Himself. It only pretends to be neutral. God *commands* the proclamation of the gospel of the universal lordship of Christ. No one has the right to undo or oppose what God commands.

Businesses—including "nice-sounding" businesses—can have policies that explicitly contradict God's commands in this area. We must face the fact that this is an evil, and that it comes from businesses and their policies, not from Christians who find that sometimes for conscience' sake they must violate those policies. (Of course, immature Christians can sometimes be obnoxious or indiscreet; but I am addressing the issue of illegitimate suppression.) This is not an evil that is easily removed. It belongs to a larger culture of evil.

Let us follow this concern a little further. Do we, in some cases, confront a culture that loves prosperity and economic pragmatism, a culture in which economic goals become new idols? The culture wants smoothly functioning businesses, and that means marginalizing the ferment engendered by religious debate. People allegedly have the "right" to have their religious views undisturbed (and unused!) in the workplace. Religion must be made irrelevant for the sake of smooth business economics. This kind of culture wants "peace" in opposition to the disruptive challenges of the gospel, a gospel that proclaims the kingdom of God and the necessity of change by submission to the lordship of Christ. This is a serious difficulty. When we confront it, we should pray for change, rather than imagining that worldly weapons are our primary resource.

Christians must also recognize that in these cases we, like the apostles, "must obey God rather than men" (Acts 5:29 ESV). That takes wisdom. The form that our obedience takes cannot be compromised merely on the basis of human rules. But in some situations it may be wisest to find a way around the rules rather than directly violating them. Christians can pray and work for change in human rules or a revised understanding of the implications of the rules. They can discuss difficulties with their superiors beforehand. The Bible counsels us to make our defense of Christian faith "with gentleness and respect" (1 Peter 3:15 ESV). With all the creativity and power that the Holy Spirit supplies, we should make every effort to talk and act winsomely. "Keep your conduct among the Gentiles honorable, so that when they speak against you as evildoers, they may see your good deeds and glorify God on the day of visitation" (1 Peter 2:12 ESV). "For this is the will of God, that by doing good you should put to silence the ignorance of foolish people. Live as people who are free, not using your freedom as a cover-up for evil, but living as servants of God" (1 Peter 2:15–16 ESV). "But even if your should suffer for righteousness' sake, you will be blessed. Have no fear of them, nor be troubled, but in your hearts regard Christ the Lord as holy, always being prepared to make a defense to anyone who asks you for a reason for the hope that is in you; yet do it with gentleness and respect, having a good conscience, so that, when you are slandered, those who revile your good behavior in Christ may be put to shame. For it is better to suffer for doing good, if that should be God's will, than for doing evil" (1 Peter 3:14–17 ESV).

Forgiveness

A Christian should also recognize from the Bible the role of forgiveness in human relationships. What should a company do with a person who has violated the law, as might have been the case with Eisai? Even if a guilty person does not repent thoroughly, it may be wise to give him another chance. Or maybe not. Here again we confront the challenge of wisely and discerningly weighing norms, persons, and situations. For example, the situation may be such that the violation was flagrant, serious, and repeated. It is time to fire the person, both for the protection of the future of the company, for the protection of the integrity of fellow workers, and for his own good (he must feel the consequences). True love, in biblical terms, cares about the person and is ready to forgive. But caring about the person may also mean bringing consequences, to strengthen the person's resolve not to sin again. This principle holds true within the Christian community, where we can experience the full power of Christian redemption. But in an analogous way it can also be applied—with careful attention to the difference in situations—to situations of "common grace" outside the Christian community. We are called on to be a blessing to non-Christians even when they remain outside the Christian faith (Gal. 6:10).

CONCLUSION

When we as Christians attempt to bring principles like these to bear within a situation of religious and ethical "pluralism," we need both to care about the blessing that non-Christians can receive from Christian principles, and to take into account the fundamental disagreements that remain in place between Christian faith and "the world." We endeavor to explain our principles winsomely, not obnoxiously thrusting forward our Christian underpinnings on those who wish not to hear them, but also being honest about the fact that our understanding is informed by deeper roots. The endeavor to do justice to both sides of the situation requires wisdom and graciousness and humility and creativity. Once again, we confront our need for the power of the Spirit of Christ.

DEPARTMENT OF HEALTH & HUMAN SERVICES

Public Health Service

Food and Drug Administration
Silver Spring, MD 20993

TRANSMITTED BY FACSIMILE

Gary Wieczorek, Associate Director, Regulatory Affairs
Eisai Medical Research Inc.
300 Tice Blvd
Woodcliff Lake, NJ 07677

RE: NDA # 20-690
     Aricept (donepezil hydrochloride) Tablets
     MACMIS #18244

Dear Mr. Wieczorek:

The Division of Drug Marketing, Advertising, and Communications (DDMAC) has reviewed two consumer broadcast television ads (TV ads) for Aricept® (donepezil hydrochloride) Tablets ("Beach" (ARU00435) and "Garden" (AAR00036)) submitted by Eisai Medical Research Inc. (Eisai) under cover of Form FDA-2253. The TV ads are misleading because they overstate the efficacy of the drug. Thus, the TV ads misbrand Aricept in violation of the Federal Food, Drug, and Cosmetic Act (the Act), 21 U.S.C. 352(n), and FDA implementing regulations. 21 CFR 202.1(e)(5)(i) & (e)(6)(i).

Background

According to its FDA-approved product labeling (PI), Aricept is indicated for "the treatment of dementia of the Alzheimer's type. Efficacy has been demonstrated in patients with mild to moderate Alzheimer's Disease, as well as in patients with severe Alzheimer's Disease."

According to the CLINICAL PHARMACOLOGY section of the PI, Aricept was tested in mild to moderate Alzheimer's disease in two randomized, double-blind, placebo-controlled studies (the Fifteen-Week and Thirty-Week Studies). In each study, the cognitive subscale of the Alzheimer's Disease Assessment Scale (ADAS-cog) was used. This subscale is a multi-item instrument that examines selected aspects of cognitive performance, including elements of memory, orientation, attention, reasoning, language, and praxis. After 24 weeks of treatment, the mean differences in the ADAS-cog change scores (scored from 0 to 70) for Aricept-treated patients compared to placebo were 2.8 and 3.1 units for the 5 mg/day and 10 mg/day treatments, respectively. The Fifteen and Thirty week studies also analyzed Aricept's ability to produce an overall clinical effect using a Clinician's Interview Based Impression of Change that required the use of caregiver information (CIBIC plus). The CIBIC plus examined general, cognitive, and behavioral function and activities of daily living on a 7-point scale ranging from "markedly improved" to "markedly worse." The CIBIC plus results in the Thirty-Week Study (Figure 3 in the PI) are presented in the following graph:

Gary Wieczorek
Eisai Medical Research Inc.
NDA #20-690/MACMIS #18244

Page 2

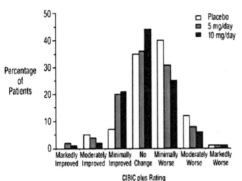

Figure 3. Frequency Distribution of CIBIC plus Scores at Week 24

In patients with severe Alzheimer's disease, the effects of Aricept on cognitive function were tested in a 24 week study (Japanese study), which evaluated patients on both the Severe Impairment Battery (SIB) and CIBIC plus. In addition, a randomized, double-blind, placebo-controlled clinical trial (the Swedish 24-Week Study) assessed cognitive function using the SIB and daily function using the Modified Alzheimer's Disease Cooperative Study Activities of Daily Living inventory for Severe Alzheimer's Disease (ADCS-ADL-severe), which is a subset of 19 items, including ratings of the patient's ability to eat, dress, bathe, use the telephone, get around, and perform other activities of daily living. After 24 weeks of treatment, the mean difference in the ADCS-ADL-severe change scores (scored from 0 to 54) for Aricept-treated patients compared to placebo was 1.8 units. The following graph shows the effect of Aricept on ADCS-ADL-severe in the Swedish 24-week study (Figure 9 in PI):

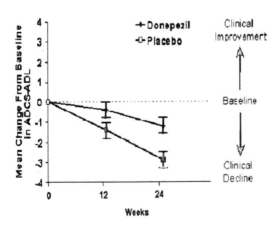

Figure 9. Time course of the change from baseline in ADCS-ADL-severe score for patients completing 24 weeks of treatment.

Aricept is contraindicated in patients with known hypersensitivity to the drug or to piperidine derivatives. Aricept is also associated with serious risks as reflected in the WARNINGS section of the PI, including syncopal episodes and gastrointestinal bleeding, especially in patients with a history of ulcers or in patients who are taking concurrent nonsteroidal anti-inflammatory drugs (NSAIDS). The most common adverse reactions associated with Aricept in severe Alzheimer's disease are diarrhea, anorexia, vomiting, nausea, and ecchymosis. In mild to moderate Alzheimer's disease, the most common adverse reactions are nausea, diarrhea, insomnia, vomiting, muscle cramps, fatigue, and anorexia.

Overstatement of Efficacy

Promotional materials are misleading if they represent or suggest that a drug is more effective than has been demonstrated by substantial evidence or substantial clinical experience.

The "Beach" TV ad presents an elderly man staring off into space, appearing distant, confused, and disinterested, while the rest of his family walks on the beach, and the man's daughter has a look of concern on her face. While this beach scene is taking place, the man's daughter makes the following statements:

- "Dad had been repeating things and acting disoriented for a while, like something was stealing him away from us."
- "We wanted to be there for him, to hold on to him." (While this statement is being made, a young boy clasps the man's hand.)

The ad then shows the man and his daughter discussing Aricept with his doctor. Specifically, the daughter states:

- "Dad's doctor said his symptoms were signs of Alzheimer's, a type of dementia, and that prescription Aricept could help." (While this statement is being made, the daughter poignantly clasps her father's hand.)

After the patient and his daughter discuss Aricept with the doctor, the man's behavior changes dramatically. The man is shown happily interacting with his family members, moving more quickly and with greater focus. For example, he pats his grandson on the head while pouring cereal, winks while feeding the dog under the table, energetically cheers and points at a soccer game while following the plays, and clasps his daughter's hand. While these scenes are taking place, the ad makes the following statements:

- "Studies showed Aricept slows the progression of Alzheimer's symptoms."
- "It improves cognition and slows the decline of overall function."
- "If it helps Dad be more like himself longer, that's everything to us."
- "Don't wait. Talk to your doctor about Aricept."

The "Garden" TV ad presents an elderly woman looking away from family members, appearing confused, aloof, and disoriented. While these scenes are taking place, the woman's daughter makes the following statements:

- "We'd been noticing mom acting forgetful and confused, like she was drifting away."
- "We wanted to be there for her, to hold on to her." (While this statement is being made, a young girl clasps the woman's hand.)

Similar to the "Beach" ad, this ad then shows the woman and her daughter discussing Aricept with her doctor. Specifically, the ad states:

- "Studies showed Aricept slows the progression of Alzheimer's symptoms."
- "It improves cognition and slows the decline of overall function."

After the woman and her daughter discuss Aricept with the doctor, the woman's behavior changes dramatically. The woman is shown interacting happily with her daughter and her grandchildren, trying on a hat, helping them plant seeds, and working with them in the garden. At the end of the ad, the daughter looks at her mother, smiling and hugging her, and the woman clasps her daughter's hand.

The totality of the above claims and presentations misleadingly overstates the efficacy of Aricept, implying a greater benefit than has been supported by substantial evidence or substantial clinical experience. As described above, the beginning segment of each ad presents patients with Alzheimer's disease looking blank, confused, distant, and walking off apart from their family members. However, after talking to their doctors about treatment with Aricept, the patients are seen interacting and communicating with their family members, happily and actively involved in activities with them. These presentations imply that, as a result of Aricept treatment, patients' cognitive and daily functioning, specifically aspects of attention and focus, orientation, communication, and social interaction and engagement, will be restored to normal.

The results from the Aricept efficacy trials in patients with mild to moderate and severe Alzheimer's disease do **not** support such a drastic improvement. According to the CLINICAL PHARMACOLOGY section of the PI, the mean differences in the ADAS-cog change scores for Aricept-treated patients compared to placebo were **only 2.8 and 3.1 units** (scored from 0 to 70) for the 5 mg/day and 10 mg/day treatments, respectively, after 24 weeks of treatment. Furthermore, the distribution of CIBIC plus scores in patients in the Thirty-Week Study (see Figure 3 in Background section) indicates that **less than 5%** of patients treated with Aricept at either dose were "markedly improved" or "moderately improved." The majority of patients experienced no change or became worse on Aricept treatment. Moreover, Figure 9 (see Background section) indicates that although the Aricept-treated group in the Swedish 24-Week Study reached a statistically significant result in change from baseline in ADCS-ADL-severe scores versus placebo, the mean difference was **only 1.8 units** (scored from 0 to 54), and patients on Aricept continued to show clinical decline over time.

Therefore, the claims and presentations in both TV ads are **not** representative of the results from the clinical trials for Aricept, and misleadingly overstate the efficacy of the drug. The inclusion of the superimposed text, "Individual results may vary," does not mitigate these misleading presentations.

Gary Wieczorek   Page 5
Eisai Medical Research Inc.
NDA #20-690/MACMIS #18244

Conclusion and Requested Action

For the reasons discussed above, the TV ads misbrand Aricept in violation of the Act, 21 U.S.C. 352(n), and FDA implementing regulations. 21 CFR 202.1(e)(5)(i) & (e)(6)(i).

DDMAC requests that Eisai immediately cease the dissemination of violative promotional materials for Aricept such as those described above. Please submit a written response to this letter on or before February 18, 2010, stating whether you intend to comply with this request, listing all promotional materials (with the 2253 submission date) for Aricept that contain violations such as those described above, and explaining your plan for discontinuing use of such violative materials. Please direct your response to me at the Food and Drug Administration, Center for Drug Evaluation and Research, Division of Drug Marketing, Advertising, and Communications, 5901-B Ammendale Road, Beltsville, MD 20705-1266, facsimile at 301-847-8444. In all future correspondence regarding this matter, please refer to MACMIS # 18244 in addition to the NDA number. We remind you that only written communications are considered official.

The violations discussed in this letter do not necessarily constitute an exhaustive list. It is your responsibility to ensure that your promotional materials for Aricept comply with each applicable requirement of the Act and FDA implementing regulations.

Sincerely,

{See appended electronic signature page}

Sharon M. Watson, PharmD
LCDR, USPHS
Regulatory Review Officer
Division of Drug Marketing,
 Advertising, and Communications

Application Type/Number	Submission Type/Number	Submitter Name	Product Name
NDA-20690	ORIG-1	EISAI INC	ARICEPT

This is a representation of an electronic record that was signed electronically and this page is the manifestation of the electronic signature.

/s/

SHARON M WATSON

02/03/2010

Our Credo

We believe our first responsibility is to the doctors, nurses and patients,
to mothers and fathers and all others who use our products and services.
In meeting their needs everything we do must be of high quality.
We must constantly strive to reduce our costs
in order to maintain reasonable prices.
Customers' orders must be serviced promptly and accurately.
Our suppliers and distributors must have an opportunity
to make a fair profit.

We are responsible to our employees,
the men and women who work with us throughout the world.
Everyone must be considered as an individual.
We must respect their dignity and recognize their merit.
They must have a sense of security in their jobs.
Compensation must be fair and adequate,
and working conditions clean, orderly and safe.
We must be mindful of ways to help our employees fulfill
their family responsibilities.
Employees must feel free to make suggestions and complaints.
There must be equal opportunity for employment, development
and advancement for those qualified.
We must provide competent management,
and their actions must be just and ethical.

We are responsible to the communities in which we live and work
and to the world community as well.
We must be good citizens — support good works and charities
and bear our fair share of taxes.
We must encourage civic improvements and better health and education.
We must maintain in good order
the property we are privileged to use,
protecting the environment and natural resources.

Our final responsibility is to our stockholders.
Business must make a sound profit.
We must experiment with new ideas.
Research must be carried on, innovative programs developed
and mistakes paid for.
New equipment must be purchased, new facilities provided
and new products launched.
Reserves must be created to provide for adverse times.
When we operate according to these principles,
the stockholders should realize a fair return.

Johnson & Johnson

U.S. Department of Health & Human Services

FDA U.S. Food and **Drug** Administration

Inspections, Compliance, Enforcement, and Criminal Investigations

McNeil Consumer and Specialty Pharmaceuticals 1/15/10

Department of Health and Human Services

Public Health Service
Food and Drug Administration
San Juan District
466 Fernandez Juncos Avenue
San Juan PR 00901-3223
Telephone: (787) 474-9500
FAX: (787) 729-5658

January 15, 2010

WARNING LETTER
SJN-2010-01

CERTIFIED MAIL
RETURN RECEIPT REQUESTED

Mr. Peter Luther, President, NA OTC
McNeil Consumer Healthcare
7050 Camp Hill Road Mb # 204
Fort Washington, PA 19034

Dear Mr. Luther:

This is regarding an inspection of your pharmaceutical manufacturing facility, McNeil Healthcare LLC, located at Road 183, Km. 19.8, Sector Montones, Las Piedras, Puerto Rico 00771, conducted by investigator J. Lopez and chemist R. Gonzalez and concluded on January 8, 2010. The inspection identified significant violations of the Current Good Manufacturing Practice (CGMP) regulations for Finished Pharmaceuticals, Title 21, Code of Federal Regulations (C.F.R.), Parts 210 and 211. These violations cause your drug products to be adulterated within the meaning of Section 501 (a)(2)(B) of the Federal Food, Drug, and Cosmetic Act (the Act) [21 U.S.C. § 351(a)(2)(B)] in that the methods used in, or the facilities or controls used for, their manufacture, processing, packing, or holding do not conform to or are not operated or administered in conformity with CGMP regulations. In addition, our inspection revealed that you failed to submit NDA Field Alert Reports (FARs) to FDA in compliance with 21 C.F.R. § 314.81 (b)(1)(ii), as required by section 505(k) of the Act [21 U.S.C. § 355(k)].

Specific violations observed during the inspection include, but are not limited, to:

1. Failure to thoroughly investigate any unexplained discrepancy or the failure of a batch or any of its components to meet any of its specifications whether or not the batch has already been distributed. In addition, you failed to extend the investigation to other batches of the same product and other products that might have been associated with the discrepancy as required by 21 C.F.R. § 211.192.

Your company has determined that the "uncharacteristic odor" complaints, some of which were associated with adverse event reports (gastrointestinal distress), for several of your OTC drug products are due to 2,4,6 Tribromoanisole (TBA) contamination in the product and/or bottles. TBA, which has a musty, mildew-type odor, is a known degradant of 2,4,6, Tribromophenol (TBP). TBP is a pesticide and flame retardant used to treat wooden pallets for transporting packaging materials and finished product. TBA is organoleptically detectable at parts per trillion. You are currently attributing the cause of the uncharacteristic odor to be contamination of the drug product containers from TBP treated wooden pallets. You have concluded that TBP from the wooden pallets degraded into TBA, which contaminated product containers and the finished product in those containers.

The contamination, first noted in 2008, occurred again in 2009, leading to recalls of several lots of Tylenol

Arthritis Relief caplets, 100 count bottles, 650 mg. More recalls are being conducted including multiple other OTC drug products.

We are aware of the complaint information available to your company, the sequence of events, and the extent of your firm's follow up measures during this period. We have concluded that your company did not conduct a timely, comprehensive investigation.

Your initial investigation into the root cause of the odor was unjustifiably delayed and terminated prematurely. Numerous complaints were received over a four month period in 2008 before they were considered a trend and before actions were initiated to determine the root cause. When microbiological testing in August 2008 did not support an initial speculation that microbial contamination was the root cause of the odor, the investigation was closed. No other possible root causes were pursued. Your firm lacked adequate justification for this decision.

Complaints of uncharacteristic odor were reported again in April 2009. Approximately 112 similar complaints were received by August 3, 2009. Although your firm had test results indicative of contamination with TBA as the source of the off odor on the complaint samples since September 2009, these results were not shared with FDA until after the initiation of the inspection and following several requests for this information made by the district office.

In October 2009, you concluded that the most probable root cause of the odor in the Tylenol Arthritis Relief caplets was the exposure of drug product bottles to wood pallets chemically treated with TBP. You did not expand the scope of the investigation to other lots and products potentially affected by this deviation. This would include, for example, products packaged in bottles from the same supplier that used the same type of wooden pallets, and other products manufactured by your facility for which odor complaints were received.

2. Failure of your Quality Control Unit to ensure a thorough investigation in accordance with 21 C.F.R. § 211.192 with conclusions and follow up accomplished as required by 21 C.F.R. § 211.198. As described above, the timing and depth of your investigative efforts regarding uncharacteristic odor complaints were insufficient to meet good manufacturing practice. Your firm's management, including the Quality Control Unit, was not proactive in response to consumer complaints. In addition, during the 2008 examination of complaint samples, your firm's analysts noted that the tablets, once removed from the bottle, did not have an unusual odor but the bottle retained a strong odor. Nonetheless, you did not pursue chemical testing at that time.

Your firm's quality management should have ensured the start of chemical testing far earlier. Failure to do so prolonged identification and resolution of the problem, resulting in continued consumer exposure. Quality problems must be thoroughly investigated, root cause determined, and appropriate corrective and preventive actions implemented as quickly as possible to limit exposure of the public to substandard drugs.

3. Failure to submit NDA-Field Alert Reports (FARs) within three (3) working days of receipt of information concerning any bacteriological contamination, or any significant chemical, physical, or other change or deterioration in the distributed drug products as required by 21 C.F.R. § 314.81 (b)(1)(ii).

Your firm received numerous uncharacteristic odor consumer complaints during the period of April 2008 through September 2008 for your product Tylenol Arthritis Relief caplets. Nevertheless, you failed to submit a FAR to FDA within three working days to inform the Agency of the nature of the problem and the steps that you were taking to address it. You did not submit the FAR until September 18, 2009, after again noting an adverse, continuing trend of numerous complaints over the course of a several month period.

The Agency is concerned about the response of Johnson & Johnson (J&J) to this matter. It appears that when J&J became aware of FDA's concerns about the thoroughness and timeliness of McNeil's investigation, whether all potentially affected products had been identified, and whether the recall was adequate in scope, J&J did not take appropriate actions to resolve these issues. Corporate management has the responsibility to ensure the quality, safety, and integrity of its products. Neither upper management at J&J nor at McNeil Consumer Healthcare assured timely investigation and resolution of the issues.

Neither this letter nor the observations noted on the FDA-483 is intended to be an all-inclusive list of the deficiencies that may exist at your facility. In addition, the Agency may send further correspondence based upon continued review of the inspectional findings. It is your responsibility to ensure that your operations at this facility and all other facilities under your control are in full compliance with all applicable requirements of federal law and FDA regulations. You should take prompt action to correct the violations cited in this letter. Failure to promptly correct these violations may result in legal action without further notice, including, without limitation, seizure, and injunction. Other federal agencies may take this warning letter into account when considering the award of contracts. Additionally, FDA may withhold approval of requests for export certificates, or approval of pending new drug applications listing your facility as a manufacturer until the above violations are corrected. A reinspection may be necessary.

Within 15 working days of receipt of this letter, please notify this office in writing of the specific steps that you

McNeil Consumer and Specialty Pharmaceuticals 1/15/10   Page 3 of 3

have taken to correct violations. Include an explanation of each step being taken to prevent the recurrence of violations, as well as copies of related documentation. If you cannot complete corrective action within 15 working days, state the reason for the delay and the time within which you will complete the correction.

Please contact the District Office to schedule a meeting to discuss your proposed corrective actions and time frames, as well as your plan for ensuring timely and meaningful involvement of corporate management (local and global) in resolving significant public health issues in the future. Please contact Margarita Santiago, Compliance Officer, at (787) 474-4789 to schedule a meeting at the FDA, San Juan District Office.

Your reply to the Warning Letter should be sent to the Food & Drug Administration, San Juan District Office, 466 Fernandez Juncos Ave., San Juan, PR 00901-3223, to the attention of Margarita Santiago.

Sincerely,

/S/

Maridalia Torrres
District Director
San Juan District

Cc:
Mr. William C. Weldon, CEO, Johnson & Johnson
Ms. Nuria Ramirez Ordonez, General Manager, McNeil Healthcare, LLC, Las Piedras, PR

Links on this page:

Peter Luther
President

(b) (4)

e-mail:

CONFIDENTIAL
February 5, 2010

Margarita Santiago
Food and Drug Administration
San Juan District Office
466 Fernandez Juncos Ave.
San Juan, PR 00901-3223

Subject: Response to the Warning Letter dated January 15, 2010

Dear Ms. Santiago:

On behalf of McNeil Consumer Healthcare, Division of McNEIL-PPC, Inc. ("McNeil"), please find our written response to the Warning Letter issued to us on January 15, 2010 (the "Warning Letter"). This document provides a summary of the corrective actions to the issues raised in the Warning Letter. The second document is the more detailed response to the FDA Form-483 ("483") issued January 8, 2010. Therefore, in considering this response to the Warning Letter, the FDA should also consider and reference the more detailed 483 response document.

McNeil and Johnson & Johnson management are taking this issue very seriously and are committed to ensuring that McNeil implements all necessary corrective and preventive actions to improve the McNeil quality systems.

McNeil shares FDA's primary concern of ensuring the safety and efficacy of our products and understands the important obligation we have to the consumers that use them. Given this obligation, our quality systems are of utmost importance to us and we appreciate the feedback and input received from the FDA in the Warning Letter. We have already begun implementing the corrective actions detailed in this response.

McNeil Investigation

McNeil acknowledges the concerns raised by the FDA in the 483 and the Warning Letter with respect to the thoroughness and timeliness of various aspects of this investigation. The corrective actions detailed below directly and indirectly address FDA's concerns and will improve the thoroughness and timeliness of our investigations in the future.

RECEIVED

FEB - 5 2010

FDA – SJN
COMPLIANCE BRANCH

2

As an initial matter, it's important to review the scope of the investigation that led McNeil to the source of the contamination, the primary root cause of the 2, 4, 6-tribromoanisole ("TBA"), and the decision to recall various McNeil products. Reviewing this investigation has been critical to our development of an effective corrective action plan. The components of this corrective action plan, which are highlighted below, and detailed in the 483 submission, are being implemented systemically throughout McNeil.

In McNeil's experience, many of the challenges raised by this particular investigation were unique. Only after we engaged ░░░(b) (4)░░░ an external forensic laboratory, that has unique testing capabilities, did we determine that TBA was a likely source of the uncharacteristic odor. After McNeil confirmed the source of the odor, we were able to launch a comprehensive investigation focused specifically on how TBA could have entered the McNeil supply chain.

While ░░░(b) (4)░░░ has the appropriate analytical equipment and methodologies capable of detecting trace amounts of TBA in parts per trillion ("ppt") levels, the nature of this testing was, and continues to be, limited to only 8 samples per day. We continue to evaluate other laboratories capable of conducting this testing; however, very few laboratories have been able to meet our ppt sensitivity requirements and no laboratories, as of the date of this letter, have been able to validate at these levels. In parallel, we are pursuing in-house development of this testing capability.

Our next challenge was to determine how TBA could have entered the supply chain. This stage of the investigation led us to review multiple potential sources of contamination, including, but not limited to caps/liners, bottles/resins, pallets, manufacturing/packaging lines, bulk product, and ingredients. We also conducted extensive literature searches and worked with toxicology experts to help us better understand the chemical and how to evaluate its potential toxicity. From this, we learned that there was no toxicity data available for TBA. Relevant Health Hazard Evaluations ("HHEs") were developed and provided to FDA. The scope of the investigation widened significantly before it narrowed. Each time our knowledge increased, we expanded our search for affected or potentially affected products.

Based on this comprehensive forensic investigation, we traced TBA from certain bottles to wood pallets, and then, more specifically, to wood used to build the pallets that was sourced from ░(b)░ and treated with 2, 4, 6-tribromophenol ("TBP"). From the literature, we know TBP can lead to the formation of TBA under certain environmental and handling conditions. Once we confirmed via analytical testing that these wood pallets were treated with TBP and were likely the primary cause of the TBA, we expanded our review to include other sites that had received these pallets and decided on January 14, 2010 to initiate the very broad recall of any potentially impacted products.

Our investigation continues and we will be providing an update to you at our February 11, 2010 meeting.

In the Warning Letter, FDA identified the following 3 specific violations that were observed during the inspection:

1. *Failure to thoroughly investigate any unexplained discrepancy or the failure of a batch or any of its components to meet any of its specifications whether or not the batch has already been distributed. In addition, you failed to extend the investigation to other batches of the*

same product and other products that might have been associated with the discrepancy as required by 21 C.F.R. Section 211.192.

2. *Failure of your Quality Control Unit to ensure a thorough investigation in accordance with 21 C.F.R. Section 211.192 with conclusions and follow up accomplished as required by 21 C.F.R. Section 211.198.* As described above, the timing and depth of your investigative efforts regarding uncharacteristic odor complaints were insufficient to meet good manufacturing practice. Your firm's management, including the Quality Control Unit, was not proactive in response to consumer complaints. In addition, during the 2008 examination of complaint samples, your firm's analysts noted that the tablets, once removed from the bottle, did not have an unusual odor but the bottle retained a strong odor. Nonetheless, you did not pursue chemical testing at that time.

Your firm's quality management should have ensured the start of chemical testing far earlier. Failure to do so prolonged identification and resolution of the problem, resulting in contained consumer exposure. Quality problems must be thoroughly investigated, root cause determined, and appropriate corrective and preventative actions implemented as quickly as possible to limit exposure of the public to substandard drugs.

3. *Failure to submit NDA-Field Alert Reports (FARs) within three (3) working days of receipt of information concerning any bacteriological contamination, or any significant chemical, physical, or other change or deterioration in the distributed drug products as required by 21 C.F.R. Section 314.81(b)(1)(ii).*

Your firm received numerous uncharacteristic odor complaints during the period of April 2008 through September 2008 for your product Tylenol Arthritis Relief caplets. Nevertheless, you failed to submit a FAR within three working days to inform the Agency of the nature of the problem and the steps that you were taking to address it. You did not submit the FAR until September 18, 2009, after again noting an adverse, continuing trend of numerous complaints over the course of a several month period.

McNeil is implementing a corrective action plan, described below, and in more detail in the 483 response, which we believe addresses each of these 3 items in a comprehensive way. We have the appropriate knowledge, resources and direction to execute these enhancements and improvements. As the President of McNeil, I understand that I and McNeil's Management Board have final oversight responsibilities to ensure that the commitments described in our responses are addressed and given priority attention by our organization.

The key elements of the corrective action plan for the Warning Letter include:
- Enhancements to the Quality System
- Organizational Changes
- Senior Management Oversight

4

Enhancements to the Quality System

Based on our investigation, we recognize opportunities to enhance our Quality System. As a result, we have immediately implemented the following improvements:

- *Changes to complaint review process:* McNeil recognizes the importance of appropriate categorization of complaints in helping to facilitate accurate, timely, and actionable trending of complaints based on reported defect types. Based on this, McNeil has reassessed all complaint categories with specific focus on categories that may require subjective interpretation. These categories have been redefined or combined to increase consistency in complaint defect coding and to ensure accuracy in trending. Accurate complaint categories will increase our ability to identify signals and trends faster, and to take action more effectively.

   All affected employees have been trained in these new complaint category definitions. The implementation of the new complaint categories will occur in February 2010.
   Concurrent to the development of the new categorization, the existing procedural requirements for quality investigators to evaluate and correct complaint categorization during daily file review have been reinforced through training. This training was completed in January 2010.

   Relevant changes to the complaint review process are reflected in SOP ▓▓▓ (b) (4) ▓▓▓ "Requirements for Complaint Handling" attached to the 483 response.

- *Changes to complaint handling procedures:* McNeil recognizes the important role of appropriate complaint handling procedures in ensuring that trends are detected early and investigated thoroughly. McNeil will continue to investigate all complaints associated with our products pursuant to SOP ▓▓ (b) (4) ▓▓ In addition, we have developed ▓▓ (b) (4) ▓▓ based on severity or frequency, for trends above baseline levels for all products. This approach in trending will enhance our ability to identify and recognize trends for product families, product lots, and across product lines. This trending will enable the early identification of issues requiring an expanded investigation, management notification and prioritization of action. This trending will be done on a continuous basis including monthly and quarterly reviews by the McNeil quality organization.

   These changes to the complaint handling procedures are reflected in SOP ▓▓▓ (b) (4) ▓▓▓ "Requirements for Complaint Handling" attached to the 483 response.

- *Change to Investigation Procedures:* We are amending the current investigation SOP to require that if an ▓▓▓▓▓▓ (b) (4) ▓▓▓▓▓▓
   ▓▓▓▓▓▓▓ (b) (4) ▓▓▓▓▓▓▓
   ▓▓ (b) (4) ▓▓ Such decisions will be documented and are intended to ensure the broadest investigatory approach. ▓▓▓ (b) (4) ▓▓▓
   ▓▓▓ (b) (4) ▓▓▓

   This change to investigation procedures will be reflected in SOP ▓▓ (b) (4) ▓▓ attached to the 483 response.

5

- *Change to Central Complaint Vigilance Quarterly Process:* We will expand our Central Complaint Vigilance Quarterly Process, where we currently review complaints, to include a more extensive review of adverse event trends across all McNeil product lines, and will formally include ███████████ (b) (4) ██████████ and ██ (b) (4) ██ This expanded process will be in place in April 2010.

  These changes to the Central Complaint Vigilance Quarterly Process are reflected in SOP ██ (b) ██ (b) (4) ██ "Requirements for Complaint Handling" attached to the 483 response.

- *Change in Field Alert Reporting Requirements for Complaint Trends:* To help ensure more timely notification to FDA of NDA-Field Alert reports, the McNeil FDA Field Alert procedure has been revised to require the issuance of a Field Alert once a confirmed complaint trend where bacteriological contamination or significant chemical, physical, or other change or deterioration in a distributed drug product cannot be ruled out. This Field Alert will be issued within 3 business days of McNeil becoming aware of a complaint trend. In addition to timely communications, this interpretation of Section 314.81(b)(1)(i) and (ii), as codified in Title 21 of the Code of Federal Regulations, will likely result in more frequent communications with FDA.

  These changes to the Field Alert Reporting Requirements for Complaint Trends are reflected in SOP ██ (b) (4) ██ attached to the 483 response.

Organizational Changes

McNeil has already begun implementing organizational changes that it believes will strengthen our focus on quality and compliance. Dr. Veronica Cruz has been appointed to the position of Vice President of Quality Assurance, OTC, effective February 15, 2010, and will be a member of the McNeil Management Board. Dr. Cruz has extensive experience in Quality within the API and pharmaceutical dosage manufacturing environment. She has supported manufacturing and distribution to global markets of OTC liquids and solids and spent much of her career in Puerto Rico, including previous experience in McNeil's Las Piedras site. She moves to this role from the position of Vice President, North America Quality Operations for Johnson & Johnson's Global Pharmaceutical Supply Group. Throughout her career, she has also developed and implemented various quality systems and processes resulting in significant improvement in the compliance level of the site quality systems.

As announced in the appointment of Dr. Cruz, she will now report directly to Sam Jiwrajka, who has been appointed to the role as head of Quality for the Johnson & Johnson Group of Consumer Companies. This move is part of changes already underway within the Johnson & Johnson Consumer organization which we believe will further strengthen our Quality operating model. Under this new model, McNeil will receive increased support from the Johnson & Johnson Consumer quality organization; however, the McNeil Management Board, consisting of executive leaders from various functions, will continue to be directly accountable for product quality and regulatory compliance of McNeil. This will allow these organizations to realize the benefits of Johnson & Johnson Consumer's scale and scope while continuing to preserve the benefits and accountabilities of our decentralized structure.

6

Senior Management Oversight

McNeil senior management is committed to more detailed and frequent oversight of our quality systems and quality-related issues with our products.

We are in the process of initiating enhanced Quarterly Executive Board Quality System reviews. These reviews will include the McNeil Management Board as well as relevant members of the McNeil quality organization, plus participants from Johnson & Johnson. While Executive quality reviews were initiated in 2009, we have identified opportunities to improve the depth and breadth of these reviews. Therefore, they will now include a review of all of our quality system elements with very specific management action plans established and tracked. This will provide senior management with the appropriate level of visibility and will ensure adequate support and prioritization of key issues.

In addition to the Quarterly Executive Board Quality System Reviews, we will be adding complaint updates to our monthly McNeil Management Board meeting. This will give the McNeil Management Board greater visibility to complaint trends earlier to ensure that they are given appropriate prioritization, attention, and action at a senior level in the organization.
These senior management quality review processes are reflected in SOP (b) (4) attached to the 483 response.

In addition to the Quality System enhancements outlined above, Dr. Cruz will lead a comprehensive assessment of the McNeil quality system in coordination with resources from Johnson & Johnson Quality & Compliance Worldwide. This assessment will be completed by the end of April 2010. Based on this assessment, Dr. Cruz will develop a plan that would continue to strengthen our focus on complaint vigilance, corrective and preventive actions ("CAPAs") and quality systems. We will share this plan with FDA to underscore our ongoing commitment to improving our quality system.

Remediation Plan related to Pallets

In addition to the corrective actions outlined above, McNeil has also developed a remediation plan specifically directed to TBA and wood pallets. Based on our determination that TBP-treated wood used to make pallets are the primary cause of the TBA contamination, a remediation plan was immediately developed which included the following:

- All existing McNeil components from the (b) (4) plant shipped on wood pallets, where the pallets could not be confirmed to be TBP-free, are in the process of being destroyed (along with the pallets themselves).

- McNeil packaging lines and warehouses are being cleaned at all sites per a protocol developed in consultation with an external TBA expert. A similar cleaning procedure was also used at the aforementioned component supplier, (b) (4)

- McNeil has required of all in-coming material suppliers that any pending shipments or future shipments are to be on heat-treated, TBP/phenol-free pallets. An inspection process has been instituted to evaluate incoming materials to confirm that they are only shipped on heat-treated pallets. In addition, documentation from wood/pallet suppliers is required to confirm that the pallets are TBP/phenol-free. Materials on pallets not meeting these requirements are not accepted into any McNeil facility. This process is also being rolled out to our third-party manufacturing sites. Monitoring of compliance with this pallet requirement will be conducted.

Conclusion

McNeil recognizes the seriousness of this situation and has identified this corrective action plan as our top priority. We are dedicated to providing the resources, time, effort and executive oversight to ensure that our quality systems meet all requirements and operate effectively and efficiently. We are confident that this corrective action plan provides the approach necessary to identify and implement systemic actions that will improve and enhance our quality processes and systems while addressing the concerns raised by the FDA in the Warning Letter and the 483.

We look forward to our February 11 meeting and the opportunity to engage with you more fully on our corrective actions and plans moving forward and on our on-going investigation. Please feel free to contact me by phone at ▮▮(b) (4)▮▮ if you have any questions or concerns.

Sincerely,

Peter Luther
President

cc: Maridalia Torres

Notes

1. John M. Frame, *Perspectives on the Word of God: An Introduction to Christian Ethics* (Eugene, OR: Wipf and Stock, 1999); John M. Frame, *The Doctrine of the Christian Life* (Phillipsburg, NJ: Presbyterian and Reformed, 2008).

2. See Abraham Kuyper, *Lectures on Calvinism* (Grand Rapids: Eerdmans, 1931).

3. Timothy Keller, *Counterfeit Gods: The Empty Promises of Money, Sex, and Power, and the Only Hope That Matters* (New York: Dutton, 2009).

4. Warning letter from FDA to Eisai Medical Research Inc., http://www.fda.gov/downloads/ Drugs/GuidanceComplianceRegulatory Information/EnforcementActivitiesbyFDA/WarningLettersandNoticeofViolationLetterstoPhar- maceuticalCompanies/UCM201238.pdf (accessed April 28, 2010).

5. "Our Credo" from Johnson & Johnson, http://www.jnj.com/connect/about-jnj/jnj-credo/ (accessed April 26, 2010).

6. Warning letter from FDA to McNeil, January 15, 2010, http://www.fda.gov/ICECI/Enforce- mentActions/WarningLetters/ucm197811 .htm (accessed April 28, 2010).

7. Response from McNeil to the FDA, February 5, 2010, http://www.fda.gov/downloads/ AboutFDA/CentersOffices/ORA/ORAElectronic ReadingRoom/UCM204455.pdf (accessed April 28, 2010).

COURAGE AND CONVICTION IN THE PUBLIC COMPANY

JEFF CONWAY

Jeff Conway has been managing Charlotte Prime, LLC, doing business as the popular Ruth's Chris Steak House Franchisee for RCSH Charlotte (SouthPark and Uptown) and, now, Savannah, since 2004. From 2001–03, Jeff served as Interim President and Chief Financial Officer of Ruth's Chris corporate office in New Orleans, Louisiana. In the decade of 1990–2000, he was President and Chief Financial Officer of Rent-Way, Inc., in Erie, Pennsylvania. For three years prior to running Rent-Way, Mr. Conway was Senior Manager to Ernst and Young in Tampa, Florida. From 1980–87, Jeff was a manager at Coopers & Lybrand in Tulsa, Oklahoma. Jeff Conway received his Bachelor of Science in Accounting at Oklahoma State University and attended high school at Tulsa Memorial High School.

ANDREW PETERSON

Since 1997, Dr. Peterson has directed distance education for graduate theological education from Charlotte, North Carolina, for Reformed Theological Seminary, Virtual Campus. Over the past dozen years, Andy has developed a "virtual campus" for the education of hundreds of graduate students at a school in the Southeast USA, Reformed Theological Seminary. With headquarters in Charlotte, the student body is worldwide. This formal degree program makes the most use of distance education of any accredited seminary in the world. Andy's professional road map has been from licensed psychologist in Pennsylvania at a community mental health center, to a professor of psychology for business psychology and teacher training courses for Grove City College, a four-year liberal arts college north of Pittsburgh, to a professor of practical theology at Westminster Seminary in California and educational technologist at Santa Fe Foundation in Solana Beach, and then to University of California, San Diego, in 1995 to establish the first Multimedia Development Center for faculty development of digital presentations.

> *Be strong and courageous, because you will lead these people to inherit the land I swore to their forefathers to give them. Be strong and very courageous. Be careful to obey all the law my servant Moses gave you; do not turn from it to the right or to the left, that you may be success-*

ful wherever you go. Do not let this Book of the Law depart from your mouth; meditate on it day and night, so that you may be careful to do everything written in it. Then you will be prosperous and successful. Have I not commanded you? Be strong and courageous. Do not be terrified; do not be discouraged, for the LORD your God will be with you wherever you go. (Josh. 1:6–9 NIV)

The public company has developed as a modern corporate structure over the last three hundred years in the lands of the Reformation and beyond, especially in the United Kingdom and the United States of America.[1] Most recently the need for Christian ethics has become urgent as government is becoming more involved with the practice of big business. The problematic effects of this intervention are becoming apparent over the past few decades in the USA. Also, the drift of important aspects of American culture away from a Christian emphasis has thrown into question those values that undergird behavior in both private and public companies. This move away from the presupposition of the Ten Commandments and the teaching of Christ has led to egregious moral failures in personal and professional lives.

This contest of worldviews has affected all of culture, including the public company. In 2001, noted Christian and business author Jim Collins documented the best success stories in his classic study *Good to Great*, where he researched the best performances by public companies that had sustained great results over at least fifteen years.[2] "The good-to-great examples that made the final cut into the study attained extraordinary results, averaging cumulative stock returns 6.9 times the general market in the fifteen years following their transition points." Actually, there were a number of rather ordinary companies that qualified as great companies by steady work through stages of buildup and breakthrough over an extended time period. They had quiet, steady leaders, a focus on getting the right people in the right seats, a willingness to confront bad news, a passion with preeminence and profitable metrics, a culture of discipline, and occasional technology accelerators.

Just published last year is the latest Collins book, now with a different tone, yet still hopeful, all in all: *How the Mighty Fall: And Why Some Companies Never Give In.*[3] This research report again has a list of sequential stages . . . this time to the decline and, even, death of some public companies.

Stage 1: Hubris Born of Success
Stage 2: Undisciplined Pursuit of More
Stage 3: Denial of Risk and Peril

Stage 4: Grasping for Salvation with "Silver Bullets"

Stage 5: Capitulation to Irrelevance or Death

Note how each one of the first four stages, while there is still hope, is failed or overcome due to a matter of business ethics. Are you prideful about business success? Must you grow immediately at all costs? Will you hear a report of one or more growing risks? Or, do you gamble it all on an untested "silver bullet"? By basing business ethics decisions on biblical principles, doing the good we ought to do, God is honored now and eternally. The likelihood of profitability is very good, though not certain. James 4 is still operative today.

> Now listen, you who say, "Today or tomorrow we will go to this or that city, spend a year there, carry on business and make money." Why, you do not even know what will happen tomorrow. What is your life? You are a mist that appears for a little while and then vanishes. Instead, you ought to say, "If it is the Lord's will, we will live and do this or that." As it is, you boast and brag. All such boasting is evil. Anyone, then, who knows the good he ought to do and doesn't do it, sins. (vv. 13–17 NIV)

This paper will add the Christian worldview as a context for rethinking the opportunity, role, and purpose of the public company in a free economy. Essential biblical principles will be adduced to show the role of the public company and the implications for ethical practice today. An extended case study of how people and systems fail will illustrate the norms, circumstances, and motives in today's difficult business world. Remedies and resolve for Christian work and life will be drawn from Scripture and selected passages of the Westminster Confession of Faith. A Christian triperspectival approach to ethical decision making will highlight a biblical balance of concerns about the commandments, situational realities, and personal intentions when under pressure to do the right thing. And the implicit stewardship theme includes how to *make* money as well as how to *give* money for good deeds.

Biblical Presuppositions from the Christian Worldview for Business

The passage in Joshua 1:1–9, is analogous to the Christian facing the ethical challenges of working in public companies. The calling is to conquer the daily business problems for a large institution to be productive and profitable.

God's Promise in the Business Situation

There was a particular situation to which Joshua, Caleb, and others were called in the narrative of redemptive history (Josh. 1:6). After wandering in the wilderness, it was time to make positive gains of territory in the land promised by God to his covenant people. An analysis of the Hebrews would have been somewhat discouraging as a benchmark for the hope of success in their mission. They were very finite, prideful, failed, and given to complaining. Yet the Lord promised that he would give them the victory of a specific mission. Take over the "Promised Land." The hope was to be in the Lord, not the human beings in the account. The command was to be faithful to God's Word in God's world.

Persistent Courage in Your Heart

The public company is a difficult arena. Risk for failure is ever present, and the consequences are great for all the long list of stakeholders. Courage is required (Josh. 1:7). Major assets and income are on the line for all the relevant players, including the following people in their corporate roles:

- Shareholders have pressure to protect personal resources and reserves as they vote on the board of directors and receive dividends. Their ownership value is a number based on cash flow times a multiple for the particular industry and situation.
- The board of directors has pressure to oversee the executive team for the shareholders, as the enterprise is to be protected short-term and long-term.
- The executive team (CEO, CFO) has pressure to meet the official projections and "whisper numbers" so that investors will buy stock for money management funds based on the reports from stock analysts. Their bank loans may be called if results fail to meet quarterly expectations.
- Mid-level executives have pressure to meet the promised quarterly

sales and expense numbers so that the analysts will recommend the company to investors as fund managers. The "cookie jar reserve" can move dollars of revenue or costs to the right month so that the quarterly numbers come out right. This is short-term vs. long-term thinking and operation.

- Staff employees are under pressure to support the mid-level executives as they work the last two weeks of each quarter to meet the numbers.
- Suppliers are under pressure to manage cost of goods for their products and promised delivery dates.
- Contractors are under pressure to keep prices low and adapt to new technologies and high expectations from their customers.
- Customers are under pressure to get sufficient service and product reliability at an affordable price.
- Commercial banks are under pressure to maintain requirements for borrowers and requirements for making loans.
- Wall Street money managers are under pressure to get reward from their investments for their customers who have invested savings into their funds, often through retirement programs.
- Wall Street analysts are under pressure to be accurate as the company executives market their company through them and a "consensus earnings estimate" is made for the investment fund managers.
- Public accountants are under pressure by management to find the "cookie jars" as well as provide a clean audit of the financial records.

Biblical Commandments as Norms

Yet the Christian who is called to work at some position in a public company always has a righteous action to take (1 Cor. 10:13). There is never a moment in God's world when there is not a right action to take. It may be difficult, painful, and seemingly futile. But God's Word, illuminated by the Holy Spirit and in the service of our Lord Jesus Christ, provides the path for ethical decision making in business (Josh. 1:8).

Following God's Word is not a passive process. Joshua is told to meditate on the Word at all times and to be careful to obey it. The theologians talk about the doctrine of perspicuity, i.e., clarity. The Bible can be understood clearly. It is not overly vague or subject to manifold orthodox interpretations in the prime areas. Surely there are disagreements on peripheral matters, but the message is close to us and clear: "It is in your mouth and in your heart so you may obey it" (Deut. 30:14 NIV).

His Presence Along the Way

Knowing God is to know Him in His world. He has created, sustained and ensured our well-being forever (Josh. 1:9). The Holy Spirit, the Comforter, was allocated to us in the divine economy of the Trinity. He enables us to turn to Christ as Savior, to keep His commandments in respect to our love for Him, and to grow the fruit that is good Christian living for all situations: love, joy, peace, patience, kindness, goodness, faithfulness, gentleness, and self-control (Gal. 5:22–23). The employee in the organization, at any level, can turn to the Spirit for these sorts of attitudes and traits.

The Christian worldview is not just an intellectual exercise, another political or lifestyle philosophy. All those areas are included in biblical teaching. But it includes the actual presence of God for help in every activity in the company. When circumstances are smooth or when they are chaotic, He is there to steady and strengthen the Christian to think, speak, and do the right things. Divine avoidance of fear (1 John 4:18) and discouragement (2 Cor. 4:7–18) is critical for good deliberation and commitment to best practices in all aspects of the business.

ROLE OF THE PUBLIC COMPANY IN GOD'S WORLD

When considering the many aspects of modern business, there are basic pillars that undergird the conceptual framework for the public corporation. Wayne Grudem has outlined a number of biblical principles that are foundational for business done to the glory of God.[4] Such business is effective in fulfilling the Cultural Mandate (Gen. 1:28) and supports the progress of the Great Commission (Matt. 28:18–20). The public corporation is an important way to organize the necessary division of labor for "subduing the earth" and promoting the Gospel worldwide along with discipling the nations in a Christian way of living based on the regeneration of individual hearts. Key pillars for the public company are biblical understandings of ownership, employment, profit, and competition. An additional element is the accuracy of market information.

Ownership

Owning shares of a public corporation is a highly symbolic and complex activity for recognizing value in God's world. The Bible talks about the morally good principle of ownership, especially in its negation in the ninth commandment, "Thou shalt not steal" (Ex. 20:15 KJV). With a division of labor that is rewarded with possessions of value, fairness ensues with a recognition of talent, time, and effort. As a pillar for the edifice of the public company, ownership facilitates motivation to participate in major efforts of huge proportions. It allows shared ownership by thousands of people or dominant ownership by just a few shareholders in some cases.

Employment

A large corporation may employ tens of thousands of people. The concept of employment brings the element of authority to the relationships in the company. This allows managers to work with groups to the end of greater revenue and lower expenses. While the employer must be careful to pay fairly (Luke 10:7), the employee must be careful to be content and work hard (Luke 3:14). As Grudem remarks, employment is "necessary for the greater production of goods."[5] And likewise, "is another way that God has created us so that we would be able to glorify him more fully in such relationships." This is all part of the Cultural Mandate to subdue the earth to God's glory and to facilitate the Great Commission, including making disciples of the whole counsel of God.

Profit

In the culture and language of the Bible, profit is a good thing. The prophet Jeremiah was not complimentary when he conveyed that Israel was "an unprofitable people." It was a curse, not a blessing, to note the deficit on their moral balance sheet. To innovate for revenue through voluntary transactions with a customer and to carefully control expenses in a thrifty operation is a good thing. The Lord does not look kindly on stewards who do not work hard with an investment toward more enterprise value; cf. the parable of the talents (Matt. 25:14–30).

> Again, it will be like a man going on a journey, who called his servants and entrusted his property to them. To one he gave five talents of money, to another two talents, and to another one talent, each according to his ability. Then he went on his

journey. The man who had received the five talents went at once and put his money to work and gained five more. So also, the one with the two talents gained two more. But the man who had received the one talent went off, dug a hole in the ground and hid his master's money. (Matt. 25:14–18 NIV)

Competition

The world of public companies is very competitive financially in sales and stock value. Rather than the static world of a "planned economy" where most companies are "too big to fail," the free market allows for an orderly culling of efforts based on the discipline of customer response. God has made human beings in a very special way, with great creativity and variety. He has also made a world that is composed of situations that vary and that require discernment to understand.

As in science and technology, when a market is allowed to exhibit its free response to products and services, the feedback leads to course corrections and a higher standard of living, i.e., subduing the earth and speeding the communication of the Gospel and biblical teaching. This creative feedback nullifies poor products and suggests new ways to master the environment with new services.

Market Information

An important aspect of a free market, where private and public companies sell their wares, is the flow of information for the business as well as the consumers. Financial statements, including detailed sales reports, are the common language for communicating the past results of a company and a basis for the projection of what's next for the future investor's consideration. While noting inevitable ambiguity at times, common accounting practices must be followed.

Trust and honesty in reporting is required for the market to work as a place of investment for future reward. Public companies have special scrutiny due to their registration, protection, and the complex processes for raising large sums of money. There must be freedom for high achievers to pursue unique and innovative ways to organize and sell the ideas. But there must be governmental courts for appeals of overt recklessness or outright fraud. If the government does not have the strict "blindfold of justice," convictions can be used for political gain. The best laws must be written . . . and the best efforts of business and courts must make the system work for productivity and for honor to God.

THE JEFF CONWAY STORY: A CASE STUDY

In the high-pressure environment of a public company, a Christian can know that every trial is aimed by the Lord for the growth in grace of the regenerate heart. (James 1:2–5; Rom. 8:28). This is the testimony of Jeff Conway (coauthor of this article) from a dramatic example of business ethics in action. He and his wife, Paula, met in high school, attended college together at Oklahoma State, and were married in Tulsa, Oklahoma. In 1979, Jeff obtained his first job as a CPA. He worked for seven years with Coopers and Lybrand and then three years with Ernst and Young.

After a decade of public accounting, an opportunity in the "rent to own" industry was discovered. A partnership was made with a former client who was a New York Stock Exchange specialist and floor governor. The business plan was to purchase a one-third interest in Rent-Way, Inc., register Rent-Way as a public company, and then use the stock of a publicly traded company to "roll up" the rent-to-own industry.

Going Public

Rent-Way was a small business with seventeen stores. It needed a capital infusion to restructure its debt and prepare the way to execute its growth strategy. A public offering document was prepared. A $7 million IPO listed Rent-Way on Nasdaq's Small Cap Exchange. Over the next nine years, Rent-Way grew to approximately 1,100 stores.

Year after year, Rent-Way completed acquisitions that fueled its growth. The first acquisition was 20 stores; the second acquisition was 40 stores; the third acquisition was approximately 100 stores; several smaller acquisitions amounted to 200 stores. As a public company now listed on the New York Stock Exchange, the quarterly struggle to meet the "whisper number" was an ever-constant pressure. Approximately fifteen analysts followed the company, and many significant institutional investors were shareholders in Rent-Way.

In an effort to become the largest company in the rent-to-own industry, Rent-Way partnered with a private equity firm and entered into an intense auction to acquire Rent-A-Center. Rent-Way eventually lost the auction to another well-capitalized competitor. The loss was disappointing. Analysts suggested the Rent-Way growth story was over. In a desperate effort to maintain its growth rate and status as a growth stock, Rent-Way merged with a troubled 400-store competitor. The scale of the acquisition and subsequent merger integration issues overwhelmed Rent-Way's culture and infrastructure. Rent-Way lost focus and basic accounting controls for a year as it struggled to upgrade systems and personnel. In the following year Rent-Way acquired another 100-store chain and opened 100 new stores.

In summary, over a nine-year span, Rent-Way grew from 17 to 1,100 stores, from 100 to 5,000 employees, and from $7 million to more than $500 million in sales. With each acquisition the company faced numerous merger integration issues. In addition, the larger acquisitions forced a restructuring of credit facilities and an upgrade of information systems to support a larger company. Rent-Way's market capitalization grew from $10 million to $750 million. Three times Rent-Way was listed in Fortune's 100 Fastest Growing Companies. Having served as CFO for eight years, the board promoted Jeff to president in 1999.

Crisis!

An accounting error reported to the board of directors in 2000 led to a series of profound events and consequences. As news of an accounting error and potential fraudulent accounting entries became public, Jeff soon found himself in the midst of a financial scandal. Articles appeared on the front page of the *Wall Street Journal*, *USA Today*, *New York Times*, and many other publications. Jeff's relatively normal life was soon spinning out of control.

Jeff was asked to resign by the board of directors. After an intense and extensive internal investigation, Jeff was cleared by the company. However, shortly thereafter, the SEC and FBI began a three-year investigation into the situation. Shareholder suits were filed. Jeff hired Jones Day, a prominent national law firm, and three attorneys began the four-year defense of government allegations. Most importantly, Jeff began the personal practice of praying daily and earnestly for guidance and discernment.

In the wake of the business disaster, and during a three-year federal investigation, two friends from a private equity firm believed that Jeff could provide assistance to Ruth's Chris Steak House. The private equity firm conducted a thorough background investigation and offered Jeff an opportunity to serve as chief financial officer of Ruth's Chris. Working for Ruth's Chris was a blessing in that it allowed Jeff to focus on productive business issues and prepare for the future. Jeff worked as CFO and interim chief executive. He led the company through a debt restructuring and the 2003 "mad cow" scare.

But, the Rent-Way case followed Jeff to Ruth's Chris as the justice system conducted a relentless and possibly politically motivated investigation. During this time, Jeff experienced the unconditional love of many family members, friends, and business colleagues. Also, there was a Christian neighbor, Steve Borderline, who reached out to Jeff. Steve introduced Jeff to a Bible study and a men's prayer group. Jeff's faith matured immeasurably during this period of high anxiety. Jeff learned to trust and rely on the Lord. Paula, Steve Bordelon, several Christian brothers, and many others gave Jeff the strength to stay focused on the Lord and to persevere during the government's investigation.

After nearly four years, the U.S. Attorney's office offered Jeff a choice. The options were to plea to conspiracy to commit a "books and records" violation or go to trial and, if convicted of even one count of fraud, face twenty-five years in prison without parole. The choice was clear, but painful. A family meeting was held to tell the girls that Dad was going away for a year. In accordance with the government's sentencing rules, eleven points were assigned to Jeff's plea. In late 2003, Jeff was sentenced to serve thirteen months of incarceration.

Prison

On December 30, 2003, Jeff and Paula made the awkward drive from their home in Mandeville, Louisiana, to Eglin Federal Prison Camp in Destin, Florida. Their good friends Steve and Diane Bordelon accompanied them on the trip. Jeff checked in at the guard house, thanked the Bordelons, and kissed Paula good-bye. He reported to prison with his Bible and wedding ring. In total, he was incarcerated for 306 interesting, bizarre, and shocking days. Prison was an eye-opening experience in terms of learning to turn to Christ, to rely on God and know the Holy Spirit as never before. It was bizarre in terms of experiencing federal bureaucracy and apparent hypocrisy. Prison was shocking in terms of experiencing random acts of cruelty and kindness; stupidity and intelligence; and sin and holiness. Many good Christian inmates reached out to Jeff. "The Holy Spirit is alive and well in prison."

It was shocking to experience the paradoxes of life as an inmate. One minute a Christian former crack dealer is making Christlike sacrifices to help fellow inmates, and the next minute a Wickham worshipping meth dealer is organizing an animal sacrifice. Jeff worked on Road & Grounds Crew #13, also known as "Pappy's Ditch Bitches." He experienced Hurricane Ivan and a one-week bizarre transfer to Yazoo City, Mississippi, to a new prison facility devoid of beds, food (other than orange juice and peanut butter), chairs, and phones. The unconditional love of Paula, Kelli, Kourtney, Kayce, Mom, Dad, and many good friends and colleagues kept Jeff going. Learning to seek God's will through prayer, Bible study, and worship gave Jeff a sense of peace and confidence that all would be just fine. Learning to turn over the trials of life to our Savior was a powerful lesson.

Release from prison was directly to a halfway house in New Orleans. Similar to the movie *Trading Places,* Jeff went from president to prep cook and learned the basics of kitchen work from Little Momma and Chiquita. He also gained appreciation for challenges inmates face when they reenter the free world.

Rebuilding a Life

Thanks to their good friend Rob Selati and business partners David Halpern and Gary Solomon, Jeff and Paula were given the opportunity to open a Ruth's Chris Steak House franchise in Charlotte, North Carolina. They sold their home and moved from Mandeville, Louisiana, to Charlotte three weeks before Hurricane Katrina struck the Gulf Coast.

In October 2005, approximately eleven months following Jeff's release from prison, Jeff and Paula opened their first Ruth's Chris Steak House in South-Park neighborhood of Charlotte. Eighteen months later, in February 2007, a second restaurant was opened in Uptown Charlotte, and twenty months later a third restaurant was opened in the heart of historic Savannah, Georgia. And now, it appears a fourth restaurant will be opened in Asheville, North Carolina.

Jeff is grateful for the opportunity to rebuild his life. He has been blessed with many good friends and forever grateful for God's amazing grace. Jeff more than ever before understands the importance of spending time daily with our Savior. Learning to trust and rely on God were the great lessons of his trial. The notion of being self-sufficient and not needing anyone's help is a horrible sin and greatly disrespects our Savior. Jeff now prays earnestly and daily for discernment to do God's will and to glorify Him in all things.

The meteoric growth of Rent-Way, the insidious temptation to please The Street, and the dramatic fall from Wall Street darling to federal inmate illustrate the perils of seeking to please Wall Street instead of earnestly seeking to please our Lord and Savior, Jesus Christ. The business world, and especially the world of high-growth publicly traded companies, is full of temptations and distractions that can pull one's focus from Christ to the carnal world. Many lessons can be learned from Jeff's experience. The foremost lesson is to seek God's Will. By prayerfully seeking God's wisdom, one can avoid many of the temptations and pitfalls of Wall Street. Secondarily, it is critical to surround oneself with colleagues and employees of character, people who place their moral integrity above the financial bottom line. Pressure exists at all levels for the many stake-holders in a public company. Data must be checked and rechecked with reliable systems. People and systems can be easily compromised in periods of high growth. In order to avoid the pitfalls and temptations common to public companies, one must seek God's will and discernment. That means reading the Bible, spending quiet time in prayer every day, and asking God for His advice. He is our shepherd and will guide us.

Another important lesson is to approach business decisions with a healthy amount of skepticism. Information and data must be challenged, scrutinized, and scrubbed to thwart the temptations to please "The Street." Be persistent in getting accurate information. Government regulation and the political nature of our justice system weave a dangerous web. The justice system is unsophisticated in understanding the complexities of business. It can be unforgiving and arbitrary. Business decisions are not always in black-and-white situations. We need to prayerfully seek the Lord's discernment and allow time for Him to work in our lives.

HOPE: OVERCOMING PRESSURE IN PUBLIC COMPANIES

In the seventeenth century, at the height of the Puritan impact on English culture, the Westminster Confession of Faith[6] (WCF) was written as a statement of Bible-based faith. It was composed by some of the best-prepared theologians and pastors in history. Today it continues to be used as a secondary standard, below the higher authority of Holy Scripture, as a test of one's holding to a consistent system of biblical doctrine.[7] It reflects a biblical world and life view that is relevant to recovery of a potent Christian business ethic.

The WCF represents a cultural consensus that crossed the Atlantic and dominated the American colonies through the end of the eighteenth century. Eventually, the Reformed lead was eclipsed by the Methodists, Baptists, and more. But it remains an abiding influence in the USA based on our founding documents, and there is even a sort of revival and resurgence in the past decade.[8] Nevertheless, the psychology of the WCF played a major role in the Puritan approach to business, and it has persisted, often as a common grace, in American society. The current question is whither now from here for business ethics in daily practice. Three topics with selected portions from the WCF will be noted for their importance in understanding the strengths and constraints on our role as Christians in business ethics today. Doing right according to God's Word is the way to overcome the pressure of working in a public company.

Biblical Sanctification

Knowing that every person is born with an original sin nature, Christ completed His sacrifice for us that we might have eternal life. Furthermore, to be born again means that even in this mortal life, Christ is perfecting us to be progressively more like Him over time. Never is absolute perfection reached this side of heaven, but we can improve and do good works, in all areas, by His grace. That would include more and more ethical thinking, speaking, and working in public companies per our individual calling. There is hope to be able to do the right thing!

> And we pray this in order that you may live a life worthy of the Lord and may please him in every way: bearing fruit in every good work, growing in the knowledge of God, being strengthened with all power according to his glorious might so that you may have great endurance and patience. (Col. 1:10–11 NIV)

1. This sanctification is throughout, in the whole man; yet imperfect in this life, there abiding still some remnants of corruption in every part; whence ariseth a continual and irreconcilable war, the flesh lusting against the Spirit, and the Spirit against the flesh.
2. In which war, although the remaining corruption, for a time, may much prevail; yet, through the continual supply of strength from the sanctifying Spirit of Christ, the regenerate part doth overcome; and so, the saints grow in grace, perfecting holiness in the fear of God. (WCF, chapter 13, sections 2–3)

Good Works

The Puritans, some of the main characters in the development and transmission of the Protestant ethic,[9] were known as "marketplace monks." Rather than the most pious living in an isolated monastery, worship was seen as part of working every day in the marketplace. The Christian's life in family, church, government, and business was an extension of the heart commitment of Deuteronomy 6:4, "loving God with heart, soul and strength.

Weber puzzled over the motivation of the Puritans, even though he quoted the WCF at length. He assumed the work was aimed at petition, suasion or appeasement of a fearsome god. Instead, business effort was the fruit of a new heart that was being sanctified. In fact, with strong assurance of faith in the grace of Christ, the Puritans did not require hard work or a bank account in order to comfort their souls about their eternal estate. The Protestant work ethic was the result of God's grace, not merit for it.

> But someone will say, "You have faith; I have deeds." Show me your faith without deeds, and I will show you my faith by what I do. You believe that there is one God. Good! Even the demons believe that—and shudder. You foolish man, do you want evidence that faith without deeds is useless? Was not our ancestor Abraham considered righteous for what he did when he offered his son Isaac on the altar? You see that his faith and his actions were working together, and his faith was made complete by what he did. (James 2:18–22 NIV)

1. Good works are only such as God hath commanded in his holy Word, and not such as, without the warrant thereof, are devised by men, out of blind zeal, or upon any pretense of good intention.
2. These good works, done in obedience to God's commandments, are the fruits and evidences of a true and lively faith: and by them believers manifest their thankfulness, strengthen their assurance, edify their brethren, adorn the profession of the gospel, stop the mouths of the adversaries, and glorify God, whose workmanship they are, created in Christ Jesus thereunto, that, having their fruit unto holiness, they may have the end, eternal life.
3. Their ability to do good works is not at all of themselves, but wholly from the Spirit of Christ. And that they may be enabled thereunto, beside the graces they have already received, there is required an actual influence of the same Holy Spirit, to work in them to will, and to do, of his good pleasure: yet are they not hereupon to grow negligent, as if they were not bound to perform any duty unless upon a special motion of the Spirit; but they ought to be diligent in stirring up the grace of God that is in them.
5. We cannot by our best works merit pardon of sin, or eternal life at the hand of God, by reason of the great disproportion that is between them and the glory to come; and the infinite distance that is between

us and God, whom, by them, we can neither profit, nor satisfy for the debt of our former sins, but when we have done all we can, we have done but our duty, and are unprofitable servants: and because, as they are good, they proceed from his Spirit; and as they are wrought by us, they are defiled, and mixed with so much weakness and imperfection, that they cannot endure the severity of God's judgment. (WCF, chapter 16, sections 1–3, 5)

Assurance of Faith

Rather than trying to achieve salvation by good works in the marketplace, the Anglo Protestants were "working out" their salvation in the sense of working out all the real implications of what it meant to be a disciple of Christ. Without compartments, all of life was seen as sacred, part of God's world. Yet with their ordinary sort of asceticism, they were devoted to family, church, and the community more than lavish spending of any profits that built up. Thus, there was capital available later for investing in new enterprises. The public market exchange was developed to coordinate the investments and their results.

Primarily, assurance of faith had its eternal importance, of course, but it did allow for a more calm and objective review of business results on a regular basis. This temperament was excellent for the development of financial statements such as the balance sheet, cash flow, and income statement, and—this is key—their regular review as enterprise value was growing. The enterprise could exist beyond the individual or family as a "good work" of one's livelihood.

> We know that we have come to know him if we obey his commands. (1 John 2:3 NIV)

1. This certainty is not a bare conjectural and probable persuasion grounded upon a fallible hope; but an infallible assurance of faith founded upon the divine truth of the promises of salvation, the inward evidence of those graces unto which these promises are made, the testimony of the Spirit of adoption witnessing with our spirits that we are the children of God, which Spirit is the earnest of our inheritance, whereby we are sealed to the day of redemption.

2. This infallible assurance doth not so belong to the essence of faith, but that a true believer may wait long, and conflict with many difficulties before he be partaker of it: yet, being enabled by the Spirit to know the things which are freely given him of God, he may, without extraordi-

nary revelation, in the right use of ordinary means, attain thereunto. And therefore it is the duty of everyone to give all diligence to make his calling and election sure, that thereby his heart may be enlarged in peace and joy in the Holy Ghost, in love and thankfulness to God, and in strength and cheerfulness in the duties of obedience, the proper fruits of this assurance; so far is it from inclining men to looseness. (WCF, chapter 18, sections 2–3)

HELP: CHRISTIAN BUSINESS ETHICS FOR THE PUBLIC COMPANY

Hope for ethical work in public companies is a wonderful thing. Help is even better in order to drive the beliefs and relief of Christian hope into daily service of the King. And the theology that is the basis of the hope is one that must be applied in order to be meaningful. It must give real help for the ethical decisions that make a company both good and great. The Reformed Christian theologian John M. Frame has repeated that "all good theology is applied theology." A recent *festschift* for his lifetime of scholarship rings the changes on that theme many times over.[10]

A keystone of Frame's approach to pastoral and social ethics is to work in a Christian worldview with three angles on the Christian life, all biblically based.[11] With (1) the norms of Scripture, the businessperson makes decisions. In (2) particular situations in public companies that require deep and broad knowledge about business and the corporation, in particular, wisdom is applied. Another facet is added when (3) the person's character is added to the full ethical analysis. Similar to the secular existential emphasis in ethics, the human element cannot be omitted for an artificial intelligence that would mindlessly apply general rules to particular situations over and over in search of wise and righteous ethical judgments.

Knowing Relevant Biblical Norms

The Creator has provided sufficient revelation for people to know the ethics of life's situations. His special revelation to us is the Bible and is intended by God to give us what we need to do "every good work." The norms about ownership, employment, etc. have been imparted to us verbally in Scripture. They provide instruction, conviction, correction, and training for making good decisions in

ethical dilemmas. All the stakeholders in a public company have this available
to them. While there is a benefit for non-Christians, the heart must be regener-
ated to apply the right norm in the right situation with a pure heart.

> All Scripture is God-breathed and is useful for teaching, rebuk-
> ing, correcting and training in righteousness, so that the man
> of God may be thoroughly equipped for every good work. (2
> Tim. 3:16–17)

Knowing Business Situations

As we come to know business, in general, and businesses, in particular, discernment grows for apt practices in the public company. There is no substitute for
an informed understanding of the elements of the business context. What are
the circumstances of the ethical dilemma? What are the goals to be pursued?
Jesus is commanding us to learn and teach others how to obey Him in all areas
of life, including business. Public companies are very complex, and their financial arrangements can be myriad. There must a competence that is equivalent to
the challenge in sophistication. Then, God's Word can illuminate the disciple,
enabling him to know and do the right thing. In this life, there will continue
to be gray areas, as growth in Christ is a process. But the Lord will teach day by
day, and we should have the humility to learn from others.

> Then Jesus came to them and said, "All authority in heaven
> and on earth has been given to me. Therefore go and make dis-
> ciples of all nations, baptizing them in the name of the Father
> and of the Son and of the Holy Spirit, and teaching them to
> obey everything I have commanded you. And surely I am with
> you always, to the very end of the age." (Matt. 28:18–20 NIV)

Knowing the Human Heart

In order to have the courage of our convictions in the public company, there
must be an ongoing process of transformation of our inner life in concert with
obedience to the extent that we know God's Word and know the situation for
application. This takes place in God's way as we live out our faith in family,
church, and state. Reading the Bible, biblical prayer, church fellowship with
other believers, observing the sacraments, and obeying the commandments are
the means of grace that the Lord uses to make us ready to move out and into

the battle here and now for His new "Promised Land."

> Therefore, I urge you, brothers, in view of God's mercy, to offer your bodies as living sacrifices, holy and pleasing to God—this is your spiritual act of worship. Do not conform any longer to the pattern of this world, but be transformed by the renewing of your mind. Then you will be able to test and approve what God's will is—his good, pleasing and perfect will. (Rom. 12:1–2 NIV)

Notes

1. Max Weber, *The Protestant Ethics and the Spirit of Capitalism* (New York: Routledge Classics, 1904, 1920); John Chamberlain, *The Enterprising Americans: A Business History of the United States* (New York: Harper and Row, 1961); David Landes, *The Wealth and Poverty of Nations* (New York: Norton. 1998);

Samuel Huntington, *Who Are We? The Challenges to America's National Identity* (New York: Simon & Schuster, 2004).

2. Jim Collins, *Good to Great: Why Some Companies Make the Leap . . . and Others Don't* (New York: HarperCollins, 2001).

3. Jim Collins, *How the Mighty Fall: And Why Some Companies Never Give In* (New York: HarperCollins, 2009).

4. Wayne Grudem, *Business to the Glory of God* (Wheaton, IL: Crossway, 2004)

5. Ibid., 132.

6. Through an Internet search, you will find many sites that reproduce the Westminster Confession of Faith in its entirety.

7. R. C. Sproul, *Truths We Confess: A Layman's Guide to the Westminster Confession of Faith*, vols. 1–3 (Phillipsburg, NJ: P & R, 2006, 2007, 2008).

8. Collin Hansen, *Young, Restless, Reformed: A Journalist's Journey with the New Calvinists* (Wheaton, IL: Crossway Books, 2008).

9. Robert Merton, "Science, Technology and Society in Seventeenth Century England," *Osiris*, vol. 4, pt. 2 (Bruges: St. Catherine Press, 1938), 360–632;

David McClelland, *The Achieving Society* (New York: The Free Press. 1961);

Lawrence Harrison and Samuel Huntington, *Culture Matters: How Values Shape Human Progress* (New York: Basic Books, 2000).

10. John Hughes, *Speaking the Truth in Love: The Theology of John M. Frame.* (Phillipsburg, NJ: P & R, 2009).

11. John Frame, *The Doctrine of the Christian Life* (Phillipsburg, NJ: P & R, 2008).

THE IMPORTANCE OF A BUSINESS LEADER'S CONTRIBUTION TO COMMUNITY LEADERSHIP

CHUCK STETSON

Chuck Stetson co-founded PEI Funds in 1992, where he is a Managing Director. Previously he was a Managing Director of Venture Capital Fund of America, leading the fund's U.S. investments and assisting in raising $50 million from U.S. and European investors. Before joining VCFA, Mr. Stetson was an investment banker, as President of Davis Skaggs Capital in San Francisco and previously as Vice President of Bache Halsey Stuart in New York and San Francisco. He pioneered private equity secondaries with a purchase of a portfolio of interests in 1978. Mister Stetson is a graduate of Yale University and the Columbia University Graduate School of Business.

In the movie about the U.S. astronauts' trip to the moon on *Apollo 13*, there was a point at which it became clear that the spaceship was not going to reenter the earth's orbit. Yet in one communication at the Houston Space Center, the man in charge told his troops, "Failure is not an option."

We have a similar crisis brewing in America, the likes of which I have not seen in my lifetime. The structures of freedom and democracy have been severely weakened over the last fifty years, and in the last couple of years at an increasingly rapid rate. Yet, there is a tsunami building five hundred miles away at sea, and when it arrives, it will demolish our health care and our pensions, and freedom and democracy will go by the boards. We saw what happened in Haiti when the structures of the buildings were weak. The buildings collapsed. We have a number of weak structures holding up democracy, and they will surely collapse unless all of us suit up and take appropriate coordinated actions.

David Gergen made an interesting point in the December 12 issue of *U.S. News and World Report*:

> Indeed, confidence in government plummeted back in the '60s and '70s and has never really recovered. It was nearly four decades ago that John Gardner first observed that at the founding, with a population of 3 million, the republic spawned a dozen world-class leaders—Washington, Jefferson, Franklin, Adams, Madison, and Hamilton among them—but today, with a population nearly 100 times that, we struggle to produce even one or two.

But it is even much deeper than that. The last line of the Declaration of Independence reads, "We mutually pledge to each other our Lives, our Fortunes and our sacred Honor." This was all for the common good of the people of America. My premise is that if we don't have the right kind of civic leadership, we will not have a civil society, thus no democracy and an impaired entrepreneurship and venture capital. Americans have always been resourceful and resilient, and we can prevent this crisis. To create the environment for successful companies, we need to address three issues:

1. Why is civic leadership critical to all businesses?
2. What are some of the bigger issues that we need to address individually?
3. What are some of the bigger issues we need to address collectively?

In this article, civic leadership is defined as "standing up for what is the right thing to do in business, both at the company level and at the community level, for the common good of all." Civic leadership is thus much more than leadership itself. It incorporates, among other things, the idea of living with our deepest differences in freedom and democracy, and at the same time giving our time, our talent, and our treasure to make a better world for all, both inside our companies (both public and private) and, particularly, in our communities. Civic leadership is built on John Calvin's principles of the depravity of mankind, upon which James Madison wrote Federalist No. 51. Our efforts need to be turned toward the biggest issues that we face.

In this article, I will be drawing on my experience over thirty years as a venture capitalist and civic entrepreneur in founding the nonprofit Essentials in Education. Scott Oliphant will give his theological overview in a separate article.

Why Is Civic Leadership Critical?

In business, we can see the effects of civic leadership at the company level in successful companies. In the early 1980s, I was a limited partner of the Mayfield Funds. The late Tommy Davis, one of the then leading venture capitalists, asked me to do a research study of his most successful companies. We looked at more than one hundred investments that Tommy had made in the 1960s, 1970s and 1980s and chose the top companies, both in terms of times return, in this case returning fifteen dollars for every one dollar invested, and of recognition as leaders in their industries. What we found and published in *Pratt's Guide to Venture Capital* was that the quality of the initial management team and board of directors was critical for the success of the company. These companies shared five common themes: (1) bedrock integrity; (2) uncompromising principles; (3) a market focus as opposed to a product focus; (4) employee concern, so that everyone was well paid and well treated; and (5) shared values, so that everyone was working as a team. This may sound simplistic, but these were what the most successful companies had. What the management team and the board had was strong values based on absolute virtues of integrity and compassion, among other things. There is moral restraint. These values have been critical for success in venture capital–backed entrepreneurial companies.

But we also need civic leadership more broadly in the business community. This involves getting involved for the best interests of all of the people. Consider a company and the town in which it is operating. If the town is not doing well, it will inevitably negatively impact the company. How can one attract top talent to move to a town that is not doing well?

In 2008, we experienced a collapse of the financial system on a scale unprecedented since the Great Depression of the 1930s. One presidential candidate argued that it was caused by greed. The other presidential candidate argued that it was caused by a need for more regulation. It was neither.

While there was some greed, leaders in the financial community failed to exercise civic leadership. We had transparency.

In 2001, 2002, and 2003, John Snow, the then secretary of the Treasury argued before Congress that it didn't make sense for people to buy homes where they couldn't afford to pay the mortgage. With $200 million of lobbying money from Freddie Mac and Fannie Mae going to Congress, Congress with great transparency said it was fine for people to buy homes that they couldn't afford. One argument advanced at the time was that they could sell them for a greater price, and that would give them greater wealth.

What is the problem? We don't have moral restraint. What do I mean?

When I first entered the investment banking business in the early 1970s, no one would have written a memorandum suggesting financing for a tobacco company or a casino. It would have been ridiculous Why? Everyone knew you didn't do it. Tobacco companies and casinos were "sin" stocks. It wasn't until 1979 that Wall Street finally financed a casino company. There was moral restraint, and that is what we need today. That is what I mean by civic leadership. We need leaders to step forward and insist upon and provide moral restraint.

The consequences for failure are severe. When Enron and WorldCom collapsed, Congress then got involved and passed Sarbanes-Oxley legislation, which has effectively ended the dominance of the U.S. in IPOs. China is now the "top dog" in IPOs because Congress effectively made us give up our leadership in the U.S. The closing down of the IPO market by Congress has particularly hurt venture capital companies by closing off what was once as much as 50 percent of the financial exits. This legislation has dramatically reduced returns and provided huge disincentives for creating venture-backed companies going forward. We need to remember that since 1971, venture-backed companies now employ 9 percent of the U.S. workforce and 18 percent of gross domestic product. We are putting at risk new employment opportunities in the U.S. as well as economic growth because of Congress's legislation. Thus, there is a lot at stake here when we don't have civic leadership that could have mitigated the financial crisis and this misguided regulation. More about that later.

Thus, as we have just seen, the most successful venture-backed companies have the right kind of civic leadership at the company level. But that is not sufficient. We must have civic leadership in the communities around us to provide moral restraint and to build a better world. When we don't have moral restraint, government steps in, and there is less freedom, and entrepreneurship and venture capital are impaired and can disappear.

SOME OF THE BIGGER ISSUES THAT WE NEED TO ADDRESS INDIVIDUALLY

What do we need to get the civic leadership we need as a country? It starts with us as business leaders. We need to believe in civic leadership and practice it. We need to mentor others and teach it to them and the next generation at business schools. Then we can make the world a better place to live.

One of my great heroes is William Wilberforce, a lead Parliamentarian in England in the late eighteenth and early nineteenth centuries. As you may recall, he was the Parliamentarian who led the fight to abolish the slave trade and ultimately slavery in the British Empire and turned a self-indulgent and decadent world into a much more civilized world that eventually became Victorian England.

Lessons Learned from William Wilberforce

First, Wilberforce practiced civic leadership, and so should we. Intuitively, he practiced what we saw in the best venture-backed companies. Wilberforce was recognized for his integrity and uncompromising principles that he brought to his job in Parliament. He was market oriented. He knew the needs of his constituents as well as the people of England, and addressed them. Wilberforce reached across the aisles and built coalitions based on the trust that people had in him.

In his job in Parliament, Wilberforce addressed the big issues of the day. Slavery is a huge evil, but often intractable. In Parliament, approximately thirty people were for slavery and thirty people were for abolition, and the rest didn't care. Wilberforce stood up morally and held firm even against strong opposition, including death threats. Equally important was turning around the self-indulgent and decadent world around him. On October 28, 1797, Wilberforce wrote down one of the greatest personal mission statements ever written: "God Almighty has given me two great objects: the abolition of the slave trade and the reformation of manners." Amazingly, he accomplished both objectives with ten friends from his village of Clapham, England, five miles south of the center of London and now a part of it, and not that much money. Many people are surprised that anything can be done with a few people and not much money. This is a message of great hope.

Second, we need to understand that a small number of people exercising civic leadership, even without a lot of money, can make a huge difference. This is the message of a one-hour documentary—"The Better Hour: The Legacy of William Wilberforce"—that a group of us produced in 2008. William Wilberforce was once a great icon of civic leadership and philanthropy around the world. He was such a household name in America in the nineteenth century that Abraham Lincoln once said that "of course, every school boy knows William Wilberforce." Several years ago, only 3 percent of Americans recognized the name William Wilberforce. History textbooks for public schools, except for a one-line mention in one textbook, take little note of this great statesman and first major philanthropist. According to one of the leading historians today, Professor David Brion Davis at Yale University, most of the historians that he knows at the university level are Marxist, and they don't like this story line of history. What they prefer is a form of despair: change is coming whether you like it or not, so get used to it. Unfortunately, that is a very inaccurate read of history that we are teaching the next generation, and we have to start doing something about it now.

Third, we need to be strategic in our giving of our time, our talent, and our treasure. Most people have overlooked the fact that Wilberforce was really the first great philanthropist in the world. Along with his full-time job in Parliament, he was actively involved in and gave to sixty-nine voluntary organizations. These organizations were the means of developing the broad-based support for changing the culture upstream from legislation.

In these organizations, Wilberforce was a key player. He was one of the top five officers of twenty-seven of these organizations, on the committee of five, governor of five, treasurer of one, and patron of one. My wife's personal favorite organization that Wilberforce created is the Royal Society for the Prevention of Cruelty to Animals, which sixty years later became the Humane Society. Wilberforce started doing all his philanthropy one hundred years before Andrew Carnegie wrote his "The Gospel of Wealth."

Fourth, we need to suit up, as William Wilberforce and his friends did, and engage in the big issues of the day. In doing so, we will need to stand up against significant opposition, including death threats, for what is right and create a better world. The last 130 years have been an anomaly historically. When premillennialists started withdrawing from the public square, they caused other Christians to withdrawn from the public square, with disastrous consequences. Instead of being "the salt of the earth" and "the light of the world" as Jesus commanded, Christians began sitting on the sidelines, focusing on our own salvation and not paying any attention to the kingdom of God, at huge cost to everyone.

Democracy at Stake for Christians

All of us are losing the moral authority that is critical to democracy as Christians, who, according to the Gallup poll, comprise 84 percent of Americans, have withdrawn from the public square over the last 130 years. It has three big implications:

1. *Big implications for philanthropy.* What do Christians who have withdrawn from public engagement give to? The focus of philanthropy has been largely on mission work. This is a very selfish focus. Christians have been looking out for themselves and perhaps a few friends, and not looking out for everyone, as their Scriptures require.

2. *Big implications for communities.* By following their current strategy, Christians have abandoned their communities—literature, the arts, movies, and the public square in general.

   During the twentieth century, Christians—the dominant faith group in America—for the most part *have allowed a culture of violence and death to develop.* Look at the movies. Very few Christians are engaged.

3. *Big implications on politics.* Christians allowed atheists to take over, with disastrous consequences. Christians allowed the genocide of 120 million people in the first half of the twentieth century at the hands of atheists Hitler, Joseph Stalin, and Chairman Mao.

But look at what else we have allowed to happen in the second half of the twentieth century. Approximately 400 million children in China and 50 million in the U.S. have been killed through abortion. We have thus killed more than 500 million adults and children of our own tribe—one-tenth of all the people now living. No century in all of history has been that cruel. Yet, Christians stood silent and allowed this to happen.

We need to learn and understand the achievements of Wilberforce and tell our friends and make sure our children and our grandchildren know about him and his great message of hope, and we ourselves need to model what Wilberforce did two hundred years ago to make a better world. We need Christians to be real Christians and engage communities with grace to make a better world

WHAT ARE SOME OF THE BIGGER ISSUES FACING US COLLECTIVELY?

At a conference of senior venture capitalists in Boston last September, I was

308 // Business Ethics Today

asked the question, "What could crush us collectively as an industry and as a country?" My response was, "Government, education, and demographics." In each instance, I believe that our businesses and communities will be severely impacted in a negative fashion, including revenues, income, and employment. Let's look at each in turn. Notice that secularism by definition has no resources. It is a free-for-all, bringing chaos out of order in the fashion of Genesis 11. The secularists need Christians to bring order out of chaos.

Government

We need to be more proactive with regulatory issues. In the U.S., Congress is trying to fix some of the moral lapses in Enron, and WorldCom did so by giving away the initial public offering market to China by establishing unrealistically strict standards for accounting. We saw earlier that the venture industry has less liquidity for existing investments and cannot be the engine that it has been for employment or the driver of growth that it has been.

But the issues are much broader than that. Religious freedom is under attack in America. The attack on religious freedom is particularly problematic since it is the glue to a civil society. John Adams was accurate when he said in 1798, "We have no government armed with power capable of contending with human passions unbridled by morality and religion. Avarice, ambition, revenge, or gallantry, would break the strongest cords of our Constitution as a whale goes through a net. The U.S. Constitution is made for a moral and religious people. It is wholly inadequate to the government of any other."[1]

In a country where 84 percent of the people profess to be Christian according to survey polls, the Congress passed "hate speech" legislation attached to a Defense Appropriation Bill and signed by the president of the U.S. that makes it a federal crime to speak in public the whole gospel. You and I can be arrested for speaking about certain parts of the Bible in a public venue. The U.S. Supreme Court in the Bob Jones decision in 1980 made it a point that public policy, i.e., hate speech, trumps the First Amendment speech.

The threats to free speech are a cloud of oppression over a community. People can't possibly perform at their best with this cloud over them.

We all have to be involved.

With respect to regulatory issues, it starts with our trade associations. In my case, I have been talking with the ingoing and outgoing chairman of the National Venture Capital Association about getting better organized to address the regulatory issues that we have and working collaboratively with other groups.

On religious freedom, there are some outstanding groups, such as the Becket Fund, that are standing up for religious freedom for all.

Education

We have done a very poor job in training the next generation. Even in our business schools, we don't teach civic leadership. We need to address teaching civic leadership in business education. In September 2008, the *HBS Alumni Bulletin* of Harvard Business School published an article titled "Building a Better MBA" in which the school, one month before its one hundredth anniversary, admitted that the MBA curriculum is broken because it is not responsive to the needs companies have, particularly in leadership. Working with the John Templeton Foundation, our largest donor at Essentials in Education, we have been meeting with deans and faculty of the elite business schools, as well as a number of major foundations, including the Bill and Melinda Gates Foundation, the William Hewlett Foundation, and others.

There is both bad and good news. In the research to date, business schools don't teach civic leadership. Ethics, when taught, is relative and refuses to recognize the universal moral laws. Even the most prominent professors, such as Michael Porter, teach a form of utilitarianism—the greatest good for the greatest number of people—which people like Peter Singer can't live with even though he espouses it, as did the late Christopher Reeve. Why are we teaching such nonsense to the next generation that will be the next captains of industry. In short, we have a huge failure to teach what is needed in business for successful companies and the common good.

The good news is that we found that between 40 and 50 percent of students are taking social enterprise courses in their second year and are interested in building a better world. We believe that we have developed a way to meet this need and provide civic leadership at the elite business schools.

When it comes to sending our children or grandchildren to schools, including business schools, or giving as alumni, we need to do our homework in the same way that we do in business. We need to ask questions. Who are the most respected teachers? We need to look at their course syllabi. What are they teaching with respect to leadership? What do they teach about civics?

Demographics

At a recent conference on corporate venturing and corporate innovation, some of the largest global companies, including Procter & Gamble and Citigroup, presented their growth strategy. I asked the chief innovations officer at each of these two companies about how they are dealing with the fact that there are one hundred countries where the reproduction rate is below the replacement rate, and that in some cases it was quite serious, such as Japan and Italy, where the rates are 1.1 and 1.3. I pointed out that the reproduction rates in Japan and Italy mean that in the next generation there will only be half the Japanese and half of the Italians in the workplace that there are today. At the same time, there will be two times the number of people over sixty-five, because of the current baby boomers, that half of today's wage earners will need to support. If the U.S. goes in this direction, where health care is already 18 percent of the economy (GDP), how can we have a fourfold increase by definition? It doesn't work. What happens to pensions? They won't work either. Who will the companies sell their products to, and what kind of products will they sell? If there are only half the workers who are making money, what will that do to shareholder values? When I raise that issue with these leading global corporations, their jaws drop. They haven't connected the dots as yet, and they don't have an answer. I tell them that they better have an answer, because shareholders will figure it out and ask why businesses are hurting their long-term shareholder values.

Interestingly enough, one consultant to the leading global companies that measures corporate innovation and growth told me that addressing demographics was beyond her expertise, so she doesn't measure it. Measuring the inconsequential data can give a false sense of security and only heightens the crisis when it comes. Are we ready for the type of earthquake that hit Haiti?

The collapse of marriage, which is occurring around the world, is surprising. In surveys of college freshmen in the United States, ninety-four expect to get married. Yet in the U.S., we are experience a collapse in marriage, as measured by the recently released Marriage Index, but it is preventable if business and others get involved. One thing that social scientists everywhere agree on is that marriage leads to greater wealth, great health, longer life, and a happier life. What is there not to like about that? Yet marriage, because of no-fault divorce and cohabiting, is in a collapse in the U.S. Research I initiated and funded has found that divorce and unwed childbearing costs $112 billion per year—$1.1 trillion over a ten-year period. It is a very conservative number, likely to be as much as $150 billion per year or $1.5 trillion over ten years. Even on a conservative basis, it costs taxpayers more than the annual cost for the war in Iraq. Separate think tanks in New Zealand, Canada, and Great Britain each copied the idea and did a study for their own countries.

If we don't get marriage right, we will continue to deal with the symptoms, including school failure, lower grades, and lower graduation rates, and incarceration rates two times greater for alternatives to marriage. In the U.S., we can't build jails fast enough. I spoke recently with the chairman of a multibillion-dollar foundation focusing on disadvantaged children from birth to eight years old. I asked the chairman, "Why are you only focused on dealing with the symptoms and not dealing with the problem?" We have to focus on allocating some money to the problem, not just the symptoms. We need to turn the faucet causing the problems off upstream or else we will continually be doing huge amounts of unnecessary cleanup.

Here are a few suggestions of things we can all do now as business leaders:

In the Community. We need to make sure that our local churches and houses of worship are teaching marriage preparation, including dating and courtship, and marriage enrichment. At the colleges and graduate schools where we send our children, do they have separate housing for men and for women? In our public schools, we need to stop sex education and replace it with instruction in dating and courtship. At Yale University, for example, we need to stop "Sex Week" in early February, which promotes pornography and free sex, all supported by the university faculty and administration. We have to be the grown-ups for the personnel of our universities.

In the Streets and at the Hill. We need to draw the line in the sand and sign the Manhattan Declaration, stating publicly that we will disobey all laws that disregard the sanctity of life, the traditional definition of marriage, and religious freedom. In doing so, we will be reclaiming the great tradition of Martin Luther King Jr.'s Letter from Birmingham Jail, which draws upon Augustine's observation that "an unjust law is no law at all."

The Manhattan Declaration, released on November 20, 2009, is "A Call of Christian Conscience" on the principles of sanctity of life, the sanctity of marriage between a man and a woman, and of religious liberty. Let me read you the last paragraph:

> Because we honor justice and the common good, we will not comply with any edict that purports to compel our institutions to participate in abortions, embryo- destructive research, assisted suicide and euthanasia, or any other anti-life act; nor will we bend to any rule purporting to force us to bless immoral sexual partnerships, treat them as marriages or the equivalent, or refrain from proclaiming the truth, as we know it, about morality and immorality and marriage and the family. We will

fully and ungrudgingly render to Caesar what is Caesar's. But under no circumstances will we render to Caesar what is God's.[2]

This last paragraph is reminiscent of the Declaration of Independence, which ends with the following words: "And for the support of this Declaration, with a firm reliance on the protection of Divine Providence, we mutually pledge to each other our Lives, our Fortunes and our sacred Honor."

Of the fifty-six who signed the Declaration of Independence, nine died of wounds or hardships during the war. Five were captured and imprisoned, in each case with brutal treatment. Several lost wives, sons, or entire families. One lost his thirteen children. Two wives were brutally treated. All were, at one time or another, the victims of manhunts, and were driven from their homes. Twelve signers had their homes completely burned. Seventeen lost everything they owned. Yet not one defected or went back on his pledged word. Their honor, and the nation they sacrificed so much to create, is still intact.

In the Courts, at the Polls, and on our Knees. In a similar way, we need to stand up for principle, and like Martin Luther King Jr., stand ready to defy unjust laws. Are you willing to take a stand and go to jail? Are you going to inquire of your elected representatives whether they have signed the Manhattan Declaration and will honestly uphold it? I have talked to some politicians, and some of them are in shock over it and the program that a group of us have put together for Fall 2010—"A Call to Pray and Act"—which includes a forty-day fast for the healing of this nation.

These are just a few illustrative examples of actions that each of us can and must do to make a better world, where business and society can flourish. There are plenty of issues that need to be addressed if we are going to have a healthy civil society and a healthy democracy. We clearly need to address these top three—government, education, and demographics. My question to you is, what are you personally going to get involved in?

Ronald Reagan said it best:

> Freedom is never more than one generation away from extinction. We didn't pass it on to our children in the bloodstream. It must be fought for, protected, and handed on for them to do the same, or one day we will spend our sunset years telling our children and our children's children what it was like in the United States when men were free.[3]

I would add to that "when we had successful companies that created an enormous number of jobs and improved their communities."

Are we going to sit by and let this happen to our children, grandchildren, our communities, and us? Or are we going to get engaged?

Notes

1. Letter to the Officers of the First Brigade of the Third Division of the Militia of Massachusetts (11 October 1798).
2. Charles Colson, Robert George, Timothy George, "Manhattan Declaration: A Call of Christian Conscience" ((http://manhattandeclaration .org/the-declaration/read.aspx), Copyright 2009.
3. Ronald Reagan, in an address to the annual meeting of the Phoenix Chamber of Commerce, March 30, 1961.

SECTION 1

CHURCH SUPPORT
FOR THOSE DOING BUSINESS IN GOD'S WORLD

SECTION 3:
CHURCH SUPPORT FOR
THOSE DOING BUSINESS
IN GOD'S WORLD

PHILIP J. CLEMENTS

The Church has struggled through the ages with how to deal with business and business people. The Reformation dramatically changed the Church's thinking from the Middle Ages perspective of business being at best a necessary evil and at worst just evil. The Middle Ages saw those who wished to be holy separating themselves from the community or renouncing work and wealth, turning to a life of poverty and begging. The Reformers found that the Bible provided worth to work as shown in this text's Section 2.

Unfortunately, the modern church and the modern seminary have a weak understanding of business and how to aid business people in the congregation. For many churches, theologians and seminaries modernity has lead to a rejection of the view of the goodness of business, as Barry Asmus and Wayne Grudem warn in their paper in chapter 6 of this text. Business is not worthy or is evil. Capitalism is an oppressive and unjust activity. Worse many churches today are adopting the abolition of private property and wealth outlined in the communist section in this text's paper, "Are Profits Moral?" Unfortunately, most of these churches, pastors and seminaries would deny this perspective and would assert that they fully teach and preach the *entire counsel* of God.

The two papers in this section endeavor to show how the Church can aid the business person in the congregation. To these papers needs to be added the closing section of the Kims' paper, "Three Offices and the Entrepreneur," in Section 2 of this text. The Center believes it is essential for the entire Christian community to participate in understanding business and aid in the development of proper Christian business ethics. The Center's research finds that Christian business ethics have led to the prosperity the world enjoys today. However, because of the church's struggle with what to do with business, outlined above, the Center feels called to organize a section of each conference to develop and teach how the church and pastors can better minister to the business person in the pew.

CHURCH SUPPORT FOR DOING BUSINESS IN GOD'S WORLD

The first paper, "Church Support for Doing Business in God's World," by Ronald Ferner and Philip Ryken sets the stage well. Ferner and Ryken were lay leader and senior pastor in the same church, Tenth Presbyterian Church, Philadelphia. Ryken has gone on to be President of Wheaton College, Wheaton, Illinois. In the opening, the authors summarize the Reformation thinking on calling and work. Their summary is a nice complement to the papers in the prior section on work.

Ferner gives an excellent background of how a businessperson develops perspectives after retiring. After a successful career in business, Ferner retired and began teaching at Philadelphia Bible University. At PBU, Ferner had to explain the merit of business as the university evaluated adding a business program. The authors outline how the church community can come to lack understanding of the role of business in God's world, using the concept of compartmentalization. This point is critical for modern business leaders who wish to understand how God's world works. For readers, Ferner's experience should be seen as the warning for the church leadership. Here is a faithful Christian with good business success, who missed a key aspect of the Christian life for many years.

The authors then turn from the practical experience of business people to the ministry of the church. Several strategies are outlined for better ministry to the business community. First is preaching that nurtures a calling to business. Importantly, the authors note that business leaders need both the public and private ministry of God's word. A pastor needs to know his people so that the pastor can appreciate the daily challenges facing the members of his congregation. As this interaction grows, the authors note that the pastor naturally will become more effective in applying God's Word to the businessperson's situations, thereby giving better counsel. Next, the paper counsels the church to equip the business person to develop a biblical worldview [Christian worldview for this text] and to understand God's Word. Business people need "to understand how to apply their business knowledge in a way that honors and glorifies God." This section of the paper lists a series of preaching topics to aid the church in ministering to the businessperson.

The paper then analyzes the important topic of the Christian witness in the business world. Outlined are both the ways the Christian business person is a witness and how the church can aid the business person in being a witness. Finally the paper explores how the church should allow the business person's talent to be used in the church. The paper does properly note that the church is not a business. Further, the business should have a mission itself to aid those in God's world.

HOW TO GET FAT IN 90 DAYS

"How to Get Fat in Ninety Days!" is a spoof title adopted by Fran McGowen and Mark Futato. While the title is designed to be catchy, the paper is quite serious about the importance of business being an extension of the mission mindedness of the business leader. This paper dovetails nicely with "Church Support for Doing Business in God's World." Following a simple outline of Bible theology on generosity and abundance, the paper jumps into the real life case of McGowen. Personal testimonies, such as McGowen's, make discussions real, as is the case here. McGowen adopted the generosity perspectives as requested by God, including the needed trust that comes along with it. The result was blessing and success for both the business and McGowen himself.

As with all such change in life discussions, caution needs to be noted that there is no secret formula for business success even for the Christian. A number of the papers in this text highlight this important truth. McGowen and Futato would affirm this as well, even though their paper reads just a bit like it is easy to adopt the principles outlined and success will show up on time, all of the time. The Center likes the way this paper is written even with this caveat, because it shows the crispness of business thinking with a strong theological framework. For the reader, McGowen's story has the same stresses we all experience, but it also reveals the blessing of being faithful while also being a very good and diligent businessperson. Let's not miss this latter point, too often the Christian businessperson does not experience the success desired due to a lack of hard work and diligence. Being a generous person, while not being diligent in business may well cause a sudden loss of capital, which God cannot solve.

CHURCH SUPPORT FOR DOING BUSINESS IN GOD'S WORLD

RON FERNER

Ron joined Philadelphia Biblical University in 1997 after retiring from Campbell Soup Company. He presently serves as Dean of the School of Business and Leadership, and Chair of the Undergraduate Business Administration program.

During his career at Campbell's, he held plant manager positions at several Campbell plants including Fremont, Nebraska; Worthington, Minnesota; and Chicago, Illinois. Ron also held management assignments at Campbell's World Headquarters in Camden, New Jersey, including Vice President–Operations/Logistics Strategy. He was transferred to Sacramento, California, as Vice President–Manufacturing, Western Region. His last assignment was at Campbell's World Headquarters in Camden, New Jersey, as Vice President–Low Cost Business Systems, responsible for improving manufacturing and customer service processes throughout the company. Ron received a Bachelor of Science degree in Food Engineering from the Illinois Institute of Technology and an MBA from the University of Chicago.

PHILIP RYKEN

Philip Graham Ryken is President of Wheaton College. He recently served as Senior Minister of Tenth Presbyterian Church in Philadelphia, where he has preached since 1995. He is Bible Teacher for the Alliance of Confessing Evangelicals, speaking nationally on the radio program Every Last Word.

Doctor Ryken was educated at Wheaton College (IL), Westminster Theological Seminary (PA), and the University of Oxford (UK), from which he received his doctorate in historical theology. When he is not preaching or playing with his five children, he likes to read books, shoot baskets, and ponder the relationship between Christian faith and American culture. He has written or edited more than thirty books, including Written in Stone: The Ten Commandments and Today's Moral Crisis.

Dr. Ryken is adjunct faculty for Beeson Divinity School and Westminster Seminary California. He is a board member for Westminster Theological Seminary in Philadelphia and Wheaton College. Dr. Ryken is a council member of Alliance of Confessing Evangelicals and a member of the Evangelical Theological Society and the Union League of Philadelphia.

n the July-August 2001 issue of the *Conference Board Review,* Laura Nash wrote an article entitled "How the Church Has Failed Business." Among Nash's conclusions:

- Businesspeople who claim to love their churches have difficulty identifying any ways in which their religion is a positive resource for them in their working lives.
- Pastors who profess admiration of their leading business congregants simultaneously describe Corporate America as a hotbed of greed and exploitation, a spiritual wasteland, a godless place.
- At best, the two professions have reached detente: they agree to disagree and keep off each other's territory.
- Faithful businesspeople assume one worldview and identity on Sunday, another on Monday morning. They cannot see how a single, church-based faith can be an ethical resource for leadership in a postmodern world.[1]

The present paper aims to address Nash's concerns about the way the church has failed business. It was coauthored by two friends from the same congregation who come from opposite sides of the business/church divide: a pastor and a businessman. Ronald Ferner's business experience includes thirty-five years with Campbell Soup Company in eight locations across the United States. During this time, Ferner and his wife have been part of ten churches, including Philadelphia's Tenth Presbyterian Church, where he presently serves on the Session with his senior minister, Philip Ryken.

The churches where Ferner has worshipped—each in a different denominational context—have used various models to interact with business in general and with businesspeople in particular. Ferner comments: "I had never given much thought to my role as a Christian who was a businessman. I had become a Christian at an early age and tried to live my life as a follower of Christ. It was not until I retired early and took a position at Philadelphia Biblical University that I began to think more deeply about my calling to business as a Christian."

Philadelphia Biblical University (PBU) will celebrate its one hundredth anniversary in 2013. The university came out of the Bible college movement and became a four-year, degree-granting institution in 1958, when it began offering a bachelor of science in Bible. Today, everyone who graduates with an undergraduate degree must earn this Bible degree. However, students may also earn a second bachelor's degree in a professional field (music—1959, social work—1974, or education—1987).

In 1997 Ferner was asked to help develop a business administration degree program that would be coupled with the existing degree in Bible. From the outset, he found that some colleagues disagreed in principle with a Bible college offering a business degree. Typically they differentiated between a calling to "ministry" and a calling to "Ministry." The term *ministry* (in the lower case) was used for laypeople and their service to Christ in the church and in the world, while the term *Ministry* (in the upper case) was reserved for pastors and missionaries.

This terminology raises important questions about business as a calling for Christians—questions that are addressed in the following:

- How does a calling to work in business relate to a Christian businessperson's calling to follow Christ?
- What is the role of God's Word in the life of a Christian businessperson?
- How can the church help a businessperson be effective in witnessing for Christ in the marketplace?
- What is the best way for businesspeople to use their gifts in the church?
- How can business itself serve as a vehicle for Christian witness?

THE CHRISTIAN'S DUAL CALLING TO FAITH AND WORK

Biblical and Theological Framework

The perceived tension between Christian faith and earthly business is nearly as old as the church itself. Even if so-called secular work has not been viewed as intrinsically evil, often it has been regarded as a second-rate way to serve the Lord, not to mention an arena for temptation and ethical compromise.

Going all the way back to the days of the early church, Christendom drew a sharp distinction between the sacred and the secular. There were two kinds of work in the world: one devoted entirely to God's kingdom and the other engaged in earthly business. Yet only people who served in some religious profession truly were called by God. To cite one notable example, the fourth-century theologian Eusebius of Caesarea stated:

> Two ways of life were given by the law of Christ to his church. The one is above nature, and beyond common human living. . . . Wholly and permanently separate from the common customary life of mankind, it devotes itself to the service of God alone. . . . Such then is the perfect form of the Christian life. And the other, more humble, more human, permits men to . . . have minds for farming, for trade, and the other more secular interests as well as for religion. . . . And a kind of secondary grade of piety is attributed to them.[2]

In other words, some people are specially called to serve the Lord, but most people do ordinary work. This bifurcation between the sacred and the secular had the inevitable and unfortunate result up through the Middle Ages of denigrating the daily, worldly work of laypeople.

Happily, the Protestant Reformation wrought a radical transformation, as Martin Luther and the other Reformers rejected absolutely the notion that nuns, monks, and other clerics performed work that was intrinsically holier or more valuable than housewives and shopkeepers. According to the English Reformer William Tyndale, from an external perspective "there is difference betwixt washing of dishes and preaching of the word of God; but as touching to please God, none at all."[3]

Rather than dichotomizing the sacred from the secular, the Reformers and later the Westminster Divines drew these two realms together by showing that every Christian has a dual calling (or vocation, from the Latin *vocatio*) to faith and work. As a result, Luther preached, "the entire world" should be "full of service to God, not only the churches but also the home, the kitchen, the cellar, the workshop, and the field."[4]

The Christian's primary calling is to follow Christ—the general call of salvation. In the words of the William Perkins, this "calling of Christianity," which is "common to all that live in the church of God," is a gracious divine summons "whereby a man is called out of the world to be a child of God."[5] The Puritans rooted this summons in the biblical doctrine of election, finding ample support for it in biblical texts that used the term "calling" (*kaleo*) to describe the divine compulsion behind Christian conversion (e.g., 1 Cor. 1:9; 1 Tim. 6:12; 1 Peter 2:9). In this sense of the word, "calling" is the Holy Spirit's way of giving people the gospel and "effectually drawing them to Jesus Christ."[6]

As an outworking of saving faith, every Christian also has a secondary calling to serve God in some particular line of business—his or her "vocation" (or *vocatio,* to use the Latin word for calling in its narrower sense). This, too, was a strong emphasis in Puritan teaching on the Christian life. According to Cotton Mather, "Every Christian ordinarily should have a calling. That is to say, there should be some special business . . . wherein a Christian should for the most part spend the most of his time; and this, that so he may glorify God."[7] Our daily work is not merely a way to make a living, therefore, but a way to fulfill our God-given calling.

If the general calling of every Christian is grounded in the doctrine of election, the special calling of every Christian worker is grounded in the doctrine of divine providence. "The Great Governor of the world," wrote Richard Steele, "hath appointed to every man his proper post."[8] Simply put, every Christian has a unique, God-given calling—"the life that the Lord has assigned to him, and to which God has called him" (1 Cor. 7:17 ESV; cf. Luke 3:12–14)—which is divinely designed for usefulness and joy.

In discussing the particular call of every Christian, the Reformers and the Puritans recognized the dignity of every legitimate form of work. Properly speaking, there is no such thing as secular work; it is all sacred. The sanctity of ordinary daily labor goes back to the ordinances of creation, when God told the first man to work the garden and take care of it (Gen. 2:15). Even though in a fallen world work has been cursed by sin (see Gen. 3:17–19; Eccl. 2:18–23), it nevertheless retains its inherent dignity. Indeed, daily work is one of the basic commandments of God (Exod. 20:9). It finds additional consecration in the vocation of Jesus Christ, who learned the value of a good day's work in His common labor as a carpenter, and who often described His life's work—everything up to and including the heavy lifting He did on the cross—in terms of a calling He had received from His Father in heaven (e.g., John 4:34; 5:17).

The implications of the Christian's dual calling to faith and work are not only economy shaping, but life transforming. If all callings are sacred, then daily business is one appropriate way to do kingdom work. The point here is not simply that Christians can serve God *in* business, but that Christians can serve God *through* business. "A true believing Christian," wrote John Cotton, "lives in his vocation by his faith. Not only my spiritual life but even my civil life in this world, and all the life I live, is by the faith of the Son of God."[9] Therefore, our business itself can glorify God.[10] William Perkins wrote to similar effect: "The main end of our lives . . . is to serve God in the serving of men in the works of our callings."[11] While we may well derive personal benefit from our labor, ultimately it is for the glory of God and the good of other people (see Eccl. 2:24; Eph. 4:28; 6:5–7; Col. 3:23–24).

The Puritans had many other useful and important things to say about God's calling to business. Here are several examples:

- They believed that when God issued a particular calling, he also provided the gifts and opportunities to fulfill that calling (John Cotton: "When God hath called me to a place, he hath given me some gifts for that place").[12]

- They emphasized the value of hard work, praising industry as a godly virtue (Thomas Watson: "God will bless our diligence, not our laziness").[13]

- At the same time, they guarded against the idolatry of work by delineating other legitimate callings in life (such as husband and wife, mother and father) and by advocating moderation (John Preston: "Take heed of too much business").[14]

- They recognized that hard work ordinarily would lead to economic prosperity, and rightly so (according to answer 141 of the *Westminster Larger Catechism*, the eighth commandment requires that we "endeavor, by all just and lawful means, to procure, preserve, and further the wealth and outward estate of others, as well as our own").

- Yet they argued that the purpose of God-given wealth was to provide for one's family and to further the public good, including care for the poor, not to pursue personal gain or spend for selfish purposes (Richard Baxter: riches "enable us to relieve our needy brethren and to promote good works for church and state").[15]

To summarize, as the foundation for everything else they said on the subject, the Reformers and Puritans regarded business as a gracious, redemptive, God-given calling for followers of Jesus Christ. These famous lines from Milton's *Paradise Lost* provide an apt summary of the Protestant perspective on vocation:

Man hath his daily work of body or mind
Appointed, which declares his dignity,
And the regard of Heaven on all his ways.

Practical Reflections

Ron Ferner did not fully understand the Christian's dual calling to faith and work until after he retired from business and started to teach at Philadelphia Biblical University. His call to business came indirectly and somewhat unexpectedly. He grew up in a Christian home, accepted Christ at an early age, and tried to follow Christ with his life. After receiving an undergraduate degree in engineering, Ferner took a job more related to business than engineering. His wife suggested that he go back to school to earn an MBA degree. Here he found that an engineering education was useful because it had taught him disciplined thinking and analysis.

What the MBA itself taught Ferner was how to do business, which he discovered that he enjoyed the most of all. Here is how he describes the challenges he faced in his early years as a businessman:

> I don't specifically remember having tension between faith and work. I enjoyed work, especially accomplishing tasks. I do remember, however, that decision making was more involved than I had thought, and that I was ill-equipped to make the "right" decision. I found that I didn't have a good methodology to make decisions, and right and wrong was never as clear as I had imagined. In addition, all of the information I needed to make the decision was never available. That was almost more ambiguity than an engineer could tolerate.

The idea of business as a calling became more important to Ferner when he joined Philadelphia Biblical University and had to justify the addition of a business curriculum to a faculty schooled in the Bible. Some of the most helpful resources on this subject include:

- Richard C. Chewning, John W. Eby, and Shirley J. Roels, *Business Through the Eyes of Faith* (New York: HarperSanFrancisco, 1990).
- Wayne Grudem, *Business for the Glory of God* (Wheaton, IL: Crossway Books, 2003).

- Michael Novak, *Business as a Calling* (New York: The Free Press, 1996).

As a church leader, Ferner's biggest finding was that a church is not a business. Although a church can use business processes, these two organizations have different goals and objectives. The main task of the church leader is to be sure that the activities of the church are congruent with the mission of the church. To explain this principle, the evangelical pastor and church leader Rick Warren quoted management guru Peter Drucker: "The function of management in the church is to make the church more churchlike, not more business-like. It's to allow you to do what your mission is."[16]

Businesspeople are on the front lines in today's world. Believers who are businesspeople are no different from other Christians, in that they need a community of believers for the support of their calling. Peter Drucker said that the most important social phenomenon of recent decades was the rise of the megachurch.[17] Why? Because the megachurch provides a supportive community for all types and segments of believers.

One of the more difficult issues that the Christian business person may face is compartmentalization. For five or six days, he or she takes on the business persona, and then on Sundays the same individual takes on the Christian persona. John D. Rockefeller (1839–1937) taught Sunday school on the first day of the week (he also tithed his salary), but he was a ruthless businessman (robber baron) for the following six days. Rockefeller believed that religion was the source for his success, but kept his religion largely confined to the Sunday compartment. This is not a healthy model for business as a calling. To live an integrated life, the Christian businessperson must maintain a healthy church-home-work balance.

In contrast to John D. Rockefeller, Philadelphia's John Wanamaker (1838–1922) lived an *integrated* life.[18] Wanamaker was a deeply religious man who believed that his faith demanded that he devote himself 100 percent to any given task or responsibility. He dedicated his life to God at age fifteen in a church on Broad Street. He founded Bethany Mission School (eventually this became Bethany Presbyterian Church) and served as the superintendent of a Sunday school that taught the Bible to five thousand children every week. But Wanamaker served God the rest of the week as well. When he established one of the world's first and largest department stores on Broad Street in Philadelphia, he delayed opening to let D. L. Moody use the building for revival meetings. Wanamaker's dual calling to faith and work is also illustrated by his service both as postmaster general of the United States and as vice-moderator of the Philadelphia Presbytery. In short, John Wanamaker lived life as an integrated Christian 24/7. He once suggested that his epitaph simply read, "servant of God."

Few of us have the exceptional gifts of a man like John Wanamaker, yet all of us are called to serve God as well as we can. The question is, where can we get the spiritual and practical support we need to live out our calling to Christ, especially if we are also called to work in business?

THE MINISTRY OF GOD'S WORD FOR A CHRISTIAN BUSINESSPERSON

Preaching That Nurtures a Calling to Business

Over time, nothing makes a bigger spiritual difference in the lives of Christian people than the faithful preaching of the Word of God. This was the strong conviction of the Puritans who wrote *The Westminster Directory for the Public Worship of God*. "Preaching of the word," they said, is "the power of God unto salvation, and one of the greatest and most excellent works belonging to the ministry of the gospel."[19] "Here the dead hear the voice of the Son of God," David Clarkson said concerning the pulpit ministry, "and those that hear do live."[20]

By the preaching of the Word, sinners are convicted of their sins, called to faith in Jesus Christ, and consecrated for Christian service. Preaching has this gospel influence in the life of every believer, of course, but it is as necessary for businesspeople as for anyone. When carried out properly, the regular ministry of God's Word has the power to shape a businessperson's spiritual perspective on work and leisure, leadership and stewardship, profit and loss, personal responsibility and public service.

In addition to preaching, there is also an important place for the private ministry of God's Word, or what the Puritans called "spiritual conference." These days, people would probably call it "pastoral counseling," except that for the Puritans, a personal conference between pastor and parishioner invariably involved teaching and applying the Bible in an explicit and intentional way—something practiced perhaps too rarely in pastoral ministry today.

Businesspeople need both the public and the private ministry of God's Word. They need a pulpit ministry that gives them the gospel, teaches them the

Christian worldview, and nourishes their dual calling to faith and work. They also need a personal relationship with a wise and caring pastor who is able and willing to help them work through the hard issues that come up for Christians in the marketplace.

To be effective, such ministry requires pastors to know their people. A good pastor will sometimes visit his parishioners at their place of business to gain a better sense of the challenges they face in their daily work. A wise pastor will also learn to ask good questions: What is your biggest on-the-job temptation? What tangible steps are you taking to balance your home life with your responsibilities at work? What has the Lord been teaching you lately about how to use your money? What spiritual issues are coming up in your conversations with coworkers? Are there any ethical dilemmas that I can help you think through more carefully from a biblical perspective? Who is the hardest person you have to work with, and how are you asking God to help you in that relationship?

One salutary result of asking good questions is that a pastor gradually becomes better equipped to make wise applications of biblical truth to real situations faced by real people. Most sermon applications should be general enough to help any and every listener, but some should be specific enough to help particular people (including businesspeople) make practical connections between biblical truth and their everyday callings in life.

According to the Reformed and Puritan view of calling, "Christian service to God does not occur only in a 'sacred' place such as a church, but also in the corporation, the commuter train or car, and life at home after the working day."[21] If this is true, then pastors need to teach the Bible in ways that help businesspeople take its truths to all the everyday places that become sacred spaces as they live out their callings for Christ.

Pursuing Spiritual Growth as a Businessperson

Needless to say, the church is not set up to help the businessperson solve complex marketing, financial, or strategic business problems. The church should work instead to equip businesspeople to understand themselves in relationship to God, to the universe, and to complex business problems.

Someone has said that great teachers create the conditions so that learning can occur. Two of the church's tasks are to help businesspeople develop a biblical worldview and understand God's Word.

What is a biblical worldview? Simply put, such a worldview sees the world through a biblical lens, so that a person's attitudes, beliefs, opinions, values, and behavior are based on the truths they receive from God's Word. In 2003 the Barna Group surveyed 2003 adults and found that only 4 percent had a functional biblical worldview. Yet having such a worldview is essential to integrating biblical principles into daily life and responding well to the challenges of the workplace.

Successful businesspeople should be well schooled in the core competencies of business. But what businesspeople need in addition to their knowledge of how business works is a clear biblical worldview to understand how to apply their business knowledge in a way that honors and glorifies God.

The Christian worldview should be integrated into every aspect of life. At Philadelphia Biblical University, the introductory business course spends time developing the student's biblical worldview. Thereafter, business principles and ethics are integrated into every business class. The integration is often difficult, but having students who are Bible majors as well as business majors makes it somewhat easier.

The solutions to a satisfying personal and business life are essentially the same, and they are well summarized in Micah 6:8: "He has told you, O man, what is good; and what does the LORD require of you but to do justice, and to love kindness, and to walk humbly with your God?" (ESV). To learn this way of living, businesspeople need both the public and private ministry of God's Word.

At Philadelphia's Tenth Presbyterian Church, Ron Ferner has been blessed to sit under the weekly teaching ministry of both James Boice and Philip Ryken. Both of these pastor/teachers have used expository preaching to give a comprehensive explanation of the biblical text, including commentary and examples. Ferner has made it a habit to take notes during sermons, and then to study the notes in his quiet time during the week.

How do these sermons relate to the businessperson in the pew? The past few years of sermons include:

- preaching on the Ten Commandments, showing the ethical implications not only for business but for life
- preaching from Ecclesiastes that develops principles of work, stress, and investment
- preaching from the gospel of Luke on the correct way to store up treasure
- preaching from Romans 8 on the proper response to suffering, which businesspeople face as much as anyone

Learning from this kind of preaching requires more from the listener than simply hearing. The businessperson must first hear and then work to integrate biblical ideas into daily life. In this way, biblical content helps to develop a biblical worldview. This is not just limited to the businessperson; every believer is called to grow deeper in believing and applying the gospel to daily life.

Christian Witness in the Business World

Challenges and Opportunities for Christian Witness

"We are what we repeatedly do. Excellence is not a single act, but a habit." This principle for excellence—often misattributed to Aristotle—applies well to gospel witness in the workplace. For Christians in business, the strongest testimony may not come from overt conversations about spiritual things, but from other people's observations of how we behave. The critical questions include: How did I handle good news? How did I react to bad news? How did I treat people in general? How did I get along with coworkers, subordinates, and superiors? Did I control my temper and govern my speech? Did I demonstrate sympathy and kindness?

We are a work in progress. Learning to react in Christlike ways does not come easily for anyone with a frustrated, aggressive personality. But it is essential if we are to maintain a clear Christian witness.

This paper began with a summary of what Laura Nash wrote in the 2001 *Conference Board Review* about how the church had failed business. Given what transpired soon afterwards, her concerns now seem prescient. Enron collapsed late that year, followed in 2002 by Global Crossing, WorldCom, Adelphia, Tyco (Dennis Kozlowski), and Arthur Anderson. These failures returned ethics to the front burner in business conversations. Articles pointed out that several of the executives involved in these scandals had taken ethics courses in their MBA programs. What had happened? It became apparent is that teaching ethics in a pluralistic society is a no-win situation. Ethical training must have something on which to base moral actions. So we return again to the biblical worldview and the integrated life.

The difference between right and wrong is not always crystal clear . . .

even to a person with a biblical worldview. Along with the foundation of a biblical worldview, the decision maker needs to have an effective problem-solving methodology. But even those two factors may not be enough. As Robert Hoyk and Paul Hersey rightly state, "But even if we have good ethical values to begin with, we can all become unethical—trapped by the situational pressures and self-deceptions."[22] What we need to know, therefore, is God himself and His purpose for our lives.

In his 2007 book *God at Work*, David W. Miller discusses the history and promise of the "Faith at Work" movement. Miller states that what draws most people to this movement is the desire to live an integrated life, where faith teachings and workplace practices are aligned. He goes on to say that some businesspeople feel that integrating faith and work is problematic and should be avoided. Others seek integration but do not have the skills or resources to know how to integrate faith and work in a meaningful and appropriate ways.

David Miller gives four ways for Christians to seek integration. He acknowledges that all typologies have their limitations, but his list is a helpful way of framing the issue. His typologies include:

1. *Ethics*: Attention to personal virtue, business ethics, and broader questions of social and economic justice.
2. *Experience*: Involves questions of vocation, calling, meaning, and purpose in and through marketplace professions.
3. *Evangelism*: Uses evangelism and the personal expression of faith; views the workplace as a mission field.
4. *Enrichment*: Uses personal and inward approaches, like healing, prayer, meditation, consciousness, and transformation.

Even for businesspeople who have well integrated their faith and their work, evangelism in the workplace can be problematic. The employer has hired the employee to do a job, and usually evangelizing coworkers overtly is not in the job description. It may be better, then, simply to live as a godly example and pray for the Holy Spirit to use this example to convict coworkers and open doors for spiritual conversation. Usually there comes a time when someone will say something along the lines of, "I noticed that your approach to that problem was different, and that things don't seem to get you down. Why is that?" Then we have an opportunity to say, "I'm glad you asked. Let me tell you why." Usually this approach is much more effective than handing out tracts by the coffee machine.

How the Church Can Assist Business Witness

There are many good ways for the church to help Christians in business fulfill their God-given calling to faith and work. We have already mentioned the foundational role that preaching plays in calling businesspeople to salvation in Christ, giving them a biblical worldview to guide their thought and conduct, and nurturing their vision to serve God by serving others in their daily work.

The church's ministry to businesspeople can and should go well beyond the pulpit, however, especially in equipping leaders for effective Christian witness in the marketplace. By "Christian witness" we do not simply mean maintaining high moral standards and leading an exemplary life, although that is part of it. We also mean giving verbal testimony to the gospel when there is an appropriate opportunity to speak with colleagues about the forgiveness of sins through the cross of Jesus Christ and the hope of eternal life through his empty tomb.

True Christian witness involves *both* a living, breathing example of Christlike godliness *and* a talking, listening communication of biblical truth. In the final analysis, no one ever comes to Christ merely through the power of another person's example. Words of gospel truth are necessary for true conversion. But in the context of the marketplace, effective opportunities to share the Christian faith will come when a businessperson establishes a well-deserved reputation for personal integrity and excellence in the workplace. Best practices in business provide the best platform for gospel witness.

There are at least two ways for the church to help. One is by providing ministry structures that *equip* businesspeople for Christian witness. For example, hosting a lunchtime Bible study and prayer time—like the one that meets every Friday at the Union League of Philadelphia—helps bring a spiritual focus to the workweek. For many years Tenth Presbyterian Church hosted an early-morning class in Christian theology, attended mainly by Center City businesspeople on their way to work. The class studied the *Westminster Confession of Faith* and *Catechisms*, seminary-level textbooks on systematic theology, and practical books that provide theological perspective on the Christian life. Churches like Redeemer Presbyterian in New York City have also found it helpful to host affinity groups for Christians who work in related careers (law, medicine, finance, etc.).[23] Presentations by leading professionals, followed by spirited discussion, give Christians an opportunity to engage spiritual issues that are directly related to their vocation. Businesspeople go away from such meetings better equipped to witness for Christ in their own sphere of kingdom work.

Another way for the church to help bring the gospel to the marketplace is by providing ministry structures that *engage* businesspeople in Christian witness. The goal in this case is not only to send people out into the marketplace, but also to provide effective vehicles for them to share the gospel with their coworkers. Philadelphia's annual Leadership Prayer Breakfast is one local example. So is the monthly luncheon sponsored by the Christian Businessmen's Connection, at which a business leader talks about leadership, shares a personal testimony, and invites people to receive Jesus Christ for personal salvation. Some Christians in business are able to host Bible studies in the workplace, giving them an opportunity to invite coworkers to learn more about Christian faith and practice.

One of the best models for business outreach is the long-running midday Bible exposition that Dick Lucas started decades ago at St. Helen's Bishopsgate, in the heart of London's financial district. Tenth Presbyterian Church has tried to follow a similar model in Philadelphia through a ministry called Faith at Work (currently on hiatus) and through hosting half-hour services in the church sanctuary before Christmas and Easter. Typically these lunchtime gatherings have opened and closed with musical soloists and featured a short evangelistic talk, with a prayer for the city.

All of these gatherings are designed to give businesspeople a welcoming opportunity to invite colleagues to find out more about the Christian faith. There is an important role in all of this for pastors and other Christian workers. By establishing a strong connection with Christians in business, a pastor becomes a go-to resource for phone calls about ethical questions in the workplace, e-mails concerning on-the-job prayer requests, and meetings with business colleagues who have spiritual questions that go beyond the expertise of the average layperson.

USING BUSINESS-RELATED GIFTS IN THE CHURCH AND THE WORLD

hen Business Goes to Church

There is another side to the business/church relationship. Christians do not just go out into the world to work; they also come to the church to worship. When businesspeople come to church, they bring exceptional gifts for ministry, as well as some potential dangers and temptations.

Consider first the dangers. To a businessperson, the church may very well look like a business. After all, the typical congregation has employees (the pastors and other staff members), management (the elder board), a customer base (weekly worshippers), and even shareholders (the church members, especially in a congregational form of church government). Viewed from a certain perspective, a church's efforts to introduce its ministry to outsiders could be considered a form of advertising. There is always a budget, of course, with either a surplus or a deficit. And the church is constantly competing for a larger market share in the community of religion.

As a result, it may be tempting for Christian businesspeople to apply business strategies directly to their service in the church without first developing a biblical philosophy of ministry or fully recognizing the distinction between the marketplace and the church. Fundamentally, the church is not a business but a family. Although we serve together as coworkers (e.g., 1 Thess. 3:2), our more basic relationship is to love one another as brothers and sisters in Christ (e.g., 1 Thess. 4:9). This ought to make a profound difference in the way churches handle everything from conflict resolution to staff members who fail to perform the duties in their job description (if they have one). Then there are the temptations that come in the area of finance, where people who apply business sensibilities sometimes fail to leave sufficient room for faith in God's promise to provide for the needs of his people.

There are temptations for pastors, too. One is to show improper favoritism to wealthy parishioners, including businesspeople. This is something the Bible expressly forbids (see James 2:1–6)—doubtless because it is tempting for ministers to depend on money to advance their ministry, or even to seek their own financial gain (see 1 Tim. 3:3). Another temptation is to confuse business acumen with spiritual gifts for leadership. The biblical qualifications for ministry state that a church elder must "manage his own household well" (1 Tim. 3:4). In the biblical world, a "household" would have included servants as well as family members, so this standard embraces many of the skills that make for good business management today. But most of the biblical qualifications for leadership in ministry do not relate directly to business at all, and it is important for churches to understand the difference.

None of these dangers should be allowed to obscure the fact that wise and growing Christians with business sensibilities can be a huge asset in the life of a local church. Smart businesspeople know how to devise effective structures for management and wise systems for accountability. This can be a healthy corrective for the tendency of many Christian ministries to be lax in self-discipline and self-evaluation. Having said that businesspeople need to leave room for faith, it should also be said that ministry leaders without good business sense are prone to be fiscally irresponsible, with devastating consequences for the cause of Christ. Tenth Presbyterian Church has benefited enormously from the gifts of business leaders in the church who know how to manage an annual budget, evaluate staff effectiveness, draft personnel policies, develop a strategic plan, conduct a capital campaign, devise innovative solutions for practical problems, ask tough questions, and pursue constant improvement in every aspect of the church's mission to Philadelphia and the world.

Business with a Kingdom Bottom Line

The church is not the only institution that is on a mission. It has also become common for businesses to identify their work in terms of mission. Here is how the secular organization Students in Free Enterprise (SIFE) describes its mission on its Web site:

> SIFE brings together a diverse network of university students, academic professionals and industry leaders around the shared mission of creating a better, more sustainable world through the positive power of business. By contributing their talents to projects that improve the lives of people worldwide, SIFE participants are demonstrating that individuals with a knowledge and passion for business can be a powerful force for change.

Philadelphia Biblical University has a SIFE team that competes with fifteen hundred other teams on campuses around the world. The team's mission statement reads, "PBU-SIFE exists to glorify God by educating and empowering others to create economic opportunity through free enterprise." When the team formed in 2000, there was a brief discussion as to whether God belonged in the mission statement. The students took their commitment to God seriously and decided to let the statement stand. Although PBU is one of the smaller schools in SIFE, its students have a dedication to excellence and have won seven regional championships in ten years.

The boldness of SIFE's mission serves as a challenge to the church. One way to see this is to substitute the words *the church* for SIFE, so that the mission statement would read:

The church brings together a diverse network of university students, academic professionals and industry leaders around the shared mission of creating a better, more sustainable world through the positive power of business. By contributing their talents to projects that improve the lives of people worldwide, *the church* is demonstrating that individuals with a knowledge and passion for business and Christ can be a powerful force for change.

When phrased this way, SIFE's mission statement becomes a dynamic statement of what Christian businesspeople can do for Christ and his kingdom. This begs the question, why do we leave this ground to secular organizations? As Christian businesspeople, why aren't we giving back to our churches, local ministries, or global missions by helping these organizations develop better processes, improved goals and objectives, more strategic plans, and effective marketing?

The world turns on business processes, and this opens many doors for Christians in business to advance the kingdom of God. Christian entrepreneurs can provide consulting, training, and capitalization for potential small business owners around the world. There are two main ways for these skills to have a kingdom bottom line: "business *in* missions" and "business *as* missions."

"Business *in* missions" consists of using business processes to support and improve operations in the church or in other mission organizations. This may consist of using accounting, marketing, supply chain management, organizational (management, leadership, strategic planning), or training skills to improve the accountability, efficiency, or effectiveness of any kingdom organization. Churches, mission agencies, local ministries, and global outreach organizations can all benefit from business expertise. What is the best way to get started? Simply by meeting with a pastor or ministry leader to explore what skill sets a businessperson has to offer and what needs a ministry may have. Another good way to get started is to sign up for a short-term mission trip and be prepared to be proactive.

The concept of "business *as* missions" is helpfully defined in the Lausanne Occasional Paper Number 59. Business as missions:

- releases people to use their gifting in business, integrated with biblical principles, to transform their own communities and nations and to carry the good news to the ends of the earth through commerce

- works both *within* a business setting (modeling behavior) and *through* its purposes and capacities (creating jobs)
- seeks to harness the power and resources of business for intentional missions impact in the community, nation, and world at large

What kinds of work does business as missions include?

- Starting a business enterprise in the developing world, which impacts a community economically, socially, and spiritually (the triple bottom line)
- Enabling such enterprises through training and availability of capital (e.g. microfinance)
- Infusing Christian values and perspective into the global conduct of business (e.g. ethics, Christian leadership principles)
- Ministering to counterparts in the marketplace with the gospel of Jesus Christ

In keeping with sound business principles, business-as-mission organizations have profit as one of their goals. This helps to make them sustainable because they are designed to operate without a constant influx of donor funds. Business as missions thus operates with a triple bottom line:

1. Profit (make the organizational sustainable)
2. Social (create jobs, grow the local economy, provide goods and services)
3. Kingdom (spread the gospel)

Business as missions is not easy to do. Starting up any business involves risk, especially when one is operating in a foreign country. The risks can be mitigated, however, with good planning and expertise. This is where Christian businesspeople are needed—people who understand their dual calling and have learned how to integrate their work with their faith, who are well trained in the biblical basis for the Christian worldview, who are committed to living and sharing their faith, and who want to strengthen the bottom line of the kingdom of God.

Notes

1. Laura Nash, "How the Church Has Failed Business," *Conference Board Review*, July/August 2001, 26–32.

2. Eusebius of Caesarea, *Demonstratio Evangelica*, quoted in W. R. Forrester, *Christian Vocation* (New York: Scribner, 1953), 42.

3. William Tyndale, *The Parable of Wicked Mammon*, quoted in Louis B. Wright, *Middle-Class Culture in Elizabethan England* (Chapel Hill: University of North Carolina Press, 1935), 171.

4. Martin Luther, from his sermon on Matthew 6:24–34, quoted in Ewald M. Plass, *What Luther Says: An Anthology* (St. Louis: Concordia, 1959), 560.

5. William Perkins, *Works*, 3 vols. (London, 1626), 1:752.

6. *Westminster Confession of Faith*, x.1.

7. Cotton Mather, *A Christian in His Calling*, quoted in Michael McGiffert, ed., *Puritanism and the American Experience* (Reading, MA: Addison-Wesley, 1969), 123.

8. Richard Steele, *The Tradesman's Calling*, quoted in R. H. Tawney, *Religion and the Rise of Capitalism* (New York: Harcourt Brace, 1926), 321.

9. John Cotton, *Christian Calling*, quoted in Perry Miller and Thomas E. Johnson, eds., *The Puritans*, rev. ed., 2 vols. (New York: Harper, 1963), 1:319.

10. This theme is more fully developed by Wayne Grudem in *Business for the Glory of God: The Bible's Teaching on the Moral Goodness of Business* (Wheaton, IL: Crossway, 2003).

11. William Perkins, *Treatise on the Vocations*, quoted in Edmund S. Morgan, *Puritan Political Ideas, 1558–1794* (Indianapolis: Bobbs-Merrill, 1965), 57.

12. John Cotton, *The Way of Life*, quoted in Edmund S. Morgan, *The Puritan Family: Religion and Domestic Relations in Seventeenth-Century New England* (1944; repr. New York: Harper and Row, 1966), 72.

13. Thomas Watson, *The Beatitudes* (Edinburgh: Banner of Truth, 1977), 257.

14. John Preston, *The Saint's Qualification*, quoted in Charles H. and Katherine George, *The Protestant Mind of the English Reformation, 1570–1640* (Princeton: Princeton University Press, 1961), 172.

15. Richard Baxter, *A Christian Directory*, quoted in Ralph Barton Perry, *Puritanism and Democracy* (New York: Vanguard, 1944), 315.

16. Peter Drucker, as quoted by Rick Warren in *Businessweek*, November 28, 2005, 104.

17. Peter F. Drucker, "Management's New Paradigms," *Forbes* 162, no. 7 (1998): 169.

18. For the full story of Wanamaker's life and work, consult the fascinating biography by Herbert Ershkowitz, *John Wanamaker: Philadelphia Merchant* (Conshohocken, PA: Combined Publishing, 1999).

19. *The Confession of Faith* (Glasgow: Free Presbyterian Publications, 1973), 381.

20. David Clarkson, *The Works of David Clarkson*, Vol. 3 (Edinburgh: Banner of Truth, 1988), 193–94.

21. Leland Ryken, "In Search of a Christian Work Ethic for the Corporate Worker," *Business and Professional Ethics Journal* 23, no. 4 (2004): 153–70.

22. Robert Hoyk and Paul Hersey, *The Ethical Executive* (Palo Alto, CA: Stanford Business Books, 2008).

23. For more information, contact Redeemer's Center for Faith and Work.

How to Get Fat in 90 Days!

The Relationship of Generosity and Prosperity in Business

FRAN MCGOWEN

Fran McGowen, founder and president of CarSense in Philadelphia, had a vision that took him beyond what his family business had been doing, successfully, for years. Fran saw the family car dealership as a mature but declining cash cow. He knew he had to use the business to fund a new stage of growth, something few family business owners realize.

McGowen envisioned a new dealership with a commitment to people and growth rather than one that sold a particular brand of car to increase its short-term profit. McGowen used prof-its from the family dealership to launch CarSense. The result: In five years, CarSense has grown to 110 employees and $70 million in revenues, and is planning its third location. By acting as if CarSense were a large, growing company, McGowen is turning it into one. CarSense has been built on differentiating itself from the traditionally disreputable car dealership community. CarSense prides itself on its simple policies, no-haggle prices, and honest salespeople.

MARK FUTATO

Doctor Mark D. Futato is Robert L. Maclellan Professor of Old Testament and Academic Dean at Reformed Theological Seminary in Orlando, Florida. He received his PhD from The Catholic University of America in Washington, DC, his MDiv from Westminster Theological Seminary in Philadelphia, Pennsylvania, and his BA from Geneva College in Beaver Falls, Pennsylvania.

Doctor Futato has published: Psalms: Cornerstone Biblical Commentary (Tyndale House), Interpreting the Psalms: An Exegetical Handbook (Kregel), Joy Comes in the Morning: Psalms for All Seasons (P&R), Transformed by Praise: The Purpose and Message of the Psalms (P&R), Beginning Biblical Hebrew (Eisenbrauns), *and* Creation: A Witness to the Wonder of God (P&R). Mark has also served on the translation team for the Book of Psalms in the New Living Translation (Tyndale House), *wrote the study notes to the* Books of Ezra and Nehemiah in Spirit of the Reformation Study Bible (Zondervan) *and to the* Book of Jonah in the ESV Study Bible, *and contributed to* The New International Dictionary of Old Testament Theology and Exegesis (Zondervan). *He has written numerous other articles and is currently writing a book on the theology of the Book of Jonah.*

How to get fat in ninety days! I doubt that you have watched any info-mercials with that lead-in lately!

Neither fat in general nor getting fat in particular is in vogue these days in our culture. There are scads of commercials and infomercials on how to lose those extra pounds one might be carrying. Reducing fat from our diets is hailed as a step in the right direction toward optimum health. So why a paper at a conference on ethics in business with a title "How to Get Fat in 90 Days!"?

In the Bible as in our culture, being fat was at times viewed in a negative light. For example, we are told that Eglon king of Moab "was a very fat man" (Judges 3:17 NIV), and his being overweight is at least indirectly associated with his death in verses 21–22, where we read,

> Ehud reached with his left hand, drew the sword from his right thigh and plunged it into the king's belly. Even the handle sank in after the blade, which came out his back. Ehud did not pull the sword out, and the fat closed in over it.

A better-known example is that of Eli, the one-time a high priest of Israel. When Eli heard that the ark of the covenant had been captured, he fell back-ward off of his seat, broke his neck, and died. The text tells us explicitly that this happened because, "he was old and overweight" (1 Samuel 4:18 NLT). Another text uses "fat" as a negative metaphor for complacency and unfaithfulness:

> Jeshurun grew fat and kicked;
>> filled with food, he became heavy and sleek.
> He abandoned the God who made him
>> and rejected the Rock his Savior. (Deut. 32:15 NIV)

Given our cultural attitudes and the biblical examples cited above, it is hard to imagine fat being used in a positive image let alone an image of pros-perity or blessing in the Bible, but such is the case.[1] For example, because Abel brought the *fat* portions to the Lord, his offering was accepted (Gen. 4:4). In another context, because the *fat* was the best part of the sacrifice, when an ani-mal was slaughtered and the edible parts were distributed, all of the *fat* went to the Lord (Lev. 3:16).

Fat is used elsewhere in the Bible in positive images. Modern translations, however, perhaps under the influence of societal attitudes, frequently leave the concrete image of fatness behind and replace it with more genteel and abstract concepts like abundance. An example is Psalm 36:8, which is typically translated, "They feast on the abundance of your house" (see ESV, NIV, NRSV). The KJV captures the concreteness of the image, when it says, "They shall be abundantly satisfied with the *fatness* of thy house."

The preceding paragraph explains the use of "enriched," or "prosperous," or "prosper" in modern renderings of Proverbs 11:25:

> "Whoever brings blessing will be enriched" (ESV)
> "The generous man will be prosperous" (NASB)
> "A generous person will be enriched" (NIV)
> "The generous will prosper" (NLT)
> "A generous person will be enriched" (NRSV)

Compare these translations with the KJV: "The liberal soul shall be made *fat*." Once again, the KJV captures the concreteness of the image of fat to represent abundance, blessing, and prosperity.

Proverbs 11:25 contains the thesis is of our paper: Whoever brings blessing to others/a generous person will be made fat/blessed/enriched/prosperous. Now, wouldn't you like to know how to get fat in this sense in ninety days?

[Okay. The ninety days is a bit of advertising hype on our part. We are not presenting an easy, get-rich-quick scheme but a practical biblical principle that connects the biblical ideas of generosity and prosperity in business. Read on to discover what this connection is.]

The story begins early in Fran's business career. Fran was not a Christian. Everything was great. Fran and his partner worked well together, and success seemed well within reach. After Fran became a Christian, a certain struggle began within him, and it would take some time before this tension would be put to rest.

Though Fran was now a Christian, he had a number of unbiblical ideas floating in his head and driving his decisions. One was the ever-so-common dichotomizing of life into the sacred and the secular. There was the sacred part that belonged to God—Fran's work with the men's committee at his local church and his work with Campus Crusade Executive Ministry. Then there was the secular part that was Fran's turf—his work in the business world, which he thought he could squeeze any way he wished in building his imagined empire. In Fran's mind these two parts of his life were not integrated or even connected except that the sacred might somehow garner favor with God and would aid Fran in his secular endeavors.

The second idea was the self-centeredness that permeates the thoughts and motivations of so many in our day. Fran had a keen focus on his success and strove to preserve every yield from his business—for himself and future advancement. Yet to Fran it seemed like the harder he worked, the more elusive prosperity became. What was wrong?

In the fall of 1982, Fran separated from his 50/50 business partner, who was not a Christian. Fran soon realized that he had complete sway to run the business however he wished. The idea of running his business as a Christian was taking root and sprouting, but this fledgling plant would take a good bit of nurturing before it would mature into a healthy plant. He persisted in pursuing dichotomized ends, serving on committees at church and pushing and straining for material success on the business side.

For the next several years Fran and his business moved along at a sluggish pace that was nonetheless still profitable, but by the early spring of 1985, the business was in serious trouble. An experienced controller Fran had hired suffered a nervous breakdown. Then after six months, Fran learned that every entry the controller had made for that period was wrong. At the same time, Fran lost two other key managers. There was no defense mechanism he could have had in place that would have protected his business against such happenings.

Fran was failing. Except for one critically timed loan from a family member, the banks would have closed the accounts and the business would have been bankrupt. Fran moved in a malaise for several months, walking around his neighborhood at times, crying, and even on occasion shouting out to God. God answered. Of course, Fran put in place a new strategic plan and cost cutting measures. He solicited solid counsel from good people. But what really happened was that in and through the tremendous pressure the Lord was applying, Fran's mindset about what he was there to do began to change, and God began to raise the business out of the ashes.

The Biblical Principle Stated

The biblical principle we will examine comes to expression in a variety of ways in the Bible. For simplicity sake, we are going to focus on one key text, the text mentioned in the introduction, Proverbs 11:25, with its concrete imagery.

The images used in the Hebrew Bible are often quite concrete, and the concreteness of the images is often lost in English translations, which have a tendency to convert the concrete language into abstract language. A translation of Proverbs 11:25 that seeks to capture the concreteness of the Hebrew text would read something like the following:

> A throat of blessing will be made fat; the one who waters abundantly surely he himself be watered thoroughly.

Let's take a look at some of the details of this short text.

The Hebrew word translated "throat" (*nephesh*) has a variety of meanings: throat, neck, breath, living being, people, personality, life, and soul.[2] The word *nephesh* could mean 'living being/person" here, and that is how it is understood by a number of translations. But given the concreteness of imagery in this verse, the more fundamental meaning of the word *throat* fits the context better. God blesses those who will be conduits for what He intends to do. But what is meant by "a throat of blessing"?

"Blessing" is itself quite concrete in the Hebrew Bible. When God blesses people, he "furnishes them with the power of fertility and growth, he grants life, happiness, and success."[3] "'Bless' can always be translated in the sense of 'giving vitality, prosperity, abundance, or fertility.'"[4] "Primarily...the divine blessing is on the covenant people . . . empowering them to exceptional fecundity . . . The blessing of God would also bring material prosperity."[5] So in short, blessing is empowerment to experience an abundant life.

Blessing in the Hebrew Bible is frequently associated with speech, and since speech comes through the throat, the image of a throat of blessing is coherent. The throat of blessing refers to the person who speaks words that result in the empowerment of others to experience abundance in life. The throat of blessing refers to the person who dispenses blessing to others.[6]

What can such a person expect to experience? Such a person can expect "to be made fat." The Hebrew verb translated "be made fat" is used in a similar way in two other texts in the book of Proverbs (13:4; 28:25). The only other place this word is used in the Hebrew Bible is in Isaiah 34:7, where it is used with a word for "fat" and is translated "soaked": "the dust will be soaked with fat." Admittedly, to be soaked in fat is not an image that has much appeal in our culture. But we must not judge the imagery of the Hebrew Bible through the lens of our cultural sensitivities. The image in Proverbs 11:25 is quite concrete: "the throat of blessing will be made fat." The significance of the image is quite clear, "the person who dispenses blessing will be drenched with abundance."

The metaphor of being made fat derives from the condition of well-fed livestock,[7] so our key text is already at least indirectly connected with the ancient business world. This connection is further solidified in the second half of verse, which uses an agricultural image of watering.[8] Proverbs 11:25 uses two different and relatively rare Hebrew words to speak of this watering. The first can be translated "water abundantly,"[9] while the second can be translated "watered thoroughly."[10] The text is saying more than if one waters one will be watered. The adverbial modifiers are important here: if one waters *abundantly*, one can expect to be watered *thoroughly*.

This one verse that uses very concrete terms establishes our principal: Whoever brings blessing to others/a generous person will be made fat/blessed/ enriched/prosperous.

Some may object that promises of material blessings are part of the old covenant but not part of the new. But the witness of the New Testament does not bear this out. As a general example, the Apostle Paul passes on the quintessential old covenant blessing of long life to new covenant children, when he says to them,

> Children, obey your parents in the Lord, for this is right. "Honor your father and mother"—which is the first commandment with a promise— "that it may go well with you and that you may enjoy long life on the earth." (Eph. 6:1–3 NIV)

Closer to the theme at hand, the New Testament uses agricultural imagery like that used in the Old Testament to teach the same principle about generosity. Jesus gave us this instruction in Luke 6:38:

> Give, and it will be given to you. A good measure, pressed down, shaken together and running over, will be poured into your lap. For with the measure you use, it will be measured to you. (NIV)

"The metaphor is from measuring out grain in such a way as to ensure that full volume is given."[11] The point of the metaphor is that "human generosity will be rewarded by divine superabundance."[12] Similarly, the Apostle Paul uses an agricultural image to teach us to be generous: "Whoever sows sparingly will also reap sparingly, and whoever sows generously will also reap generously" (2 Cor. 9:6 NIV).

These agricultural images that come from an agriculturally based culture certainly applied to the business world of the ancients and thus apply to the modern business world as well. The book of Proverbs itself makes this application to the business world in the verse that follows our key text, which says, "People curse those who hoard their grain, but they bless the one who sells in time of need" (Proverbs 11:26 NLT).

Back then, as now, it would have been tempting to hold onto grain in a time of need in the hope that scarcity would drive up prices and profits. But generous people who are interested in blessing others take a different tack and experience a paradoxical gain.[13]

THE BIBLICAL PRINCIPLE ILLUSTRATED

Let's return to Fran's story to see how this principle worked out in his life and business. We left Fran wondering why it seemed like the harder he worked, the more elusive prosperity became, wondering what was wrong. There were, no doubt, a number of things wrong in the business. One thing was clearly wrong, however. The business was not being operated according to the principle set forth in Proverbs 11:25. Rather, Proverbs 11:24 was functioning to one degree or another: "One man gives freely, yet gains even more; *another withholds unduly, but comes to poverty*" (NIV, emphasis added).

From the day Fran shouted out to God and heard God's answer, "It's my [God's] business—do my bidding there," things began to change. One of the first things that happened was that Fran's sacred/secular dichotomy began to dissolve. Fran began to see his business not as the secular part of his life that enabled him to do the sacred stuff but as one of the ministries that God had called him to. His business, though a different kind of calling, was just as much a calling to kingdom work as was his ministry in the local church and with Campus Crusade.

Seeing his business life as a key component of his calling in life entailed another significant change. Fran began to see his employees as people of value and dignity, not simply as tools to use in creating his empire or as mere objects of evangelism. (Ironically, when Fran's view of his employees changed, their hearts also changed, and they became more open to the gospel.) Since Fran now saw his employees as people of value and dignity, it was natural for Fran to begin to put into practice the principle of Proverbs 11:25. One of the first things he did was to institute a pension match for employees. Employees could contribute up to 2 percent of their income into a retirement plan, and the business would match that contribution. A few years later Fran decided to contribute 20 percent of the business profits to employee 401(k) accounts. Generosity was taking deep root as a core value in the business.

This principle of generosity carried over to the business venture Fran is currently in. When he started this new business with his founding partner (a fellow Christian) they designated 15 percent of the business profits for kingdom work outside of the business itself. This generous giving was easy when the business profits were modest, but it got harder when profits dictated significantly larger giving checks. Yet they stayed committed to the principle, and the profit numbers kept growing.

Fran also increased his personal giving to the point where his wife began to wonder about his course of action. Fran asked her to agree to an increase each year and to watch and see what God would do. They found that at the end of each year they had more than when they started, and at times they couldn't fully understand where the increases had come from.

Along the way Fran discovered that for well-rounded success, it is most important for him to be in the Word of God every day and to strive to follow that Word in all areas of life. Joshua 1:8 became a guiding text,

> This book of the law shall not depart from your mouth, but you shall meditate on it day and night, so that you may be careful to do according to all that is written in it; for then you will make your way prosperous, and then you will have success. (NASB)

While it is true, in general, that we are not to test God (see, for example, Deuteronomy 6:16 and Luke 4:12), in regard to generosity, God himself has invited us to test him through the prophet Malachi:

> "Test me in this," says the Lord Almighty, "and see if I will not throw open the floodgates of heaven and pour out so much blessing that you will not have room enough for it." (NIV)

In his business, Fran has experienced the faithfulness of God in keeping this promise. He has also experienced the truthfulness of Proverbs 11:25. As he has dispensed blessing to others, he himself has "been made fat." As he has watered others abundantly, he himself has been watered thoroughly. Fran recognizes that they have a wonderful brand image, great locations, a strong business model, excellent people in the company, etc. And he also recognizes that these are not the foundational generators of success. Rather, they are the outpourings that God has given as Fran has walked by faith in God and has striven to put the principle of Proverbs 11:25 into practice.

CONCLUSION

Fran's experience has demonstrated that putting the principle of Proverbs 11:25 into practice works. But this principle does not just "work." It works by faith, as Fran realized. There is a related proverb that says, "he that putteth his trust in the LORD shall be made fat" (Prov. 28:25 KJV). Whatever we do in life we do by faith in the son of God who has loved us and has given himself for us (see Galatians 2:20).

The principle of generosity that is articulated in Proverbs 11:25, while applying to our business ventures, applies to every area of our lives. The text does not specify the form that generosity can take.[14] The beauty of the image is in part found in its ambiguous nature. We can dispense blessing in a variety of ways, from giving money to giving help to giving advice to giving a listening ear to giving a shoulder to cry on, to giving a Bible in each car sold, etc. And as we give, we can expect to get.

This is not to say that we give for the sole purpose of getting, but getting is a biblical entailment of giving. The concept of win-win you see is not simply a habit of highly effective people.[15] It is a habit of highly effective people because it is a biblical principle that God has woven and into the fabric of the world that He has made.

How to get fat and ninety days! There is no quick and easy way to "get fat" in ninety days. But there is a principle that is a key component:

A person who dispenses blessing will be made fat;
the one who waters abundantly—surely he himself be watered
thoroughly.

Notes

1. Leland Ryken, Jim Wilhoit, and Tremper Longman III, eds., *Dictionary of Biblical Imagery* (Downers Grove, IL: InterVarsity, 1998), 273.

2. Ludwig Koehler et al., *The Hebrew and Aramaic Lexicon of the Old Testament* (Leiden: Brill Academic Publishers, 1999), 2.712.

3. Ernst Jenni and Claus Westermann, eds., *Theological Lexicon of the Old Testament* (Peabody, MA: Hendrickson, 1997), 1.273.

4. G. Johannes Botterweck and Helmer Ringgren, eds., *Theological Dictionary of the Old Testament* (Grand Rapids, MI: Eerdmans, 1974), 2.294.

5. Willem VanGemeren, ed., *New International Dictionary of Old Testament Theology & Exegesis* (Grand Rapids, MI: Zondervan, 1997), 1.259.

6. For "of" in the sense of "dispenses" see Bruce K. Waltke, *The Book Of Proverbs: Chapters 1—15.* (Grand Rapids, MI: Eerdmans, 2004), 505, footnote 166.

7. Crawford Howell Toy, *A Critical and Exegetical Commentary on the Book of Proverbs* (Edinburgh: T&T Clark, 1988), 235.

8. *Ibid.*

9. Koehler et al., *Hebrew and Aramaic Lexicon*, 3.1195.

10. *Ibid.*, 2.436 and 3.1195.

11. Leon Morris, *The Gospel According to St. Luke: An Introduction and Commentary*, 1st ed. (Grand Rapids, MI: Eerdmans, 1974), 132.

12. Joseph A. Fitzmyer, Joseph A. Fitzmyer, *The Gospel According to Luke: Introduction, Translation, and Notes*, 1st ed. (Garden City, N.Y: Doubleday, 1981), 641.

13. Waltke, *The Book of Proverbs*, 508.

14. Tremper Longman III, *Proverbs* (Grand Rapids, MI: Baker Academic, 2006), 263.

15. Stephen R. Covey, *The 7 Habits of Highly Effective People: Restoring the Character Ethic*, Rev. ed. (New York, NY: Free Press, 2004).

INDEX

SCRIPTURE INDEX

9 781936 927005